# A Well-Founded Fear

# A Well-Founded Fear

*The Congressional Battle to Save Political Asylum in America*

### Philip G. Schrag

Routledge
*New York London*

Published in 2000 by
Routledge
29 West 35th Street
New York, NY 10001

Published in Great Britain by
Routledge
11 New Fetter Lane
London EC4P 4EE

Copyright © 2000 by Routledge

Printed in the United States of America on acid-free paper.

Library of Congress Cataloging-in-Publication Data

Schrag, Philip G., 1943–
    A well-founded fear : the Congressional battle to save political asylum in America / Philip
G. Schrag.
      p.   cm.
    Includes bibliographical references and index.
    ISBN 0-415-92156-2 (hb.). — ISBN 0-415-92157-0 (pb.)
    1. Asylum, Right of—United States—history.    2. Refugees, Political—Legal status, laws,
etc.—United States History.    I. Title.
KF4836.S37    2000
342.73'083—dc21

00-35014
CIP

*This book is dedicated to John Fredriksson, Micheal Hill,
Elisa Massimino, Karen Musalo, Michele Pistone,
Deborah Ann Sanders, Carol Wolchok, and dozens of
other advocates, in the nation's capital and beyond the Beltway,
who work tirelessly, year after year, to preserve
the United States as a refuge for victims of persecution.*

# Contents

# Introduction

The Republican Congress elected in 1994 brought to Washington more than its Contract with America. Speaker Newt Gingrich's platform for his party's ascendency included ten highly visible changes that he hoped to make in the American political landscape, including a constitutional amendment to balance the budget, a five-hundred-dollar-per-child tax credit, limitations on punitive damages, and term limits for members of Congress.[1] Congress eventually passed into law a few of the Contract's terms. Others died quietly. Meanwhile, many veteran Republican legislators who had served for a decade or more as members of a relatively powerless minority, particularly in the House, returned to Capitol Hill in January 1995 as chairs of the committees or subcommittees that in Democratic hands had repeatedly rejected their initiatives. Whatever might happen to the most visible issues highlighted by the Contract with America, they were suddenly in a position to enact into law a large number of other Republican proposals that previously never had a chance of passage.

Restricting immigration wasn't mentioned in the Contract with America. But it was one of the many gleams in the eyes of some of the members of the newly ascendent majority. And it wasn't merely a Republican idea. Anti-immigrant sentiment was on the rise throughout the land. The voters of California had just passed an initiative to restrict the public benefits that could be used by unauthorized immigrants. A bipartisan commission headed by a liberal icon, former Democratic representative Barbara Jordan, recommended not only cracking down on illegal immigration but cutting back on legal immigration as well. The Clinton administration began to write a bill to tighten immigration standards and procedures.

In the opening months of the new Congress, Republican leaders drafted lengthy bills to change American immigration policy drastically. Some provisions imposed greater controls along the Rio Grande border. Some reduced the quotas for future would-be immigrants. Some limited welfare benefits to immigrants. But among the hundreds of pages of what these leaders hoped would become a new immigration law were three provisions that would create new barriers to entry by a particularly vulnerable class of people: refugees from political or religious persecution.

1

Although some of the earliest European settlers in America had themselves traveled to the new world to escape from persecution, the United States had for much of its history made immigration progressively more difficult for refugees. The record of the United States toward Jews fleeing Nazi Germany is particularly problematic. But in the years following World War II, the nation had gradually adopted a fairly progressive refugee policy.

Now, as part of a more general immigration "reform," congressional leaders sought to reverse that trend in three ways. They wanted to restrict immigration quotas for refugees who sought, while still abroad, to be designated for resettlement in the United States. They desired to curtail the availability of judicial hearings for aliens who reached the United States on their own and asked for asylum at border crossings and airports. And they wanted to tighten drastically the procedural rules for those who entered the United States (legally or illegally) and applied for asylum at a later time.

The two men who had just become the chairs of the House and Senate Immigration Subcommittees sponsored restrictions that were so severe that they would in effect have ended asylum in America. Within ten months after the Republican takeover of Congress, with virtually no press attention or public debate, most of the cutbacks that these two men had aimed at refugees had been approved by their subcommittees and by the full House Judiciary Committee. By November 1995, advocates for refugees had—to borrow an important phrase from the Refugee Act of 1980—"a well-founded fear": that America would close its doors to people who were forced to flee their own countries because they had become, or were about to become, victims of human rights abuses.[2]

This book is the story of what happened to the refugee provisions in those immigration bills, and why. It is partly a history of refugee policy-making, particularly during the 104th Congress. It is partly a tale of congressional process, in the tradition of several other case studies of legislation.[3] It is partly a story about citizen action; that is, how human rights groups, refugee advocates, and religious organizations created and worked in new coalitions to try to prevent Congress from limiting the rights of refugees. And in part, this is the personal memoir, like some other first-person case studies I have written, of one of the advocates.[4]

Through this study of a struggle over public policy, I would like to persuade others, in this age of intense cynicism about the political process, that despite PACs, vast contributions from wealthy people to political parties, and the dependence of our politicians on the expensive medium of television in their election campaigns, our national Congress is still an amazingly open institution in which many different voices can be heard. I was moved to write this account by an incident in a law school class that I taught during the early stages of the legislative struggle. My law students had all nearly completed a law school course in which they had personally represented refugees who were seeking asylum in the United States. They were wonderful students: brilliant, dedicated, persevering. Through their extraordinary efforts, they had won ten of the twelve cases on which they had worked (and an eleventh case was soon won on appeal). But to this point in the course, they had learned about asylum law almost exclusively from the perspective of a litigator; I wanted them to look at the public policy issues as well. So I asked them to read the provisions of the then-pending immigration law that would have most drastically changed the law with which they had been dealing for several months, provisions that, if then in force, would have turned their clients' victories into defeats. They were horrified. After we discussed the policy concerns driving the proposed legislation, I asked them to imagine that they had just taken a job as the assistant to the director of a small, poorly funded human rights organization. What would they suggest to the director that the organization do about this proposed legislation?

I thought that even if they had not learned much in law school about influencing legislation, they could easily have answered my question, at least partially, on the basis of what they had learned in their high schools and colleges. All of us, I expected, had experienced endless civics classes where we had learned that when we care about a public issue, we should write to members of Congress, send letters to the editor, and get in touch with other organizations that might help. But the very students who had displayed amazing creativity in handling and winning difficult refugee litigation drew a near blank on this question of legislative process.

The response was even more discouraging when, after discussing some of the actions a human rights organization might take, I asked a more personal question. In this new problem for class discussion, they were told not to assume that they worked for a human rights organization. They were just themselves, students who had successfully represented refugees. Now, after several months of study, they knew more about asylum law, and about how refugees would be affected by the new legislation, than 99.99 percent of the population of the country. Furthermore, it was clear from the discussion to this point that all of them disapproved of the proposed law. By virtue of their new expertise, had they any desire, or even any moral obligation, to participate in an effort to defeat the law, perhaps by sharing their knowledge or opinions with members of Congress? I expected them to realize that many of their clients' stories and circumstances were unique case studies demonstrating why the new law would bring about unjust results, and that by sending those stories, even with the clients' identities obscured, to key members of Congress, they might help to head off the pending bills. Again I drew a near blank. Only one member of the class intended to write a letter or do anything else to try to affect the legislation.

When I probed further, I discovered the reason for this passivity. I was correct in assuming that they thought that the proposed legal changes were very bad policy. But my students, who were so confident when arguing before an asylum officer of the Immigration and Naturalization Service or before a judge of the Immigration Court, felt utterly powerless with respect to the national Congress. It wasn't worth writing or trying to take any other political action, they said; no one would care what a student had to say. Members of Congress were controlled by powerful interests. Or, at the very least, legislators paid attention only to people with special access. Perhaps after a decade or more, when they were experienced lawyers with substantial practices, they could influence legislation, but such an idea seemed preposterous at this stage of their lives.

Then I realized that my hour of disappointment with these students' responses represented only part of the problem. I had reason to be disappointed by my own response to the new legislative initiatives as well. For about six months before this class took place, I had been dimly aware that a very restrictive immigration bill was being written on Capitol Hill, and that it included some provisions that would adversely affect refugees, a group about whom I cared deeply. But I too had done nothing about it. I had been busy supervising my students, and I had treated the new law as someone else's problem. Until mid-semester, when I prepared the readings for the class on current policy issues, I had not even bothered to learn in any detail what the new law would provide. I was a professor of law, I had taught the legislative process, and thirty years earlier I had been a summer intern in a senator's office. But to me, like my students, Congress (particularly the new Republican Congress) seemed remote, mysterious, and impenetrable.

During the year following that class, working with many others, I threw myself into a campaign to preserve the overseas refugee program and to save asylum. This book chronicles what we did, the extent to which we succeeded, and the extent to which we failed. It is not a comprehensive cookbook for future citizen action, but it does imply that genuine public participation in the legislative process is feasible (at least when the law at issue does not involve the distribution of large public subsidies to wealthy individuals or corporations), and it suggests some techniques for mounting a systematic campaign to influence a pending bill. If any future students, teachers, other citizens, or, for that matter, noncitizen residents of the United States read this book and conclude that they can become involved in national lawmaking, my principal purpose will be achieved. The book is not a how-to manual, but in addition to suggesting that Congress is quite responsive to organized advocacy from whatever source, it may also provide future advocates with some specific ideas about advocacy techniques. Therefore, I have included, among the several appendices, some of the documents that were written and distributed as part of the case against more severe restrictions on refugees.

A second goal of this book is to provide to students of the congressional process a window into the world of the advocates who try to affect the process. Most previous case studies have focused intensely on the legislators themselves, or on their staff members, and they have tended to give short shrift to outside advocacy organizations. A notable exception is the work of former Federal Trade Commission chairman Michael Pertschuk, who in 1986 began to contribute literature to this genre that gave due consideration to the role played by public interest advocates.[5] I hope that this volume contributes to the tradition he began.

## My Participation in the Opposition to the Legislation

I was one of hundreds of public interest advocates who opposed parts of the 1996 immigration law. I attended many strategy meetings, served on numerous committees to draft statements, and made my share of phone calls to congressional offices. In addition, at two junctures[6] I was more than a minor player. I could not write an accurate book without including a description of my own participation in the effort, and my involvement has enabled me to provide a level of detail about the process that I might well have missed if I had not been involved and had tried to reconstruct the battle after it was over. But my activism does present the risk inherent in any memoir: that because I was a particular advocate located in a particular place, my view of what happened may be skewed by my point of observation. This possible distortion may be magnified by the fact that my office was in Washington, so I became involved in the "inside-the-Beltway" advocacy carried out by the Washington offices of several large national nonprofit organizations. These organizations could not have been effective without their institutional presence in congressional districts around the country and the support and participation of their thousands of members. If I had lobbied against this bill as the director of a regional office of one of those organizations, the book probably would have devoted more pages to local advocacy efforts and might have given less attention to what happened in contacts with members of Congress or their staffs. I am convinced that advocacy in Washington and pressure on members of Congress in their home districts are both essential aspects of a successful legislative strategy (about which I say more in the final chapter), and I hope that reporting my own participation in the process does not undercut that essential conclusion.

## The Structure of the Book

The book has three parts. Part I describes the increasing pressure from 1990 through 1995, in the country and in Congress, for some retrenchment of the nation's openness to immigrants, including refugees. Chapter 1 provides historical context. It describes the history of the nation's refugee policies, with particular attention to the enactment of the Refugee Act of 1980 and the controversies over asylum and refugee policy during the Reagan and Bush administrations. Chapter 2 describes the Clinton administration in its first two years and its efforts to devise an immigration policy against a background of repeated crises involving alien smuggling and acts of terrorism attributed to asylum-seekers. In chapters 3 and 4 a new Republican majority in Congress seizes the initiative. Through 1995, this majority writes harsh refugee provisions into its immigration bills and, over the objections of the Clinton administration and human rights advocates, pushes the legislation through three subcommittees and committees on its way to final enactment.

The portion of this book that includes my personal experience begins with part II. Chapter 5 describes my belated awareness of the dangers in the pending bills. It relates my effort to galvanize nonprofit organizations into collective action to prevent Congress from imposing a short deadline on asylum applications. Chapter 6 describes the creation of a new coalition, the Committee to Preserve Asylum, to organize collective advocacy. It introduces Michele Pistone, who led the effort. Chapters 7 through 11 show how the committee, along with other organizations and coalitions, tried to influence the bill through the remaining stages of the legislative process. Some of these efforts were successful and some were not, but each stage of the proceedings was dramatic, suspenseful, and intensely challenging.

This book has a part III because the story of legislation does not end when a bill is passed. Chapters 12 and 13 describe the hard-fought struggles over the administrative regulations, forms, and operating procedures that the Immigration and Naturalization Service would use to implement the new law. Chapter 14 connects the new legislation, and related immigration laws and rules passed in 1997 and 1998, to the still-shifting political tides. Chapter 15 draws from the case study some tentative conclusions about legislative advocacy by public interest organizations.

## The Scope of the Book

I have attempted to provide a reasonably comprehensive account of the process by which Congress dealt with the three refugee issues in the 1996 immigration law: the proposed ceiling on the number of refugees who could be admitted annually, the "summary exclusion" process for aliens who arrive without visas, and deadlines on asylum applications. But this account is necessarily incomplete in at least two ways. First, it is probably somewhat more complete with respect to advocacy by nongovernmental organizations than with respect to the interplay among government officials. I have undoubtedly missed some of the byplay within the federal administration, within the Congress, and between those two branches of government. I have tried through interviews with congressional staff members and administration officials, and through the collection of a considerable amount of material that leaked into the press, to provide a reasonably thorough account of what pertinent members of Congress and of the administration were doing about the refugee issues, but there may have been some secret negotiations or trade-offs of which I am not aware.[7]

Second, the refugee issues discussed in this book were but three out of the hundreds of immigration amendments proposed in the lengthy House and Senate bills. I chose to write a book that treated the refugee issues in depth rather than an encyclopedic account of all of the controversies generated by these bills. Of course, the members of Congress who worked to pass the law and some of the organizations that opposed or tried to change the legislation cared not only about the refugee provisions, but also about many other issues in the House and Senate bills; in particular, quotas on legal immigration, the future status of aliens who had been in the United States "illegally" for many years, and social welfare benefits for legal and unauthorized aliens. To the extent that these issues became prominent, and particularly to the extent that attention to them affected the debate on refugees, I have discussed them in this narrative. Thus, this account gives some attention, but with much less detail, to the battles over maintaining legal immigration levels, permitting states to keep unauthorized aliens out of public schools, and restricting welfare benefits for immigrants. Perhaps another scholar will take up the challenge of reconstructing the entire battle over the immigration law, but that task could result in a work of well over a thousand pages. Meanwhile, this more modest effort will suggest the intensity and complexity of the struggle.

## Terminology

People who work in the field of immigration tend to use many acronyms and technical terms. I have tried to minimize the number of such expressions in this book. To assist the reader with those I had to incorporate, I have included a glossary at the end of the book. Two terms deserve special mention. The word "refugees" has at least three meanings, and they are often confused. In common parlance, the word refers to those who flee their homelands for almost any catastrophic reason, including war, famine, flood, ethnic strife, or persecution. American law does not use the word in such a broad sense, and neither does this book. The term "refugees" in this book refers only to people from another country who have been persecuted, or have a well-founded fear of being persecuted, because of their race, religion, nationality, political opinion, or membership in a particular "social group." American law also distinguishes between people subject to persecution who are recognized as refugees while they are still abroad, and those who apply for refugee status when they are already in the United States or at its borders. Refugees in the latter category are technically called "applicants for asylum," rather than "refugees," even though they also fit the legal definition of a refugee. This book usually uses the term "refugees" to refer to people who qualify for refugee status: that is, those who are recognized as refugees while still abroad, and those who come to the United States and can qualify for asylum. A few passages describe the overseas-refugee program. In those passages, the context makes clear that I am using the term to refer to the beneficiaries of that program.

The terms "alien" and "illegal alien" are also difficult, but for different reasons. American immigration law defines "alien" as any person who is not a citizen of the United States. Thus, it includes citizens of other nations and stateless people, whether or not they are physically in the United States, and if they are in the United States, whether they entered properly or not. The term has been used for many decades, is deeply embedded in our law and language, and is a useful shorthand for a complicated concept. Yet it is offensive to some people, connoting "other-ness" or even antithesis to American identity, as in the phrase "alien to our way of life." The term is, of course, also commonly used to refer to beings who aren't human at all: creatures from other worlds in the literature of science fiction. Professor Kevin R. Johnson has argued powerfully that the use of this term, in the law and in secondary literature about the law, "helps to reinforce and strengthen nativist sentiment toward members of new immigrant groups."

But Johnson acknowledges that "the term is regularly used, often with some reluctance or at least the felt need for explanation, in immigration discourse."[8] Perhaps in the next few years the word, as applied to humans, will be replaced by another. Meanwhile, though I am uncomfortable with it, a less familiar word or phrase could make this book more difficult to read.

The phrase "illegal alien" is not, however, found in the statute. In common parlance, it refers to a person who is in the United States without having been admitted through the processes established by law. The phrase is problematic because although we usually equate the term "illegal" with criminal activity, being present in the United States without a valid visa is not a criminal act.[9] In recent years, scholars have begun to use the phrases "undocumented alien" and "unauthorized alien" to refer to those who have entered the United States without permission. This book uses the latter phrase.

## A Note on Sources

Legal scholars thrive on footnotes. This book has a very large number of notes to sources. In a very small number of places, however, I make statements for which the source is an unnamed congressional "staff member," and in an even smaller number of places a statement isn't footnoted at all. The reason for these omissions is that some congressional staff members and a few advocates would only agree to be interviewed (or to reveal particularly sensitive information) on "background"; in journalistic parlance, without attribution to them by name. In my opinion, it was more valuable to report their information or observations without attribution than to withhold it because they would not allow their names to be used. Some scholars would undoubtedly make the opposite judgment, reasoning that anonymous information cannot be reliable. It's a close call. I did not use such information unless it meshed consistently and convincingly with the fabric of what I learned from documents and other sources about the process by which the refugee provisions were addressed by Congress.

Another issue involves the accessibility of documentary sources. The great majority of sources that I cite are public documents. Some are memoranda that I have on file. A few of the documents are public but are difficult to access. Specifically, House and Senate committees make transcripts of their "mark-up" sessions, in which they actually negotiate and vote on the precise language of legislation. But they do not publish the transcripts or permit anyone to copy them or scan them electronically, even for a fee.[10] They do, however, allow members of the public to go to their offices and read the transcripts, and even though they forbid copying they allow note-taking, including verbatim reproduction! Recently (and apparently after some small controversy among staff members, at least in some committees), permission to take verbatim notes by pen or pencil has extended to taking verbatim notes by laptop computer. Accordingly, my research assistants spent many long hours copying over relevant committee debates by retyping them on laptops, and portions of this book are built on the fruits of that tedious work.

A final note involves the page number references to the *Congressional Record*. The *Record* is published in a "daily" edition and republished, years later, in a bound edition with different pagination. The page numbers in this book refer to the daily edition.

## Acknowledgments

This book is the story of hundreds of people throughout the United States who worked to persuade Congress to stand up for fair treatment of refugees. Each of those people contributed to a joint effort, and each of them could recount incidents that are not included in this book. I appreciate what they did to moderate this law, and I hope that I have captured the spirit of their labors.

Many people, some of whom were part of the "coalition" effort and some of whom were not, helped me with the book itself. I would like to thank Stuart Anderson, Diana Aviv, Maurice Belanger, Joshua Bernstein, the late Joyce Chiang, Bruce Cohen, Patricia First, Carmel Fisk, John Fredriksson, Micheal Hill, Angela Kelley, Alan Kraut, Bronwyn Lance, Arnold Leibowitz, David A. Martin, Jana Mason, Elisa Massimino, Bill McGeveran, Ally Milder, Joel Najar, Michele Pistone, Kevin Price, Eugene Pugliese, "Mary Rawson," Grover Joseph Rees, Aliza Rieger, Alan K. Simpson, William Slattery, Dan Stein, Kathleen Sullivan, David Yassky, and Wendy Young for their time and for the information they gave me during interviews. Special notes of gratitude go to Professors T. Alexander Aleinikoff and David A. Martin, not only for their recollections of some of the events, but also for their helpful comments on an earlier draft of the manuscript, and to Lenni Benson, Peter Juviler, and Carolyn Patty Blum for their editorial suggestions. I appreciate the cooperation of Michele Pistone and the National Immigration Forum in sharing their pertinent archives. I am deeply indebted to my indefatigable research assistants Beth Boisvert and Lisa Brill, and to Karen Summerhill of the Georgetown University Law Library for her periodic help with requests for assistance in tracking down unusual documentary sources. I appreciate the continued encouragement of my colleague David Koplow, who suggested that I write this volume; the support of Georgetown University Law Center and its dean, Judith Areen, who granted me a research leave to work on this book during the fall of 1997; and, as noted above, the path-breaking work of Michael Pertschuk on the subject of public interest lobbying. Most of all, I am enormously grateful to my children, Sam Lerman and Sarah Schrag, and to my wife, Lisa Lerman, a law professor at Catholic University. With good cheer they urged me to keep working despite far too many absences from home, first while I helped to hack away at this legislation, and later while I wrote its story.

# Prologue

Mary Rawson, a teacher and mother, lived in a small town in an African country. As a teacher, she came face to face with hungry, half naked, and anemic children who dropped out of school when they became too ill to attend or could no longer pay the required fees. She watched children in her Sunday School class die from malnutrition and preventable childhood diseases such as malaria, cholera, and typhoid fever. She discussed the condition of these children with other members of her women's group and pointed out the need for the government to be more involved in its citizens' survival and the quality of their lives. Gradually, the women perceived that the government was not doing what it should to promote the safety, education, and well-being of children. They agreed that the government should be pressured to provide children with free vaccines, free elementary education, and clean drinking water.

Feeling a strong need to improve the prospects for these children, Ms. Rawson started a larger organization devoted to children and their rights. Representatives from this group addressed large crowds of people, spoke to heads of villages, and disseminated copies of the United Nations Convention on the Rights of the Child, which the government had ratified but not implemented.

As anchorwoman of a weekly radio talk show for children, Ms. Rawson became more prominent, and she fell under the eye of her government's security forces. She was periodically arrested, questioned, and released. These experiences only deepened her commitment to her work.

She helped to organize a three-day training session on children's advocacy in the nation's capital. The U.S. Embassy sent observers. The meeting seemed very successful, but when she got into a taxicab to return to her hotel, the taxi driver took off in the wrong direction. "Where are you going?" she asked. "We are going to get there," the driver reassured her. But the taxi drove to an unfamiliar neighborhood, where men pulled her out of the car and pushed her into a building. Inside, uniformed men tied her to a rack and turned her upside down, her skirt spilling over her head. The men beat her arms, her legs, and the soles of her feet with plastic hoses, while cursing, threatening, and mocking her.

The beating produced bloody cuts and scars that remain with her to this day. After a few hours, they dumped her on the street, yelling at her to cease her activities. She spent several weeks in a clinic, receiving treatment for her bruised and swollen body.

Humiliated, angry, and more determined than ever, she continued to advocate for children's rights. Her torture had drawn more attention to her group and the work it did for children. New chapters sprang up all around the country. Ms. Rawson shuttled between these groups, giving talks, handing out flyers, and distributing more copies of the UN Convention. She came to the attention of the U.S. Embassy in her country and was selected by the U.S. Agency for International Development to go on a study and observation tour of institutions that advanced children's rights in the United States. When she landed in New York, none of her luggage arrived. A friend later located it in a locked office in her country's airport. Despite the torture at home and the warning implied by the seizure of her luggage, she did not think of trying to remain in the United States. Like other members of her women's group, she knew that if even one person defected from the group, it would create a crevice that the police would widen and eventually use to break the group.

She returned home with a renewed commitment to reform, eager to try to make her government offer some of the services that she had observed in the United States. Now that she had been to America, she could speak out with new strength and new authority. But she knew that the authorities could spy on meetings, so their locations were secretly whispered from one woman to another.

Even riding buses through towns proved risky. The street corners were filled with uniformed policemen, backed by secret police who wore no identifying insignia. Buses were often stopped, the passengers told to show their identity cards. When she showed her card, the police invariably gathered to examine it closely, to talk about it, singling her out. Her name had evidently been entered into what was known colloquially as the "black book," the registry of suspected trouble-makers. Occasionally she was arrested and beaten on her feet, though not as severely as before.

Meanwhile, her radio show was becoming well known. She was attracting a greater following. At a national conference to discuss drafting a constitution, she spoke in favor of recognizing children's rights. Afterward, she was again arrested and again beaten.

Late one night in the spring of 1994, after midnight, she returned home from a political meeting. She was elated because the turnout had been high and she had distributed many flyers. She had just undressed for the night when she heard a loud banging on the front door, accompanied by curses and threats. Her husband knew that the commotion could only be another arrest. He told her to run. Dressed only in her night clothes, she dashed through the kitchen and out the back door. She spied one of her neighbors driving the town's bread van. She pleaded with him to help her to flee. He thought she was being pursued by thieves, let her get into the back of the van, and sped away. She found a woman who gave her some fabric to wrap around herself and she hid in a trailer park. She despaired that her children, waking, would think that she had simply vanished and abandoned them. She had not been able even to say good-bye.

In the trailer park, she found someone who would drive her to a village where she could hide. Soon she learned that the police had picked up her husband for interrogation, demanding that he produce her. On nights when her host suspected that the police would be searching near the town, she hid outdoors, between huge roots of mangrove trees in a swamp, covered by mud, devoured by mosquitoes. Days passed. At last her husband sent some clothing, her passport, and word that she must leave the country. Her host assisted her to board an airplane for Paris, with a quick connection to New York.

At John F. Kennedy Airport, an immigration inspector scrutinized her passport. Her visa, which the American embassy had given her when she toured the United States, permitted multiple entries into the U.S., but only for professional conferences and work. Had she come for a conference? If so, what conference? She admitted that she had not come for a conference. She said that she had come to visit her brother, who lived in Washington, D.C. In that case, the inspector said, she would have to pay an eighty-dollar visa waiver fee.

She did not have the money, she told him. But her brother was waiting on the other side of the customs barrier. Immigration officials paged the brother over the public address system. He arrived, paid the fee, and drove her to Washington. In the car, for the first time in weeks, she was safe, no longer subject to imminent capture. Now, at last, she could think about how much she missed her husband and children, thousands of miles away. For the first time since her escape from home, she wept.

The first months in the United States were miserable. She wondered whether the American police would cooperate with her own country's police, whether she would be picked up and sent home. For six months, she remained inside her brother's apartment, not risking being seen, hoping that things would soon change in her country so that she could return to her family. She did not telephone her husband or children, reasoning that the police would be listening, and that a call from her could endanger them. Finally, her uncle, who had also fled to America, told her that he was applying for asylum, and that she should do so too. So after more than six months in America, she went to her uncle's volunteer asylum lawyer. That lawyer said that he did not have time to represent her. But he referred her to the the Asylum Law Project of the Washington Lawyers Committee for Civil Rights and Urban Affairs, directed by Deborah Ann Sanders, an asylum expert. Sanders and her legal assistant, Ruth Spivack, interviewed Ms. Rawson and asked her to write out some of the details of her story. When they read what she had written, they told her that they would help her locate a volunteer lawyer.

After some time, they located a attorney who might assist her, and Ms. Rawson met with this lawyer. After interviewing her again, the lawyer checked with others in her corporate law firm, and the firm agreed to represent Ms. Rawson as a pro bono case. But more time passed, because just when the firm had approved the representation, Ms. Rawson's lawyer moved to a different firm. She had to get new approvals. Then, over the course of several weeks, her lawyer prepared voluminous documents, such as reports from human rights workers, to substantiate Ms. Rawson's claim.

Finally, more than eight months after she had arrived in the United States, Mary Rawson applied for asylum. Fortunately, the delay did not affect her claim, because the law did not impose any deadline on applications for asylum. She was interviewed by an asylum officer of the Immigration and Naturalization Service. He refused to grant asylum. He reasoned that she must be lying. If she had been beaten as she described, she would not have returned to her country from her tour of U.S. medical and childcare programs. He charged her with overstaying her visa and initiated proceedings to deport her to her own country.

The deportation proceeding gave her the opportunity to tell her story, one last time, to another official, an immigration judge in the Department of Justice. This time, however, a lawyer for the Immigration and Naturalization Service was also present, opposing her asylum request. The judge listened carefully to her story, and to the cross-examination conducted by the government's lawyer. A physician testified that the scars on her body were consistent with the beatings she described. The judge believed her and granted asylum.

*In this account, Mary Rawson's true name has been changed, and her country obscured, because her children are still at risk in her hometown. She has not seen them since 1994.*

*Part I*

# The Opening Salvo

# 1

# From Plymouth Rock to Kennebunkport
## *1620–1992*

Since its very beginnings, America has been a refuge for the persecuted—a "city on the hill" beckoning the victims of political, religious, ethnic, and other forms of repression. That tradition continues to this day.

—U.S. Commission on Immigration Reform (1997)[1]

In 1995, certain powerful members of Congress mounted a strong campaign to restrict immigration generally; they also sought to make it more difficult for refugees to seek asylum in the United States. These efforts were not unique to the 104th Congress. For much of American history, with the exception of a brief, remarkable thaw from 1965 to 1990, lawmakers imposed ever-increasing limitations on immigration into the United States. Some of the restrictions, particularly those in effect during the 1930s, had a devastating effect on people who had been forced by the threat of persecution to flee their native lands.

Every American schoolchild learns that some of our most famous founding fathers were refugees seeking religious and political freedom. The Pilgrims who landed at Plymouth Rock in 1620 were members of a sect that had separated itself from the Anglican church. Threatened with arrest because of their supposedly radical views, they emigrated to Holland and then to Massachusetts.[2] Between 1629 and 1642, twenty thousand Puritans, members of religious groups prosecuted and occasionally imprisoned in England for their doctrinal and liturgical deviation from the Anglican Church, also emigrated to Massachusetts, and a still larger number went to the southern colonies.[3]

Other colonies also received what we now think of as religious and political refugees. The first Lord Baltimore, a Catholic, actively promoted Maryland as a safe haven for Catholics because they could not freely practice their religion in Protestant England.[4] In the 1650s, Sephardic Jews, whose ancestors had settled in Dutch-controlled areas of Brazil after having been expelled from Spain, were forced to flee when the Dutch lost control of the territory. They helped to settle Dutch New Amsterdam, now known as New York.[5] In 1688, Protestant Huguenots, fleeing after Louis XIV revoked the Edict of Nantes, arrived in the

17

Western Hemisphere. Many settled in South Carolina, and others founded what is now New Rochelle, New York.[6] William Penn established the colony of Pennsylvania in part to create a refuge for Quakers.[7] During the fifty years before the American Revolution, approximately two hundred thousand Presbyterian Scots and Irish sought protection in the colonies from British persecution in their homeland.[8] During the same period, successive groups of German religious minorities, including Mennonites, Moravians, Schwenkfelders, and Inspirationalists, also sought freedom from religious persecution in the American colonies, particularly in Pennsylvania.[9] In the 1760s, after the British arrested large numbers of Nova Scotian Acadians of French descent, destroyed their homes, and declared the men "enemies of the state," many Nova Scotians fled to what is now Louisiana.[10]

After independence, refugees were a small but steady part of an ever-expanding stream of emigrants to the United States, drawn by seemingly limit-less economic opportunity as well as by political and religious liberty. Royalist refugees from the French Revolution built a settlement in Pennsylvania that they called Asylum.[11] Norwegian Quakers emigrated to the United States in 1825 to seek greater religious toleration.[12] Germans who had supported the unsuccessful revolution of 1848 fled in substantial numbers to America to avoid imprisonment and death as retribution for their political activities.[13]

For a hundred and fifty years before the American Revolution, and a hundred years thereafter, immigration—whether by refugees or anyone else—was relatively unrestricted. America needed soldiers to defend itself and laborers to develop the continent.[14] During this period, Congress passed no laws imposing restrictions on immigration, leaving immigration to state regulation. Some of the states attempted to close their borders to certain kinds of immigrants that they deemed undesirable. For example, beginning in 1788 several states banned the importation of persons who had ever been convicted of a crime. In the first third of the nineteenth century, Massachusetts and New York passed laws to prevent the immigration of those likely to become paupers. And before the Civil War, several northern states (including Indiana, Oregon, and Illinois) along with many of the slave states barred immigration by free Negroes.[15] But neither the states nor Congress imposed numerical restrictions on immigration, discriminated against people with particular religious or political beliefs, or (with the exception of the antebellum state laws preventing the immigration of free Negroes) excluded people of a particular race or nationality. For a long time after independence, despite a few organized efforts to prevent European Catholics from immigrating into the United States, most people who sought a better life in the United States, including those who were fleeing oppressive governments, were welcomed into our constantly expanding nation.[16]

Then, in the late nineteenth century, as it has so many times since then, California began to lead the country in a different direction.[17] Chinese immigrants began to arrive in California shortly after the 1849 Gold Rush.[18] Many more came to work on the transcontinental railroad. They were welcomed by the railroad and mining companies, which urgently needed laborers, but they were attacked verbally and physically by organized groups of whites, some of whom resented their competition for employment. They were specially taxed and kept out of public schools. When a severe depression hit California in the 1870s, anti-Chinese sentiment and activities increased markedly. California's politicians, including those in Congress, and Stephen J. Field, a particularly influential Supreme Court justice from California who had presidential ambitions, pressed repeatedly and successfully for a new treaty to restrict Chinese immigration and for limits on the rights of Chinese people already resident in the United States.[19]

In 1882, the California delegation persuaded Congress to exercise the power granted by the new treaty. Congress passed the Chinese Exclusion Act, barring Chinese laborers, including skilled workers, from immigrating for ten years, but permitting those already here to remain, leave, and return.[20] Within a few years, Congress made the bar on Chinese immigration permanent, and it repealed the exception for those who had already immigrated but wanted to leave and return.[21] One particular Chinese immigrant was barred from landing even though he had been en route home to San Francisco when the "leave and return" provision was repealed. He challenged the constitutionality of the law. In an opinion written by Stephen J. Field, the justice who nine years earlier had been a leading advocate of restricting Chinese immigration, the Supreme Court upheld the law. The Court reasoned that if "the government . . . considers the presence of foreigners of a different race in this country, who will not assimilate with us, to be dangerous to its peace and security, their exclusion is not to be stayed because at the time there are no actual hostilities with the nation of which the foreigners are subjects." The Court ruled that although the Constitution did not explicitly vest Congress with the power to regulate immigration, such power was an inherent "incident of sovereignty."[22] The Court therefore established that Congress could control immigration and exclude immigrants, a "plenary power" it has exercised ever since. A corollary of this much-criticized "plenary power" rule is that aliens who arrive at the border or land at American airports seeking permission to enter the country do not have the same right to fair procedure, deriving from the due process clause of the Constitution, that citizens and lawfully admitted aliens enjoy.[23] If Congress chooses to create procedures through which the government treats some of these aliens unfairly, while determining whether to admit them, the courts have little if any power to intervene.

Two years after the Court's decision, Congress embraced its invitation to exercise federal control over immigration. It created the position of superintendent of immigration, left intact the ban on Chinese immigration, and imposed a new ban on immigration by persons "likely to become a public charge."[24] At just about this time, America began a period of rapid industrial growth, requiring immense amounts of labor. In response to the availability of relatively high wages, immigration from Europe began to soar. Competition among the steamship companies reduced the cost of transoceanic travel to less than fifteen dollars, the average wage for just a month's work,[25] and from the 1880s to 1920, approximately twenty-four million people came to the United States.[26] Halfway through this period, Emma Lazarus's famous poem inviting the world to "give me your tired, your poor, Your huddled masses yearning to breathe free" was attached to the base of the Statue of Liberty, which had been dedicated in New York harbor in 1886.[27]

But just as the West had reacted against the immigration of the Chinese, and shortly afterward, the Japanese,[28] many people in the rest of the country resisted the rapid influx of new Americans from southern and eastern Europe, many of whom were Catholic, and two and a half million of whom were Jewish. Nativist groups and labor organizations, including the American Federation of Labor, demanded an end to European as well as Asian immigration.[29]

Patriotism and anti-German sentiment produced by World War I fanned the flames. The Immigration Act of 1917 included a literacy test for new immigrants and created a "Asiatic barred zone" (including India and Southeast Asia) from which all immigration was banned.[30] When the wartime economic boom ended, demands for further immigration restrictions swelled. These calls were reinforced by experts in "eugenics" such as Dr. Harry H. Laughlin of the Carnegie Institution of Washington and the Eugenics Research Association, who advocated the "selection of immigrants on the basis of biological fitness"[31] and who complained that without eugenic screening we "were getting too many immigrants of unassimilable races, but especially too many individuals, regardless of race, who lacked inborn the intellectual and spiritual qualities of the founders of the Nation."[32] Proposals to suspend immigration altogether were scrapped in favor of the Quota Act of 1921. Under this law, annual immigration of Europeans of any particular nationality was limited to 3 percent of the number of foreign-born Americans of that national origin as reflected in the 1910 census, and only 1 percent of the entire immigration quota could be filled by non-Europeans.[33] Immediately, the proportion of immigrants from southern and eastern Europe was halved, while the percentage of immigrants from northern and western Europe more than doubled.[34]

But this legislation, designed to be temporary, did not sufficiently settle the problem for many Americans who, like Calvin Coolidge, believed that "America must be kept American" and that "biological laws tell us that certain divergent people will not mix or blend."[35] In 1924, Congress made the quota system permanent, but it changed the formula so that it would even more greatly favor immigrants of English stock. The 1924 legislation reduced the quota to 2 percent, and it temporarily based each nationality's allocation on the 1890 census, rather than the 1910 census, to reflect better the period before massive immigration from central and southern Europe had occurred.[36] Although after 1929 the 1920 census was used as a baseline, the basis for calculating the quota was changed from the number of "foreign born" people of a given nationality already in the United States to the number of people of each "national stock," thereby including native-born Americans of British and German ancestry in the count for the British and German quotas.[37] Italians now had a quota of less than 6,000, though Italian immigration had exceeded 150,000 in the years before 1920.[38] For the first time, Japanese people were formally excluded by law.

Events of the years before, during, and immediately after World War I produced the economic boom and bust that eventually influenced national immigration laws. The political and military conflicts of that period also created a large number of Armenian and Russian "refugees," people who seemed different from most other European immigrants of the preceding century because they were fleeing from war and persecution.[39] As a result, governments began to perceive refugees as a category of would-be immigrants needing distinct humanitarian treatment,[40] and the League of Nations created a legal definition of the term "refugees."[41] But despite intense awareness in Europe of a postwar "refugee" problem, the new American quota laws made no exceptions for would-be immigrants who had been forced to flee their countries.

Over a period of about five years in the late 1920s, Congress and the American bureaucracy refined the quota system, perfected the implementing procedures, and developed one more restrictionist wrinkle. Even if they fit within the quotas, people "likely to become a public charge" were barred from immigrating. This "LPC" provision had been law since 1891, but it had been interpreted to preclude only those who lacked the physical or mental skills needed to hold a job. In 1930, President Herbert Hoover re-interpreted the clause to bar those who, as a result of current market conditions, were unlikely to obtain employment.[42] This new policy gave American consular officers, to whom would-be quota immigrants had to apply for visas, a vast discretionary or judgmental power over which people from a particular country would fill the quota, or whether it would be filled at all.

It is one of the great, sad ironies of history that in the early 1930s, just as all the American restrictionist machinery was finally in place, Adolf Hitler became chancellor of Germany and began to persecute the Jews, first in his own country, and then in the countries that, by negotiation or war, fell under his domination. Because so many Americans were of German ancestry, Jews trying to escape from Hitler's Germany might have been able to emigrate to the United States, within the German quota. But the Great Depression had begun. Many Americans believed that more immigration would mean even fewer jobs for those already in residence. Others believed in a eugenic anti-Semitism. There was little public sentiment in America for the easing of immigration restrictions as a result of Hitler's deeds, and much organized agitation to maintain the barriers preventing Jewish refugees from resettling in the United States.[43] In 1938, public opinion polls found that 60 percent of Americans objected to the presence of Jews in America, 20 percent wanted to drive Jews out of the country, and only a third would oppose an American anti-Jewish campaign.[44] State Department officials, some of them personally anti-Semitic,[45] passed word to the consular officials in Europe that they should use delay, and the discretion afforded them by the LPC clause, to refuse visas to Jews trying to flee from Hitler's repression. George Messersmith, the American consul general in Berlin, who was not strongly anti-Semitic but reflected the "bureaucratic indifference to moral or humanitarian concerns" that was widespread within the State Department and the nation as a whole, wrote his superiors in Washington that the purpose of granting visas "is not, as some interpret it, to maintain the United States as an asylum or refuge for dissatisfied and oppressed people in other parts of the world irrespective of their capacity to become good and self-supporting citizens of our country."[46]

The United States did admit about a quarter of a million European refugees, most of them Jews, in the eleven years between 1933 and 1944.[47] But this number was small in comparison to the number of people threatened by Hitler.[48] As a result of the 1924 quota legislation, the State Department's interpretation of the LPC clause, and the force of restrictionist public opinion—which militated against changing the law or its interpretation—60 percent of the German quota went unused in the prewar years.[49] And matters only got worse. In 1939, Congress turned back a bill to admit twenty thousand German refugee children.[50] As late as June 1940, when Hitler's armies were overrunning France, Assistant Secretary of State Breckinridge Long wrote secretly, "We can delay and effectively stop for a temporary period of indefinite length the number of immigrants into the United States. We could do this by simply advising our consuls to put every obstacle in the way and to require additional evidence and to resort to various administrative devices which would postpone and postpone and postpone the granting of the visas."[51] By 1942, Germany was systematically murdering Jews from nearly all of Continental Europe, but even where escape was possible, the American quota system and its administration made refuge in the United States virtually unachievable.

The United States issued pious declarations of hope that refuge could be found for those trying to escape from totalitarian tyranny. At America's initiative, representatives from more than thirty nations had gathered in Evian, France, in 1938 "to consider what steps can be taken to facilitate the settlement in other countries of political refugees from Germany [including] persons who desire to leave Germany."[52] This event was "hailed by the American and European press as the great humanitarian event of the year."[53] But the industrial nations did not change their laws or procedures to permit greater immigration. As the Holocaust Memorial Museum succinctly describes the commitments made by the governments represented at Evian,

Great Britain would admit few Jews and kept Palestine closed to large-scale Jewish Immigration. Canada was willing to accept farmers, but this did not help the urban Jews of Austria and Germany. Australia declined to assist because it "does not have a racial problem and [is] not desirous of importing one." The Venezuelan delegate was reluctant to disturb the "demographic equilibrium" of his country: no Jewish merchants, peddlers, or intellectuals were wanted there.

The Netherlands and Denmark offered only temporary asylum. The United States finally agreed to admit—for the first time—the full legal quota for immigrants from Germany and Austria. The Dominican Republic alone offered to receive a substantial number, 100,000 Jews.[54]

In the years before and after the Evian Conference, the legal structure cemented into place by the Immigration Act of 1924 took its toll most severely on the Jews of Europe.

The Evian Conference did establish an Intergovernmental Committee on Refugees.[55] World War II prevented that committee from doing much for refugees, but the idea of concerted international action on behalf of refugees had been given greater currency. When the war ended, Americans were shocked by photographs of Jewish concentration camp survivors who had been reduced to near-skeletons, and by revelations that Hitler's officials had murdered six million Jews. And refugee concerns were not mere history: millions of refugees still roamed Europe and other continents, or waited for relief in displaced persons camps, unwilling or unable to return to their former countries.[56] The world's governments responded by creating new temporary international agencies to supersede the Intergovernmental Committee. Shortly thereafter, when the advent of the Cold War and the Soviet takeover of central and eastern European countries made it likely that refugees might continue to flee totalitarian governments for some time, they established a more permanent United Nations High Commissioner for Refugees (UNHCR).[57]

In the postwar agreements, the definition of a refugee was made to depend, not on political or social categories, but on a case-by-case determination. Despite the objections of the Soviet Union, which did not want political dissidents to be afforded any special privileges, the "essence of refugee status came to be discord between the individual refugee applicant's personal characteristics and convictions and the tenets of the political system in her country of origin."[58]

A critical paragraph of the charter creating the position of the High Commissioner defined the mandate of that official as extending to any person who "as a result of events occurring before 1 January 1951 and owing to a well-founded fear of being persecuted for reasons of race, religion, nationality, or political opinion" is "unable or ... unwilling" to return to the country of his nationality.[59] Soon after it was written, this paragraph became of great importance, because it was essentially incorporated into a treaty designed to describe the relationships between nations and refugees. In the 1951 Convention Relating to the Status of Refugees, a refugee was defined as someone who, as a result of pre-1951 events "and owing to well-founded fear of being persecuted for reasons of race, religion, nationality, membership of a particular social group or political opinion," was outside his country and "unable, or owing to such fear, unwilling to avail himself of the protection of that country."[60]

Several limiting aspects of this definition and of the convention that included it are worthy of note. First, the countries of the world were unwilling to undertake an open-ended commitment to future refugees; the definition pertained only to refugees created by World War II and its immediate aftermath. Second, not even all such refugees would necessarily be covered; countries signing the treaty were given the additional option to limit the definition of "refugee" to those displaced by pre-1951 events "in Europe."[61] Third, the definition excluded people who were fleeing from famine, natural or man-made disasters, or war; although it added the "social group" category to the four that had been listed a year earlier, a peson would have to earn refugee status by having a well-founded fear based on one of the five listed grounds. This feature would enable the Western countries to focus world attention more or less continuously on the political failings of the Soviet bloc countries, because the West could, at will, admit dissidents who fled those countries and justify their actions as based on the convention.[62] Fourth, the convention actually required very little of its signatories. If a signatory nation admitted a person as a refugee, the convention required certain minimal standards of treatment, such as providing them with no less favorable access to public housing or education than the nation provided to other foreign nationals, and the same welfare rights it provided to its own citizens.[63] The convention did not, however, require a signatory nation to accept any refugees onto its territory. On the other hand, if a refugee somehow found his way to the territory of a signatory, that nation could not expel or return the refugee to the border of a territory where his "life or freedom would be threatened on account of" one of the five listed grounds incorporated in the refugee definition.[64] However, the country could try to deport the refugee to a third country in which he or she would be safe.

Despite the limited nature of the convention's requirements, the United States did not sign it. In fact, the American response to the postwar refugee crisis was rather minimal. Congress did not pass a Displaced Persons Act until 1948, three years after the war ended, and although that act permitted the admission of up to two hundred thousand refugees, its definition of who could be resettled in the United States "precluded the issuance of visas to ninety percent of the displaced Jews who entered Germany, Austria and Italy."[65] Four years later, over President Truman's veto, Congress amended the national origins immigration quota system to reduce the annual quota to one-sixth of one percent of those in the United States in 1920 who were of the ancestry in question.[66]

The 1952 legislation did not include any exceptions or special provisions for refugees. But in 1953, Congress did pass a special Refugee Relief Act to allow the admission, outside the quota, of a limited number of "escapees" who had fled persecution in Communist-dominated countries or the Middle East. Congress specified that the act was not a "precedent or commitment . . . to participate . . . in any international endeavors aimed at a permanent solution of the problem."[67] In addition, the 1952 law included a somewhat vague "parole" authority under which the attorney general could temporarily admit a person to the United States "for emergent reasons or for reasons deemed strictly in the public interest."[68]

When the United States encouraged Hungarians to revolt against Soviet occupation in 1956 and then failed to support the Hungarians militarily, two hundred thousand new refugees were created. President Eisenhower offered asylum to 10 percent of them, but only about a third of those could be given visas under the Refugee Relief Act. Eisenhower then used the parole authority to admit the rest of them en masse, a probable circumvention of the immigration laws that set the stage for increasing legislative-executive tension over refugee admissions in years to come.[69]

Then came the 1960s, that brief, remarkable period ushered in by the civil rights movement, in which the nation looked seriously at the needs of its least advantaged people. In the 1960s, Congress passed civil rights acts to assure equal opportunity to people of all races in public accommodations, employment, voting, and housing; laws providing for Medicare and Medicaid; statutes providing for a war on poverty, including funds for community action agencies and Model Cities grants; subsidies for Supplemental Security Income; and a wealth of other programs to assist those who had suffered from prejudice and misfortune. Immigration was not immune from the generous spirit that stirred the nation. Four months before his assassination, President Kennedy asked Congress to pass a complete overhaul of the immigration laws, and to repeal the national origins system.[70] He did not live to see this proposal become law, but his brother, Senator Edward M. Kennedy, carried this work forward. Immediately upon his induction into the Senate in 1963, Senator Kennedy was appointed to serve on the Judiciary Committee. By virtue of its oversight of the Justice Department, in which the Immigration and Naturalization Service (INS) was housed, this committee had responsibility for immigration law and policy. Kennedy was also placed on its immigration subcommittee. Within a short period of time, he was one of a handful of senators who cared about and understood what had already become a very complex immigration act. Within two years, Kennedy was acting chair of the subcommittee, and he was able to steer through the Senate, and through Congress, a radical change in the tilt of American immigration law.[71] Kennedy prompted Congress to replace the race-based immigration system that had been a mainstay of U.S. immigration policy ever since 1882. The 1965 law repealed all racial restrictions. Congress imposed an annual quota of 170,000 immigrants from the Eastern Hemisphere and a separate, lower quota on immigration from the Western Hemisphere.[72] Some people, such as spouses and parents of U.S. citizens, could be admitted outside of the quota. (The number of legal immigrants gradually increased to a total of about a million per year by 1992).[73] Within the quota, specific subtotals were set aside for preferred categories of immigrants, such as spouses and unmarried children of legal resident aliens and people with special skills. Refugees got their own quota at last: 6 percent of the total. But in this subcategory, unlike the others, geographical and ideological restrictions were retained: to qualify, a refugee had to depart from a Communist-dominated country or the Middle East.[74] In any given year, no single country could send more than 20,000 emigrants to the

United States. European prosperity reduced emigration from that continent, while the new law facilitated immigration from other regions. Over time, the pattern under which a disproportionate share of American immigrants had come from Europe was reversed. Annual immigration from Asia rose from an average of 15,000 in 1951–60 to 274,000 in 1981–90. Annual immigration from northern Europe fell from 105,000 to 55,000 in the same periods.[75]

The expansive atmosphere of the 1960s infected the international community as well. The nations of the world negotiated a 1967 protocol to the 1951 Refugee Convention. It eliminated the temporal restriction under which people who had been made refugees after 1951 were not considered refugees under the convention, and it also eliminated the optional European focus of the convention, giving it worldwide applicability.[76] With the advice and consent of the Senate, the United States ratified the protocol. It thereby agreed, as a matter of international law, not to return refugees to countries where their lives or freedom would be in danger.

The refugee provision of the 1965 legislation, with its ceiling and geographical restrictions, proved inadequate almost immediately. President Lyndon Johnson invited Cuban refugees to seek protection in the United States, and because they did not originate in Europe, he had to use the parole authority, not the new immigration law, to admit them.[77] But congressional critics argued that the use of the parole power to admit large groups of refugees circumvented the new law, and pressure slowly built for the enactment of a law that would more fully address the issue of refugee protection.[78] Other critics protested that the parole power could be used and was being used ideologically, taking into account the Cold War foreign policies of the nation but not the humanitarian needs of refugees; from 1957 to 1968, the parole power was used to admit 232,000 people fleeing Communist-dominated countries, but only 925 people from all other countries combined.[79] From 1968 to 1980, the respective numbers were 608,000 and 7,000.[80] Despite dissatisfaction with the refugee provisions of the 1965 law, it would take Congress until 1980 to replace them.

Meanwhile, although the Refugee Protocol required only that countries not deport refugees to countries where they faced serious danger, a new idea had entered the political arena: asylum, a more durable set of rights in the receiving country. Asylum "results in lasting permission to remain, not just non-return to the country of persecution."[81] No U.S. law authorized the government to offer asylum, but shortly before it entered World War II, the United States had permanently resettled particularly important intellectual and political leaders, as well as refugees who had been endangered by the invasion of western Europe. By indulging in the fiction that they were temporary visitors, the Roosevelt administration had created a minuscule asylum program, circumventing the 1924 legislation.[82]

Throughout the 1970s, congressional committees held hearings on several proposals for a new statutory framework for accepting refugees who applied overseas and, after 1977, procedures for obtaining asylum in the United

States.[83] These proposals became more urgent after North Vietnam's victory over South Vietnam in 1975, which resulted in the evacuation of 130,000 refugees, most of whom were resettled in the United States through an exercise of the parole power because, as in past crises, the refugee sub-quota of the 1965 legislation had been exhausted.[84] This mass parole, like many others before 1980, was criticized by members of Congress for two reasons. First, it seemed a circumvention of the law. In addition, leading legislators did not think that the administration had adequately consulted with them as required by law. The administration, for its part, resisted such consultation, stating that the consultation requirement precluded prompt action during emergencies, and that Congress failed to respond when the administration did request its advice.[85] Congressional complaints about inadequate refugee admission consultations would become common in future years, leading to considerable legislative distrust of the Immigration and Naturalization Service.

During the Carter administration, Congress and the executive branch consulted not only on the scope of refugee admissions but also on the shape of the emerging legislation. The administration wanted unfettered discretion to admit as many refugees as it deemed desirable in light of foreign policy and humanitarian considerations. Congress wanted statutory controls on the number of refugee admissions and mandatory consultations, or perhaps to retain the ability to veto administration actions.

The resulting Refugee Act of 1980, which included a compromise between the legislative and the administrative branches of government on these issues, represented the most progressive step, with respect to refugee protection, ever taken by an American Congress. The act was the result of years of work by Senator Kennedy (whose accession to the chairmanship of the full Judiciary Committee in 1979 made passage of the law possible)[86] and by a small group of members of the House of Representatives.[87] The act built into American law the Refugee Convention's definition of a refugee, expanding it slightly to include those who had been persecuted, as well as those with a well-founded fear of future persecution, on the basis of one of the five listed grounds. Congress repealed the 1965 sub-quota for overseas refugees, and it restricted the president's power to use his parole authority to admit large numbers of refugees at his discretion.[88] At the same time, Congress created a new, less restrictive overseas refugee program. Until 1982, the administration could admit fifty thousand refugees each year, a number far lower than might be needed to meet humanitarian needs, but one that could "garner popular and political support for the Act's passage."[89] The act included provisions through which the president could breach this limit, and the president did so in a very significant way.[90] After 1982, "refugees of special humanitarian concern" (a phrase that seemed to emphasize the refugees' needs rather than Cold War policies) could be admitted, based on their overseas applications, without any statutory numerical ceiling and without regard to whether they were likely to become a public charge, though Congress and the administration would consult annually to determine the number who would be admitted during the following year. In the event of a crisis, the president could provide for additional admissions, again after consulting with Congress. The consultations, not the law, would determine any regional allocation of the negotiated refugee ceiling. Reflecting its dissatisfaction with the nature of previous communications, Congress specified several detailed consultation procedures. For example, the president's representatives in the consultations had to have cabinet rank, and various written reports had to be made to Congress two weeks before the discussions took place.[91]

The act's new provisions for refugees who had already reached the United States (as opposed to those who applied from abroad) were in some ways an even greater advance from previous law. To make American statutory law consistent with the Refugee Protocol the country had signed thirteen years earlier, Congress made "withholding of deportation" mandatory. Under this doctrine, a refugee could not be returned to a country where he or she would be in danger.[92] But Congress went further, providing that the attorney general could grant asylum to such a refugee.[93] Congress recognized that situations of danger did not quickly disappear, and that it was desirable to enable refugees to begin new lives, without having to fear involuntary deportation if persecution at home became less likely. When conferring asylum, the attorney general could also extend it to a refugee's spouse and minor children. Furthermore, a year after obtaining asylum, a refugee could become a permanent resident; and five years after the initial admission, the permanent resident could become a naturalized American citizen.

Within months after he signed the Refugee Act, President Carter and the Democratic Senate majority that had passed the law were swept from office. Ronald Reagan became president of the United States. Because the Republicans now had a majority in the Senate, Strom Thurmond of South Carolina replaced Edward M. Kennedy as chair of the Judiciary Committee. Alan K. Simpson of Wyoming became the new chair of the Senate's Immigration Subcommittee.[94]

Very quickly, the new Reagan administration's handling of both the overseas refugee admissions program and the new asylum system became the subject of intense criticism from the growing human rights community. The vast majority of the refugees who were admitted to the United States from overseas came from only two regions, and those two were sites of Cold War conflict: Southeast Asia (still teeming with those who had fled the war in Vietnam) and the Soviet Union.[95] Furthermore, the government adopted internal guidelines under which nearly all of those who were chosen for resettlement in America were people with family or previous political ties to the United States, rather than those whose needs for resettlement were greatest.[96] But rather than questioning how refugee admissions were being allocated, Congress requested the administration to reduce its numerical targets.[97]

Human rights groups discovered that asylum applications filed by refugees who reached the United States, like refugee applications filed abroad, were apparently being decided in accordance with Cold War foreign policy concerns, rather than the humanitarian standards of the new law. By 1982, the United States was supporting governments in El Salvador and Haiti that many people regarded as oppressive; granting asylum to a person claiming to have been persecuted by the Soviet Union was consistent with U.S. foreign policy, but determining that an American ally was a human rights violator was, at the very least, awkward for a junior official. In fiscal year 1983, the INS granted asylum to 78 percent of Russians and 44 percent of Romanians seeking this status, but only to 2 percent of Haitian and 3 percent of Salvadoran applicants.[98] Before granting asylum, INS officials were required by the new regulations to consult with the State Department, and they almost always concurred with State Department opinions. One INS adjudicator admitted frankly that he "would never, never, overrule the State Department."[99] A General Accounting Office report concluded that "applicants from different countries who claimed to have suffered similar mistreatment did not have similar approval rates."[100]

Furthermore, with respect to aliens who arrived at an airport or seaport and asked for asylum, the Reagan administration in 1981 reversed a long-standing practice of allowing them to remain at liberty pending a determination of their future status. Rather than jailing only those deemed security risks or likely to abscond, it began a practice of routine incarceration.[101]

If Congress was going to address emergent problems in the administration of the new Refugee Act, the task would fall, in the first instance, to Alan Simpson, the new chairman of the Senate's Immigration Subcommittee. Simpson, who had only entered the Senate in 1979, benefited more than most from the Reagan landslide the following year; as a very junior senator he became a subcommittee chairman, and within a very short time, he would become the single most influential member of Congress on the subject of immigration.

Simpson's background was colorful, even by Senate standards.[102] His great-grandfather, Finn Burnett, had been an Indian fighter and a friend of Sacajawea, the Indian guide for Lewis and Clark. His grandfather had befriended, and later successfully prosecuted, Butch Cassidy; he had also obtained a gun to shoot and kill a cowboy who had insulted him, but he was acquitted of first-degree murder because, as Alan Simpson told a reporter, the jury decided that the cowboy deserved to be killed.

Simpson's father Milward had gone into Wyoming politics, serving as a Republican in the state legislature, as governor, and eventually as U.S. senator. Alan was born in 1931. As a teenager, he got into some trouble. Once he was put on federal probation for two years for shooting mailboxes, and he was arrested for fighting at the University of Wyoming.[103] After he graduated in 1954, he married Ann Schroll, and then served in the army in Germany to fulfill an ROTC commitment. He missed Wyoming terribly and hated his military service; as he told his biographer, in the earthy language for which he was well known in the Senate, "There I was married to this marvelous chick, and I was smoking three packs a day and drinking beer like it was going out of style."

After completing law school in Wyoming, he worked as a divorce lawyer and ran successfully for the state legislature, which met for forty days every two years. After ten years, he became the majority floor leader, and then Speaker, after which he made his first run for the U.S. Senate.

When he arrived in Washington in 1979, he was an instant hit with his colleagues and with the press. Journalists, in particular, were "infatuated with his earthy humor." A *Washington Post* columnist called him "one of the most refreshing breezes that occasionally gentles their way through the Congressional pomp."[104]

He did not plan to make immigration policy his major issue, and he was appointed to the Immigration Subcommittee largely by chance. Immigration "was not an issue that I sought to have visited upon me. It was one that just fell in my ambit and is probably one of the most unpopular, ghastly, non-political, non-nothing—you can make no gain from it. . . . But I'm goofy enough to like to mess around in it."[105]

When Simpson took over the Immigration Subcommittee, the government was admitting overseas refugees from only two regions, it had a new policy of jailing asylum applicants, and it was systematically denying asylum to refugees from repressive regimes that enjoyed U.S. diplomatic support. But he did not regard these policies as major problems. The big issue, in the opinions of Simpson and the Reagan administration, was that the number of annual asylum applications was rising rapidly.

Shortly after the Refugee Act passed, human rights violations and civil conflicts in Haiti, Guatemala, El Salvador, and Nicaragua escalated. Large numbers of people who might reasonably claim to be refugees under the new act could, without too much difficulty (compared with similarly situated Asians or Africans), reach American shores. Asylum applications rose from 3,700 in 1978, to 16,000 in 1980, and 63,000 in 1981.[106] The administration was not prepared for the rapid increase; the government had not hired or trained enough asylum adjudicators. It simply failed to decide many cases. Therefore, a large backlog began to build up. By 1983, approximately 166,000 asylum claims were awaiting resolution.[107]

The Reagan administration did not perceive any need to hire more personnel; rather, it wanted to "streamline" asylum and exclusion procedures.[108] Under the law that existed at that time, any person arriving in the United States without proper papers would have an opportunity to show an examiner of the Immigration and Naturalization Service that he was entitled for some reason (such as eligibility for asylum) to remain. If turned down, the refugee could appeal to the federal courts. In one of his first initiatives as chair of the Immigration Subcommittee, Senator Simpson sponsored a bill, which soon passed the full Senate Judiciary Committee, to curtail the rights of such would-be immigrants. Under the bill, the INS official in charge of a particular case would make "some inquiry" as to why the alien was "unlawfully seeking entry." But the Judiciary Committee noted that "it is the intention of the Committee that this be a general inquiry and should not include advice of any right to claim asylum or leading questions with respect to persecution."[109] Further questions were to be asked only if the alien's answers, without prompting, "provide[d] evidence" that he might be entitled to asylum. If the alien didn't say the words evincing asylum eligibility, he would be deported forthwith, without a hearing or appeal. If he did say the right words, he would be interviewed further regarding asylum eligibility, but if he were turned down, he could not appeal to a court.[110] The new process would be known as "summary exclusion."[111]

Senator Simpson's bill included another idea as well for curbing asylum applications. When the United States began proceedings to deport an alien, that person would have only fourteen days thereafter in which to file the first portion of an asylum application (and another twenty-one days to complete the application). Someone who missed this two-part thirty-five-day deadline would be barred from seeking asylum.[112]

This bill passed the Senate in 1982, but it did not pass in the House, so it did not become law. In 1984, major immigration bills, including asylum restrictions, passed in both houses of Congress but died when a Conference Committee was unable to reconcile them before the Congress adjourned.[113] The bills were controversial, among other reasons, because they included asylum restrictions.[114] When Simpson reintroduced the legislation in 1985, he told the Senate that he had "removed some of the provisions which have seemed to be a less important part of the immigration debate, in order to focus our intentions on the most essential elements of the bill. Changes in our system of legal immigration and asylum adjudication have been deleted."[115]

Therefore, when Congress passed a major Immigration Reform and Control Act in 1986,[116] the act left in place all of the Refugee Act's provisions for refugees and asylum applicants. Simpson's efforts to limit asylum had failed.

More accurately, his efforts had failed temporarily. The fight was not over, but Simpson accepted a temporary truce. The battle outlined in the early years of the Reagan administration would preview the struggle that would simmer for another fourteen years. The three refugee issues that Congress first debated between 1980 and 1982—ceilings on overseas refugee admissions, summary exclusion procedures, and time limits for asylum applications—would become the very issues over which the battle lines would be drawn in late 1990s.

Although the 1986 law did not change the asylum rules directly, its provisions nevertheless deeply affected the future controversy over asylum procedures. The law provided amnesty to most "undocumented" aliens who were then in the United States (that is, those who had never received permission to immigrate). But to deter future "illegal" immigration, the law required noncitizens to have work permits and imposed fines on employers who hired unauthorized workers. To understand how these rules affected asylum, it is necessary to return to the subject of the backlog of asylum applications.

New filings of asylum cases had declined between the early 1980s and the mid-1980s, and the INS's asylum backlog fell every year from 1984 through 1990.[117] But as the employer sanctions provisions of the 1986 law began to take hold, aliens who crossed the Rio Grande in search of jobs found it more difficult to obtain them. There was, however, one way in which such a person could get a work permit. Although a person arrested at an airport or border could file an asylum application "defensively" to try to avoid deportation, a person who had entered the United States without being apprehended could file an "affirmative" asylum application. A person who filed an affirmative application for asylum was entitled, under INS regulations, to receive a temporary work permit until the application was adjudicated. After 1986, this sole exception to the new work authorization restrictions provided a powerful incentive for filing an affirmative asylum application, however weak the merits of that claim might be. Furthermore, the incentive would become stronger if the time required for the INS to adjudicate applications grew longer, because the alien's ability to avoid deportation, and her temporary work authorization, would also be stretched out. In addition, the more aliens filed claims because of this incentive, the more the INS would fall behind in its processing, further increasing the potency of the incentive to file for asylum.

The INS might have eliminated the incentive by assigning more employees to process asylum claims, thereby eliminating its backlog and adjudicating new claims shortly after they were filed. In 1990, when the agency created a new type of official, a trained "asylum officer," to handle asylum cases, it had a particularly good opportunity to do so. But the "INS's top officials assigned only 82 positions for asylum officers ... grudgingly increased to 150 in 1992 ... with a bare minimum of staff support."[118]

By trying to hurry through its backlog without seeking or obtaining adequate staff support, the INS actually magnified its administrative problems. Apparently, the agency rejected many Central American claims in an overly summary fashion.[119] Applications from people who had fled from Guatemala and El Salvador were successful only 2 percent of the time, compared to about 20 percent for all applications. In the late 1980s, the government's treatment of Central American asylum applicants came under increasing judicial scrutiny. One case that reached the Supreme Court resulted in a decision that actually made more lenient the standard that the government had been applying to asylum applicants. Appealing his deportation, a Nicaraguan asylum-seeker, whose brother had been tortured by the Sandinistas for his political activities, argued that the attorney general had interpreted the "well-founded fear of persecution" standard in too crabbed a way, as if Congress had required asylum-seekers to prove a "clear probability" that they would be persecuted if returned to their home countries. The Supreme Court agreed, noting that "one can certainly have a well-founded fear of an event happening when there is less than a 50% chance of the occurrence taking place." It gave the example of a person from a hypothetical country in which "every tenth adult male person is either put to death or sent to some remote labor camp."[120] In his concurring opinion, Mr.

Justice Blackmun went further, criticizing the INS for its "years of seemingly purposeful blindness."[121] Similarly, in 1989, a lawsuit blocked the deportation of 27,000 Central Americans who had received only superficial and cursory asylum interviews, without proper conditions of confidentiality or adequate language interpretation.[122] And the following year, in a lawsuit that became known as the "ABC Case" because of the initials of one of the religious organizations that brought the suit, the government agreed to settle a class action alleging bias against Central American asylum applicants. Under the settlement, it consented to readjudicate virtually all prior denials of applications by Salvadoran and Guatemalan applicants, approximately 150,000 cases.[123] Reapplications pursuant to the settlement further swelled the backlog of pending affirmative cases. But "stunningly, top INS officials never actually budgeted additional officers or otherwise made any specific plans to deal with the coming onslaught of ABC cases."[124]

The result was almost mathematically predictable. After 1990, the backlog once again increased. It had stood at 72,000 cases at the beginning of fiscal year 1990, but it reached 97,000 in 1991 and, in the wake of the ABC settlement, 204,000 in early 1992.[125] With the backlog constantly growing, an unadjudicated asylum application appeared to be a ticket to indefinite residence, along with an authorization to be employed, in the United States.

Meanwhile, just as the INS was beginning to understand its partially self-inflicted wound involving affirmative asylum applications, the agency was beset by a related but somewhat different crisis involving "defensive" asylum claims. Since 1981, it had been jailing, pending hearings, people who arrived at airports without proper travel documents and immediately claimed asylum. But the funds that Congress had budgeted for INS jail cells were finite, and the number of aliens arriving without proper passports and visas, and asking for asylum, began to exceed the jail space available. The INS district director for New York, William S. Slattery, complained that it was no longer necessary to wade the Rio Grande; a would-be immigrant need only buy an airline ticket and land at John F. Kennedy Airport. More than ten thousand undocumented aliens were arriving there each year, and many of them were asking for asylum. The INS controlled only 190 jail cells in New York. Immigration judges, who decided their cases, had fourteen-month backlogs. Each person jailed was costing the INS a hundred dollars a day, so the INS could not detain most of them, and the majority of those who were not detained never appeared for their scheduled hearings. If the INS spent its limited funds for more detentions, there would be fewer INS airport inspectors, resulting in "long lines and waits for the ten million passengers ... who arrive at Kennedy each year." As a result, according to Slattery, "anybody in the world who wants to come can come."[126]

Human rights advocates proposed a solution to this problem. They suggested that the INS station some of its trained asylum officers, who since 1990 had been specially trained to decide affirmative cases, at the airports. These officers would screen the apprehended asylum seekers. The purpose of the screening would be to separate those with strong asylum claims from those whose cases seemed completely without foundation. This preliminary screening would not cause anyone to be sent home immediately, as under Simpson's old summary exclusion proposal, but would determine which people should be released into the community pending a hearing, and which should be jailed until their hearings because they were unlikely to prevail in their cases. That "would introduce rationality to the process," said Arthur Helton of the Lawyers Committee for Human Rights.[127]

The INS actually adopted this policy in 1992, but its own bureaucracy frustrated its implementation. The INS general counsel who had helped to develop the pre-hearing screening and release program later complained that "many INS employees view the job as simply trying to keep people out of the country. They don't distinguish between people who have been persecuted and people who have not. The enforcement people see the asylum branch and the general counsel's office as softies who have no real world experience and are an easy mark for fraudulent claims."[128]

The hardliners within the INS had a different solution to the proliferation of asylum claims by those apprehended without visas at airports. They urged the agency to return to Congress to ask for authority to initiate summary exclusions. Then, most of the aliens could be deported forthwith, rather than held for eventual hearings before judges. But the Democratic party had again achieved a Senate majority after 1986, and Simpson had lost his chairmanship of the Immigration Subcommittee. Summary exclusion legislation did not seem realistic. "It's on an INS wish list, but it's forbidden by law and it's unlikely the law will change," Helton predicted.[129]

Just as the Bush administration was struggling with administrative problems involving both affirmative and defensive asylum applicants, a new congressional priority began to change the other branch of refugee processing, the overseas refugee program. With respect to refugees applying for American sanctuary from abroad, the compromises established by the Refugee Act of 1980 had worked well for nearly a decade. But the 1980s were years of increasing repression against Soviet Jews, and some members of Congress believed that the United States was not doing enough to enable "refuseniks," Jews who wanted to emigrate from the Soviet Union, to come to the United States.

These members of Congress perceived two problems. First, under the Refugee Act, the government was directed to make case-by-case determinations about who was a refugee, based on whether the particular individual who wanted to immigrate into the United States had a well-founded fear of persecution. Before 1988, the INS did not always require individual processing. Rather, agency officials assumed that Soviet Jews, Armenians, and certain Vietnamese met the test. In August, 1988, however, someone in the government "blew the whistle."[130] Attorney General Edwin Meese began requiring that members of these groups, like everyone else in the world, meet the individual test for refugee status. The percentage of Soviet Jews granted refugee status suddenly dropped from 93 percent to 62 percent. Some members of Congress wanted to restore the presumption that formerly had been extended to the groups in question.

Second, the General Accounting Office told Congress that the question of which particular Soviet Jews received refugee status depended not on the merits of the case, but rather on "the INS officer's knowledge of conditions in the Soviet Union, how long the interview was, and whether the INS officer asked open-ended or specific questions."[131] Restoring the presumption would avoid these inequities.

In 1989, Democratic New Jersey senator Frank Lautenberg persuaded Congress to change the law to make it easier for Soviet Jews to immigrate as refugees. The "Lautenberg Amendment" to the fiscal year 1990 Foreign Aid Appropriations Act provided that people fleeing from Indochina and "aliens who are (or were) nationals and residents of the Soviet Union and who are Jews or Evangelical Christians" should be given refugee status upon showing "a credible basis for concern about the possibility" of persecution, rather than a well-founded fear of persecution.[132] The wording of this amendment lowered the standard of refugee eligibility, but only for the groups it named.

At first, the Lautenberg amendment was uncontroversial. It passed the Senate on a vote of ninety-seven to zero.[133] But Senator Simpson did sound a warning. He thought it a "mistake" to single out certain groups for "special treatment" and he regarded lowering the persecution standard as "not consistent with the Refugee Act."[134]

Because the Lautenberg amendment affected only the foreign aid appropriation for one fiscal year, rather than the permanent Refugee Act, it would have expired in September 1990. Before it expired, however, Senator Lautenberg proposed to renew it for two more years. Simpson was not eager to see the amendment renewed. He argued that many of the Jews being resettled from the Soviet Union as a result of the amendment, at U.S. government expense, could have immigrated, at their own expense, as close relatives of U.S. citizens.[135] Nevertheless, the amendment was renewed for two years in 1990, and for two more years in 1992, when its protection for Jews in the Soviet Union was rewritten, taking into account the new map of the world, to apply to Jews in Russia and the other states of the former Soviet Union.[136]

While controversies over asylum processing and overseas refugee admission standards simmered, the Bush administration also had to face a front-page refugee crisis. On September 30, 1991, Haiti's armed forces overthrew Jean-Bertrand Aristide, the country's democratically elected president. Military forces then "arbitrarily detained, routinely tortured, and summarily executed thousands of Haitians who had supported Aristide."[137] Large numbers of Haitians began to flee their country in small boats, seeking refuge in the United States. The U.S. Coast Guard intercepted the boats, as it had during other mass flights from Haiti in the 1980s. On board, INS officials conducted interviews lasting only about five minutes to determine whether a would-be refugee had a "credible fear" of persecution. This rough standard was an understandable attempt to make a quick, threshold determination, but it had no basis in law.[138] If they passed this test, refugees were taken to the United States, where they could try to prove a well-founded fear of persecution in an ordinary asylum interview. But the INS officials determined that nearly all of the refugees were fleeing miserable economic conditions or generalized civil strife, not persecution, and the Coast Guard therefore returned most of them to Haiti. The Haitian Refugee Center of Miami, a refugee advocacy group, sued the Bush administration, claiming that neither the Refugee Act nor the international protocol were satisfied by cursory interviews conducted by INS officials with inadequate information about human rights in Haiti.

After a federal court issued an injunction (later reversed) against repatriating the Haitians under these conditions, the government established a refugee camp at the U.S. Naval Base in Guantanamo Bay, Cuba. It conducted screening interviews at the naval base, but these interviews were also challenged as inadequate, in part because the refugees were not allowed to consult with lawyers. Over a few months, violence in Haiti increased and still more Haitians took to the sea. More than thirty-six thousand refugees were eventually plucked out of the ocean and interviewed summarily at the naval base.

The refugee camp on the base became overcrowded, and sanitary conditions declined. Diseases, including HIV-related illnesses, proliferated. After seven months, President Bush realized that the system he had set up for dealing with the Haitian crisis was not working, but he was not willing to bring the refugees to the United States for medical treatment and standard asylum interviews. Instead, from his vacation home in Kennebunkport, Maine, he ordered the Coast Guard to surround Haiti and to return all fleeing Haitians to their country. Pursuant to the "Kennebunkport Order," the refugees would no longer receive even cursory asylum interviews.[139] When Coast Guard cutters arrived with refugees in the harbor at Port-au-Prince, the Coast Guard officers used fire hoses to force them off the boats, into the hands of Haitian military officials who were waiting to arrest them.[140] In court, the government argued that because the refugees were being intercepted before reaching American shores, neither the Protocol to the Refugee Convention nor the Refugee Act of 1980 protected them, and therefore, the United States had a free hand.

In late 1992, with the asylum backlog growing, INS officials complaining that New York and other airports provided open entry to anyone who arrived claiming asylum, the Senate's consensus about Russian Jews beginning to unravel, and press criticism about the administration's handling of the Haitian refugee crisis mounting,[141] it might have seemed that asylum and refugee policy could not soon become significantly more controversial. Such a conclusion would have been quite erroneous.

# 2

# Clinton's Turn
## *1993–1994*

Our borders leak like a sieve.
—President Bill Clinton[1]

Even before he took the oath of office as president, Bill Clinton had to back-track on a campaign promise to refugees. Clinton had locked up the Democratic nomination before President Bush issued the Kennebunkport Order. Distinguishing himself from his rival, he denounced it in strong terms. "I am appalled by the decision of the Bush administration to pick up fleeing Haitians on the high seas and forcibly return them to Haiti before considering their claim to political asylum," he said. "If I were president, I would—in the absence of clear and compelling evidence that they weren't political refugees—give them temporary asylum until we restored the elected government of Haiti." He called the Kennebunkport Order a "sad example of the administration's callous response to a terrible human tragedy."[2]

Two months later, after a federal appeals court had issued an injunction against enforcement of the order (an injunction that the Supreme Court later stayed and then reversed), Clinton praised the court because it had "made the right decision in overturning the Bush administration's cruel policy of return-ing Haitian refugees to their oppressors in Haiti without a fair hearing."[3] A few weeks later, he added that he wanted to "reaffirm my opposition to the . . . cruel policy of returning Haitian refugees to their oppressors in Haiti without a fair hearing for political asylum."[4] And a week after being elected president, he said that the "blanket-sending them back to Haiti . . . was an error. And so, I will modify that process . . . I'm going to change the policy."[5]

Human rights advocates had additional reasons to expect that Clinton would rescind the Kennebunkport Order immediately after taking office. Although none of the lawyers who had worked on the case against the Order were members of the Clinton transition team for immigration policy, two of them were appointed as consultants to the team, and Yale professor Harold Koh, who had directed the litigation, worked with other experts to prepare rec-ommendations for the president that were circulated among senior transition team members.[6] Some of the team members told human rights groups that "whatever was announced would be to [y]our satisfaction."[7] Shortly thereafter, the *New York Times* reported that Clinton would order the government to begin again to process asylum claims at Guantanamo Bay.[8]

But during preparations for the inauguration, Clinton staff members heard reports that Haitians were building nearly a thousand boats and were hoping to land in the United States during the ceremony. They worried that the inaugural celebrations "will be marred by news footage of Haitian boat people drowning in stormy waters," a concern underlined by an unconfirmed report that a Haitian boat had recently sunk off the Bahamas.[9] When they investigated the possibility of reopening the Guantanamo Bay refugee camp that President Bush had closed in favor of returning boat people to Haiti without interviews, they discovered that it had been dismantled to provide tents to Florida in the wake of a devastating hurricane.[10]

A week before he was inaugurated, "the unthinkable happened."[11] Clinton broadcast a radio message to Haiti announcing that the Coast Guard would continue to carry out the Kennebunkport Order under his new administration.[12] Refugee and human rights advocates were "devastated."[13] Arthur Helton, of the Lawyers Committee for Human Rights, said that the decision reflected the "fear—even paranoia—among the Clinton team about an influx of boat people."[14] Some said that the decision represented a "caving in to pressures from politicians, especially from Florida, who had begun a noisy campaign warning of the perils they faced from a surge of poor immigrants."[15]

The new president's first days in office were not easy. He was "pummeled" by the press, which accused him of backtracking on campaign promises, including those to the Haitian refugees.[16] His plan to issue an executive order to allow homosexuals to serve in the military was leaked to the press,[17] angering the Joint Chiefs of Staff who read about it for the first time in their newspapers.[18] On his fourth day as president, his new secretary of defense wrote him a confidential memorandum saying that his proposed repeal of the homosexual ban would also be strongly resisted in Congress, and that memorandum, too, was immediately leaked by an opponent of the repeal.[19] The next morning, a gunman with an assault rifle fired on Central Intelligence Agency employees as they waited at a stop light before entering the CIA's parking lot in Langley, Virginia. He killed two people and wounded three.[20]

The gunman, Mir Aimal Kansi, a well-educated Pakistani national from a wealthy family, had entered the United States on a temporary business visa in March, 1991. Approximately a year later, he applied for asylum. His application included few details of the political persecution he claimed to fear in Pakistan. Because the INS was not staffed at a level sufficient to interview promptly the large volume of asylum applicants in the early 1990s, he was never assigned a date for an interview to determine the validity of his application.[21] Nearly two years after entering the United States, he committed the slayings and then promptly fled to Pakistan (where he remained until he was abducted by federal agents in 1997 and returned to the U.S. for trial).[22]

Just one month later, a powerful car bomb exploded in the underground parking garage of New York City's World Trade Center. At the time, it was, in terms of fatalities and damage, "the largest scale bombing on U.S. soil in modern history."[23] Six people died; more than a thousand people were injured.[24]

Within a short time, an asylum applicant was implicated in this act of terrorism as well. Ramzi Ahmed Yousef had been seen driving in the Ryder rental van used in the car bombing, and he had disappeared a few days later.[25] He was thought to be one of two men who lit the fuse.[26]

Yousef had arrived at Kennedy Airport from Karachi, Pakistan, on September 1, 1992, a day like many others, when thirty or forty passengers without valid travel documents were apprehended by INS officials at the airport. On the flight with Yousef was Mohammad Ajaj, a Palestinian with a false Swedish passport. Ajaj's passport was an obvious forgery, so his baggage was inspected. He had few articles of clothing, but he was carrying a large assortment of manuals on how to make bombs, and videotapes of suicide car bombings. Ajaj was sentenced to six months in prison for the passport fraud.

Yousef was more fortunate. Although he lacked a visa, he had a valid Iraqi passport. At the airport, he claimed asylum. He could have been detained, but the small detention facility was full, as usual, so he was released pending an asylum hearing that would eventually be scheduled.[27]

Yousef soon became a follower of Sheik Omar Abdel Rahman, the leader of the Al-Salam mosque, located over a Chinese restaurant in Jersey City. Rahman, who preached fiery sermons advocating the overthrow of the Egyptian government, had been arrested and acquitted in Egypt in connection with the assassination of Anwar Sadat, the former Egyptian President.[28] He too had entered and remained in the United States under unusual circumstances. During a four-year period, he had applied for seven visas at U.S. consulates in Africa. On all but one occasion, his requests had been granted. In each case, his name should have raised questions because of his previous ties to possible criminal activities. However, the officials who granted the visas were not foreign service officers, but Central Intelligence Agency employees holding second "cover" jobs as consular officers. Although there is no evidence that the CIA wanted to assist Rahman, they issued the visas routinely.[29] In 1990, the State Department discovered its error and revoked his visa, but he re-entered the United States, perhaps with a different visa, and applied for permanent residence. The INS granted that application, but it revoked his status in 1992 when it discovered that he never should have been allowed to enter the country. At the same time, it began proceedings to deport Rahman, but Rahman applied for asylum, a case that was pending when the World Trade Center bomb went off.[30]

Yousef flew to Pakistan hours after the blast, and he became the Number One fugitive on the FBI's most wanted list.[31] Rahman was arrested four months after the World Trade Center bombing and charged with plotting to blow up the United Nations Building, the Holland and Lincoln Tunnels, and the George Washington Bridge.[32]

William Slattery, the New York INS district director who for years had been complaining, unheeded, about spurious asylum claims at Kennedy Airport, was ready to make the most of the facts of the Kansi and Yousef cases, and of the fear of foreign terrorists that both inspired. Slattery was the son of a New Jersey firefighter, an ex-Marine, and a former member of the border patrol that had served in Texas to keep foreigners from crossing the Rio Grande. He'd been a deportation officer in Philadelphia and then an INS assistant commissioner during the Reagan administration. In 1990, he had been assigned to the top INS job in New York, and he had quickly established a reputation as a hard-liner, bent on jailing illegal immigrants to the extent possible. Immigrants' advocates had accused him of imprisoning Somali war orphans and Chinese dissidents; the American Civil Liberties Union had charged that he "denied [detainees] meaningful access to legal representation" and subjected them to "arbitrary and punitive segregation."[33]

But for Slattery, the INS's well-known lack of adequate detention facilities, coupled with the opportunity to avoid instant deportation by asking for asylum, was simply an inexcusable loophole through which aliens with enough money for a plane ticket to New York could evade the legal limits and procedures for immigration. Before the murders, he had tried warn the nation that Kennedy Airport had replaced the Rio Grande as the best place to slip across the U.S. border.[34] After the CIA shooting and the World Trade Center bombing, he was ready to launch an all-out media campaign. As an enforcement official rather than an official spokesperson or political appointee, he was forbidden by the INS from giving press interviews to state his opinions.[35] But he believed that he needed "to play the media card to get the attention of Congress." Therefore he "allowed the media to force me to submit to interviews."[36]

He began with a conservative magazine, the National Review. Shortly after the CIA shooting, he gave an interview to Ira Mehlman for a story that magazine would run on misuse of the asylum law. "During fiscal 1992," Slattery complained to Mehlman, "I detained only 1,169 of the 15,000 inadmissibles who came through JFK." Although the INS planned to quadruple the amount of detention space available to Slattery by fall, he termed the expansion "woefully inadequate."[37]

In principle, expanding detention facilities and increasing the number of immigration judges who adjudicated asylum claims could have solved the problem that Slattery identified. With enough judges, aliens arriving without visas and claiming to be refugees could have had their cases adjudicated in a month or less, rather than having to wait eighteen months to have a hearing, and the cost of incarcerating such a claimant for a month would be have been a small fraction of the cost of a lengthy detention.[38]

But Slattery did not believe that he could obtain the detention facilities that he would need to house fifteen thousand inadmissible aliens per year, even if the period for each detention were reduced. Since the early 1980s, jail space for aliens had not been paid for by congressional appropriations. The funding was provided by a small user fee, then six dollars per person, collected by airlines from each international passenger as part of the price of an airline ticket. The user fee funds paid not only for detention spaces, however, but also for "facilitation"; that is, for the INS and customs inspectors who worked in airports. The traveling public and the airlines cared a lot about facilitation, which directly affected how long an arriving international passenger had to wait in line after a flight. Furthermore, facilitation was very expensive, a result of unusual overtime pay provisions left over from legislation that had been on the books since 1931.[39] The airlines, which had considerable political clout in determining how the fees they collected would be used, lobbied successfully for the government to use most of the money for facilitation, as opposed to the detention of passengers who arrived without proper documents.[40]

Slattery, therefore, did not make a great effort to try to get Congress to create more judicial positions or build substantially more detention facilities. But he recalled the idea that Senator Simpson had championed unsuccessfully in the early years of the Reagan administration. "Instead of building a prison for 5,000 people, you could more cheaply have summary exclusion," he reasoned.[41]

After the World Trade Center bombing, Slattery accelerated his press efforts. He pointed out to *Newsday* that although Sheik Rahman did not disappear after applying for asylum, two-thirds of Kennedy Airport's asylum applicants never showed up for their hearings.[42] He advised the *Los Angeles Times* that "only 7% of all inadmissible aliens are detained. That means people know they've got a 93% chance of walking right through into the United States."[43] He told the *New York Times* (which ran its article as a first-page Sunday story) that "Congress must change the law to allow him to send most of them packing after a quick hearing at Kennedy.... The aliens have taken control. The third world has packed its bags and it's moving."[44]

Slattery got help from the Federation for American Immigration Reform (FAIR), the nation's leading anti-immigration lobby. John Tanton, a Michigan opthalmologist, had founded FAIR in 1978 because he believed that "too many Third World immigrants were entering the United States, having too many children, and assimilating slowly."[45] The organization grew steadily, attracting half of its members in California.[46] In its early years, FAIR had commented actively on immigration issues. It had, for example, opposed any amnesty for aliens already in the United States without permission.[47] But it did not itself become a subject of public controversy until 1988, when a memorandum that Tanton had written two years earlier was leaked to the public. Tanton's memo agonized over the supposed consequences of Latin American immigration. "Will Latin American migrants bring with them the tradition of the mordida (bribe), the lack of involvement in public affairs, etc?" the memo asked. It suggested that if Latin American Catholics reproduce more quickly than other citizens and "get a majority of the voters," they might "pitch out" the concept of the separation of church and state. And on the declining political influence of older immigrant groups with lower rates of reproduction than Hispanic Americans, Tanton's memo warned that "this is the first instance in which those with their pants up are going to get caught by those with their pants down."[48] Revelation of the memo brought a storm of criticism and led Linda Chavez, a former Reagan administration aide, to resign as president of U.S. English, another organization Tanton had founded.[49]

At virtually the same time, FAIR took another blow when a writer for the *San Diego Union,* based in the heartland of FAIR's support, reported that one of FAIR's principal funding sources was the Pioneer Fund, a New York organization "created in 1937 ... to popularize what it called 'applied genetics' in present-day Germany—that is, Adolph Hitler's massive program for forced sterilization for persons judged to be of inferior heredity."[50] In fact, the first president of the Pioneer Fund had been Harry H. Laughlin, who had so often testified in Congress in favor of the nationality-based restrictions of the Immigrant Act of 1924.[51]

By 1993, however, criticism of FAIR had receded in memory, particularly outside California, and FAIR was again on the offensive. Ira Mehlman, the author of the *National Review's* feature on asylum law, was FAIR's "media outreach" director. Despite Mehlman's position with the organization, he noted in his *National Review* feature on Slattery and the Kennedy Airport problems that he'd written the article "in his private capacity."

Slattery and FAIR had overlapping but not identical goals. Slattery was a professional manager, trying to fix a broken border control system.[52] He did not express any opinion on the appropriate level of legal immigration. FAIR stood for immigration restriction, and closing the Kennedy Airport loophole was a small part of its larger agenda. Dan Stein, who had become FAIR's executive director, believed that the inscription on the Statue of Liberty was a "sentimental vestige" of yesteryear. "Forget about the lamp and the door," he said. "We cannot accommodate even a fraction of the people who want to move here." Like Slattery, however, he favored eliminating the hearing rights of asylum applicants. Echoing John Brown's prediction of the coming civil war to abolish slavery, he declared that "unless the system changes, we're going to have a bloody battle and it's either going to be settled by effective political leadership or it's going to be settled in the streets."[53]

The most important publicity effort in which Slattery and FAIR were involved was the CBS-TV *60 Minutes* broadcast of March 14, 1993. The program began with host Lesley Stahl revealing that Sheik Rahman was "just one of hundreds of thousands of foreigners who have found an almost foolproof formula to stay in the United States." Stahl's principal guests, who spoke between film clips of terrorists and clips of immigrants walking through Kennedy Airport asking for political asylum, were Stein and Slattery. Stein said that "every single person on the planet Earth ... can stay indefinitely by saying two magic words: political asylum." He claimed, erroneously, that only one or two percent of those seeking asylum were legitimate refugees.[54] He asserted that even if no more asylum-seekers arrived, it would take the INS eighty-five years to clear its backlog of cases. Although Slattery had been forbidden from expressing opinions on the broadcast, he agreed with Stahl that "you don't know what [these aliens] have done, you really don't even know their real names, and minimum, they're in this country for eighteen months." One of Slattery's officers told Stahl "privately" that "there's no way of finding out if these people are murderers, terrorists, or if they have AIDS. We just have to let them in." Stahl concluded the feature with pictures of four men who had arrived and claimed asylum while she was conducting her airport interviews; they were leaving the airport "very happy." She added, to her viewers, "To walk freely into the United States and then stay as long as you want, it only matters that you get here."[55]

The *60 Minutes* broadcast itself generated "massive media attention,"[56] and FAIR was ready the very next morning with a press release and a detailed legislative proposal.[57] Within two days, the broadcast transformed asylum procedure from an arcane subject of interest only to those who followed administration of the immigration laws into a hot political issue. "Members of Congress already had the impression that [asylum] was out of control, and then came the broadcast," said a legislative assistant to a member of Congress who served on the House Immigration Subcommittee. "It solidified their impressions. It had a huge impact on the Hill because most members of Congress and members of their staffs watch most TV news stories. Most of them are media junkies. Even if a member didn't watch the broadcast himself, he was likely to hear about it from colleagues right away. And then there was a flurry of calls from constituents who were angry about what they had seen on TV. At that point, every member of Congress had to have his staff member write letters to constituents saying that it was terrible that asylum was being abused."[58]

Coincidentally, a House subcommittee was holding a hearing on terrorism the morning after the broadcast. The lead witness was James L. Ward, a deputy assistant secretary of state who was serving as acting secretary for consular affairs because President Bush's appointee to that position had resigned, but President Clinton had not yet nominated his own candidate. Representative Douglas Bereuter, a Nebraska Republican, asked Ward about Senator Simpson's old summary-exclusion idea, which had been reintroduced in the House in 1992 by his colleague Bill McCollum.

The political officials of the new Clinton administration had not yet developed a policy on summary exclusion, and Ward had to be careful. Yet a bomb had very visibly exploded and had killed people, it apparently had been detonated by an asylum-seeker, and Bereuter had remarked that a large audience was watching the hearing on the C-Span cable network. Even though Ward himself had not seen the *60 Minutes* broadcast, already he had "had people talk to me about it," and he knew the political impact the show would have. It would be awkward to punt. Ward began by noting that he couldn't speak officially for the Department of Justice, of which the Immigration and Naturalization Service was a component part. He asked the committee to accept his testimony as "that of an informed observer." In that capacity, he expressed his view that what *60 Minutes* had shown "is a clear example of what happens ... and in fact the Department of State two years ago went on record with the Immigration Service as supporting them in coming up with what we term 'summary exclusion' ... and I think the Congressman's legislation in my, again, layman's opinion ... fits the bill rather nicely. I would hope that both the Department of State and the Department of Justice would be able to support a reintroduction of that bill."[59] The political issue was now out in the open and on the record: would the Clinton administration be as tough on immigration, in this regard, as the Bush administration had been—or at least as the Department of State under the Bush administration had been?

Another official was even better prepared than Ward to respond to the *60 Minutes* broadcast. Bill McCollum was ready to legislate. McCollum, a lawyer from Orlando, Florida, who had chaired the local Republican party, had first been elected in 1980, after unseating a Republican incumbent who had been caught in a scandal. A member of the Judiciary Committee, McCollum's principal legislative efforts had been to lead the fight against the Brady handgun control bill, and to oppose the 1990 increases in quotas for legal immigration. Over the years, his safe seat had become even safer; his conservative views were consonant with most of the voters in his 81 percent white district, and after having been most recently reelected with 69 percent of the vote in 1992, he was headed for an unopposed race in 1994. Because the House had what seemed like a permanent Democratic majority, he'd lost a lot of battles, but meanwhile he had become vice chair of the House Republican Conference, and he had become well known for his "bulldog perseverance."[60]

Two days after the *60 Minutes* broadcast, McCollum held a press conference to announce that he was reintroducing his summary exclusion bill. He lost no time in tying his proposal to the nation's fear of foreign terrorists. The bill "addresses a problem that many of you saw raised on *60 Minutes* this past Sunday," he told the press. "If you watched the *60 Minutes* thing, you watched that Paki fellow wander off to go get a cab or something.... This brings us back to the fact that—you'll remember it was a Pakistani who has been accused ... it looks like that Pakistani who was involved with the shooting out here at the CIA came in under exactly these conditions.... Who knows whether somebody might be a potential terrorist we're letting in today, with all these numbers coming in?"[61] Days after McCollum introduced his bill, Alan Simpson introduced a similar bill in the Senate.[62]

Over the next three months, the Clinton administration tried to develop its immigration policy, but it was hampered by its own slow pace in nominating senior officials and the slow pace of Congress in confirming them. Clinton did not nominate Doris Meissner to become his commissioner of immigration until June 19, and she was not confirmed until October.[63] During this period, as "most senior immigration jobs [were] empty, the agency [was] being run by holdovers from the Bush Administration ... and into the vacuum local INS directors, career officials like William S. Slattery in New York ... moved to reassert their power and law-enforcement priorities."[64] Human rights advocates were alarmed by the president's willingness to leave immigration to Bush officials and the civil servants, particularly Slattery. From the Lawyers Committee for Human Rights, Arthur Helton noted that "Slattery cannot conceive of an alien who has a legitimate claim of persecution, and he has been much admired during this interregnum by other career bureaucrats for reasserting the old-timers' cynicism about political asylum."[65]

Slattery's "railing against the humanitarian leniencies of the asylum system"[66] may not have reflected disregard for human rights so much as a desire to correct or at least lay blame elsewhere for a problem for which he and his colleagues might otherwise be criticized. Human rights groups had long complained that the INS did not give high enough priority to asylum adjudication and had created its own backlog problem by not asking Congress for sufficient resources. By going public, Slattery "turned the tables, blaming the supposedly crafty immigrants who stormed the gates."[67]

Congress as well as INS career officials were active during this critical period. "Hearings proliferated on what was suddenly being portrayed as an asylum crisis."[68] Democratic staff members of the Senate Judiciary Committee said that Dan Stein's "call has been heard loud and clear" and predicted that summary exclusion would be enacted.[69] Meanwhile, the asylum application backlog continued to grow. Although it already included 244,000 cases in May, 1992, the INS projected that it would rise to 350,000 cases in 1993.[70]

In late May, the Senate's Immigration Subcommittee held a hearing on asylum policy. Its witness was Chris Sale, a career official then serving as acting commissioner of immigration until Clinton's own candidate could be nominated and confirmed. Although the president had not yet addressed summary exclusion and had not nominated a commissioner, it seemed impossible to postpone taking a stand on summary exclusion. Without accepting the language or details of the pending Simpson bill, Sale endorsed the "principles" of developing "effective procedures for expedited removal" of aliens who arrive in the United States without valid visas, and of "threshold determinations of eligibility (rather than full-fledged hearings) to permit those with plausible claims to remain in the United States to present those claims." Temporizing, she said that the administration "look[s] forward to working with the subcommittee on this matter." When Senator Simpson noted that "you did not seem to endorse . . . my bill" even though "we delayed the hearing to give [the administration] time to get some things together," she replied that Simpson would eventually get a more definitive statement, because "we are in fact working at the highest levels now on an interagency basis, under the guidance and leadership of a subcommittee of the National Security Council."[71]

Ms. Sale's assurances of an orderly interagency process concealed considerable behind-the-scenes turmoil. David Martin, a professor of immigration law who became a consultant on asylum reform a few months later and was appointed as the INS's general counsel in July, 1995, later wrote that a host of agencies and players became involved, including a great many White House staff, each with a different angle of approach and each at a different level of understanding and sophistication with regard to immigration and asylum issues. Apparently the painful series of meetings had seemed endless. Often, I was told, just as certain issues were reaching resolution, new players would enter the game—worrying that the package was either too tough or not tough enough, or otherwise demanding that some component be rethought.... A friend who had played a lead role in the internal debates remarked to me on my first day on the job: "We've both called for more attention to immigration from the top levels of the White House. Sometimes the worst thing that can happen is for your wishes to come true."[72]

Summary exclusion legislation seemed to be becoming an inevitability. Even Senator Edward M. Kennedy had apparently accepted the concept, after sending two of his assistants to Kennedy Airport to assess the problem there. After the visit, one of them reportedly favored "a quick airport hearing for [asylum] applicants and the immediate return of those whose claims have no merit."[73] Kennedy developed his own summary exclusion proposal, a variant of the Simpson bill that provided greater procedural protections for asylum applicants.[74]

As if the heat on this subject were not already high enough, another dramatic incident sent it still higher. Six days after the Senate hearing, the freighter *Golden Venture* ran aground on a sandbar two hundred yards off Rockaway Peninsula in Queens, New York. Its 286 passengers had fled from China, some seeking refuge from China's rule imposing sterilization or abortions on most Chinese who have more than one child, others merely seeking a better life in the United States. Each of them had saved a small fortune to pay the smugglers who conveyed them to the United States, and they had endured a horrifying and dangerous journey to New York. When they hit the sandbar, they jumped into the sea and ran for shore. Ten of them died in their first moments in the United States. Most of the rest of them eventually asked for asylum.[75]

Unluckily for the passengers, their sandbar was in William Slattery's district. Most asylum-seekers who arrived in the New York district without visas had been released, of course, because of the lack of detention facilities. But Slattery saw the arrival of the Chinese in New York, rather than on the West Coast, as part of a "deplorable trend"; letting them go free could encourage other smuggling attempts. Even though he lacked jail cells in which to hold all of them, he insisted that they be detained, and White House officials were not inclined to appear to disagree with his recommendation. "On orders from the White House," the survivors were sent to detention centers in Pennsylvania, Maryland, and Texas.[76] During the next four years, ninety-nine of them would lose their asylum cases and be deported to China, and about one hundred others would be released or resettled in Latin America. The remainder, represented for the most part by volunteer lawyers recruited by human rights organizations, pressed their legal claims for asylum. But they remained in detention with those claims still unresolved until 1997, when the president decided that keeping them in jail served no useful purpose.[77]

The day after the arrival of the *Golden Venture*, discussions of "quick fixes" became more urgent.[78] Members of Congress also paid even more attention to asylum issues. Senator Kennedy said that inaction on reformation of the asylum system had now become "indefensible."[79] One member of Congress particularly affected by the new development was Charles Schumer, the representative in whose district the *Golden Venture* had landed.

Schumer was something of a political prodigy, having been elected to the New York State Assembly at the age of twenty-three and to Congress before he turned thirty. In a dozen years, he had become well known as an energetic and creative member. He had helped to draft the bailout legislation after the savings and loan crisis and had been the floor manager for the Brady bill to delay handgun purchases. With a 95 percent rating for 1992 from Americans for Democratic Action, he could almost always be counted as a liberal, but he would occasionally latch onto a conservative position. He favored the death penalty, for example, to the consternation of many of his fellow New York Democrats.[80]

Schumer was no stranger to immigration issues or to the asylum controversy. His district, in Brooklyn and Queens, was "where the descendants of the 1890–1924 migrants live."[81] He was a member of the House Immigration Subcommittee, and he had helped to pass the 1986 immigration law, including its amnesty for millions of Latin Americans who had settled in the United States without permission.[82] Furthermore, Kennedy Airport was located less than five miles from his district, and he had long been aware of William Slattery's complaint of a leaky urban border. But his solution, unlike Slattery's, had not been to curtail the asylum adjudication process for immigrants without proper visas. Instead, Schumer wanted to preclude that process altogether, by arranging for INS officials to pre-screen passengers' travel documents in foreign airports, preventing those without valid visas from ever reaching the United States and claiming asylum.[83] This proposal had been criticized both by human rights advocates, who argued that it would hurt legitimate refugees who were unable to procure valid travel documents from repressive governments, and by conservatives, who pointed out that it would not have stopped terrorists such as Sheik Rahman or Mir Aimal Kansi, both of whom arrived with U.S.-issued visas.[84] He needed a new, more credible plan.

During June, Schumer talked with McCollum and with Romano Mazzoli, the chairman of the House Immigration Subcommittee. While Schumer had been advocating pre-inspection and McCollum had been pressing for summary exclusion, Mazzoli had a third idea. Only a small part of the asylum case backlog was the result of applications from travelers like Yousef who had been identified at airports as lacking proper documentation. Most of the applications in the backlog had been filed by people who had spent months or years in the United States. Some of them were bona fide refugees; others had applied to obtain work permits pending the resolution of their claims. Mazzoli's concept was to impose a new, short deadline on those affirmative asylum applications. This idea, like summary exclusion, had roots in the proposals first aired by the Reagan administration and Senator Simpson in 1982, but Simpson's 1982 deadline would have applied only to aliens who were already in deportation proceedings, not those living in the United States who applied affirmatively for asylum. Mazzoli thought that "an individual seeking refuge should have an obligation to come forward, not use it as a rationalization 15 years later to avoid deportation. If you go back to the original idea of asylum, imagine a Russian ballerina coming to the United States and saying, 'I want to stay here.'"[85] Mazzoli recognized that not every asylum applicant would be able to assert or prove eligibility for asylum immediately upon landing in the United States. "Of course you should give them a little bit of time to orient themselves," he reasoned. "How much time is enough? It comes down to how astute you think people are."[86]

The result of the Schumer-McCollum-Mazzoli negotiations was to put all three of their ideas in one bill.[87] In a press conference, they claimed that "with the three of us, it has a good chance of becoming law."[88]

Three weeks later, the administration decided on its policy. David Martin later remarked that the "very setting for the public unveiling ... revealed the remarkable political prominence the issue had achieved.... It was announced at a press conference where the president, the vice president, and the attorney general all spoke."[89] The president announced his support for new legislation to curb illegal immigration. Americans, he said, "will not surrender our borders to those who wish to exploit our history of compassion and justice."[90]

An administration official, speaking on "background" so that he or she could not be identified in the press, revealed the details of the administration's proposed version of summary exclusion. A person who claimed asylum after being apprehended at an airport without proper documents would have an interview with a member of the asylum corps, the group of INS officials who had been given special human rights training. That official would determine "whether or not they in fact have a credible fear of persecution, whether or not there is a substantial likelihood" that they could qualify as a refugee. If the officer denied the claim, the decision would be "reviewed by an appellate officer who works for an agency that is independent from INS." If the decision went in favor of the alien, "the strong likelihood is that they will be given work authorization prior to their completing the refugee process" by appearing before an immigration judge for a full asylum hearing.[91]

The details of the president's proposal represented two important compromises among factions in the inter-agency battle that had preceded it. Those favoring a summary process, rather than sending all apprehended asylum claimants to judges for full hearings, had won the main battle: the administration had endorsed summary exclusion. William Slattery was delighted; "getting this idea started is the initiative that I'm most proud of."[92] But those sensitive to the possibility of human error by biased or overworked inspectors had obtained important concessions. Under the Refugee Act, the asylum determinations for people subject to deportation were made by judges who were part of the Justice Department but independent of the Immigration and Naturalization Service, and an applicant who lost before the judge could obtain review by the federal courts. Federal judicial review was no longer assured, and "many new administration players" didn't trust a front-line INS officer to replace two layers of judges. Accordingly, two important aspects of the administration proposal were its provisions that trained asylum officers, not border inspectors, conduct the summary interviews, and that administrative review of any adverse decision would be undertaken by officials who were not part of the INS.[93]

The president's proposal was warmly welcomed by Representative Mazzoli, and Senators Kennedy and Simpson were said to be negotiating on the text of a bill that they might jointly sponsor to achieve the president's objectives. But immigration and human rights experts were alarmed. Carol Wolchok, the director of the American Bar Association's Center for Immigration Law and Representation, pointed out that many refugees couldn't be expected to tell their stories immediately on arrival; they are "people who survived because they didn't share their confidences." Lucas Guttentag, director of the American Civil Liberties Union's Immigrants' Rights Project, remarked that the "proposal is a badly misguided response by the President and some in Congress that panders to America's most primitive fears about immigration."[94] The director of the Lutheran Immigration and Refugee Service complained that the credible-fear standard subjected refugees to forcible repatriation "before all the facts of the case are made known," while the U.S. Catholic Bishops' Office of Migration and Refugee Service accused the president of reneging on his moral leadership in refugee protection.[95]

Representative Schumer, on the other hand, thought that the president had not gone far enough, and that the administration's program "had a few things missing.... Our bill says [that if you are already in the United States] you have 30 days to come forward or you don't have the right to asylum."[96] Two days after the president's press conference, the INS issued a press release saying that the INS was indeed considering several other ideas to supplement the reforms that Clinton had announced. Among them were "a time limit on applying for asylum, with narrowly defined exceptions."[97] Although the press release itself made it clear that the elements being considered by the agency were "not final," Duke Austin, an INS spokesman, implied that the agency in fact favored a time limit on asylum applications. "It only makes sense to have some kind of time limit," he said. "[I]f you are a true asylee seeking refuge, there is no reason why you wouldn't do it when you get here."[98] Though he appears not to have made it clear at the time, Mr. Austin may have been voicing his own views rather than those of the agency; he left the INS a year later to become spokesman for FAIR.[99]

At the end of its press release, the INS made public an action that would prove, in the long run, to make an enormous difference in the asylum process; it had hired, as a consultant to help reform the asylum system, Professor David Martin of the University of Virginia Law School. Martin had become personally familiar with asylum processing during the Carter administration, when he had worked on the claims of Haitian refugees as a special assistant in the human rights office of the State Department.[100] Since then, he had become a leading scholar in the field of immigration law. He was the author of a major article proposing asylum processing reforms and the co-author of an important immigration law textbook.[101]

For a few months, asylum became a less prominent political issue. Senator Kennedy introduced the administration's proposals as a Senate bill,[102] but he and Senator Simpson did not introduce legislation jointly. Doris Meissner, the president's nominee for INS commissioner, won confirmation and began to work. David Martin began to develop a set of ideas that could dramatically reduce the number of new asylum applicants and the backlog of old cases without new legislation. His key idea had three parts. First, the INS would deny a work permit to a new asylum applicant unless the government took more than six months to resolve the applicant's case. Second, the agency would give priority, in ruling on new applications, to newly filed claims, rather than starting with the oldest cases in the backlog; that way, it would have a chance of resolving such cases within the six-month limit. Finally, an affirmative asylum applicant who had no other right to be in the United States and did not persuade the interviewing INS asylum officer to grant asylum would immediately be put into deportation proceedings before an immigration judge. A judge who was not convinced that the applicant deserved asylum would order the person deported. Under Martin's proposals, an asylum application would no longer generate a work permit; instead, a weak asylum application by an unauthorized alien would bring the person to the attention of the authorities, and if the application was denied, the alien would be ordered deported. Because asylum applications would be much less attractive, the number of such applications would presumably fall drastically, making it possible for the government to decide most cases within six months and not have to award work permits.[103] An additional attraction of Martin's system would be that because the backlog would have lower priority than newly filed cases, the agency would be able to grant asylum to obviously meritorious applicants much more quickly.

But just as asylum had seemed to become more quiescent, another murder brought it back into the headlines. On March 1, 1994, Rashid Baz, a Lebanese national who had entered the United States on a student visa and then married an American citizen, was driving his car across the Brooklyn Bridge. Suddenly he drew two pistols and fired them in fusillades, one through his car window, at a van carrying a group of Hasidic Jewish students, killing Aaron Halberstam, sixteen years old. Baz then crossed the bridge, heading into Brooklyn, and sped into a stall of the automobile repair shop operated by Hilal Mohammad. Mohammad recognized Baz as a driver for one of his clients, the Pioneer Car Service.

Baz began ranting at Mohammad, saying that he had shot a couple of black teenagers who had tried to rob him. Mohammad tried to rebuff him, but Baz threatened him with a gun. Afraid of Baz's rage, Mohammad threw the spent shells from the back seat into his Dumpster and got Baz to leave.

Mohammad had entered the United States from Jordan six years earlier, on a six-month work visa. He had remained after it expired. Despite paying four thousand dollars to two lawyers, he had never obtained any lawful immigration status. His wife was pregnant with their fourth child. He feared that if he called the police, he would be identified and deported. He had Pioneer's owner retrieve the car, but witnesses who had heard about the shooting had meanwhile reported seeing a car with a broken window drive into the shop.

Baz and Mohammad were both arrested, and Baz was eventually sentenced to 141 years in jail. As for Mohammad, rumors flew. According to ABC News, Mohammad was believed by the FBI to be a member of the terrorist group Hamas. Some of New York's newspapers reported that the police thought him a heroin smuggler. These rumors later proved untrue, but the climate was so bad that when the district attorney offered probation in exchange for a guilty plea, Mohammad accepted. He was out of jail, but deportation loomed. He requested asylum, claiming that his life was in danger in Jordan because he had been a member of Al Fatah but had left it because he rejected its ideology.[104]

Devora Halberstam, the victim's mother, was determined to bring to justice anyone who had any complicity in her son's murder. She thought that Baz's life sentence was too mild and wanted him put to death, although New York law did not permit death sentences at that time.[105] She was equally outraged at the possibility that Mohammad might be granted asylum, and she worked hard to prevent it. Fortune graced her campaign, because she was able to enlist the assistance of Senator Alphonse D'Amato (who was willing to make what the press called an "unusual public criticism [of the judge] in a pending legal matter") and a congressman whose district was just a few miles from the scene of the slaying, Charles Schumer. Schumer joined Ms. Halberstam in statements to the press complaining that the asylum proceedings were unduly lengthening the time it was taking to deport Mohammad, whose asylum bid eventually was denied.[106] Schumer was more angered by Mohammad's asylum claim, and by how long it took to be resolved, than by the asylum claims of Kansi and Yousef. The slaying of Aaron Halberstam involved racial hatred, a child victim, and a New York landmark bearing the name of his own district's borough.

At the INS, officials building on Martin's efforts were working quickly to accelerate the asylum process. At the end of March 1994, less than a month after the Brooklyn Bridge murder, the INS published its proposed regulatory changes in the *Federal Register,* the first step in giving them legally binding effect.[107] Human rights advocates disliked the changes because they knew that many asylum applicants would have difficulty surviving without being able to work while their applications were pending, even if the government could decide their cases within six months, and they tried to persuade the agency not to make the change.

Meanwhile, Senator Simpson was nursing two new grievances about the refugee laws. They involved the overseas refugee program. Simpson had supported the Refugee Act in 1980, and he had originally gone along in 1989 when his colleague Senator Lautenberg had made it easier for Soviet Jews and Vietnamese people to win refugee status for resettlement in the United States. But he had grown increasingly concerned about the large numbers of overseas refugees the United States was admitting, because the federal government was paying only part of the cost of resettling them, leaving the balance to be covered through the health and welfare budgets of the states. Each time his colleague Frank Lautenberg had pressed for periodic special treatment of specific groups of refugees, Simpson had become increasingly doubtful about the wisdom of renewing the Lautenberg amendment. In the 1992 annual consultation between the administration and Congress, Simpson had urged the Bush administration to "reduce the flow through the refugee pipeline ... for a year or two." He had also complained that most of the refugees being admitted pursuant to the amendment were not fleeing any type of "active, current persecution."

In addition, Simpson had complained that the administration was not taking seriously the periodic congressional input into consultations. "It is difficult for me," he had said, "to see these consultations as a serious effort on the part of the administration to receive and consider the views and concerns of Congress when, without justification or explanation [they] are apparently simply ignored."[108]

Simpson had reiterated his two objections in 1993, when he complained that the fifty-five thousand refugee slots allocated for people from the former Soviet Union and Eastern Europe were excessive in view of the political changes since the Cold War had ended. Not only was the United States accepting most of its refugees from only two regions (the former Soviet bloc and Southeast Asia), but thanks to the "in-country" processing sites that the State Department and the INS had set up in Moscow and Ho Chi Minh City,[109] most "refugees" were people who had not even fled their countries. With more than 75 percent of the United States' refugees emigrating from within their own countries, rather than having fled, the overseas refugee program had, in Simpson's view, become "for the most part an immigration program in refugee clothing."[110] Simpson was not alone in his view. Mazzoli echoed some of Simpson's sentiments, saying that "we now have 75 percent of the refugee processing occurring inside the countries. This is an indication of an immigration program, not necessarily a refugee program."[111]

The Lautenberg amendment was scheduled to expire, after another two-year renewal, at the end of September 1994, but Lautenberg proposed to extend it again, through fiscal year 1996, justifying its need primarily by the strong showing that the party of the ultra-nationalist, anti-Semitic candidate Vladimir Zhirinovsky had made in Russia's parliamentary elections, and by reports of fires in two Jewish buildings in Russia.[112] For the first time, Simpson formally opposed renewal. He argued that special treatment for selected groups of would-be refugees (particularly Soviet Jews, who as a result of the amendment received 80 percent of the refugee immigration slots) was unwarranted; that it had prompted a "wave of dubious conversions" in Russia, and that the Soviet Union was history and Russia was now "our friend of friends." The amendment, he said, causes the United States to act on behalf of "powerful specified groups." It had turned U.S. refugee policy into "pure politics." Furthermore, many of the people given refugee status under the amendment were not really refugees, fearful for their lives; many of them even stayed in Russia to wind up their affairs for six to twelve months after winning U.S. refugee status. Unlike other immigrants to the United States, they were then resettled in the United States at the expense of the taxpayers rather than their American relatives. Despite these arguments, Simpson predicted, he would lose by a vote of eighty-five to fifteen. Simpson lost—and the vote was eighty-five to fifteen.[113] He was, however, determined to try again.

In his 1994 attack on the Lautenberg amendment, Simpson explicitly said that his proposal to kill its renewal would affect only the composition of the immigrant pool, not the total number of refugees or other immigrants admitted to the United States. Meanwhile, though, anti-immigrant sentiment had been rising steadily for three decades, a social trend that imparted real power to political demands for a retrenchment. In 1965, when Senator Kennedy had steered through Congress his sweeping repeal of the system of national origins quotas, polls determined that only 33 percent of Americans had favored decreasing the level of immigration. By 1977, this figure had risen to 42 percent. It rose again to 49 percent by 1986. By 1993, when Clinton administration officials had gathered to determine the new administration's immigration policy, the figure had climbed to 61 percent according to a Times-CBS poll, and 69 percent according to the Gallup poll.[114] Americans' perception that their economy was tightening and that jobs were harder to find contributed to growing anti-immigration sentiment in the late 1980s and early 1990s; 60 percent of poll respondents said that welcoming immigrants was impractical because of hard conditions in the country.[115] The poll takers learned that much of the anti-immigrant furor was "colored by a perception—contrary to the facts— that most immigrants are in the United States illegally," but politicians did little if anything to correct the public's misimpressions.

The feeling that the U.S. should reduce its levels of immigration, and particularly that it should halt the flow of those who were entering outside of the visa quotas, was strongest in California, where whites were just a decade away from ceasing to be a majority of the population. In 1986, Californians had approved a referendum making English the state's official language.[116] In the early 1990s, California voters felt themselves to be in the grip of a protracted recession, though in fact the state had lost less than 5 percent of its jobs compared with more than 11 percent in Massachusetts and Connecticut, and 7 percent in New York and New Jersey, and by the spring of 1994, "California was roaring back."[117]

California governor Pete Wilson fed the flames. In 1993, he had "lashed out at the state's illegal immigrants. Not since Earl Warren vociferously advocated interning Americans of Japanese descent during World War II ha[d] a Golden State chief executive sought to advance his political fortunes at the expense of an unpopular minority."[118] By the end of the year, three-quarters of Californians viewed illegal immigration as a "grave threat."[119]

In the early summer of 1994, Wilson's prospects for reelection that year looked poor. He trailed the Democratic candidate, Kathleen Brown, by twenty points. But as Wilson discovered that he could play on Californians' fears of new immigration, he "made illegal immigration the main plank" of his campaign.[120]

A voter initiative helped Wilson to make immigration a major issue in the gubernatorial election. Alan Nelson, who had directed the INS during the Reagan administration, and Harold Ezell, who had been the INS's western regional commissioner under Nelson, drafted what became Proposition 187, a voter initiative to deny public benefits to unauthorized aliens. At the time, Nelson was working half time as a lobbyist for FAIR, but FAIR claimed that it was not behind the initiative.[121]

Proposition 187, which received enough signatures to be put on the November California ballot, was designed to discourage illegal immigration by prohibiting the state government from providing welfare, public education, and nearly all medical services to unauthorized aliens. Informal polls showed the initiative to be immensely popular with the state's voters, enjoying more support than either Wilson or Brown.[122] Wilson saw his chance and called the initiative "long overdue,"[123] even making illegal immigration "the central issue" of his campaign. Brown opposed the initiative.[124] Senator Dianne Feinstein, a Democrat in a close struggle for reelection, opposed the initiative but said that she would work to pass her pending bill, similar to one sponsored by Simpson, that would crack down on illegal immigrants in many other ways.[125]

Brown's lead vanished, and Wilson won reelection, taking 61 percent of the white votes but winning over only 23 percent of Hispanic voters.[126] Proposition 187 carried easily, garnering 59 percent of the total vote,[127] though it was opposed by three-quarters of Hispanic voters.[128]

In this climate, with Congress and the Clinton administration vying to fix an asylum system that was widely regarded as seriously flawed, and the public at large increasingly hostile to immigration generally, it might seem that a law restricting asylum would have passed in 1994. If the Mazzoli-McCollum-Schumer bill was too severe for the Clinton administration and the Democratic Congress,[129] at least the bill that Senator Kennedy had introduced on the administration's behalf in 1993 might have been enacted. But neither house passed a bill affecting asylum or refugees in 1993 or 1994.

Several reasons account for congressional inaction in the 103d Congress. First, a much bigger issue simply occupied much of the available attention of the most senior policy makers, including Senator Kennedy and the president. The president's proposed health care reform, the major initiative on which he had campaigned, and in some ways the most important test of his political power, was in the process of being mangled and killed by the Congress.[130] For both branches of government, virtually all other new legislative initiatives were secondary.

Second, within the INS, ardor for summary exclusion, as announced by the president and embodied in the Kennedy bill a year earlier, had dampened considerably. "Some of political steam went out of the summary exclusion effort," David Martin concluded, "perhaps in part because the Coast Guard was able to intercept other Chinese smugglers' ships before they reached U.S. territory,"[131] so the *Golden Venture* episode did not evolve into a pattern. Also, Commissioner Meissner finally took office toward the end of 1993, and although she was bound by the president's announcment to support some form of summary exclusion policy, she had reservations about the particular bill that Senator Kennedy had introduced at the agency's behest before she assumed office.[132] As a result, she did not press for enactment of a summary exclusion bill until August 1994. By that time, it was too late in the congressional session for legislators to enact restrictions over the objections of immigration advocates.[133]

Third, the Kennedy Airport crisis eased. For two reasons, the number of people arriving each week without proper papers declined dramatically. Slattery had been given another three hundred detention spaces, and word probably filtered out that New York was no longer the risk-free port of entry it had been. Also, the INS had quietly begun to train airline officials of U.S. and foreign carriers to examine passengers' travel documents before they boarded aircraft bound for the United States. As a result, a smaller proportion of those with counterfeit or forged passports or visas arrived in New York.[134] (Of course this new procedure may well have excluded some genuine refugees who lacked proper documents, along with a much larger number of people who could not have won asylum in the United States).

Solving the problem of people arriving at airports without proper papers would fix only part of the government's asylum problem, because people claiming asylum at airports were only about 10 percent of those who sought asylum each year. The much larger fraction of applicants were those who filed affirmative applications after having entered the United States, some of them without proper visas. This group accounted for the overwhelming majority of both new applications and applications languishing in the ever-growing backlog. But David Martin believed that the administrative reforms that the INS was putting into place, particularly decoupling asylum applications and work permits, would significantly reduce the magnitude of the backlog problem.[135]

During the spring and summer of 1994, human rights and refugee organizations complained that many features of the proposed new rules, particularly the denial of work permits to future asylum applicants and the government's proposal of a $130 filing fee, were too harsh, forcing asylum applicants to go hungry for up to six months while their cases were being decided.[136] They persuaded the INS to drop the fee,[137] but Martin regarded denial of work permits as central to his plan to discourage unfounded filings. Withholding of work permits remained part of the regulation, which took effect on January 3,

1995.[138] Refugee advocates did not think that they could win a lawsuit to invalidate the new regulation, and no suit was ever filed.

By that time, however, a tornado had torn through the American political system. President Clinton's approval rating had fallen steadily through 1994.[139] Newt Gingrich, the House Republican strategist who planned his party's campaign, cleverly conceived of a "Contract with America," signed by virtually all Republican candidates for the House, to demonstrate that the GOP was united behind a positive platform, and one that could be distinguished from business as usual. In the congressional election of 1994, the Democrats lost their majorities in both the Senate and the House, with the larger body going Republican for the first time in forty years.[140] The Republican victory meant, of course, not only that each that each house would have a Republican majority, but also that each committee and subcommittee would have a Republican majority, and that the chair of each such committee would be a Republican who for years had sat as the leader or a very senior member of that committee's political minority.

The nation was not used to having a Democratic president and a Republican Congress. No one knew quite what would happen. But astute observers recognized that because Congress held most of the lawmaking cards, the combination was considerably more conservative than the regime of Republican presidents and Democratic Congresses to which the country had long become accustomed.

In every area of public policy, therefore, commentators and longtime participants in the lawmaking process expected a dramatic shift to the right. Immigration was no exception. Alan Simpson would be taking over from Edward Kennedy as chair of the Senate's Immigration Subcommittee. Lamar Smith of Texas would be taking over from Mazzoli as chair of the corresponding House subcommittee. The majority lineup in the Immigration Subcommittee in the new House was so conservative that Alan Simpson was considered "likely to be the voice of moderation on immigration matters in the 104th Congress."[141]

FAIR was elated. "We expect to see the tightening up of the whole deportation process, eliminating needless appeals, presumption in favor of detention, curtailing of asylum, and summary exclusion at the border," said its director Dan Stein.[142]

Advocates for immigrants couldn't honestly disagree with that assessment. Jeanne Butterfield, the senior policy analyst for the American Immigration Lawyers Association, predicted succinctly that "there will be a whole list of horribles put into a spiffy new package."[143] The Clinton administration, caught off guard, was essentially speechless. A week after the election, its officials said that they hadn't decided how to deal with the immigration policy changes that the election was certain to bring.[144] In just twenty-two months, President Clinton's turn to be the principal shaper of American immigration policy had already come and gone.

# 3

# Mr. Smith,
# Already in Washington
## January–August 1995

We're going to say to people who are not skilled, not educated and distant family members that we just don't have room for everybody in the world; we have to put the interests of America first.

—Lamar Smith[1]

Lamar Smith, the new chairman of the House Immigration Subcommittee, was, like many of the new leaders in the House, a Texan. The center of his district had been settled by refugees—Germans who fled their land when the democratic revolution of 1848 had failed. But 150 years later, the district consisted mainly of suburbs north of San Antonio and of Austin, ranch lands, and some oil country. It was 82 percent white, and solidly Republican, having voted for Bush over Clinton by more than two to one in the 1992 presidential election.[2]

Smith was well aware of the opportunity the voters had given him when they voted for Newt Gingrich and his famous Contract. Smith was a Yale graduate, a former business writer for the *Christian Science Monitor*, and a lawyer.[3] First elected to Congress in 1986, Smith had shown himself to be a staunchly conservative Republican. He had fought against the Brady gun control bill,[4] tried to cut every appropriation act, and unsuccessfully opposed increasing legal quotas in the 1990 immigration reform.[5] But until now, he had never been part of a political majority in the House. His main role in immigration debates had been "offering losing amendments."[6] Never before had he had the opportunity to play a leading role in national immigration policy. But now "I wake up with a smile on my face," he said. "I look forward to going to the office. It's nice to be in a position to help decide issues."[7]

Smith believed that during the 1920s, "racism, religious and ethnic bigotry, and bogus theories of eugenics [had] infected the debate over immigration, even in the halls of Congress,"[8] but that the 1965 liberalization of the immigration law had also been "unduly influenced" by an inappropriate consideration, the nation's concern at that time with ending racial discrimination.[9] He was determined to preside over an overhaul of the law, to "restor[e] credibility to the U.S. system of enforcement against illegal migration [and] set ... priorities for legal immigration that are in accord with the national interest."[10]

Smith was also well aware that the Republicans could lose their House majority in the 1996 election. Bill Clinton had squandered his party's two-year control of Congress. Republicans like Gingrich and Smith were determined not to waste any time. Only ten issues had been advertised in the Contract, and changing the immigration law was not among them. But Smith's back pockets, like those of every new committee and subcommittee chair, bulged with old bills and proposals that had never stood a chance in a Congress controlled by Democrats. Some had been introduced in prior years and consigned to die without further consideration in various committees. Others had never been introduced, because they had been beyond the pale of political feasibility. Until now.

On the other side of the Capitol building, Alan Simpson knew that his day had also come. Simpson had enjoyed enormous popularity throughout most of his Senate career and was still very well liked by his colleagues on both sides of the aisle. Indeed, in a poll of congressional staff members in 1990 he was termed the third most effective senator.[11] But Simpson had suffered three major political setbacks in the early 1990s. During the Gulf War, without verifying his source, he had called Peter Arnett, a CNN reporter, an Iraqi "sympathizer" and had falsely said that Arnett's Vietnamese brother-in-law had been active in the Viet Cong.[12] He brought more criticism on himself, from more sources, than he'd seen in many years; a *Washington Post* editorial complained that "Alan Simpson has dipped into the slime."[13] A few months later, during nationally televised Judiciary Committee hearings on Professor Anita Hill's allegations about the conduct of Supreme Court nominee Clarence Thomas, Simpson complained, without substantiation, that "I really am getting stuff over the transom about Professor Hill. I've got letters hanging out of my pockets. I've got faxes. I've got statements from Tulsa saying 'watch out for this woman.'"[14] He later conceded that "I was not myself."[15] Then, after the 1994 election, he ran for reelection as the Senate Republican whip (the number two position), a job he'd held for a decade. Had he won, he would have become the majority whip, and he would have become the majority leader when Bob Dole later resigned to run for president. But by one vote, he lost to his colleague Trent Lott in a secret ballot among Senate Republicans.[16]

For Simpson, that loss was not "free of pain."[17] He was committed to represent Wyoming in the Senate for at least two more years, but he no longer held the leadership position that he had long enjoyed.

His loss was mitigated by the fact that he could now take over as chair of the Immigration Subcommittee. The last time he'd held that position, he had been instrumental in passing the 1986 immigration reform. He had told reporters that passing that law had "really tickled my butt."[18] In 1995, he would have a chance for an even better tickle, because this time he would not be constrained by a Democratic House.[19] Like Smith, he was in a hurry; within days after losing his leadership post he announced that "this baby is red hot and we're going to move."[20]

Smith and Simpson would be able to cooperate in changing the immigration laws, not only because they came from the same party and shared a commitment to reducing immigration, but also because they enjoyed a warm working relationship.[21] In addition, one of the two senior immigration experts on Simpson's staff, Cordia A. Strom, moved across Capitol Hill to become the chief counsel of Smith's subcommittee. Before working for Simpson, Strom had been a staff attorney, under Dan Stein's supervision, for the Immigration Reform Law Institute, FAIR's nonprofit alter ego for litigation.[22] She had a close relationship with both chairmen, and like a pollinating bee, she would be able to convey ideas and strategies between the two committees and their staffs.[23]

For its part, FAIR saw in the chairmanships of Smith and Simpson an unparalleled opportunity to change the law, because those two men could, by virtue of their offices, control the process of drafting the bills. "We knew that it was a clear advantage to have two strong reformers [chairing] the two subcommittees," Dan Stein said. "When you have the drafting advantage you have a big advantage."[24]

Simpson rode the first horse out of the starting gate. Three weeks after the Congress convened, he unveiled his proposal to curb "illegal" immigration—with another bill, to reduce the quotas for legal immigration, scheduled to follow.[25] Simpson had said that he wanted a bill that "will not be ugly, because there are plenty of provisions out there that have an ugliness to them."[26] Indeed, this initial version of his bill was not as bad as some immigration advocates had feared. Some of the bill's provisions were benign, such as its authorization of additional funds for the INS to patrol the nation's Mexican border, and its increased penalties for alien smugglers. Others were more controversial. For example, the 1986 law that bore Simpson's name had imposed sanctions against U.S. employers who hired unauthorized aliens, but many employers continued to employ such persons, claiming they couldn't distinguish between valid and counterfeit employment authorization documents. Simpson called for the government to create a national computerized database system through which employers would have to verify identities before hiring any worker.[27] The bill also made deportable any legal alien who received public assistance for more than twelve months, but it did not deny all benefits to aliens, and it exempted child health and emergency benefits from the deportability rule.[28]

Refugees fared worse than most other would-be immigrants under Simpson's plan, however, as he returned to themes he had hummed almost as long as he'd been a senator. He proposed to impose a statutory ceiling, at fifty thousand, on the number of refugees who could be admitted annually through the overseas-refugee program.[29] His bill also provided summary exclusion interviews, rather than hearings before immigration judges, for those who arrived in the United States without visas. As in the administration's 1993 proposal, the bill specified that immigration officials could deport such people immediately if, through prompt interviews, officials determined that they could not prove "credible fear" of persecution.

Simpson scheduled a hearing on his bill, to be held seven weeks after he introduced it. Several of the organizations that advocated for immigrants and refugees began to meet and to prepare for this hearing, their first opportunity to organize opposition to what they saw as its excesses, and to educate the press. But they suspected that Representative Smith's bill would be much worse, and they tried, through requests to his staff, to get some advance word on what it would contain. In this they were largely unsuccessful. As one advocate put it, the draft bill "was very tightly held. Smith wasn't even bringing most of the other Republicans [on his subcommittee] into a discussion of what should be in the bills."[30]

"Ostensibly, hearings are important primarily as fact-finding instruments," the leading scholar of congressional procedure has written, but in fact "major bills have usually been the subject of public debate and media coverage[,] the positions of the administration and the special interest groups are well known ... [and the] hearings often are poorly attended by committee members.... Witnesses usually read from prepared texts, while the committee members present often feign interest."[31] Nevertheless, a hearing is an important event, because legislators believe holding a hearing to be a prerequisite, except in the rarest of circumstances, for passing a bill; because hearings give legislators a chance to obtain public support for their positions; and because corporate and nonprofit organizations use them for mobilization purposes as well.[32]

Simpson began his hearing[33] by saying that in the early 1980s the committee had held twenty-two hearings on similar issues, and he didn't want to have that many again.[34] In fact, he held only one. In his opening statement, he took direct aim at the Lautenberg amendment: "The people are also worried about ... the way claims of persecution made by persons from certain countries are judged by different standards, with the result that many are granted a status not possibly available to others who come from elsewhere. I call them State Department refugees."[35]

This statement tipped Simpson's hand, because nothing in his bill would have repealed the Lautenberg amendment. Such a provision would have brought opposition to the bill from the majority of senators who had recently voted to renew the amendment. Instead, his proposal to reduce the refugee quota by about 50 percent was probably designed to cause the Lautenberg amendment to implode without being repealed. If only fifty thousand refugees could be admitted worldwide, and the State Department admitted approximately fifty thousand Jews and Evangelical Christians from the former Soviet Union and people fleeing from Southeast Asia as it had been doing in recent years,[36] no other refugees could immigrate. That situation would be politically and morally untenable, so the State Department would have to allow fewer refugees to qualify under the Lautenberg amendment.

Speaking for the Clinton administration, Attorney General Janet Reno, the first witness, told Simpson that "you have been wonderful to work with, and I look forward to a continued cooperative effort." She did not address the proposed cut in the refugee cap, but, reflecting the influence of INS Commissioner Doris Meissner and the fact that airport pre-screening and other measures had already reduced by a third the rate at which people arrived at Kennedy Airport without proper papers,[37] she did signal a change in administration policy on summary exclusion. The administration wanted to have "standby" authority to use summary exclusion procedures, if necessary, when the number of arriving aliens "exceed[s] our inspection capacity," rather than being required to use those procedures, at all airports, to deal with every person arriving without a visa. This would "not require the full staffing" that Simpson's proposal would impose. In other words, the less drastic administration version would save money for the taxpayers.[38] In fact, the INS had already tried, behind the scenes, to persuade Simpson to change his bill to grant the administration only standby summary exclusion powers. But Simpson had rejected the request.[39]

Simpson heard from non-governmental witnesses on both sides of the subject of refugee cuts. Charles Keely, a Georgetown University professor who specialized in international migration, supported Simpson's proposed cut, because in the past, the U.S. had "encouraged outflows [from communist countries] for ideological reasons," but now "ethnic and advocacy politics cannot continue to make refugee admissions a humanitarian pork barrel designed to satisfy constituencies under the rubric of honoring Cold War commitments." Keely called for the repeal of the Lautenberg amendment and for the U.S. to accept only a "fair share" of the world's refugees "for whom death or physical harm is imminent." This "fair share" would be "well below" the fifty thousand that Simpson had proposed.[40] Dan Stein, the executive director of FAIR, also supported Simpson, because the refugee cap would "put discipline in the system."[41]

Two witnesses took issue with the cap. Elizabeth Ferris was vice chair of the Committee on Migration and Refugee Affairs of InterAction, the umbrella organization for the hundreds of agencies around the country that engaged in refugee resettlement and assistance. To begin with, she wondered aloud why a proposal to limit this category of *legal* immigrants was part of Simpson's bill to control *illegal* immigration, instead of being deferred for his bill to cut all of the legal quotas. Of course she could not draw Simpson out on this, because witnesses generally do not put questions to senators. Ferris argued that the number of refugees had actually increased since the end of the Cold War, from fifteen million to twenty-two million; that the U.S. should be able to respond more quickly when political events created refugees; that a cap would politicize the refugee program by making the protection of each group of refugees depend on lobbying by that group's supporters; and that a cap would "have consequences" to American leadership in the world.[42] Elisa Massimino, the legal director of the Washington office of the Lawyers Committee for Human Rights, added that if the people being admitted as refugees weren't the most deserving individuals, the process for selecting them should be changed in lieu of reducing their numbers.[43]

Massimino, however, focused most of her attention on the summary exclusion proposal—a logical division of labor with Ferris because, whereas Ferris's constituent agencies assisted people admitted through the overseas refugee program, Massimino's organization helped asylum seekers. Citing internationally accepted interpretations of the Protocol to the Refugee Convention, to which the U.S. was a party, she suggested fourteen amendments to Simpson's bill that would be necessary to make a summary exclusion procedure compatible with international law. Her principal suggestion was to lower the standard that Simpson would apply. An asylum applicant who entered without proper documents should be denied a full hearing only when his or her claim was "manifestly unfounded," not whenever the applicant failed to demonstrate "credible fear."[44]

A month after the hearing, the nation was shocked by an act of violence that dwarfed even the World Trade Center bombing. Early on the morning of April 19, 1995, the federal office building in Oklahoma City was destroyed by an enormous truck bomb, killing 168 people, several of them children in a daycare center. Timothy McVeigh, who had been born in America, was eventually convicted of setting off the blast,[45] but in the days immediately after the explosion, many politicians and anti-immigration advocates assumed that it was another example of leaky borders, and they used the bad news to justify passing laws to make immigration more difficult. James Phillips of the Heritage Foundation said that the blast would "raise the threshold for admission into our country." Henry Hyde, who chaired the House Judiciary Committee through which Smith's bill would have to pass, said that "our country is like a hotel lobby. You can walk in, walk out." The press predicted that as a result of the bombing, Simpson's summary exclusion procedure would be "revived and even strengthened."[46]

Simpson may have recognized that he now had more room in which to maneuver. His subcommittee was scheduled to meet to "mark up" his bill on June 8. In a "mark-up" session, a subcommittee or committee proceeds to consider a bill section by section. Any member may propose amendments (or amendments to amendments), which are then debated and voted upon. After all amendments have been considered, the committee votes either to kill the amended bill or to "report" it; that is, to send it onward to the next stage of the legislative process. In this case, the mark-up had a twist. Six days before the subcommittee mark-up, Simpson revealed that he had changed his own bill in significant ways, and was in the process of making still more changes, and he announced that the subcommittee would consider his new version of the bill, not the one on which the hearing had been held.

Simpson did not formally introduce the new version before the mark-up, so it was not made available to the public through publication in the *Congressional Record*. Instead, the text continued to roll right up until the mark-up began.[47]

When finally unveiled, the revised version had an unpleasant surprise for refugee advocates: it included not only the refugee cap and summary exclusion, but also a provision to deny asylum to anyone who applied for it more than thirty days after entering the United States. The time limit reflected Simpson's view that "if you are truly a refugee, you need to seek refuge [and] you don't need to sort it out."[48] The bill made an exception only for claims based on circumstances that arose after the alien's entry, and which the alien filed promptly after learning of the new circumstances.

Refugee advocacy agencies were caught off guard by the thirty-day proposal, but they were well prepared to fight Simpson on the refugee cap, which had been in his bill for months. Representatives of organizations concerned with refugee resettlement and immigration had been meeting in Washington for weeks to develop arguments and strategies against the Simpson bill. These representatives called themselves the "family immigration coalition."[49] They had studied the makeup of Simpson's subcommittee and noted that it had only seven members—Republicans Alan Simpson, Charles Grassley, Arlen Specter, and Jon Kyl, and Democrats Edward Kennedy, Paul Simon, and Dianne Feinstein. To defeat the refugee cap, they would need only four votes (including Kennedy and Simon, two liberals on whom they could count). Feinstein could not be counted on as a certain ally; she had "lobbied hard" to join the subcommittee so that she could help to pass restrictive legislation.[50] The best chance of obtaining two additional votes would be to find at least one Republican to take the lead in challenging Simpson, and another Republican who would follow.

Preventing a statutory refugee cap was of keen interest to refugee service organizations, and particularly to those concerned with Russian Jews. Reducing the refugee cap would not only weaken the American response to the needs of refugees throughout the world, but as Simpson was well aware, it would create competition for limited refugee slots between Jews emigrating from the former Soviet Union under the Lautenberg amendment and all other refugees. Fortunately, both Jewish and Lutheran organizations had good connections to both Grassley and Specter.

When officials of these organizations first saw Simpson's bill, they'd gone to see Kolan Davis, Grassley's aide, to ask that Grassley oppose Simpson on the cap. But Davis said that Grassley couldn't do so; Simpson had already extracted from all of the Republican members of the subcommittee a promise not to try to amend the bill in any significant way during the mark-up.

The refugee organizations decided to try to push Grassley to break his precommitment. The Council of Jewish Federations took the leading role in developing opposition to the cap.[51] The Council knew that if anyone could change Grassley's vote, it would be the Union of Councils for Soviet Jews (UCSJ).

Grassley had first been elected, along with many other new Republican senators, in the Reagan landslide of 1980. In 1982, *Washingtonian Magazine* rated all the senators and concluded that in the category of "intelligence" Grassley was the "worst" of the lot.[52] The *Des Moines Register* then publicized the fact that Grassley's staff had protested to the *Washingtonian* that the senator "almost got his Ph.D." The *Register* added that the House Republican campaign committee was using the incident to teach press secretaries "how to turn a stubbed toe into a full-scale foot amputation."[53] This terrible press account brought Grassley to his political low tide, but Ally Milder, a Jewish member of his staff, helped him up from the bottom.[54]

Milder had gone to the Soviet Union for the first time in 1976, when she had been a college student. In a pre-trip class, she'd met Shirley Goldstein, who had gone twice before and had become involved in the issue of Soviet refuseniks, Jews who were victims not only of Soviet discrimination but also of their government's unwillingness to allow them to emigrate. Milder and Goldstein spent their time in Moscow visiting well-known refuseniks and dissidents such as Yelena Bonner. Following this trip, Milder concluded that the Republican Party was tougher than the Democratic Party on matters involving human rights in the Soviet Union. She started working in Republican politics in her home state of Nebraska, supported Ronald Reagan's presidential ambitions, and went to law school. By 1982, she was a lawyer on the staff of the Senate Judiciary Committee.[55]

Milder recognized that Grassley needed to improve his standing with the public. Working with the UCSJ, she persuaded him to go with her to the Soviet Union and visit would-be Jewish refugees in their homes, although the U.S. Embassy in Moscow did not cooperate with such visits. Like Milder, Grassley took with him several Torahs and Stars of David for those he would visit, and some of them were confiscated by Soviet customs officials. The trip resulted in excellent publicity in Iowa, where human rights was a popular issue. It also greatly helped his political standing with Democrats. He followed up the trip by starting a congressional caucus to help Soviet Jews, and he changed his position from opposing to supporting foreign aid for Israel. He made frequent appearances at international conferences on refugee issues, and freeing Soviet Jews became a continuous concern. The combination of his conservatism and his willingness to champion refugee causes made him unbeatable for reelection.[56]

In 1987, Grassley had appeared at a meeting sponsored by the UCSJ, to question the newly freed dissidents Anatoly Shcharansky and Yuri Orlov about conditions for Jews in the Soviet Union.[57] Since then, the Jewish organizations had gone to him for help from time to time. They had discovered that while Grassley, a conservative, was reluctant to spend federal funds, he would help them to keep America's doors open to victims of persecution. In 1995, shortly before the mark-up, the UCSJ asked Grassley to meet with its Washington representative, and with Arnold Leibowitz of the Hebrew Immigrant Aid Society. At the meeting, Grassley agreed to change his vote and to oppose a statutory numerical limit on refugees.[58]

In addition, the Lutheran church had resettled many refugees in Iowa, where they had made a positive contribution to the state. Some Iowa Lutherans who were personal friends of Grassley had sponsored Vietnamese refugees in the late 1970s. During the weekend before the mark-up, Grassley was in Iowa. The Lutheran Immigration and Refugee Service arranged for his Lutheran friends there to see him. By the time he returned to Washington, Grassley had decided that he would not only vote against Simpson, but that he would make the motion to strike the cap.[59]

Arlen Specter, too, had long supported Jews trying to leave the Soviet Union. In 1911, his own father had fled Russia in poverty and had been welcomed in America.[60] In addition, Specter was very familiar with the refugee resettlement process, because he had served as the ranking Republican member of the subcommittee that appropriated funds to support refugees during their first several months in the United States. A considerable portion of those funds were spent in his state of Pennsylvania, and a statutory cap on refugees would reduce this source of income to his state.[61] Furthermore, he had raised substantial campaign funds from the Jewish community in Pennsylvania and New York.

Specter would not meet with the Jewish organizations. No one knew in advance how he would vote.[62] But if Grassley, Specter, Kennedy, and Simon voted to remove the refugee cap from the bill, Simpson would lose on this issue. Unsure what Specter would do, the refugee organizations also sought the vote of Dianne Feinstein, a much less certain ally because of the strong anti-immigrant sentiment in California. Like Specter, Feinstein enjoyed a good relationship with Jewish organizations in her state, but when the director of the Jewish Federations of San Francisco met with her, Feinstein said that she might have to part company from the organization on this vote.

While refugee advocates mounted these quiet campaigns against Simpson in Washington and in the states of his subcommittee members, another factor also undermined his effort to impose a statutory cap. This battle had been fought in the Senate before, in a slightly different way—just a few months earlier in the vote on renewing the Lautenberg amendment. Simpson's eighty-five to fifteen loss had put an overwhelming majority of senators on record as supporting a continuing substantial flow of refugees from Russia. Members of the subcommittee were aware that the main short-term impact of a statutory refugee cap might be that Russian Jews would thereafter constitute an even greater percentage of overseas refugees. Then the needs of other refugees might create pressure to kill the Lautenberg amendment when it next came up for renewal. By voting with Simpson, senators would put themselves under pressure to cast an unpopular vote against Soviet Jewry at a later time.

As the mark-up approached, the refugee advocates were fairly confident that they had the four votes they would need for a majority. But just before the mark-up, a new development altered their calculations.

As part of the 1990 immigration act that had expanded the legal immigration quotas, Congress had voted to create a bipartisan Commission on Immigration Reform. The commission had been moribund for years, but at the July 1993 press conference in which he had embraced summary exclusion, President Clinton had announced that he would appoint a new chair to the commission, to invigorate the effort to give direction to federal immigration policy.[63] He had appointed Barbara Jordan, a liberal former Democratic member of Congress, to chair the body. The day before the mark-up, with much fanfare, Jordan delivered the commission's plan to the president. To the surprise of many it reflected Simpson's views on several major immigration issues.

Jordan's commission called for Congress to cut legal immigration from its current level of 830,000 (down from more than a million in 1991), to 550,000. The panel also recommended reducing the number of refugees from 112,000 to an annual "target" of 50,000—the very number specified in Simpson's bill. The commission apparently believed that the number of refugee admissions would fall even lower than 50,000 when the large programs for the resettlement of refugees from Southeast Asia and the former Soviet Union came to an end, and that it could shore up the United States' moral commitment by locking in a number as high as 50,000.[64] But the commission's long-range view was taken as an immediate imperative by politicians eager to appear responsive to the public's desire to do something about immigration. President Clinton endorsed the commission's recommendations the very day they were made, saying they were "consistent with my own views."[65] The advocates were "outraged."[66] Maynard I. Wishner, president of the Council of Jewish Federations, said that if the U.S. followed the recommendations it would be "turning its back on its moral commitments and its history."[67]

The day's newspapers reported the proposals just as the subcommittee was sitting down to vote on a statutory numerical limit on refugees. But the advocacy groups had done their homework well, and they had already obtained assurances from a majority of the subcommittee's members. By the time the mark-up convened, Simpson knew that he was likely to lose on this issue.[68] Indeed, he had foreseen a loss, though not necessarily a loss in his own subcommittee, three months earlier, during the hearing. There, he had told a sympathetic witness that he would say to the "groups" that "you can go to the floor and you can win on that and portray anyone against it as being, you know, shriveled, but I will remember who is doing it. Other than that, I have no strong feelings in that area."[69]

Despite his pessimism about the outcome, Simpson did his best. The refugee issue came up right away. Grassley's discomfort at having to disagree with his fellow Republican was evident as he opened the debate; "You probably get tired of us saying how great a bill you have and then the first amendment that comes up is to strike a provision that I think you feel very strongly about." But Grassley did make his motion to knock out the cap, saying that in 1994, over 32,000 Jews had been admitted to the U.S. from the former USSR; the cap would therefore "cause, undoubtedly, the abandonment of thousands of refugees around the world." Kennedy supported him.

Simpson began by praising Kennedy. When the Refugee Act was passed in 1980, he said, "I was simply the playwright standing back in the wings. I am intrigued by a man that had a great grasp of refugee and immigration issues." Then, noticing Kennedy, "I see you smiling."

"Well, we go through this each time," Kennedy said. "I am waiting for the shoe to drop on the other side."

"When it drops," Simpson said, "a 15B shoe will drop." Simpson went on with his familiar theme, that the Soviet Jews were not really refugees, but simply subsidized immigrants. Then he complained about the advocacy groups: "The domestic refugee groups who care very deeply about these people—people in my church, the Episcopal Church, the Catholics, the Lutherans have done wonderful things over the years [but] they have so influenced refugee law and politics that I fear we will lose public support for refugee admissions unless we take some action. . . . We could well lose the program altogether."

As the moment for voting approached, everyone was reasonably certain that Simpson would lose, but no one knew how Feinstein would vote. Feinstein, too, did not know. "I am really quite torn on this because I really see the wisdom of what the Chairman is saying," she agonized. "Half of the refugee population ends up in California [and] there isn't school space, there isn't housing. I was hopeful I would have a little more time before this vote would come up."

Simpson called the roll. It turned out not to be close. The vote was five to one to strike the cap; Kyl was absent, and only Simpson voted for his own proposal. But he had not given up. "We will press forward and see if we can make the case at another level, as we say."[70] He might have meant the full Senate Judiciary Committee or the full Senate, but more probably, he was thinking about the House of Representatives, where Lamar Smith was in firmer control than Simpson of his Republican colleagues. If the House passed a refugee cap, Simpson could later try in a House-Senate conference to restore it to the final legislation.

Although refugee advocates had beaten back, at least temporarily, Simpson's effort to cap overseas admissions, they had not organized a similar attack on summary exclusion, and they had been taken by surprise by Simpson's last-minute inclusion of a thirty-day deadline on asylum applications. No senator even proposed amendments to these parts of Simpson's bill,[71] and the bill as a whole was approved, and sent to the full Senate Judiciary Committee, by a vote of four to two, with only Kennedy and Simon dissenting.

Meanwhile, Smith's staff had been drafting his version of an immigration bill that would be considered, in the first instance, by his House subcommittee. Out of the public eye, Cordia Strom and her colleague Edward Grant were combining into one bill the dozens of proposals that had been advanced over the years by the Federation for American Immigration Reform, former INS officials who had served in the Reagan and Bush administrations, and, more recently, a congressional task force on immigration policy appointed by Speaker Gingrich.[72] Pro-immigration advocates frequently asked Strom to let them know what she was putting into Smith's bill, but she refused to show them any early drafts.[73] They got their first look at the House bill when it was published a few days after Simpson's mark-up.

Simpson had deferred cuts in legal immigration quotas for a separate bill, to be considered later, but Smith combined legal and illegal immigration in a single bill that was more than three hundred pages long.[74] FAIR was delighted with both the scope and length of the proposed legislation. "We knew that we would be better off with a single bill," Dan Stein later recalled. "It is easier to pass one bill than two, and an omnibus bill takes on a life of its own."[75] Also, "The sheer size of the initial bill, the scope and magnitude of the proposed changes, covering legal, illegal, asylum and refugee reforms, made it possible for us to support the bill in its entirety while overwhelming the opposition's resources."[76]

Eight other members of his subcommittee joined Smith when he unveiled the bill at a press conference. The eight included John Bryant, a conservative Texan who was the ranking member of the subcommittee's Democratic minority. Bryant's co-sponsorship of Smith's bill signaled that it would be virtually impossible to make significant changes in the bill, at least at the subcommittee stage.[77] Furthermore, Smith announced that the subcommittee would hold its hearing on the bill's hundreds of proposed legal changes in just a week's time.[78] He wanted not only his subcommittee, but also the full Judiciary Committee, to approve the bill before Congress took its August recess.[79]

To the advocates who favored immigration, the bill was as bad as they had feared. It promised to cut legal immigration by a third, eliminate immigrant visas for brothers, sisters, and adult children of U.S. citizens, and require citizens sponsoring other family members to have an annual income equal to at least 200 percent of the poverty level for the sponsor, the sponsor's family, and the alien's family, a test that a third of Americans could not pass.[80] It barred nearly all means-tested public benefits (such as Medicaid) for unauthorized aliens, even prohibiting states from providing such benefits, although because education is not means-tested, it did not bar such aliens from attending public schools. It created a national computerized employment eligibility verification system, but it did not propose a new type of identification card.

The bill included two provisions restricting refugees. Although the idea of a statutory cap on overseas refugee admission had been considered "dead" after it was overwhelmingly defeated in Simpson's subcommittee,[81] Smith was emboldened by the immigration commission's report to resurrect it in his subcommittee. His bill imposed a fifty-thousand ceiling, like the one just defeated in Simpson's subcommittee. It also provided summary exclusion, rather than hearings, for people arriving without visas, except those who persuaded INS officials at the border or airport that they had a "credible fear" of persecution. Unlike the bill that Simpson's subcommittee had just approved, however, it did not impose a deadline on asylum applications.[82]

Smith was not eager to expose his bill to lengthy hearings. He allowed only a single day of testimony to hear from and question eighteen witnesses, though he had held other hearings, on particular topics, before revealing his bill. By happenstance, the House had remained in session throughout the night before the hearing, so the subcommittee members were exhausted. Only Smith was on hand to open the hearing, and only four of his colleagues dropped by during the day to be recorded as present. "We'll need to limit your opening remarks to 5 minutes," he warned the witnesses. "It's going to be a long day." As it turned out, however, the day was not long. Smith and his colleagues began after 10 A.M. He dismissed most of the witnesses with very few questions after their five-minute "opening remarks," so even with a lunch break of an hour and a half, he was able to adjourn the hearing by 3 P.M.[83]

The first witness was the Clinton administration's principal spokesperson, Executive Associate Immigration Commissioner T. Alexander Aleinikoff, who began by praising Smith's bill as a "bipartisan effort to craft immigration legislation in the national interest." However he noted, the bill "was introduced only a few days ago, so we have not had the opportunity to do a complete analysis of the bill's provisions," which the administration would submit at a later date. In his allotted five minutes, Aleinikoff principally highlighted the areas of agreement between the Clinton administration and Smith. He did not mention legal immigration or refugee admissions, although in a written statement for the record he opposed the refugee cap and said that the administration needed more time to study the report of the Commission on Immigration Reform, and in response to a question, he tried to create room for the administration to backtrack from the commission's proposed cuts, saying that the president viewed its report as "a framework, not a blueprint." Another Justice Department official who accompanied him mentioned summary exclusion, but rather gently: "We believe that there must be appropriate processes to protect aliens who assert claims for asylum.... The administration's proposal, in many respects, coincides with [your bill, but it allows the government] to decide when and how to use this means of exclusion."[84]

The bill touched so many areas of immigration policy that most of the other witnesses used their five minutes to address the cuts in legal immigration, and few of them mentioned refugee issues. However, three non-governmental witnesses spoke about them. John Swenson, the executive director of the United States Catholic Conference, stated that "persons fleeing persecution or other refugee-like situations have a special moral standing," and he argued against a statutory cap. Smith countered that the large numbers of refugees coming to the United States in recent years "are the result of specific groups of people that we feel are now mostly here, whether it be the Vietnamese or Russian Jews and so forth."[85] Bill Frelick, from the U.S. Committee for Refugees, provided the essential arithmetic. "Estimates of the current former Soviet caseloads stand at approximately 135,000 to 160,000, which will need admissions of 40,000 per year for the next 3 to 4 years. There's no telling what might happen [after that], although continued political destabilization, hypernationalism, and anti-semitism have to be considered as real possibilities. Currently about 30,000 refugees are admitted from [other regions, so the cap] would squeeze out some of the world's most vulnerable refugees, among them, Somalis, Rwandans, Bosnians, Iraqis and Cubans." Frelick also argued that the summary exclusion provision "really runs contrary" to the Refugee Convention, "which says that if a refugee can show good cause why he used false documents, that he should not be penalized in any way."[86] And FAIR's Dan Stein said, succinctly, "Refugee caps, long overdue. The special interests have undermined the integrity of the refugee selection system. Restoring caps is the only approach."[87]

With the hearing behind him, Smith could get on with the real business, marking up the bill in his subcommittee, so that it could be passed on to the House Judiciary Committee and then the full House. He convened the subcommittee in mid-July, just two weeks after the hearing ended, and kept it in session several evenings over the course of a week.

Smith had the votes in his subcommittee to do just about anything he wanted. Like many House subcommittees, the Subcommittee on Immigration was not broadly representative of the House of Representatives. When they join the House, new members of Congress are allowed to express preferences for their committees and subcommittees; those who join the Immigration Subcommittee are usually those who feel passionately, one way or the other, about immigration. The committee's membership tended to come from states with large numbers of immigrants; in 1995, five of the seven Republicans, and three of the five Democrats, represented just three states—Texas, California, and Florida. As a result, in the 104th Congress as in other sessions, the Immigration Subcommittee tended to be disproportionately composed of Republicans who felt strongly that immigration should be curbed, and Democrats who believed, with equal fervor, that it should not be restricted further. As soon as the Republicans achieved a majority in the subcommittee at the beginning of 1995, the anti-immigration forces were well in control, particularly because Smith picked up the support of John Bryant, the ranking Democrat. He could count on an eight-to-four majority on most issues, nine-to-three when Schumer went along with him.

At the mark-up, therefore, the Democrats, most of whom were still shell-shocked after losing control of the House for the first time in forty years, had little hope of amending the bill, and they saved most of their fire for the full committee.[88] They did not even try, for example, to force a vote—which they would have lost—on retaining the existing quotas for legal immigration.[89] But conservative Republicans felt no such restraint. As at Simpson's mark-up in the subcommittee's Senate counterpart, a proposal to impose a deadline on asylum applications made a surprise appearance. Although Smith's bill had not included such a provision, Representative McCollum dusted off the deadline provisions of the bill that he had introduced with Mazzoli and Schumer in 1993. He proposed similar provisions as an amendment to the bill. The McCollum amendment precluded an alien from applying for asylum, unless she had filed a "notice of intention to file" it with thirty days after arriving in the United States and had then filed it within sixty days thereafter. Like Simpson's bill, it made an exception where circumstances had changed in the alien's own country. The amendment also changed the standard for granting asylum. Instead of awarding it whenever a person showed a well-founded fear of persecution, the amendment allowed asylum only when the applicant proved that it was "more likely than not" that she would be persecuted.

Five months earlier, the INS had put into effect David Martin's regulatory reforms, which were intended to eliminate the employment authorization carrot that asylum critics claimed had been provoking unfounded asylum applications. McCollum's decision to recycle Mazzoli's time limitation on filing claims may seem puzzling in view of the recent change. Three reasons may help to explain his action.

First, McCollum may have known about the regulatory reform but simply not have cared whether or not it was working. At that stage, at least, he may have thought about the problem in moral terms, rather than as a solution to the administrative problem of an overloaded processing system. "There was the idea that people have a duty to come forward," his staff assistant recalled. "There should be some responsibility on their part to make themselves known."[90]

Second, the INS may not have known or reported accurately to Congress just how successful its reforms had been. On July 5, it had announced that the reforms had produced a "14 percent drop in the number of asylum claims filed, as compared to January–May, 1994."[91] This statistic greatly understated the effects of the reform. The 1995 component of the comparison apparently included claims that had been filed years earlier by Guatemalans and Salvadorans, which were being re-filed early in 1995 for readjudication under the federal court settlement of the "ABC" case. In fact, the INS had received 55,074 new (non-ABC) asylum applications in the first five months of 1994, and only 30,533 such applications in the same period of 1995,[92] a drop of 44 percent, not 14 percent. Even this more meaningful figure would have understated the effects of the reform, however, because the application statistics for the first two months of 1995 (as well as the last two months of 1994) were bloated by filings stimulated by the reforms themselves, as aliens tried, some unsuccessfully, to beat the January 4, 1995, deadline for receiving employment authorization simply by applying for asylum. If the INS had compared applications in March, April, and May of 1995 with the same period of 1994, it would have discovered that applications had fallen by 62 percent, from 33,355 to 12,798.[93]

Third, news of the success of the regulatory reforms, or even of their existence, may not have reached Carmel Fisk, the staff member who reincarnated the Mazzoli provision as the McCollum amendment, until after the subcommittee voted on the bill. Fisk had done McCollum's immigration staff work in 1994, but she had left at the end of the year to take care of her child. During the first half of 1995, McCollum had no staff person working at the Immigration Subcommittee. A member of his regular office staff tried to fill in, but this staff member "didn't have much background in immigration."[94] As the Smith bill headed for its July 13 subcommittee mark-up, McCollum's office called Fisk at home and asked her to return to help him with the bill. She agreed to do so, but she did not arrive until shortly before the mark-up.[95] During her period at home, she did not follow immigration issues closely. "I had a lot going on," she recalled. "I was eight months pregnant and had a two-year-old at home. They called me a week or two before the subcommittee mark-up. They were basically using stuff we had prepared in the previous Congress."[96]

Armed with the news of the "14 percent drop" resulting from the reforms, an INS lawyer, Joyce Chiang, tried prior to the mark-up to brief whichever staffer in McCollum's office was working on the Smith bill. Fisk hadn't yet returned to work for McCollum, so she briefed Karl Kaufmann, another of McCollum's legislative assistants, who had joined the staff that year.[97] But it was Fisk, not Kaufmann, who would, within the next several days, resuscitate Mazzoli's deadline. Chiang was not able to brief Fisk until July 24, several days after the subcommittee completed its mark-up of the bill.[98]

McCollum himself may not have become aware of the administration's reforms until considerably later. Two months after the mark-up, a delegation of conservative advocates met with McCollum to express their concerns about the immigration bill's provisions for a national identity card. At the end of the meeting, Stuart Anderson, a policy analyst for the CATO Institute, asked McCollum about his asylum deadline amendment that by then had been approved by Smith's subcommittee. He pointed out that the deadline would cause great hardship for people fleeing forced abortion, a concern shared by many conservatives. McCollum replied that any person who missed the deadline could ask Congress to pass a "private bill" to allow the person to avoid deportation. Anderson pointed out that the INS had changed its regulations to deny automatic employment authorization to asylum applicants, and that the administrative reform appeared to have taken care of much of the problem of spurious applications. McCollum said that he wasn't aware that the regulations had been changed.[99]

At the subcommittee mark-up, Smith and the other Republicans, as well as Schumer, were receptive to McCollum's proposal. Two Democratic representatives, Howard Berman and Xavier Beccera, objected to his amendment, arguing that the new rules would make many real refugees ineligible for asylum. But Berman and Beccera were hopelessly outnumbered in the subcommittee, and the amendment passed by voice vote.[100]

Berman also tried to ease the standard that would be applied by the INS in Smith's summary exclusion provision. Under the Smith bill, aliens subject to summary exclusion would have asylum claims decided by the INS on the spot, without hearings, and a claimant could obtain a full hearing before an immigration judge only by showing a "credible fear" of persecution. But the Smith bill also went further by giving "credible fear" a special definition. To pass the test, the alien would have to persuade the INS official that it was "more probable than not" that he was telling the truth, and that in the light of his statements, there was a significant possibility that he could win asylum. Berman wanted to enable an alien to win by showing that it was "probable" that the alien was telling the truth, and that there was a "reasonable" rather than a "significant" possibility of winning. Smith and McCollum claimed, however, that

Smith's language had been "very carefully thought out," and Berman's amendment failed on a voice vote.[101]

After considering these and about thirty other amendments, the subcommittee passed Smith's bill by voice vote, sending the legislation, including McCollum's amendment, to the full House Judiciary Committee. But the process had taken four meetings over the course of a week. Although Smith had controlled the outcome, he had not managed to move the bill through the subcommittee as quickly as he would have preferred. Congress was about to take its traditional August recess, so the Judiciary Committee would be unable to convene before mid-September. That would give pro-immigration forces some time to regroup and to try to build opposition.

The National Immigration Forum used the month of August to organize national lobbying on all aspects of the Smith bill. The Forum, a national coalition of 222 ethnic, religious, labor, and service organizations, had been founded in 1982 to "preserve America's long standing commitment to the rights and opportunities of immigrants and refugees."[102] In 1993, when McCollum and his colleagues had tried to restrict asylum, the Forum had kept its members informed, but it had not engaged in lobbying. By 1995, it had become clear that many aspects of America's immigration policy might be reversed, and its officers decided that the Forum had to become more active in the halls of Congress.

On August 1, the Forum sent its members an "urgent action alert," noting that the subcommittee's bill would "gut family immigration, slash refugee admissions ... [and] decimate due process for asylum seekers." It warned that "the best, and probably last chance" to change the bill would be in the Judiciary Committee. Putting the best possible face on the devastation of immigrants' rights wrought by the subcommittee, it heralded, "Our voices are being heard ... most significantly, the full Judiciary Committee mark-up was put off until after the August recess." It urged its members to undertake all of the standard citizen actions. Specifically, it asked them to try to meet with their representatives, if only for ten minutes, during the recess; to meet with the editorial board of their local newspapers to ask for editorials opposing the bill; and to start campaigns to write letters to representatives. It also asked them to bring as many people as possible to Washington for "lobby days" on September 11 and 12, just when the Judiciary Committee would be starting its own mark-up. "The goal is to have at least 300 people swarm Congressional offices" to demonstrate support for "fair and generous immigration and refugee policies."[103]

The campaign to stop the Smith and Simpson bills had begun. But the congressional Republicans appeared to have the momentum, and the power to have their way.

# 4

# Mark-up Hell
## September–November 1995

My Dad was an immigrant, and it's a good thing, but things run out.
> —Representative Sonny Bono (R-CA),
> during House Judiciary Committee con-
> sideration of the immigration bill.[1]

On September 11 and 12, 1995, the "lobby days" organized by the National Immigration Forum (NIF), about 350 people converged on the House of Representatives office buildings, where they saw their representatives, or, in many cases, their representatives' staff members who were responsible for immigration policy. Even before the lobby day started, NIF officials were optimistic that they could win support from a few Republican members of the Judiciary Committee, enough to reverse some of the most important decisions that the subcommittee had made. "As a result of visits by advocates," NIF told its members, several key Republicans have begun to express misgivings ... and may now be inclined to split the bill, rethink the refugee cap and family immigration categories [and] soften the asylum and summary exclusion provisions." After lobby day, NIF told its members that the effort had been a "grand success," and that their visits had left members of Congress with "plenty to think about as they consider some of the egregious provisions."[2]

NIF had not merely unleashed its membership on the Hill; it had equipped them with materials to leave with legislators, maps of Capitol Hill, reporting forms, and most important, a set of prioritized issues. It would have been impossible for NIF to train its members to argue about the details of the several dozen contentious issues in the legislation, so it provided them with sample messages on four issues: maintaining existing quotas for immigration by relatives of people already lawfully in the United States, protecting refugees, rejecting a national employee identification system, and, above all, "splitting" the House bill.[3]

Splitting the bill meant decoupling proposed cutbacks of legal immigration from those provisions of the bill, such as the sections providing for more border guards, that sought to prevent illegal immigration. A "split" would create separate immigration bills to deal with the two different types of immigration.

Splitting was a high-priority tactic of immigration advocates for three reasons. First, a bill to combat illegal immigration seemed certain to pass in the 104th Congress, probably by a wide margin. If a single bill also included a retrenchment of the legal immigration quotas, that less popular measure could be swept into law on the back of the illegal immigration controls, without full consideration of its own merits. Second, even the provisions designed to control illegal immigration included what the immigration advocates regarded as excesses, such as the national identitification system and the summary exclusion provisions. But as long as the organizations had to concentrate on preserving opportunities for their constituents' relatives to immigrate, they were certain to be less effective in trying to control those excesses. Third, the high-tech industries, particularly computer, software, and pharmaceutical firms, relied heavily on foreign-born scientists and engineers. These firms would not lobby to preserve quotas for immigrants' relatives, but they did want Congress to preserve existing quotas for skilled workers. A split-the-bill strategy would draw the fault line between legal and illegal immigration, not between family and business immigration. It therefore offered the possibility that business groups would help to preserve family immigration, and vice versa.

The NIF took two other important steps, not relying only on its lobby days. First, it sought and received help from Rick Swartz, its founder. Swartz had begun his career in the mid-1970s in a large Washington law firm but had soon become a staff attorney with the Lawyers Committee for Civil Rights Under Law. There he had helped to handle a class action for four thousand Haitians aggrieved by the INS's asylum procedures. He had also helped members of Congress to write a law to reimburse Florida for federal social services for the Haitians and Cubans who arrived in large numbers in 1980. In 1982, Swartz founded the Forum to provide an institutional voice for immigrants in national affairs. For about ten years, he'd served as its president, bringing into its fold more than a hundred national organizations and thousands of local affiliates. He advised both the Bush administration and the Clinton campaign on refugee issues, and a *National Law Journal* study named him one of the nation's twenty most prominent immigration attorneys. Then, in the early 1990s, he had begun to work with conservatives. He'd left the presidency of the Forum, opened a political consulting firm, and become an advisor to the Hoover Institution at Stanford. He was hired to advise Microsoft and Intel, both of which worried that Congress would limit immigration by skilled workers. He received encouragement and funding from the Political Club for Growth, a conservative organization that had helped to bankroll Newt Gingrich's political action committee.[4] The conservative organizations particularly detested any hint that immigration enforcement would lead to Americans being required to carry a national identity card, but as part of a wider effort, they were also willing to argue against further restrictions on legal immigration.[5] By late summer, 1995, Swartz had enough political and business connections to try to forge a coalition of the right and the left on immigration issues, centered on the split-the-bill strategy. If Swartz could indeed create such a coalition, the Forum and its allies might obtain unusual political clout.

The Washington staff of the Forum also organized experts to brief the staff assistants of House Judiciary Committee members about the subcommittee bill, so that those assistants would not be dependent on Smith's staff to interpret the often arcane text. Swartz helped arrange for staff members of two conservative Washington think tanks, Steve Moore of the CATO Institute and Stuart Anderson of the Alexis de Tocqueville Institution, to join several more predictable pro-immigration advocates at one such briefing.[6] The conservatives tended to emphasize their opposition to the restrictions on business immigration, while the liberals argued against restrictions on family unification and refugees. They found common ground in fighting the nation's general aversion to immigration, and they began to coordinate tactics, causing a stir despite their somewhat differing interests. On the second of the NIF's two lobby days, executives from sixty-five corporations also descended on congressional offices to demonstrate their desire for continued immigration by skilled employees.[7] "Most of these groups have never worked together before," Swartz said proudly.[8]

Swartz was able to bring some libertarian non-profit organizations and a few high-tech companies into the emerging "left-right" coalition, but his contacts among mainstream U.S. corporations were more limited. For those contacts, the pro-immigration community turned to Warren Leiden and Jeanne Butterfield of the American Immigration Lawyers Association (AILA). Businesses that needed visas for key employees from abroad often turned to specialized immigration lawyers to help solve their problems. The top officials of the lawyers' trade association therefore asked the group's members to request their corporate clients to help fight new restrictions.[9] Eventually, some of the trade associations for business organizations began attending meetings of the family immigration coalition and coordinating their lobbying with them.[10]

Smith himself was unmoved even by the combined efforts of the left-right coalition and the family coalition. If immigration advocates were going to avoid a one-third cut in legal immigration levels, they would have to find the votes to beat him, rather than win him over. The best chance to do that might be in the full Judiciary Committee, they reasoned, rather than on the House floor, because it would be easier to educate 35 Representatives than all 435 of them.[11] Furthermore, Speaker Gingrich would be able to impose rather firm discipline once the bill got to the House floor. The Rules Committee, which the House leadership controlled, could limit floor amendments or even prevent the House from considering any amendments to the committee-passed bill.[12]

The Judiciary Committee had fifteen Democrats, but only twelve of them were strongly pro-immigrant, and the twelve included Schumer, who could not be relied on for asylum-related issues. Immigration advocates would have to win over at least six of the twenty Republicans. Therefore, the best chance for changing the bill significantly in the Judiciary Committee would be to persuade the committee's conservative chairman, Henry Hyde of Illinois, to support amendments to the bill that had emerged from Smith's subcommittee. The chairman's vote for an amendment would give other Republicans political "cover" to support the amendment as well.

Hyde represented conservative, high-income suburbs west of Chicago. His district was 88 percent white and only 1 percent black. First elected in 1974, Hyde had become one of the most respected members of the House. Through the 1980s he had adopted his party's positions on most issues; he had "destroyed" the nuclear freeze resolution, tried to amend the U.S. Constitution so that Congress could ban flag-burning, and worked to restrict the rights of criminal defendants. But his name had become a household word as a result of his successful advocacy of the "Hyde Amendment," prohibiting the use of federal welfare funds to pay for abortions.[13]

Ironically, the views that led Hyde to oppose abortion also gave immigration advocates their hope that they could make him an ally. Hyde was a devout Catholic whose anti-abortion views were but a part of the pro-family, pro-child orientation that he shared with the Catholic leadership. He was personally close to the Catholic hierarchy in Chicago, particularly the liberal Cardinal Joseph Bernardin, a son of immigrants who had denounced Proposition 187, arguing that immigrants contributed more to the American economy than they took from it.[14] Internationally, the Catholic Church was strongly in favor of liberal national immigration policies.[15] European and Latin American immigration had helped to boost the church's membership in the United States for well over a century.

Immediately after the Republicans had won control of the House, Newt Gingrich had given Hyde the Judiciary Committee chairmanship, jumping him over a more senior member. That same week, Pope John Paul II had given Hyde a private audience.[16] There was some reason to hope, therefore, that Hyde's Catholic outlook and the respect in which he held church leaders would make him receptive to moderating Smith's bill. Micheal Hill, a lobbyist on the staff of the U.S. Catholic Conference in Washington who had previously worked as a legislative assistant for a Democratic representative, seized the moment. Before the Judiciary Committee's mark-up began, Hill arranged a meeting in Chicago between Hyde, Bishop Edwin Conway (representing Cardinal Bernardin), and himself.

In the meeting, Conway and Hill sought Hyde's support for maintaining the quota for family immigration and deleting the summary exclusion provisions from the bill. To help Hyde understand how the summary exclusion provisions were at odds with the teachings of the church, they explained that a pregnant Chinese mother who had fled to the United States to avoid a forced abortion might be returned to China, to undergo the abortion, because under Smith's bill she would no longer be assured that a judge would hear her case for asylum.

Hyde had then expressed concern about the refugee provisions. He made no explicit promises, but advocates who heard about the meeting hoped that he would at least help to kill or moderate the summary exclusion section of the bill.[17]

Meanwhile, the Clinton administration was scrambling to agree internally on its position on the Hyde bill. Five days before the mark-up, the Justice Department sent committee members an eighty-one-page single-spaced letter, describing its position on most of the issues raised in the bill. On the biggest issue in the bill, the administration supported a reduction of family and business immigration from 830,000 to 490,000 people. It did oppose a statutory cap on refugees, but it couched its objection not in terms of the United States' responsibility to the large number of refugees in the world but, more bureaucratically, because such a provision would be "an unwarranted restriction on the process and on the President's responsibility to determine issues of foreign policy."

The administration now had to restate its policy on summary exclusion of aliens who arrived without visas. The president had announced in his 1993 press conference that he favored summary exclusion, but in Senator Simpson's hearing, the administration had opposed having to administer such a program, preferring "standby" authority to be used, if necessary, when so many immigrants arrived at once that normal hearings before judges could not be provided. In this third iteration, commenting on the Smith bill, the administration told the committee that it "believes that there is an immediate need for such a provision and strongly supports its enactment," that it "prefers" its own standby concept because Smith's version would entail an "unnecessary use of resources," but that it "is prepared to work with the Committee to resolve differences." The administration was not trying to signal an intention to capitulate,[18] but its endorsement in principle of the committee's approach, and its mild criticism of universal summary exclusion, may have set the stage for it to be rolled.

The administration's tepid critique of summary exclusion contrasted markedly with its forceful stance against the Smith bill's other incursion on refugee treatment, the deadline for affirmative asylum applicants that McCollum had added to the bill in the subcommittee. The letter devoted seven pages to a powerful attack on the McCollum amendment, which, it said, it "strongly opposed" because McCollum's changes would "dramatically transform the character of asylum proceedings" and could even "have the unintended result of reversing significant progress that we have made." The administration told the subcommittee that it had revised its regulations at the beginning of the year to establish "procedures that permit the quick identification and granting of meritorious claims and the referral of all others to immigration court for deportation proceedings [and] the decoupling of eligibility for employment authorization from the asylum application process." In other words, asylum applicants now had to win their cases before they could get jobs, and a person with a weak case no longer had an incentive to apply. But to understand this point, a member of Congress who received the letter would have to parse a seventy-word sentence on page 55.[19]

Furthermore, the administration told committee members in its bureaucratic jargon, asylum interviews "are being scheduled at a rate of 162 percent of the level of new receipts." English translation: for the first time in many years, the backlog of applications was getting smaller.

After telling the Republican committee that the Democratic president had solved the problem, the administration turned to what it thought was wrong with the McCollum provision. McCollum's elimination of the "well-founded fear" standard for asylum, and his substitution of a tougher "more likely than not" standard, could make U.S. law "inconsistent with our international legal obligations under the 1967 Protocol." The administration also opposed the requirement that an asylum-seeker file an intention to apply within thirty days of arrival. However it did not argue that most asylum-seekers could not comply with such a stringent deadline; it argued only that such a provision would be difficult to administer because aliens who had entered the country illegally could lie about their date of entry.[20]

The administration's letter may have supplied the Democratic minority with some arguments to use against the bill during the mark-up, but few Republican members cared about how the Clinton administration thought Smith's bill could be improved. In addition, many members did not pay much attention to what the administration said about immigration policy. Some did not care about the administration's views because they assumed, erroneously, that they had been unduly influenced by interest groups traditionally aligned with the Democratic Party,[21] while others ignored them based on the opposite and equally incorrect assumption that they reflected principally the views of the INS, an agency much maligned on both sides of the aisle.[22] In the words of one Democratic staff member, "Nobody trusts the Immigration and Natural-ization Service, neither the right nor the left. INS is seen as incompetent by the right, and bureaucratic and heartless by the left."

When the mark-up began, refugee advocates rubbed elbows with business lobbyists in a hearing room so packed that there was, literally, standing room only.[23] They knew that they would be there for days. Elisa Massimino from the Lawyers Committee for Human Rights; Angela Kelley from NIF; Carol Wolchok, the American Bar Association's immigration expert; Micheal Hill of the Catholic Conference; Cecilia Munoz of the National Council of La Raza; and officials of the Council of Jewish Federations sat side by side, making notes for faxes or weekly reports to their memberships and, as the days proceeded, making increasingly active efforts to affect the outcome.

These organizations had spent years getting to know the Democrats who had controlled the House, but they had never courted the Republicans who were now in charge. In the House Judiciary Committee mark-up, this omission came to haunt them. "You would walk into the mark-up and you would see the entire immigration community sitting on the right side of the room with the Democratic staffers," said John Fredriksson, who lobbied for the Lutheran Immigration and Refugee Service. "Visually it was all wrong. It was one of the reasons we failed. We weren't ready to cross over politically."[24]

Within the first three days of mark-ups, it became clear that for several related reasons, Smith had almost as much control of the full committee as he'd had of his own subcommittee, although the margins by which he won nearly all of the votes were smaller. In the 1990s, the Judiciary Committee was, even in Hyde's opinion, "one of the most ideologically polarized and partisan committees in the House."[25] Full committee members who were not on the subcommittee were ill prepared to challenge the subcommittee's product because they were less able to discuss the intricacies of the Immigration and Nationality Act. Also, Smith personally buttonholed most of the Republicans and asked for their support, and most of the Republicans did not want to buck what seemed to be their party's tough stand on immigration or to expose differences among Republicans. Accordingly, the Republicans tended to vote as a bloc, supporting Smith's bill, even though one or two Republicans occasionally sided with the Democrats. Democrats, too, tended to stick together, but their numbers were smaller and a few of them sided with John Bryant in his support of Smith.

One of the first significant divisions in the full committee was over Ohio Republican Steve Chabot's effort to eliminate the system through which employers would have to check government databases before hiring employees. Though some businesses and conservative organizations strongly opposed what they called "1-800-BIG BROTHER," seeing it as a stalking horse for a national identity card, Chabot's amendment to knock out the system lost seventeen to fifteen.[26] Similarly, a Democratic amendment to give the Department of Labor power to crack down on employers who hired undocumented workers was defeated on a party-line vote.[27]

On its second day, the committee reached the first of the three refugee issues. The Smith bill's summary exclusion procedure specified that an alien arriving at an airport without a visa would be interviewed on the spot by an INS official, and if the official and the official's supervisor did not believe that the alien had a credible fear of persecution, the alien would be returned immediately, without any hearing.[28] Jerrold Nadler, a New York liberal Democrat, did not try to eliminate summary exclusion altogether, but he attempted to provide a hearing to at least some of the people affected. The Smith bill, he said, would deny "elementary due process" to people who "fled some tyrannical regime under the guns of the secret police or escaped across the border ... exactly the people who are least likely to have proper documents duly stamped and notarized by the gestapo or the KGB or the Khmer Rouge."[29]

Nadler's amendment would have allowed the alien to seek review of a summary exclusion decision within forty-eight hours, and the alien would receive a hearing before an immigration judge unless the judge decided that the asylum claim was "totally lacking in substance" or "manifestly lacking in any credibility."[30] Smith objected that Nadler's standard was too "generous" and would delay what should be a truly "summary" process. Howard Berman, a liberal California Democrat, jumped to Nadler's defense, saying that the INS had dealt with the Kennedy Airport problem and the adjudication backlog it had created. An INS official was in the room. If allowed to speak, the official might have described the degree to which the administration had been successful. But

Smith and Hyde had turned down the administration's request to be allowed to speak during the mark-up sessions.[31] Hyde told Berman that he could, if he wanted, consult with the INS official about the processing backlog, in Hyde's own office, and then "regale us with what he's learned."

Berman thought that the INS had worked down its backlog of airport asylum applications and he looked to the INS official for confirmation. "Could we ask INS to nod their head yes or no?" he asked. "Are those still the figures? Is that still the backlog? I thought your ..." The INS official signaled Berman, apparently indicating that the backlog was still great. Berman was nearly cornered. But he thought he'd read somewhere in an INS report that the problem was being solved. He asked Hyde if he could have a moment to look through his papers. "You surely can," Hyde said. "Strongly encouraged." And Hyde began humming. Berman could not find what he was looking for, and other members began to lose patience. Nadler's amendment was so soundly defeated on a voice vote that he didn't even bother to ask for a roll call.[32]

Minutes later, Representative Patricia Schroeder sought to "lower the standard just a tad." She proposed to change the alien's burden of proving a credible fear from having to show that it was "more probable than not" that he was truthful to showing that it was "probable" that he was truthful. It is not clear that this amendment would really have changed anything, but it too was defeated on a voice vote. Smith easily turned aside another Democratic amendment, which would have allowed the federal courts to review summary exclusions.[33]

The immigration advocates could now see that Smith would make determined efforts to protect his bill from liberalizing amendments, and that Hyde was not in their camp, even as to summary exclusion.[34] Massimino, Wolchok, and Hill turned themselves into a subcommittee to try to protect asylum-seekers. They began to draft amendments, and amendments to Republican amendments, and at night, after the mark-up ended, they would try to meet with the committee members' staff assistants to persuade them to fight another battle. Few Republican staff members would even bother to talk with them.

"Every day I went from despair when I studied the provisions of Smith's bill, to elation when I learned that a congressman was willing to offer our amendment," Massimino recalls. "Then I'd watch in horror and return to despair when the amendment, almost always offered by a Democrat, was defeated on a party-line vote."[35]

Smith's control over the bill was assisted by the fact that the committee's deliberations were not the subject of national attention. Aside from immigration insiders, no one knew what was happening in the mark-up. A *Wall Street Journal* column complained that the "Smith-Simpson effort is sliding through Congress under media radar, shielded by larger debates on Medicare, taxes, and welfare."[36]

The issue that most concerned the business executives who read the *Wall Street Journal* was Smith's effort to stem the flow of skilled workers. Smith sensed trouble, and to break the left-right coalition, he offered business a separate deal. He would compromise on the quota for employment-based visas, if the business groups would promise to stop trying to split the bill. The business groups accepted the deal.[37]

The religious and ethnic groups felt double-crossed, and they had to scramble harder for votes to split the bill. With business groups gone from the coalition, a minor rift developed between the groups who cared most about family reunification for immigrants already in the United States and those who cared most about avoiding a statutory refugee cap. The latter wanted Berman, who drafted the key amendment, simultaneously to go after all of the bill's restrictions on legal immigration. However, Berman wanted to maximize the number of votes he might obtain, and he calculated that anti-refugee sentiment might bring down an otherwise attractive attack on Smith's least defensible provisions. Therefore, Berman's split-the-bill amendment did not eliminate Smith's provisions capping overseas refugees and restricting asylum-seekers' procedural rights. Even so, the effort to split the bill failed on what was essentially a party-line vote. Only one Republican supported Berman, and only two Democrats deserted him.[38]

The immigration advocates had made no headway at all on summary exclusion and (except for the sop thrown to business) had lost in their attempt to avoid massive cuts in legal immigration. The committee next reached the question of imposing a deadline on asylum applications. Texas Democrat Sheila Jackson-Lee proposed extending the deadline from thirty days to six months. "To expect a traumatized woman fleeing rape in Bosnia to submit a notice of intent to file for asylum within 30 days ... flies in the face of the reality of her situation," she argued. McCollum opposed her, arguing that Kansi, the CIA assailant, had been able to remain in the United States after filing a belated asylum application. Her amendment failed, nine to fourteen. McCollum wasn't worried about the committee Democrats' attacks on his asylum limitations, but the administration's strong objection to it, conveyed by INS General Counsel David Martin, who had met with him several times,[39] prompted him to offer his own substitute for the version of his amendment that the subcommittee had approved. He acknowledged that the INS's regulations had "reduced the number of new [affirmative] asylum cases significantly" but said that there was "still a need to do considerably more." A time limit was "very important." Contrary to the thrust of Jackson-Lee's amendment, however, McCollum now *reduced* the allowable time period from a total of ninety days in the subcommittee bill (thirty to file a notice of intention, and sixty more to file the actual application) to a total of just thirty days. Asylum seekers "should be expected to seek protection as soon as possible," he urged. He acknowledged that while he would satisfy the administration on its other objections to the subcommittee's asylum provision, he could not agree with the executive branch that no deadline was needed.

To the horror of the refugee advocates, Schumer—who had co-sponsored the omnibus asylum amendment in 1993 with McCollum and Mazzoli—gave his "strong support" to the McCollum amendment. "Asylum's a great thing about America," he said, "but that doesn't mean that there aren't some responsibilities on citizens who—or not citizens, but individuals who seek to invoke that very special privilege."[40]

With Schumer on the wrong side, it fell to Barney Frank to defend asylum. Frank represented the liberal Brookline and Newton suburbs of Boston, and the city of New Bedford. In fifteen years in Congress, he had become well known and well liked for his debating skill and his sense of humor. His own voters had shrugged off his admission that he was gay, and he had survived a censure motion, made by Gingrich in 1990, after Frank's housemate and personal aide had been discovered to be a male prostitute. Third in seniority among Judiciary Committee Democrats, he had become, in the Gingrich Congress, one of the minority party's most visible spokesmen.[41]

Frank first took issue with the restrictiveness of McCollum's only exception to the deadline, an exemption allowing people to file late if circumstances had changed for the worse in their countries, after the thirty-day deadline had expired. Hoping to appeal to Hyde's interest in curbing abortion, he raised the specter of a "woman subject to a restrictive birth policy who finds out [after the deadline] that she's pregnant." He suggested that an exception should also be made for changes in personal circumstances as well as changes in overseas conditions.

McCollum wasn't impressed. "Most of us conclude, and I believe this, that, by far and away, the vast majority of those who come here seeking asylum will know when they set foot on the soil that that's what they want . . . and opening the door for any change in circumstances opens the door for a lot of mischief."

"What about pregnancy?" Frank demanded. "Suppose a Chinese woman comes here and finds she's pregnant? That's not a change in China."

"If we start making an exception . . . that allows for attorneys, and so forth, to play a lot more mischief with this."

Zoe Lofgren, a California Democrat, interjected with a case she herself had handled as a lawyer, a case in which country conditions had not changed, but her client could not have proved her fear of persecution within thirty days. "It turned out that the Khomeini regime was slaughtering Jews in Iran, but it took some considerable time to find factual evidence to sustain that claim," Lofgren said.[42]

McCollum persisted. "In sitting around, jogging, and trying to do the treadmills, or whatever, thinking of these things, you could think of quite a number . . . and you're opening the door, in my judgment, very wide."

The first part of Frank's amendment to be put to a vote was his effort to broaden the exemption. Frank's choice of forced abortion as a way of illustrating why McCollum's amendment was too narrow was clearly troubling Hyde, and when the roll was called, several Republicans passed, perhaps waiting to see how Hyde, called last because he chaired the meeting, would vote. When Hyde's turn came, he voted for the Frank amendment, and the Republicans who had passed followed his lead. Frank's amendment was approved, the first small victory for refugee advocates on the House side of the Capitol.

Then Frank turned to the length of the deadline. Jackson-Lee's six-month amendment having failed, Frank saw that trying to eliminate the deadline altogether would go nowhere in the committee. But thirty days, he argued, was much too short. With his characteristic charm, he argued that people differ in how they react to the stresses of persecution: "You can see that by the rate of resignation from the Congress. There are people who are more upset by being harassed and persecuted, and some of us who hang on." Trying to make some inroad on McCollum's strict timetable, he proposed a sixty-day deadline. Even this was too liberal for McCollum, who claimed that "you're going to have as many people who are going to file in 30 days as they would in 60." Schumer chimed in again, saying that "there's been so much abuse there that I think we should err on the side of the 30 days." This time, Frank was defeated, on a voice vote.

Undaunted, Frank raised a third issue about the subcommittee's asylum provision. The subcommittee's bill would have barred asylum for anyone who could be deported to some third country where he would not be in danger. He pointed out that this provision precluded the government from granting asylum to any Jew, because Israel accepts any Jewish refugee under its Law of the Return. He pointed out that it made little sense to turn away Jewish refugees who chose to come to the U.S. because they spoke English and had U.S. relatives. The U.S. should have the discretion to permit them to remain.

McCollum disagreed. "I don't think we ought to be taking a lot more people than we have to," he said. Hyde took issue with Frank's example, saying he'd once asked a "nice-looking young couple" who were Russian refugees why they wanted to go to the United States rather than Israel. "There's a war on in Israel," the couple had replied. Hyde didn't think this a good enough reason, particularly since "Israel desperately needed people, 20 million Arabs threatening to push them into the ocean."

But one of Hyde's colleagues, Republican Bob Goodlatte, interceded, urging a "middle ground." Instead of barring asylum altogether, he asked, why not allow the attorney general to grant it in a case of "unjust hardship?"

"That's fair," McCollum said.

The door was opening very slightly, and Berman pushed it further. "Don't do it just on the test of extreme hardship for the applicant. There may be some U.S. national interest involved."

Another Republican, Steven Schiff of New Mexico, chimed in with an example. "Let us suppose that a high-ranking official from a hostile country defects. We may want that person here."

Frank saw the opening he needed and quickly rewrote his amendment. Instead of giving the U.S. government what seemed to be unguided discretion to admit or refuse refugees who could go to a third country, he suggested that the committee allow the government to grant asylum, despite the possibility of safety in a third country, when the attorney general found it to be in the "public interest" to do so. McCollum accepted the amendment, ensuring its passage.[43]

Shortly thereafter, the committee took up the final refugee issue, the subcommittee's prohibition on admitting more than fifty thousand refugees a year. For weeks, the refugee organizations had been searching for a Republican sponsor to lead a challenge to Smith on this issue. The Council of Jewish Federations reported that its New Mexico chapter could talk with Schiff about it. When chapter officials did so, they found that he knew nothing about the issue and although he expressed some interest in it, he did not seem willing to be their standard-bearer. When the refugee organizations couldn't find anyone else, they approached Schiff a second time. He was worried about his relationship with Hyde, and he waffled. When the committee's mark-up began, the organizations still lacked a Republican supporter.

But during the days of mark-up, there had been many recesses during which members had to leave the committee room to vote on the floor. The representatives of the Jewish refugee organizations followed Schiff during those breaks and continued to teach him about their issue. He gradually learned it. He now knew, for example, how many refugees there had been in past years, and how many were expected in the future.[44] Schiff's education was assisted by Grover Joseph Rees, who had been INS general counsel in the Bush administration. After the Republican victory in 1994, Rees had become staff director of the House Subcommittee on International Operations and Human Rights. That subcommittee had no direct influence on immigration bills, but its chairman, Christopher Smith (no relation to Lamar), was keenly interested in any ways in which U.S. legislation impacted on human rights issues, and Rees brought to Christopher Smith's subcommittee his deep knowledge of the intricacies of immigration law. Rees worked up a fact sheet showing that if the cap were enacted, "you'd have to cut the number of ex-Soviet Jews and Indochinese in half, cut Bosnians and Cubans, and not let in any Chinese refugees."[45]

When the committee reached the refugee cap, Schiff proposed an amendment to keep the fifty-thousand target in the bill but to allow the administration to exceed it as a result of the annual refugee consultations. Essentially, his amendment would have allowed the administration rather than Congress to continue to control the quantity of refugee admissions. For the first time in the mark-up, Hyde gave his own opinion on one of the issues before his committee. He disagreed with Schiff, saying that it was appropriate for Congress, rather than the president, to decide the ordinary limit on refugee admissions. The refugee advocates' spirits sank; the chairman's intervention would surely turn other Republican votes away from Schiff.

By this time, the committee had been in session for six days. Members were getting tired, and Hyde noted that the table under the pending amendments was still "sagging." Attendance had never been perfect, and as a result of one of Newt Gingrich's procedural reforms, the House no longer permitted voting in committee by giving a "proxy" to another member. As a result, a Republican amendment such as Schiff's, if supported by most Democrats, might pass, over Smith's opposition, simply because some of the more conservative Republicans weren't in the room when the vote was called. Or the amendment might fail because the absence of a few Republicans was counterbalanced by the absence of a few Democrats. As in a political election, therefore, each side did what it could not only to persuade neutrals, but to bring its committed supporters to the polls.

The non-governmental advocates were very active in this game, but it wasn't easy. "On the day of the refugee cap vote, we knew the vote was going to be very close," recalls Jana Mason, the advocate from Immigration and Refugee Services of America. "Beccera wasn't feeling well. He had his [baby] daughter with him, and he kept lying down. Nadler was in the bathroom. We kept advising Schiff not to call for a vote yet; not all our supporters were in the room. We had people following members around, going into the bathroom with them to make sure they didn't disappear before the vote was held. And we kept counting."[46]

Mason's team did not have enough members to shadow every Democrat and watch every bathroom. When the vote was held, two of the committee's most liberal Democrats, Jackson-Lee and Jose Serrano, were missing. Still, several Republicans were willing to follow Schiff's lead, so the vote would be close. During the vote, one of the last Democrats to enter the room was Rick Boucher, a Virginian who was expected to vote for Schiff's amendment. As he walked in, Boucher looked at John Bryant, the senior Democrat on the Immigration Subcommittee and the only Democrat, up to that point, to have opposed Schiff. Bryant signaled thumbs down. Boucher voted against the Schiff amendment. It failed, fifteen to sixteen, keeping the fifty-thousand-person refugee cap in place. Boucher later told his Democratic colleagues that he'd made a mistake and had meant to support Schiff.[47]

Mason and her allies thought that they'd had the votes to kill the cap and had been defeated only by bad luck. They could try again, but the committee's procedure precluded consideration of an amendment that, in the opinion of the Parliamentarian, was essentially the same as one that had already been defeated. Four of them "were standing in the hallway, trying to change it enough so that the Parliamentarian would allow it to be voted on," recalls Mason. They came up with a new Schiff amendment. It would have allowed a fifty thousand cap to be exceeded if there were "compelling circumstances" that were justified by humanitarian concerns. The Parliamentarian probably would not have accepted it, but Smith had heard of Boucher's error, and he graciously allowed Schiff to try again.[48]

Five days later, this Schiff variation came up for a vote. This time, Boucher voted for the amendment, but Jackson-Lee and Serrano were again absent, along with the full committee's most senior Democrat, John Conyers, and one Republican who favored removing the cap. As a result, the effort again failed.[49]

On the tenth and final day of the mark-up, the immigration advocates made one last attempt to recover from their losses on summary exclusion. They drafted a "human rights" amendment to exempt from the summary exclusion process anyone who came from a country with a pattern of serious human rights violations. Jackson-Lee offered the amendment; McCollum and Smith spoke against it, and it was defeated on a voice vote.[50]

All that remained was to vote on the bill as a whole, to send it forward to the full House. The outcome was a foregone conclusion. All of the Republicans and three Democrats voted for the bill. What made matters even worse, from the viewpoint of the immigration advocates, was that while the Judiciary Committee was deciding to cut back legal immigration, the Senate had passed a sweeping welfare reform bill, one title of which also severely restricted legal aliens. The Senate-passed bill barred most legal aliens (except those already in the United States) from receiving most kinds of welfare benefits (such as disability benefits for the poor) during their first five years in the United States.[51]

Despite the votes of House Judiciary Committee Republicans on Berman's "split-the-bill" amendment, not all GOP legislators favored the restrictions on legal immigration; the business community's unease, in particular, was beginning to be felt. The day after the House Judiciary Committee approved the bill, ten of the most conservative Republican members of the California delegation, including Dana Rohrabacher and Robert Dornan, wrote to Hyde, asking him to split the bill on the House floor because "the linkage of legal to illegal immigration has resulted in a backlash of resentment from our legal immigrant communities."[52] Smith rushed to put down the public division within Republican ranks, and within a few days, one of the Californians recanted, another softened his views, and thirty-five other Republicans, including the chairman of the powerful Rules Committee, wrote a counter-letter advocating that legal and illegal immigration be linked together to provide the political impetus necessary to cut back on legal immigration.[53]

The House bill was headed for the floor, but the arduous committee work wasn't quite over. The day after Republicans circulated their counter-letter, Simpson introduced the half of his immigration reform that he'd postponed drafting until after his subcommittee had completed work on illegal immigration. His bill was remarkably similar to Smith's, reducing legal immigration by about a third. He hadn't been a party to the deal Smith had cut with business, either; his bill cut the quota for business immigration and imposed a new ten-thousand-dollar tax on each immigrant hired, provisions that were especially damaging to Silicon Valley.

Immediately, Simpson reconvened his subcommittee. "Strap your seat belts on," NIF faxed its membership. "We're going back to Mark-up Hell."[54] Even with the high-tech industry beginning to be reanimated by Simpson's legal immigration bill, the immigration advocates' ability to influence the subcommittee proved no greater than in the struggle over the earlier illegal immigration bill. Simpson's subcommittee approved the bill by a vote of five to two; once again, Feinstein supported him, and only Kennedy and Simon dissented.

The subcommittee's final act was to combine its two bills into one, so that unless its action were reversed by the full Judiciary Committee, the Senate, like the House, would have a single omnibus bill that was tough not only on illegal immigrants, but also on asylum-seekers, relatives of prior immigrants, and skilled workers who wanted to work for American companies.[55]

In November 1995, public attention was focused on a federal budget stand-off between Congress and the president that had resulted in a protracted closure of many federal agencies. The congressional committees' decisions to reduce legal immigration received relatively scant coverage, and how they had determined to restrict American refugee policy was even less visible. The advocacy groups knew, however, that their backs were against the wall. Both bills cut back drastically on legal immigration, made it difficult for traumatized refugees to avoid summary exclusion, and imposed a severe thirty-day deadline on affirmative asylum applications. In addition, the House bill slashed the overseas-refugee program. There remained only one more chance, before these bills got to the Senate floor, to try to moderate them: the full Senate Judiciary Committee.

And just then, Senator Simpson dropped one more bombshell. A week after he pushed the second bill through his subcommittee, he announced that he would not run for reelection.[56] Now a bill was sure to pass before the 104th Congress expired at the end of 1996. Alan Simpson, a man much admired by his colleagues on both sides of the aisle, had turned restricting immigration into his valedictory legacy.

*Part II*

# The Heat of Battle

# 5

# Someone Else's Problem
## November 1995

The third child is so overwhelmed by the magnitude of the problems of the world that she doesn't even know where to begin, and so she does nothing, not even ask. And we tell her, "It is not up to you to complete the task, but neither are you free to desist from it."

—My family's Passover Haggadah[1]

In the spring of 1994, I knew nothing about immigration, refugees, or asylum. I taught law at Georgetown University, where, among other things, I directed a clinical program called the Center for Applied Legal Studies. Students who enrolled in this program—essentially a double course for one semester—learned how to practice law by representing low-income clients, without charge, under the supervision of two other lawyers and myself. The types of cases we handled were contested claims for social security disability payments, and lawsuits by or against consumers.

I'd supervised students working on these two types of cases for nearly fifteen years, and I was restless. The issues had become repetitive. More problematically, although the clinic was fully subscribed, student applications for the clinic had been declining steadily. In the early 1970s, when I had first begun to teach, students were eager to work on cases involving social welfare benefits and consumer issues. By the mid-1990s, these concerns remained important to clients but appealed less to my students.[2]

The students themselves had conducted a petition drive to tell the law school what kind of new clinic they wanted. Issues involving international human rights were in the headlines every day, and students wanted to try to help alleviate the suffering of people subject to torture and other forms of persecution. Hundreds of them signed a petition asking Georgetown to create, in addition to my clinic and ten others, a clinic that would address international human rights.

Budget constraints prevented the law school from building yet another clinic, but I realized that by converting my clinic into one that worked on these issues, I could respond to the students and also renew myself intellectually. I interviewed several of Washington's human rights lawyers to find out what they

91

did, and how students could contribute. I learned that human rights lawyers did many different kinds of work, but because nations often took decades to act, the lawyers' tasks took years to complete. For example, some human rights lawyers drafted international treaties and urged nations to negotiate and then sign them, and other lawyers wrote exposés of abusive conditions in other countries and petitioned the United Nations to investigate. Law students working on such projects would graduate long before their work produced any tangible results.

One area of human rights work, however, had a much shorter time frame. Human rights activists in other countries sometimes not only failed to move their own countries but so alienated their governments that their lives or freedom were in danger. Many of these brave people stayed in their native lands, sometimes undergoing imprisonment or torture, but others fled, seeking either a temporary safe haven or a new start in a democratic country such as a Western European nation, Canada, or the United States. I learned that the United States government had established a formal structure through which asylum claims were decided, and that some human rights lawyers represented asylum applicants. Also, although asylum cases had in the past often languished in the bureaucracy for years, the INS was in the process of developing new regulations that would speed cases through the system within months. The new system would be bad news for aliens who didn't win asylum, but it would provide just the right time frame for students in my one-semester clinic.

I decided to investigate refugee issues more carefully. One of the first steps I took was to visit the United States Holocaust Memorial Museum in Washington. It had been open for a year and was already the most visited museum in the world. But it took my new professional restlessness—and my father-in-law's visit from Boston—to prod me into going.

That first visit had a profound influence on me. The museum offers a visitor a moving experience on many levels, as it tells the story of the Holocaust through three floors of photos, videos, artifacts, and a frighteningly detailed model of a gas chamber and crematorium from one of the Nazi concentration camps. But I was particularly struck by several exhibits documenting official American indifference to the horrors of Nazi persecution of the Jews. I saw, for example, the museum's sad photo of the luxury hotel in which the delegates to the 1938 Evian Conference had produced so little, and the letter from the War Department to an American Jewish leader, reporting the government's decision not to waste bombs on the train tracks leading into Auschwitz. But the saddest and most shocking exhibit on American policy was the large exhibit on the voyage of the *St. Louis*. I now know that this is a somewhat famous historical episode, and that Hollywood even made a movie about it. But at the time, I had never heard of this ship.

The *St. Louis*, I learned, was an ocean liner that sailed from Germany to Cuba in the spring of 1939. The Nazi government allowed 937 Jewish refugees to board it, confident that other governments would not want to make their lands available as places of refuge for Jews and would not allow the passengers to disembark. In that event, Germany could demonstrate that its anti-Semitic sentiments were, in fact, widely shared. Other nations' refusals to accept the *St. Louis* passengers for resettlement might reduce the attention that the international press was devoting to its discriminatory policies. The ship was, in fact, the last chance for Jews to leave Germany before World War II virtually sealed the border a few months later.

Unbeknownst to the ship's captain and passengers, the president of Cuba had invalidated the Jews' landing permits, apparently because his corrupt minister of immigration had not shared the bribes he'd received for issuing them, and because Germany had whipped up anti-Jewish sentiment in Cuba.[3] The ship waited in Havana harbor for several days during which the Cuban authorities repeatedly denied permission to dock. When he was forced to depart, the German captain, a man with impressive loyalty to his passengers, headed north, while through telegrams and newspaper reports, passengers and a Jewish refugee organization pleaded with the United States government to allow the passengers to disembark. Next to the museum's display of photographs of the ship and its passengers, and the original telegrams from the passengers, a caption tells what happened next:

> Sailing close to the Florida shore, passengers could see the lights of Miami. U.S. Coast Guard ships patrolling the waters ensured that no one jumped to freedom. The German captain, Gustav Schroder, appealed in vain to the United States for permission to dock. From June 2 to 6, Captain Schroder steered the *St. Louis* back and forth between Miami and Havana, hoping that the Cuban or American government would grant asylum to his refugee passengers.

But at this point, polls showed that 83 percent of the American public was opposed to allowing more refugees to enter. Secretary of State Cordell Hull declined to let the ship land. President Franklin D. Roosevelt let that decision stand. The ship returned to Europe, and although Britain, France, Belgium, and the Netherlands made last-minute decisions to accept the refugees, half of them were killed in death camps after Germany launched its westward invasion the following year.[4]

The museum's lobby housed a temporary exhibit about the massacres then being undertaken for the purpose of "ethnic cleansing" in Bosnia. The exhibit was deliberately small to make the point that the Holocaust was an unparalleled historical event. I could barely look at it. The exhibit on the *St. Louis* had made its mark on me. The picture seemed clear enough. Like most other countries, the United States had been passively complicit in the Holocaust. Severe persecution of ethnic minorities was still taking place around the globe. I was aware from my research on human rights lawyers that the United States had an asylum law, under which some victims of human right violations could obtain safe haven here. In most cases, however, our government didn't believe the asylum applicant or thought that her flight was not the result of the kind of persecution our law recognized. And I was in a position to help today's version of the St. Louis passengers, if not by the boatload, than at least one at a time. By representing asylum applicants, my students and I could literally save their lives.

Shortly after my museum visit, I attended a short talk about asylum law by Jeanne Butterfield, who had just been appointed as the political action director of the American Immigration Lawyers Association. There I learned how asylum fit into immigration law, and how the procedures worked. Asylum had become very visible through press accounts of alleged abuse, Ms. Butterfield said, but in fact people to whom asylum was granted were an almost insignificant fraction of American immigrants—about eight to twelve thousand people per year, compared with just under a million legal immigrants, and perhaps three hundred thousand others who evaded patrols at the Mexican border or entered legally and overstayed temporary visas. Only a small fraction of asylum applicants, she said, were people who were apprehended at airports without proper papers and then asserted asylum as a defense to deportation (or as the law then called it, "exclusion," because they had not yet technically entered the U.S.). The vast majority were people who had entered the United States, legally or illegally, had been here for quite some time, and had then filed affirmative applications for asylum. After being interviewed by INS asylum officers, about a fifth of these affirmative applicants won asylum.

The remainder were subject to deportation. Until 1994, many were never actually put into deportation proceedings, in part because the INS could rarely locate the people who had been denied asylum, and therefore could not give them notice of deportation proceedings. But under the regulatory reforms designed by David Martin and being put into place by the INS, asylum officers' decisions not to grant asylum to affirmative applicants would be coupled to deportation proceedings before judges. An asylum applicant would not be told at her oral interview whether or not asylum was granted. She would have to return approximately ten days later, when she would sign a receipt for an envelope enclosing a written decision. The envelope for a losing applicant would also contain a court order requiring her to appear for a deportation hearing, and the receipt would prove that the order had been delivered. Then, in the deportation hearing before a federal immigration judge—a person on the Justice Department payroll but independent of the INS—she would have a final but more complete opportunity to make her case for asylum. Unlike the typical forty-five-minute asylum officer interview, the hearing could last several hours, or even several days if the evidence warranted an extensive presentation. The asylum applicant could have the full assistance of counsel, although the government would not provide a lawyer for her. She could present witnesses and cross-examine any witnesses against her. She could ask the judge to consider substantial amounts of documentary evidence to support her claim. On the other hand, the INS would also be represented by counsel, and at this point the INS counsel would be doing her best to discredit the asylum claim and deport the applicant. Particularly at these deportation hearings, the asylum applicants' last chance to avoid deportation, legal representation was necessary, and the percentage of represented applicants who won their cases was much higher than the percentage of people who went into court without help. However, many asylum applicants had little or no money, and there was an acute shortage of lawyers willing to help impoverished clients.

Butterfield's presentation reinforced my belief that my students could simultaneously learn how to practice law, help people in great need, and, because proving an asylum case requires the advocate to become steeped in the human rights record of a client's country, become involved in international human rights issues. I spent the next year training myself, collecting library materials, writing manuals, and in many other ways preparing to convert my program, starting with the 1995 fall semester, into an asylum law clinic.[5]

I was so busy that although I was well aware of the congressional election of 1994, I did not think about its implications for the work on which I was about to engage. In the spring of 1995, I saw a notice that an organization that I had not previously encountered, the National Immigration Forum, was holding a conference on asylum. As part of my preparation to teach my clinic, I went. At the conference, several speakers bemoaned the bills that Senator Simpson and Representative Smith were writing, bills that threatened nearly every aspect of immigration, including asylum. I was, however, overwhelmed by having to learn a new field of law in a year. I paid scant attention to what a Texas congressman wanted to do to change that field in the future. I was retooling myself as a lawyer and teacher; the pending legislation was someone else's problem. I was glad that a National Immigration Forum and an American Immigration Lawyers Association existed, and that they would try to head off regressive national legislation. I could leave such matters to them.

Nearly a hundred students applied for the twelve spaces in my new asylum law clinic; clearly, I had tapped into an area in which they were eager to work. We opened our doors in late August 1995, with sixteen clients from Lebanon, Bosnia, Moldova, and several African countries. Half of our clients were filing affirmative applications and being interviewed by asylum officers; the others were in deportation proceedings, trying to persuade immigration judges that they merited asylum. We felt our way together through a new area of practice, and our naïveté showed, but the students rose to the occasion magnificently, working an average of fifty-two hours a week for their clients, even though most of them were also taking two other courses, writing papers for law journals, or engaged in other activities. They doggedly investigated human rights violations in their clients' countries and documented the personal histories that their clients claimed, in one case even arranging to have a client's medical records smuggled out of her country so that they could be used as evidence. One student, who herself had been granted asylum as a child, was hit by a car, but after a week in the hospital she continued her work eagerly, though she occasionally grimaced with pain. The hard work paid off, too. The students won all but one of their cases.

Midway through the semester, I took the students on a field trip to the Holocaust Memorial Museum, so that they too could see the origins of U.S. refugee law and how their work fit into a historical progression. After our discussion of the origins of American refugee law, I thought that I should also offer a class on contemporary issues in refugee policy. But what were those issues? At that point, I remembered the conference I'd attended in the spring, and the bills that some Republicans were proposing. I looked into the content and status of the bills, thinking that the pending legislation might make a good teaching vehicle.

I was horrified to learn that Congress was on the verge of slashing overseas refugee admissions, eliminating hearings for many people who arrived at our airports without visas, and barring asylum for anyone who didn't ask for it within thirty days of arrival. The thirty-day cutoff was particularly shocking. None of the clinic's clients had applied within thirty days of their arrival. That alone wasn't definitive, because a legal requirement for prompt filing might have led some of them to file sooner. But as I thought about our clients, I didn't think that they would have been able to file so quickly.

Joseph was a typical client. He had fled Zaire, flown to Canada with false papers, and, upon arrival, had used those papers to cross the border into the United States. But he had lived in the United States for more than a year, slowly acclimating to this country, before seeking legal assistance to apply for asylum. Then he had been referred from office to office until he had landed at our door.

When my students first interviewed him, he was evasive. They could not pry from him the reasons for his flight. Only after several weeks of interviews did he trust them enough to tell his story. Then they learned the horrors of his life.

Joseph was a Jehovah's Witness, and he had been unwilling to give Zaire's brutal dictator, Mobutu Sese Seko, the absolute loyalty Mobutu demanded, or to accept his government's ban on the practice of his religion. As a student in Zaire, Joseph had written an article criticizing Mobutu's regime. He was imprisoned for twenty months. After his release, he helped plan a rally against Mobutu. For this he was thrown into a prison camp where soldiers burned him with cigarettes. When they interrogated him, they applied electric shocks to his penis, causing him to scream uncontrollably and nearly pass out. They held him for six months in the camp, during which time they gang-raped him three or four times a week. He suffered from terrible rashes and constant diarrhea. Finally, one of his relatives bribed the necessary officials. Joseph was released, and his guards put him on a ferry to the neighboring country, Congo-Brazzaville. His family also bought the false papers that enabled him to get to Canada.

The students' immediate supervisor, my colleague Joshua Davis, later explained why Joseph did not apply for asylum until more than a year after his entry into the United States, and why, even after he had come to our office, weeks passed before he revealed the facts that were the basis for his successful asylum application.

> Joseph's reticence was in part the result of the pain he felt when reliving the nightmare of his life in Zaire.... Joseph's hesitance was also in part caused by an amazing innocence he had maintained through his ordeals. He had been raised in a Christian tradition that forbids using the words necessary to describe the methods used to torture him. And, most difficult of all, the mix of Joseph's psychological and religious upbringing caused him to feel an odd complicitous guilt for the defilement of his body. After many of the incidents of his torture, when he was left trembling on the floor, coated in his own blood, Joseph would describe himself as feeling "dirty." Only after the students had helped Joseph to work his way to offering a coherent account of the terrible fate that had befallen him was he ready to present his case persuasively to an asylum officer.... On the day of the interview with the asylum officer ... for the first time in countless hours of narrative, when Joseph described the terrible events of his young life, he allowed himself to cry.[6]

If I was right in thinking that like Joseph, many true refugees had good reasons for not applying for asylum immediately, the thirty-day cutoff was not just a minor tinkering with the administration of the asylum laws. A thirty-day rule was, for all practical purposes, the end of asylum.

But, I wondered, even if Congress thought that the overall level of immigration should be reduced, why would it tighten the rules for the 1 percent of immigrants who were victims of persecution? From the perspective of American political ideals, and from the point of view of wanting to include in our society those who took democratic ideals seriously, weren't victims of persecution precisely the group with the best claim for immigration?[7]

Not only was the new legislation very bad for refugees, I discovered, but it was racing through Congress. The bills had already been approved by the House and Senate Immigration Subcommittees, and even while I was reading the bills, the House Judiciary Committee was also approving them. But surely, I thought, immigrant and refugee organizations were going to stop this law from being passed. What was going on behind the scenes?

I called several national organizations to find out. I learned that a coalition of refugee organizations was working very hard to kill the cap on overseas admissions. They had succeeded in the Senate and had nearly succeeded in the House Judiciary Committee. But the pro-immigration advocates who cared about summary exclusion and the thirty-day rule were simultaneously working on numerous other provisions in the bill, had less political experience and clout than the refugee organizations that were focused on the proposed ceiling, and were being routed by the Republicans who were running the committees.

I was the new kid on the block, and although I had once taught a course about Congress, I had no lobbying experience. But I was angry at the thought that, under cover of tightening the procedures (which I doubted was necessary at all in view of the new regulation barring employment), Congress might abolish asylum. Also, I realized that if I stood by and did nothing while Congress closed the border to refugees, I would be as complicit as Cordell Hull in the deaths of those who were subsequently excluded. I asked some of the organizations if I could help. The more the merrier, they said, but they were already doing all they could, and losing.

I thought of two things I could do. First, although several organizations and coalitions were working to fight the bills in general, and the refugee cap in particular, no organization was especially focused on the thirty-day rule, and the several small organizations that helped asylum-seekers in the Washington area had not yet become involved in lobbying. Maybe by recruiting more allies and concentrating forces against this particular section of the law, groups concerned with asylum could have a greater impact.

Once a month, I attended a meeting, hosted by the INS's local asylum director, at which the asylum advocates for local refugee services, by this time including myself, discussed administrative issues, such as the difficulty of reaching an INS asylum officer on the telephone when a problem arose involving an application. After one of these meetings ended, I asked the organizational representatives to stay for a few minutes, and I explained the looming crisis. They agreed that the situation was awful, and I proposed that we try to form some sort of task force to lobby against the thirty-day cutoff. Deborah Anne Sanders, the director of the asylum project of the Washington Lawyers Committee for Civil Rights and Urban Affairs, agreed to host such a meeting. She well knew what the real effect of a thirty-day deadline would be, because her organization had found legal help for Mary Rawson[8] and countless others who had sought asylum months or years after arriving in the United States. Everyone offered to call other human rights and refugee experts to ask them to attend.

The other action I could take was to try to expose the McCollum and Simpson amendments to brighter light. I wrote an op-ed column denouncing the thirty-day rule and sent it to the *Washington Post*, which hadn't covered this issue at all. I knew that the chance of my column being accepted was small; over the years the *Post* had often rejected pieces I'd submitted. But it couldn't hurt to try.

Early in November 1995, about seventeen of us convened in Sanders's conference room. Several of those in attendance worked in small, local agencies that represented asylum applicants, such as Spanish Catholic Charities and the Hispanic Legal Action Center. A few people who had been working on the bills filled in those of us who had not followed them closely. Jeanne Butterfield and Elisa Massimino explained that the groups concerned with Soviet Jewry, and their allies in other refugee organizations, had helped to kill the refugee cap in a

Senate subcommittee but that no organized opposition had focused on asylum, and that most members of Congress had little concern about asylum. Many legislators regarded asylum applicants as "illegal" immigrants. The Clinton administration agreed with our concerns about the thirty-day rule, but to date it had been entirely ineffective.

They also pointed out to us that as a practical matter, our best hope lay with the Senate Judiciary Committee, consisting of ten Republicans and eight Democrats. Since at least Feinstein and perhaps Alabama's conservative Democratic Senator Howell Heflin could not be counted on, we needed to get at least three or four Republican votes.

My heart sank. The task seemed impossible. Couldn't we instead persuade Senator Simpson that the thirty-day provision was undesirable and harmful?

Be our guests, the experts told us. So far, however, Simpson had seemed unresponsive to reasoned arguments or political pressure from anyone, even the business community. He would have to be beaten, not converted. And we might have only five weeks in which to work, because Simpson seemed eager to get the bill through the Judiciary Committee before the Christmas recess.

No one in the room had the slightest idea how to pressure, persuade, or even talk with Republican senators. The conversation shifted to instrumental goals. We might not be able to kill the asylum deadline altogether in the Senate committee, but perhaps we could influence its details. What, some asked, could we live with?

The experienced lobbyists immediately threw cold water on the very idea of discussing "bottom lines." "Never tell them your real bottom line," Massimino advised. "They'll take that as an opening position and start bargaining you down." Butterfield added that in her experience, even supportive legislative staff members didn't have a lot of time for dickering and wanted to get to the end point right away. "They'll ask for your bottom line in the first conversation."

Somewhat uncomfortably, I brought up the fact that however difficult it might be to change the momentum on an asylum deadline, asylum-seekers also had an interest in defeating the summary exclusion provision. Someone pointed out, however, that it was more difficult to address two issues at once, particularly when we might not be able to make any impact on even one issue. I had anticipated that the meeting would have to address this difficult issue of priorities. If we worked on both issues, we might dilute our own effectiveness. But if we chose only one of the two issues, we might help one group of asylum-seekers (e.g., those already in the U.S. who were affirmatively applying) and abandon another (those stopped at airports, subject to the summary exclusion rule). Nevertheless, we could not afford to be paralyzed by indecision. I proposed that we concentrate on the thirty-day rule, for several reasons. It was much less complicated and therefore easier to explain to Congress and to the public; it affected more asylum-seekers (because many more refugees applied

affirmatively than were apprehended at airports); and it hadn't yet been ana-
lyzed or discussed among senators, because no one had challenged it in the
Senate subcommittee mark-up.

Others were troubled about seeming to give up on summary exclusion,
because although the numbers of people affected were smaller, it was even
more unreasonable to expect a refugee to tell his story within a few minutes of
arriving at an airport than to seek asylum within a month. And a person who
was too afraid or disoriented to explain his fear of persecution to the INS official at the airport would be sent home on the next plane. But we agreed to start
by concentrating what resources we had on the thirty-day rule. If we seemed to
be doing very well on that issue, someone added, we could later add the other
issue to our agenda. We shared a muted laugh at the suggestion.

At the end of the meeting, the talk inevitably turned to holding another
meeting. At that point, it became obvious that this group, or task force, or committee, or whatever it was, needed a leader. Although I had been a catalyst, I
knew that I should not be that leader. Unlike everyone else at the meeting, I
represented no one and had no organizational base or administrative
resources. It would be difficult for me even to send out meeting notices or reli-
ably to provide meeting space, much less be the central focus for what could
eventually become many daily telephone calls and faxes. I looked around the
room. For three reasons, the best candidate for leadership was Elisa Massimino,
the legal director of the Lawyers Committee for Human Rights. First, the
Lawyers Committee ran the largest non-profit asylum advocacy program in the
country. Its New York and Washington offices each had agreements with
dozens of law firms through which the committee screened cases for volunteer
lawyers, trained the lawyers and provided them with manuals, forms, and a
telephone consultation service, and reviewed the volunteers' draft documents.
At any given time, the committee was involved in nearly eight hundred asylum
cases. Second, asylum was not the committee's only human rights work, but it
was a large part of it, so the committee was unlikely to lose interest in this project or become diverted in other directions before it was over. Third, although I
did not know Ms. Massimino very well, I had heard from several colleagues
that she was an outstanding human rights advocate.

There was just one problem. In one month, Ms. Massimino was scheduled
to begin a maternity leave that would last for several months. In proposing Ms.
Massimino to lead our work, I assumed (quite erroneously, it turned out) that
the Senate Judiciary Committee would mark up the bill before Massimino left
at the end of November. If the mark-up were postponed until December or
until the early part of 1996, she would not be on hand to provide the leadership
we needed. Nevertheless, she seemed the best possible leader for the new group,
and during the meeting I asked whether she would assume the task.

She agreed, but of course she noted that she would not be able to continue for more than another month. However, she reported, Willkie Farr and
Gallagher, one of the firms whose lawyers occasionally volunteered for asylum

cases, had offered to lend one of its senior associates to the Lawyers Committee to fill in for her while she was on leave. This lawyer had no congressional experience, but she was very able, and Massimino was certain that she could learn whatever skills were necessary. The name of her replacement was Michele Pistone.

I was troubled that Ms. Pistone lacked legislative experience, but in view of my own lack of experience, I could hardly complain. Nor was there any real alternative, because Massimino had instantly accepted, on behalf of herself, her organization, and her stand-in, the leadership role I'd urged. I could only hope that Pistone would turn out to have the qualities that Massimino ascribed to her.

A few days later, we got a huge break. The *Washington Post* ran my column, giving it a Sunday slot where it would have the largest possible audience, and a position at the top of the editorial page. Though newspapers often change authors' headlines, the *Post* even used my proposed title, "Don't Gut Political Asylum."

It would be impossible for refugees to file so quickly, I argued in the column. Many don't speak English. They aren't allowed to work. They must immediately find ways to feed themselves and their children and to find minimal housing. Months may pass before they learn about asylum or how to apply for it. Then they have to understand the eight pages of fine-print instructions and fill out the seven-page form. But filling out the form isn't enough. To make a winning case, they must follow the INS's own advice to "attach additional written statements and documents" to support their factual claims, including "newspaper articles, affidavits of witnesses or experts, periodicals, journals, books, photographs, official documents, other personal statements, or evidence regarding incidents that have occurred to others." I pointed out that my students spent a month or more of full-time work just obtaining affidavits or collecting basic documentation such as birth and death records, and that they usually had to make repeated international telephone calls and exchange many faxes with witnesses before developing enough evidence to support a winning application. Finding appropriate experts and getting their written statements took even more time. The attachments to a typical successful application consisted of hundreds of pages of documents. And the proposed law was not only unreasonable, but unnecessary, in view of the facts that asylum accounted for only about 1 percent of U.S. immigration, and that the recent regulatory reform had already ended the abuse to which the new law was directed.[9]

The most obvious value of the op-ed was, of course, that it reached hundreds of thousands of readers, some of whom undoubtedly were members of Congress or staffers who worked for them. However, I saw two other uses for the piece, which led me to make dozens of copies. First, it was a blissfully short statement of the case against the thirty-day rule; it gave our new group a good leaflet to put into the hands of anyone who cared to learn our views. Second, virtually no one on Capitol Hill had ever heard of me, and I was worried about

getting legislative staff members to talk to me or take me seriously. But because
the *Post* is Washington's most important newspaper, I thought that the reprints
might give me some degree of credibility. I might be able to use them as over-
sized calling cards.

The day after the column appeared, I sent a copy to each member of the
Senate Judiciary Committee, and in each case I requested a meeting with a staff
member. I had no illusion that the senators would study, read, or even receive
the reprints, but perhaps at least their staff members for immigration issues
would peruse them or even call me. I was disappointed, but in view of how
busy senators' offices are, not entirely surprised, when I received no calls at all. I
also sent a copy to several conservative columnists, starting with Henry
Kissinger and George Will because I'd fortuitously shared the *Post*'s op-ed page
with them. The only reply came from an assistant in George Will's office, but
after that initial display of possible interest, his assistants declined to follow up
or to let me speak to him.[10]

I did receive a response to the op-ed from an interesting quarter, however.
Immediately after it appeared, I was called by a producer from a television
show called *Pork* on the America Talking cable network. Would I agree to a
half-hour debate, on the thirty-day issue, with Representative McCollum and
FAIR's Dan Stein?

I had never heard of the network or the program, and I was wary of accepting. This show would have a very small audience, I assumed, so I would hardly
make any impact. Also, I didn't yet consider myself an expert on asylum, and I
might make some kind of blunder that would discredit me in McCollum's esti-
mation. On the other hand, those same factors argued in favor of my appearance. If few people watched, any mistakes I made would have minimal impact.
And McCollum himself had never had to defend his provision in public. He
might be pressed into making some sort of concession.

I arrived at a studio in downtown Washington, where I met Stein. In person
he was an amiable fellow, not at all like the angry anti-immigrant orators of the
1920s whom I'd seen in documentary films. McCollum was in the Capitol's TV
studio. We would be able to hear each other, but I wouldn't see what McCollum
looked like until I went home and watched my tape of the broadcast. So I sat
down to argue with a disembodied voice.

I should have realized from the title of the program that the producers' bias
was to show that the federal government didn't work, and that therefore, John
David Klein, the moderator, might subtly side with McCollum's "reforms" over
my defense of the existing law. I wasn't quite prepared, however, for the degree
of Klein's skepticism.

McCollum led off, citing Kansi's CIA murders as proof that asylum was
being abused. Thirty days was enough because "I would expect the Immigration Service to make the form much simpler."

Klein gave him an assist: "Now the thing is, once you apply for asylum, you
can stay here almost permanently on a constant basis just constantly appealing
it even if you are turned away, isn't that correct?"

"Well that's right," McCollum replied. "You still have lots of people who are using and have used the system to just stay here."

Then Klein introduced me and asked me what I thought of the thirty-day plan. I said that in my clinic, I hadn't met a client yet who could have applied within thirty days.

"I'm sorry, Philip," Klein said (he called McCollum "Congressman"). "A lot of folks at home are going to find that a little difficult. When you come in you're being told if you want political asylum, you apply within thirty days. Why would they have difficulty doing that?"

"First of all," I said, "they are not told that."

"But they will be told that under the new law, but go ahead," Klein argued.

"There is nothing in the congressman's bill that says they are going to be told that."

Klein had gone out on a limb and seemed unnerved. Seeking reassurance, he asked, "Let me ask the congressman. Will they be notified?"

"Yes they will," McCollum said. "We had quite a colloquy with my colleagues on the other side of the aisle. The Immigration Service would be required to tell people who came in that they could apply for asylum and this is how long it would take."

Despite my lack of legislative experience, I knew the difference between a colloquy and a law, and from my conversations with those who had been at the mark-up, I wasn't even sure there had been any conversation about the particular issue of notice. "It's not in your legislation, Congressman."

"Well it may not be in the legislation but it's certainly going to be in the report language. And I think the Immigration Service is going to do that."[11]

At this point I was glad to have gone on the show. If the provision did become law, its author was now on record as believing that the INS should notify people of the time limit, an expensive and perhaps impossible task, particularly with respect to aliens who arrived in the U.S. undetected. I was determined to press the point further.

"May I ask the congressman a question?" I asked.

"Sure, jump in," Klein said.

"Is the notice going to be only in English or in the many other languages that asylum applicants speak?"

"Well I don't know that," McCollum conceded. "We're not going to try to dictate that. I would hope that the procedure is fair."

"But I represent a client who only spoke Somali when he arrived in the United States," I protested.

Klein interrupted to help McCollum. "Mr. Schrag," he said (less familiarly), "If we get bogged down in whether or not the United States makes a good effort, there probably will be some people who will fall through the cracks. Ain't no legislation perfect. But up to this point let's just say it is perfect. Do you have any objections to this?"

"Some of these people are victims of torture, some of them are very seriously ill as a result of that torture, or psychologically damaged," I said.

I went on to describe the other problems I'd listed in the *Washington Post* column.

"Mr. Schrag, or Philip, let me ask you something," Klein interjected. The great majority of applicants didn't win asylum, and many of the losers remained in the U.S. Wasn't something wrong?

This was a valid point, and I explained how David Martin's regulation denying work permits was solving that problem by eliminating the attraction of filing a false asylum application.

Klein turned to Dan Stein and asked whether he agreed with McCollum.

Stein played his part. "We think what he's got is a good start but it needs to be strengthened still," he said. He argued that asylum should be abolished and replaced with a system under which those arriving in the U.S. to seek refuge could never become citizens, no matter how long they were allowed to stay. They should always be subject to being returned when conditions improved.[12]

I felt energized by the debate. McCollum, I realized, had seemed all-powerful and larger than life. He was a very powerful member of Congress, but he did not have good answers to all the questions that could be raised about his proposal, and his idea was based on a very erroneous view of the capabilities and knowledge of most asylum-seekers. Perhaps other members of Congress would yet take a less rigid stance. But for that to happen, I thought, we asylum advocates would have to show much more muscle.

To help make that happen, Massimino and I reached beyond the local service organizations and the small number of national organizations that had attended our first meeting. We started calling all the other organizations we could think of, everyone in Washington who might care to defeat McCollum's provision, particularly national human rights groups such as Amnesty International, Human Rights Watch, Physicians for Human Rights, the American Civil Liberties Union, and every possible type of religious organization. The Lawyers Committee for Human Rights also had good contacts at Washington law firms; perhaps one of the firms that had volunteered for individual asylum cases would offer us other types of support for this legislative project.

In response to our calls, several groups offered to send representatives to a larger meeting, and Gary Sampliner, a partner at the law firm of McKenna and Cuneo, offered conference facilities in his spacious downtown firm. We were on our way to becoming a more substantial operation. But just when it became clearer that we had a little breathing space because the Senate Judiciary Committee mark-up would not take place right away, it also became clearer that much would depend on the resources and abilities of organizations I did not know well, and particularly on the talent of a person I had never met. Massimino was on the verge of turning over her desk, for what would probably be the duration of the effort, to her stand-in, the woman whom I had blindly propelled into the leadership of our legislative project.

# 6

# The Committee to Preserve Asylum

## December 1995

The first step was to get organized.

—Michael Pertschuk and Wendy Schaetzel[1]

Michele Pistone grew up in a middle-class family in the suburbs of New York. She often was looked after by Colombian housekeepers who aroused her curiosity by talking with her about their country. When they returned to Colombia, she asked whether she could visit with them, but her parents did not take the idea seriously. When she was twelve, however, her grandfather, an Italian immigrant, died, and her grandmother took her to Europe for the summer, a trip that reinforced her interest in other cultures. Her parents did not encourage this interest. "My father had a friend who was Chinese and I asked him if I could live with them so I could learn Chinese," she recalls. "My whole family thought I was crazy. I was never able to do it."

When she was in high school, college, and law school, she spent semesters or summers living in Spain, Japan, Italy, Mexico, and Peru, and she traveled to China and Thailand. During one of those summers, she was with a Peruvian friend in his country when they came upon a peaceful political demonstration. Suddenly, the police arrived in a pickup truck and began arresting the demonstrators. Shocked, she wanted to approach the scene, but her friend quickly whisked her off in the other direction, telling her that it was too dangerous to witness the arrests. She was troubled for years that she had seen people rounded up and carried off for their peaceful advocacy, and that she had been helpless to prevent it.

She did well in law school, and at her father's urging, she sought, received, and accepted the offer of a job in the corporate department of Willkie Farr, a major New York law firm. She was supposed to work on mergers, but the recession of the early 1990s was just beginning, so with time on her hands, she was delighted when a more senior associate proposed that she work on a pro bono asylum case that the Lawyers Committee for Human Rights had asked the firm to accept. The client had fled from Somalia. Pistone didn't know where it was.

Civil war had just broken out in Somalia, a war serious enough to prompt President Bush, two years later, to send the marines. But the U.S. papers hadn't yet reported much about it. Her client's father had just become the head of his clan because a rival clan had murdered his predecessor. With murderous intent, the rival clan had begun a search for her client's father and for her client as well. The INS had apprehended her client at an airport, because he lacked a U.S. visa. It had put him in jail and was in the process of deporting him. Pistone won asylum for him, and when his relatives escaped from Somalia, she won asylum for them as well. Meanwhile, she moved to Washington, where her firm had set up a telecommunications law department. For about three years, her job was to obtain licenses from the Federal Communications Commission so that one of Willkie's clients could launch telecommunications satellites, but she continued to give free representation to Somalian asylum-seekers, and she became the expert on human rights in Somalia for the Washington office of the Lawyers Committee, where Massimino served as legal director. Saving the lives of her African clients seemed far more satisfying than the work her clients were paying her to do. Her father could not understand her greater concern for Somalian refugees than for American corporations. "Now that the Italians are here," he told her, "we can shut the doors."

In the fall of 1995, Massimino asked Pistone to replace her for several months during her maternity leave. She described the work in terms of coordinating the Lawyers Committee's human rights research and education and overseeing the asylum work done by the committee's law firm volunteers. Unaware of the lobbying project that was about to unfold, Massimino did not mention the pending immigration bill. Pistone had no idea that fighting Smith and Simpson on asylum would dominate her life for more than a year, first at the Lawyers Committee and then back at her firm, or that it would lead her to leave the law firm permanently for a new career as a professor teaching immigration and human rights law.[2]

Pistone was eager to do full-time human rights work for a while, and her firm paid her full salary while it loaned her to the Lawyers Committee. Ten days before she was due to start, Massimino asked her to attend a meeting about the new law, the second meeting of the group concerned with asylum procedures. She recalls being "totally confused" at the meeting. "People were talking about different senators and congressmen and I didn't really know what their role was. That's also where I met you."

The meeting was not very productive. Its main decision was to try to convene another meeting, about ten days later, and in the meanwhile, again attempt to enlarge the group. By the time the next meeting was held, Massimino had begun her maternity leave, and Pistone had just started her new job. She arrived in the conference room at the law firm of McKenna and Cuneo. The conference table was huge, so long that a person at one end of the table almost had to shout to be heard at the other end, and this time, as the group assembled, the room was filled with people. In addition to the local refugee service organizations, officials attended from the National Immigration Forum, the Centers for Victims of Torture, the American Immigration Lawyers Association, the American Civil Liberties Union, Amnesty International, and the Washington legislative offices of half a dozen major religious organizations. "I was just taking a seat at the side of the table with everybody else," Pistone remembers. "You came over to me and said that I should sit at the head of the table, because I would be running the meeting. This was a shock. When you are an associate at a law firm you don't really run anything."[3]

After only minutes to prepare, she took on her new leadership role. But soon the meeting took on a strange character, as the conversation revealed that the room really held three groups. The first was our ragtag gang of asylum advocates who knew next to nothing about how to deal with Congress. The second consisted of the national organizations that had been lobbying on other aspects of the bill, with only the most limited success, for several months. A third, smaller group was comprised of professional lobbyists from the law firm hosting the meeting, who knew a great deal about standard lobbying practices, but very little about asylum. We in the first group knew we were green, but the second and third groups reinforced our belief that we had a lot to learn. "They spoke to us [in the second person] as if they weren't part of us, telling us what we should be doing," Pistone says. The chasm was widened by gaps in perception. Some of the service providers had a hard time believing that Congress would actually do away with asylum, while the veterans of mark-up hell knew that Congress might well do that and much, much more.

Although Pistone and I were surprised by the somewhat remote stance of our advisors, we were impressed by the content of their advice. The experts made it very clear that there was a "right" way for a new organization to start a lobbying campaign. First, we needed a name. Second, we needed a clear statement of who we were, what we wanted, and why it was a good idea. This statement should be no longer than two pages, they told us, because congressional staff members rarely had time to read longer documents. It should be signed by all of the organizations supporting us, to show our political strength. Once we had this document, we could start to use standard tactics for getting our message across: conversations and visits with staff members and, if possible, members of Congress; field organization and pressure; and a media campaign. We would also eventually need allies within the Senate Judiciary Committee itself and a legislative strategy, including a fallback strategy in case we could not succeed.

We agreed to take their suggestions, but we thought we might be short on time. It was already late November, and Simpson was trying to get Orrin Hatch, the Judiciary Committee chairman, to hold the full committee mark-up before the Christmas break. The mark-up might in fact slip until early in 1996, but we couldn't be certain. We had to follow the model that the experts told us about, but we also had to start contacting members of Congress, using the *Washington Post* op-ed as a temporary statement of the issues, until we had a formal organizational statement.

Working in groups is a necessity, both because groups are usually better than individuals at devising solutions to problems, and because political power can be concentrated through coordination in groups. But work in groups takes more time than individual work, because the process of reaching reasonable consensus is laborious and time-consuming. Even agreeing on a name for who we were took time. I'd proposed, alliteratively, that we constitute ourselves as the Project to Preserve Political Asylum. But one of the religious organizations pointed out that describing asylum only in "political" terms left out religion, one of the major reasons for flight from persecution.[4] Someone else noted that a "committee" sounded more solid than a "project." After some discussion, we became the Committee to Preserve Asylum, or CPA. Pistone offered the Lawyers Committee's office as the CPA's address. At the instant we agreed upon our name, I was struck, as I had been in the past, that one of the real, unappreciated glories of the American political system is that when people with a shared political goal want to create an organization to pursue their ends, they can just pick a name, print up some stationery (or just select a nice computer font), and go to work. They don't have to apply for permission, rent an office, register with the government, or pay a fee.[5]

Then we had to write our statement, but we realized that getting a large number of organizations to sign it was at odds with injecting all of our arguments against the thirty-day rule. The longer and more detailed the statement, the greater the risk that staff members or board members of the various organizations would quibble with the language or the gist of the arguments, drawing out for weeks the process of agreement on a final text, and perhaps making consensus impossible. Our experts advised us that most organizations had stringent bureaucratic rules regarding "clearance" on the text of any words that appeared *above* their group's signature, but were less fussy about any attachments that *followed* the signature. We therefore decided to write a quite general one-page covering letter that would enclose our two-page position statement. We would also enclose several case histories of actual refugees who won asylum, but who, like Joseph, could not reasonably have applied for it within thirty days of arriving in the United States.

Another problem was whether the position paper should attack the thirty-day rule or argue against any deadline at all. It was relatively easy to show that many asylum applicants could not apply within thirty days. But if we charged hard at the thirty-day rule that McCollum, Smith, and Simpson had written, they might change it to sixty or ninety days, which would be nearly as bad. Then, anyone reading our literature might toss it away as obsolete or unresponsive. In the end, we hedged, ridiculing a limit as short as thirty days, but also saying that no deadline was needed (in view of David Martin's regulatory reforms). We included some non-humanitarian arguments that we hoped would appeal strongly to those who hated government waste. We quoted the INS's own statement that it didn't want to spend time and money adjudicating time limits. We also pointed out that any deadline would impede the INS's ability to deport unauthorized aliens with non-meritorious asylum cases, because those who missed the deadline would no longer have an incentive to identify themselves to the government in an application for asylum.

We delegated the drafting to a smaller subcommittee, but inevitably, even our seven-sentence covering letter took a lot of work to develop. As chair of the subcommittee, Pistone produced and edited many drafts, but even after the subcommittee was satisfied, some of the groups that were asked to sign it insisted on changing a word or a phrase. For example, we'd begun by saying that we were an ad hoc coalition of religious groups, human rights organizations, and immigration and civil rights advocates. But organizations of doctors who cared about human rights victims wanted explicit recognition, and we agreed that mentioning them added to our credibility. So we added "concerned physicians" to the description of our identity.

To collect case studies, CPA members agreed to canvass their organizations' archives of closed, successful asylum cases. Of course, we recognized that case studies are anecdotal rather than statistically significant evidence of a problem. But our experts advised us, and we novices also knew as newspaper readers, that Congress (like the public in general) is often more easily moved by the stories of a few actual people than by statistical summaries. Indeed, the stories of a few individual terrorists such as Kansi seemed to be fueling the whole movement to restrict asylum.

The veterans of several months of mark-up hell told us, however, that we had to be careful about which case studies we used. Republicans tended to think that no one from Central America was a legitimate asylum applicant. Many members of Congress thought that rape was not persecution, so rape victims from Bosnia could not be used. Hyde and others did not regard Jews from the former Soviet Union as real refugees, so they should not be used either. We should start by looking for cases of belated applications by prominent political dissidents, preferably from China, Cuba, or Russia, and work down from there.

Similarly, our case studies had to avoid mentioning that the shortage of legal services for impoverished asylum-seekers was one of the reasons why some of them could not file applications very promptly. Access to lawyers was indeed part of the problem, as in the case of Mary Rawson, who finally overcame her fear of revealing her experiences but then had to wait for several weeks while her lawyer obtained clearance to represent her from two different firms. We were told, however, that many members of Congress had little patience with lawyers, and refugees could expect no sympathy because of the failure of the American legal profession to provide enough pro bono services.

The experts also advised us to instruct our constituents not to send case studies directly to members of Congress. Everything should be screened by our group, lest McCollum and Simpson get stories that they could discredit, either by showing them to be inaccurate or incomplete, or by arguing that the refugee really could have applied sooner for asylum.

The last immediate problem was how to find organizations to endorse our letter. Almost incidentally, one of the more experienced people at the table mentioned "fax trees," a term that was new to me. It seemed that several of the national organizations, including NIF, the American Immigration Lawyers Association, and Amnesty International, had either sets of fax numbers for other organizations stored in their machines, or an organized system through which they could send a fax to ten organizations, each of which would forward it to ten others. By giving our final letter, once it was ready, to a few organizations, we could get it distributed to hundreds of other organizations within three days. And while some of these organizations gave higher priority to other threats in the immigration bill, they graciously agreed to distribute our letter for us.

It took a week for the subcommittee to finish drafting the "sign-on" letter and statement. Pistone sent it out on the fax trees and began collecting and selecting powerful case studies. "Mrs. Y," a famous Tibetan popular singer, was fired from her job and put under constant surveillance by the Chinese government when she refused to participate in a celebration of Chinese suppression of Tibetan demonstrations. Though pregnant, she fled on foot over the Himalayas to Nepal and eventually came to the United States. She avoided applying for asylum for fear that her relatives still in Tibet would be persecuted if she were granted that status. She sought an employment-based visa on the basis of her musical ability, but nineteen months later, she gave up that unsuccessful effort, and she sought and won asylum. "Dr. M," a Sudanese physician, was kidnapped and beaten by the National Islamic Front because he joined the Doctor's Union. He fled to the United States but suffered from such severe depression upon arrival that he could not seek asylum. He found a volunteer lawyer, but it took the lawyer two months to get corroborating documents from Sudan. The doctor filed for asylum five months after entering the U.S., and he won. Pistone collected three pages of stories such as these, and waited for signatures to arrive.

She was amazed by how many endorsements rolled in. Two weeks after she sent out the letter, Pistone had signatures from eighty-nine organizations across the country, including dozens of community organizations serving refugees and several national organizations such as Human Rights Watch, Church World Services Immigration and Refugee Program, the American Jewish Committee, and the Lutheran Immigration and Refugee Service.[6]

On the very day that the letter was ready for distribution on Capitol Hill (and to its signatories for use back home), Senator Hatch put the immigration bill on the calendar of the Judiciary Committee, saying that mark-up would begin as soon as possible after the Senate reconvened in January.[7] Pistone's copier hummed. She delivered the CPA's letter to the offices of Judiciary Committee members just as the Senate was taking its break, an interlude that gave staff members slightly more time to read the mail. (A copy of the letter, with the case studies omitted to save space, is reproduced as appendix B.)

The Committee to Preserve Asylum now had an identity and a mission statement. It was sending out its message. But whether it could swing a single vote remained to be seen.

# 7

# "What's a Senator?"
## December 1995–March 1996

Persecution takes many forms, including torture and death. I do not believe the American people will regard those consequences as the appropriate level of punishment for a missed deadline.

—Washington University professor Stephen H. Legomsky, one of the nation's leading experts on immigration law[1]

I had no idea where to begin. We had just named our new Committee to Preserve Asylum, but weeks would pass before we'd be able to draft its statement, collect signatures, or communicate officially with senators. Simpson might be able to get a mark-up in December, while we were still mobilizing. We had to make our issue visible right away.

Success would depend on recruiting four Republican senators from the ten on the Judiciary Committee. Not only didn't I know any Republican senators, but I barely knew any Republicans. I stereotyped most Republican senators as Simpson clones.

I looked over the list of Judiciary Committee members (reproduced in appendix C). The only reputed Republican moderate was Specter. I didn't want to start with him, because if I could find a more conservative ally on the committee, Specter seemed likely to follow, but it was much less likely that a conservative would follow Specter.

For advice, I called my friend Peter Schuck, a professor at Yale Law School who had been one of the first scholars to study and write about immigration law. He didn't know anyone in Republican senators' offices, but he suggested I call Joseph Rees, the staff director of the House subcommittee that dealt with human rights. Rees had been INS general counsel under President Bush and had stayed in that position through the first six months of the Clinton administration. Peter assured me that Rees was deeply concerned about refugees, including asylum-seekers.

Although the subcommittee that Rees served didn't have jurisdiction over immigration, he was very aware of the Smith and Simpson bills. His subcommittee's chairman, Christopher Smith of New Jersey, was, like Hyde, a devout Catholic and a strong critic of China's forced abortion policies. Smith

111

had traveled to Africa to investigate religious persecution against Christians. Both Smith and Rees were eager to help reduce the bills' impact on legitimate refugees.[2]

Rees advised me to call the office of Senator Spencer Abraham. He didn't know who was handling the Simpson bill there, but he'd heard that Abraham wasn't happy with Simpson's intention to restrict legal immigration.

All I knew about Abraham was that he'd been deputy chief of staff for Vice President Dan Quayle. He was also the most junior member of the committee, ninety-eighth out of one hundred in Senate seniority. It seemed unlikely that he'd be much help. But I had nothing to lose.

I called Senator Abraham's office, but I knew that I wouldn't be able to talk to the senator personally, and I didn't try. All members of Congress have substantial staffs; the larger a senator's state, and the more seniority the senator has, the larger the staff. I knew that staff members handle most of the interactions between a legislator and members of the public, and that many of them have a great deal of influence over how their bosses will vote on legislation or proposed amendments.[3] Using Rees's name, I got through to Ray Kethledge in Abraham's office and explained my concerns about the thirty-day rule. Kethledge heard me out and said that Abraham disagreed with several aspects of Simpson's bill. He had his hands full because he might introduce amendments to other provisions, but if I could find another Republican to sponsor a motion to strike the asylum deadline, Abraham would probably vote for the motion. Barely able to contain my exuberance, I asked if he had suggestions for other people I might call. He gave me the name of Joe DeSanctis, his counterpart in the office of Senator Mike DeWine of Ohio. DeWine, like Abraham, was a conservative, midwestern freshman on the committee.

I was stunned. I'd been on the telephone for ten minutes, and although Kethledge hadn't made any promises, I was apparently already a quarter of the way to getting the swing votes we'd need in order to count a majority of committee members against the thirty-day rule. It was so easy! I had no idea that I'd started with the senator who would become Simpson's main challenger, and that months would go by before I'd find even one more Republican ally.

Quickly I dialed DeSanctis, and invoking the introduction from Kethledge, I asked whether he'd read the op-ed that I had sent to DeWine. He had not, but he asked me to fax him a copy, which I took to be a good sign. I summarized the issue over the telephone. He said that his boss had an open mind, that he would pick and choose among sections of the bill, and that he might even vote against some sections, but that he would not offer any amendments. I asked him to meet with me, but he put me off, saying that it would be premature to meet until the mark-up was scheduled. I was happy that DeSanctis had not defended the thirty-day rule, but unlike Kethledge, he had not been willing to predict that his boss would oppose it. Furthermore, I could now start to detect a potentially troubling pattern. When the time came, several senators might be willing to vote for a motion to strike this provision, particularly if a Republican would make the motion so that it did not become a partisan issue. But finding a Republican to make the motion might prove more difficult than rounding up the votes.

Meanwhile, the Committee to Preserve Asylum asked senior INS officials for a meeting, because, working separately, neither the committee nor the agency had persuaded the House Judiciary Committee to scrap McCollum's proposal. Perhaps together they could be more effective. The INS was convinced that David Martin's regulation, ending employment authorization for asylum applicants, had discouraged thousands of applications from people who could not possibly win asylum. But we pointed out that the INS had not compiled clear statistics, had not displayed well whatever statistics it had compiled, and had not persuaded Congress or the public that there was no longer a problem that had to be solved by legislation. During the meeting, Phyllis Coven, the INS's international affairs director, suggested an inspired idea.[4] In just a few weeks, Martin's regulation would have been in effect for exactly one year. The INS could hold a birthday party: a press conference to announce the success of the regulation, to publish new, well-displayed statistical information, and to articulate the case against the McCollum proposal. Indeed, the INS could give Congress credit for having brought the asylum problem to the attention of the administration, which subsequently wrote responsive regulations.

Over the next several weeks, I called the offices of Senate Judiciary Committee members, but compared to my first call with Kethledge, the results were always discouraging. After hearing why I was calling, one staff member put me on perpetual hold and then refused to accept all subsequent calls from me. Several asked me to send another copy of the op-ed but said they were too busy to meet. Some said it was too soon to meet, but more experienced hands warned me that if I waited, as the staffers suggested, until the mark-up was imminent, they would say that it was too late to meet because their senators had already made up their minds.

A few staffers, however, agreed to meet with a small delegation from the Committee to Preserve Asylum. Often we asked one or two refugees to come with us, people like Mary Rawson who had won asylum but, due to personal or political circumstances, had not applied until long after they had arrived in the United States. Our first meeting was with Senator Specter's aide, David Brog. On this occasion we brought with us a man from a third-world country who had waited more than a year to apply for asylum. This refugee explained to Brog that he had been an official in his country, but that he and his allies had been deposed, and threatened with death, by the leaders of a military coup. He had fled to a neighboring country, where he lived in a refugee camp. However, as a member of his country's government in exile, he'd traveled to New York to address the United Nations. While he was there, his own country pressured the country in which he'd been living in exile to cancel his passport. He was stranded in the United States. He could have applied for asylum immediately, but he knew that his application would be used by the government of his own country to show his people that he had deserted them and was resettling in the United States. So he asked the State Department for some sort of temporary permission to remain, short of asylum. He also asked the government of Norway, with which he had a connection, for similar temporary status. After considering his request for a year, the United States and Norway both told him that the only protective status he could request was asylum in the United States, the country in which he was in fact living. He applied for and received asylum. But more than a year had passed between his arrival in New York and his decision to seek asylum. He could not have won asylum if Senator Simpson's bill had become law.

Brog listened attentively to the refugee's tale and promised to take up the issue with Specter. We had similar reactions in other Senate offices: polite attention, promises to talk to the boss, and no real encouragement.

A group of us, including the same refugee, were leaving the Dirksen Senate Office Building after such a meeting with Fred Ansell, Senator Thompson's staffer. As we passed the last door on the ground floor, just before the exit, we noticed its legend: "ALAN SIMPSON—WYOMING."

"Let's go in and have it out with the great man," said Deborah Sanders, the director of the asylum law project of the Washington Lawyers Committee for Civil Rights.

"We could just wait out here," said Gary Sampliner, the partner who had arranged for his law firm to host our meetings. "Sooner or later he'll have to come out to go to the bathroom." This was pure jest, for we all knew that Senators had private restrooms in their suites.

But as if on cue, the door opened and a tall stringbean of a fellow emerged. We all knew his face. My instinct was to get out of his way as soon as possible. But Sanders is the most gutsy woman I've ever met. "Hello, Senator," she said, smiling.

"Hi," he said, smiling, ever the politician. "What brings you here?"

"Actually," she told him, "we've come to ask some senators to vote against one section of your immigration bill. And if you could just give us two minutes, we'd like to tell you what we think is wrong with it."

He seemed mildly shocked, but even more curious. I was more than a little embarrassed. It didn't seem polite to accost a senator in the hallway, when he was obviously on his way to a meeting or vote. On the other hand, this really was the classic kind of "lobbying," hanging out in the lobby for a chance to talk to legislators, as it was practiced before campaign contributions gave greater access to those who could buy it.[5]

"I'll give you five," he said. "But just five."

Sanders explained what was wrong with a time limit on asylum.

Simpson listened politely. When she finished, he asked, "When are you people going to get honest about the definition of a refugee?"

All of us were surprised by this question, and I think none of us had any idea what he was talking about. "Could you explain what you are referring to?" I asked.

"The Lautenberg amendment!" he said, his voice rising. "You know that most of the people being given refugee status aren't really refugees, and they are using up spaces that could be given to people in Africa and Asia who really need to be resettled here. Calling the Russian Jews refugees is just bullshit! Bullshit!"

This conversation had taken so many surprising turns in four minutes that I was reeling. I didn't know what the Lautenberg amendment had to do with asylum. I hadn't known that Simpson was so concerned for third-world refugees. And above all, I was embarrassed that a senator was using barnyard language in front of our foreign guest.

"I don't understand the relationship . . ." I started.

"I'll tell you what," Simpson said to all of us. "You go back and tell the groups. Tell them that if the groups get serious about the definition of refugee, this cowboy will play fair and square with them about the asylum deadline." And with that he was gone.

The encounter left me with so many questions. Had Simpson only put the deadline into his bill to use it as a bargaining chip for something else? If so, what did he really want? Was the deadline all part of a plan to keep out the Jews? Or was Simpson genuinely concerned that the Lautenberg amendment was squeezing out deserving third-world refugees? Finally, was Simpson's real plan to divide the coalitions that were forming to fight his bill? We could do as he suggested and urge the Jewish groups that had just joined our CPA to give up the Lautenberg amendment, for which they'd struggled for years, in order to preserve asylum. But certainly they'd refuse, and they might resent our suggesting that they abandon their old cause for our new one. Simpson's proposed deal wasn't even worth mentioning in one of our meetings; we couldn't deliver it even if we wanted to do so.

A few days later, the mail brought another surprise, the only response I ever received to the op-ed reprints that I'd sent to Judiciary Committee members. "Although I am a co-sponsor of [Simpson's] bill," the letter read, "please be assured that I will give careful consideration to your concerns about the hardship a 30-day rule might impose on refugees, who often arrive in the United States without knowledge of the asylum process or the ability to communicate in English." The signature on the letter was Strom Thurmond.

I stared and stared at the letter and the signature. I hadn't even bothered trying to call Thurmond's office, assuming that one of the Senate's most conservative members would support Simpson down the line. Yet the letter seemed to be asserting as the author's own statement, not just paraphrasing my letter, that refugees would have trouble applying for asylum quickly.

I wasn't in my office the next day, because my six-year-old daughter, Sarah, was ill and it was my turn to stay home with her. But I couldn't wait to call Thurmond's office. So I seized a moment when Sarah seemed to be occupied. I closeted myself in my study and called to ask for his aide for immigration policy.

I reached Melanie Sabo, who confirmed that she'd drafted the letter for Thurmond. I asked her to talk with me for a few minutes about the issue. I wanted to assess whether Thurmond was really sympathetic, and whether he might make the motion to strike. If Thurmond was in our corner, we couldn't lose.

According to Sabo, Thurmond could conceivably oppose Simpson on this issue, because thirty days seemed much too short a time for traumatized refugees. However, she added, the letter reflected her own sentiments more than a fully considered position by Thurmond himself, and although she might recommend that he vote against a thirty-day limit, she could not say what Thurmond would do when the time came.

Just then, Sarah opened the study door, climbed into my lap, and began to ask me to play with her. I put my fingers to my lips, reached for a Post-it, and printed a note to her. "Could you please wait? I'm talking to a senator's office."

Sarah reached for a Post-it of her own. Laboriously putting one letter after another, she wrote, "What's a senator?"

I pointed out to Sabo that opposing the thirty-day limit might be good politics in South Carolina, because many applicants for asylum were anti-Communists who had fled from Nicaragua, Cuba, or other leftist-dominated countries. Meanwhile, I found another Post-it and wrote, "A senator is someone who helps make laws."

Sarah wrote, "What are laws?"

For the next ten minutes, I tried to arm Sabo with arguments about why Thurmond should be our leader, while simultaneously conducting a correspondence course on American government. I'm not sure I succeeded very well with either task, and by the end of the call I was a nervous wreck.

By this time, the CPA was getting into gear. It had delivered its letter and case studies to Senate offices, and Pistone opened the beyond-the-Beltway phase of the campaign. She assigned one CPA member to each of the seventeen states represented on the Judiciary Committee. That member's task was to get as many people from the state as possible to call and write to the senator, request personal meetings during the Christmas break, and generally raise a ruckus back home about the hardship of the thirty-day rule. Many of the organizations that had signed CPA's letter had headquarters or members in the seventeen states, so it was possible to use our own letter as a source of leads for building local pressure. In addition, some of the national organizations represented on the CPA did their own lobbying. For example, Physicians for Human Rights canvassed doctors among its membership who had treated refugees suffering from torture-induced trauma. The organization collected the physicians' testimony in a book that it delivered to all of the Senate Judiciary Committee members.[6]

The new year, 1996, opened with the press conference that the INS had promised. Commissioner Meissner heralded the good news: as a result of the year-old Martin regulations, asylum applications had fallen by 57 percent, compared with the prior year, and the INS was now able to conduct interviews with 84 percent of new claimants within sixty days after they applied.[7] Neither the agency's press release nor the commissioner's opening statement mentioned the proposed legislation. But a planted question from the audience inquired about it, giving Meissner the opportunity to reply that "you don't need a thirty-day rule. It's an over-reaction."[8] Meissner followed up the press conference by visiting House and Senate offices to offer personal briefings on the success of the new regulations.

The *Washington Post* gave significant coverage to the announcement. It featured the story on page two, and it editorialized a few days later that "considerable distance has been covered in improving procedures."[9] The press thereby reinforced what senators and their staffs were hearing from the administration, the CPA and the refugees that it brought to one office after another, and in some cases, their constituents back home.

As the mark-up neared, however, the CPA encountered three new difficulties. First, while senators' staff members continued to be quite accessible, interested, and in most cases, obviously sympathetic to CPA members' concerns, most of them explicitly said that their bosses hadn't considered refugee issues yet and, in view of the many subjects that senators had to vote on, probably wouldn't do so until the eve of the mark-up. They assured us that they would brief their bosses, orally or in writing, about the thirty-day rule, and in some cases, they hinted that they would recommend a vote against Simpson. But they could not promise us anything, and we could not get in to see the senators themselves.

Our best chance of seeing senators personally was not in Washington, where their schedules were packed from morning until late at night, but in their home districts, where they went for the Christmas and President's Day breaks, and on many weekends. Pistone encouraged refugee advocates to try to obtain in-state meetings with senators whenever possible. But there the CPA's second difficulty arose. Simpson had refused to make a separate deal with the business community, as Smith had, and the coalition of family reunification advocates and pro-immigration businesses had been revived.[10] The business and family immigration lobbyists were also trying to get in-state meetings with the senators on the Judiciary Committee. In many cases, the senator was willing to schedule only one in-state meeting with pro-immigration advocates. The family and business immigration advocates, and their split-the-bill message, always received primacy on the agenda of this single meeting, and refugee advocates were consigned to the tail end of the session, when time was short and the senator was already thinking about other issues. For example, Senator Hank Brown confined refugee issues to the last five minutes of a meeting he held in Denver.

CPA's third problem involved developing a fallback strategy. Having such a strategy was necessary. Democratic staff members continually warned that the well-liked Simpson could not be beaten outright during his final year in the Senate. Pistone never accepted this logic, reasoning that Simpson would get nearly all of the three hundred sections of his bill, and the CPA was not trying to beat him outright but simply to remove one obnoxious provision. Nevertheless, the fact of life seemed to be that Simpson would have to get at least a face-saving provision, and maybe more. On the other hand, any fallback could be dangerous, because as soon as Senate staff got wind of it, they would try to pocket it, reducing the degree of friction between their bosses and Simpson. Then they would ask for the next set of concessions. If we did develop a fallback strategy, it had to be kept secret until the last possible minute.

Early in the process, we decided to delegate the fallback strategy to someone who was out of town, so that the Washington advocates wouldn't even be thinking about fallbacks while they lobbied to strike the deadline altogether. We asked Professor Jean Koh Peters, director of the immigration clinic at Yale Law School, to think about fallback positions, independent of the rest of the CPA.

Peters and her student David Fry soon experienced the ethical qualms that all of us shared about legislative compromise. "We have some misgivings about the entire venture," Fry wrote. A compromise providing a much broader exception to the thirty-day rule than the "changed circumstances" exception already in the bill "fails to address the real issue, which is that the thirty-day deadline is utterly unconnected to the merits of the claim. [T]he group in Washington should consider ... whether our client pool would not be better served in the long run if we propose only more meaningful amendments, even if they have less chance of success."[11] Despite these reservations, Peters and Fry went to work to write a back-pocket compromise and a rationale justifying its adoption.

Simpson had wanted a Judiciary Committee mark-up before Christmas. January came and went, but the committee's chairman, Orrin G. Hatch, still had not set a date. Simpson pushed him to put the mark-up on the committee's calendar early in February, but Hatch did not seem eager to accommodate him.[12] The continued uncertainty about when the mark-up would occur kept the CPA off balance, because some of the senators and staff members declined to focus on proposed amendments to the bill until a mark-up was at least scheduled.

But the CPA used the additional time to bring more refugees to Capitol Hill, to keep talking with staff members, and to keep looking for a Republican sponsor for the motion to strike. It also asked human rights experts to make their opinions known to senators.[13] Increasingly, senators' staffers told Pistone and her fellow CPA members that they personally thought the provision should be struck, but they doubted that their senators would want to lead a battle against Simpson. Often, they asked how many votes the CPA had collected, implying that they could more easily recommend that their senator get into a battle if the senator was sure to come out on the winning side. Most senators hadn't yet been briefed, so even though the staff members were swinging our way, we could not count senators' votes.

The staff members also let Pistone know that they had been hearing opposition to the asylum deadline from their constituents, and that even some of the offices least warm to our entreaties told her that she was doing an impressive job. Some said that they had received more calls about the asylum deadline than about any other immigration issue except splitting the bill. This feedback reinforced Pistone's determination to keep the cards and letters coming. The CPA's campaign was helped by the fact that although FAIR supported the thirty-day deadline, FAIR was stretched too thin to expend many resources to defend it. FAIR's principal objective was to build support for the Smith and Simpson bills generally. It could not, at the same time, vigorously oppose all of the attacks by refugee advocates and other pro-immigration forces, on various provisions of the legislation. FAIR had "only about $3.5 million dollars in annual resources, so all [it] could do was put out one-pagers on most amendments."[14]

Several staff members said that between a thirty-day deadline and no deadline, they would recommend eliminating the deadline, but that they would favor, as a compromise, a longer deadline. Senator Thompson's staff member, for example, told a CPA member that he would personally favor a one-year deadline. "The feeling in Tennessee," he said, "is round 'em up and ship 'em out."[15]

Neither the CPA's increasingly effective lobbying nor some senators' desire for a compromise escaped Simpson's notice. His counsel, Richard Day, met with the other senators' staff members early in February and announced that Simpson was not wedded to his own proposal. Day invited other senators to propose amendments to it, so long as they did not kill the very idea of a deadline. No one in the meeting, however, took issue with the premise that a deadline had to remain in the bill.

While she worked on the Republicans, Pistone did not neglect the Democrats. Based on staff comments, it seemed that our initial premises were correct. We could count on the six liberal Democrats, but Feinstein would probably vote with Simpson, and there was no way to know how Heflin would vote. Heflin had announced his retirement; he was therefore free from reelection pressures and could vote his conscience. I started making blind calls to Alabama immigration lawyers who were listed in the membership directory of the American Immigration Lawyers Association.

With one of them, I hit pay dirt. He turned out to be a close friend of Heflin's legislative assistant. Knowing that he was an Alabama immigration expert, the assistant had sent him a copy of Simpson's bill and asked for his written comments. After I explained the problems with the thirty-day rule and sent him the CPA's literature, he said that he would recommend that striking the deadline be one of Heflin's top priorities. A few days later, Pistone met with the legislative assistant. At the end of the meeting, he told her that he was going to recommend that Heflin vote for a motion to strike.

Kennedy's staff told Pistone that Kennedy would be willing to make the motion, but they agreed with us that it would be more likely to succeed if it had Republican sponsorship. What Republican would be willing to challenge Simpson? Based on the receptions we'd received from staffers, the most likely candidates were Hank Brown, whose assistant had been very understanding, and Mike DeWine, whose staffer Joe DeSanctis had been non-committal in person and unwilling to meet us until the mark-up was scheduled.

Pistone learned that Brown in fact had two assistants who worked on immigration issues, and that the one who had been sympathetic was the more junior, less influential aide. She requested and obtained a meeting with David Miller, the more senior assistant, and I tagged along.

Pistone made the case against the thirty-day rule. After listening politely, Miller said nothing positive about her presentation. Instead, he barraged her with skeptical questions. Without a limit, wouldn't many people just wait to see whether they were caught, and claim asylum as a last, desperate way to prolong their U.S. residence? Hadn't the INS proved incapable of managing the asylum docket under current law? What would be Pistone's fallback position if she did not get what she wanted? Pistone answered each question well, but I was certain that we were wasting our time and wanted to leave as soon as possible. However, after questioning her for half an hour, Miller ended the meeting by saying that he would recommend to Brown that he sponsor the motion to strike the thirty-day rule, or that he co-sponsor it with Kennedy.

I was amazed, but I realized that without saying so, he'd been playing the devil's advocate, to make sure that if Brown joined our camp, he would not be surprised by arguments he could not answer satisfactorily.

Still, we had no commitment from Brown, so we had to continue our search for a sponsor. Now that the mark-up had been scheduled, we could try DeWine again. This time, although he still hadn't met us in person, DeSanctis said that he'd be willing to recommend that DeWine offer the motion to strike the thirty-day rule, or that he co-sponsor it with Kennedy. As usual, he said we couldn't count on DeWine's sponsorship yet, because the senator hadn't approved it.

The suspense was terrible, but for the first time, we began to see ten or eleven possible votes on the eighteen-member committee. We counted seven Democrats, plus Abraham, Brown, DeWine, and Specter, who had said nothing, but whom we assumed would go along if two or three more conservative Republicans were with us. Pistone reported the conversation with DeSanctis to Kennedy's office.

By this time, the beginning of the mark-up was days away, although we knew that the committee might take several days of sessions before it reached the asylum issue. For several weeks, Senator Abraham, himself the grandson of Lebanese immigrants who had arrived in the United States with less than five dollars in their pockets,[16] had been quietly gearing up to lead the minority of Republicans who would oppose Simpson's plan to curtail legal immigration.[17] Just before the mark-up began, Abraham announced that he would lead the effort to split the bill.[18] Simpson at last realized that the coalition of business and non-profit organizations had the votes to defeat his cutbacks on legal immigration. He announced that he would jettison all of the restrictions on business immigration, hoping to make the same deal with business that Smith had made in the House. But Abraham applied counter-pressure to the business community to keep it with him, and this time, business remained in the split-the-bill coalition.[19]

In the wee hours of the morning of February 29, people began lining up in the hall outside the room in which the mark-up would take place. Most of them were "place-holders," people hired by law firms to stand on line for hours so that they could yield their places to business lobbyists at 10:00 A.M., when the mark-up was about to begin. When Pistone arrived at 8:00 A.M., the line was down the hall and around the corner. There seemed little hope of getting into the room, but she told one of the place holders that she was an associate with Willkie Farr, a true statement even though she was on loan to the Lawyers Committee. The place holder knew that his company wanted to get business from the firm, so he let her cut into the line in front of him. In the mark-up, she watched a remarkable drama unfold. Abraham tried to get an immediate vote on his split-the-bill amendment, before Simpson could make pro-business amendments to siphon away Abraham's votes. Simpson argued that Abraham's snap motion "hinders my ability to ... go through the bill sequentially, to do it in a rational way." Abraham replied that the question of whether legal as well as illegal immigration should be restricted was a "threshold issue." When Hatch hinted that he might allow a vote on Abraham's motion because Abraham had been the first senator recognized to speak, Simpson invoked "a personal privilege of this committee," and asked the members to "support me against the Chairman."

Hatch realized that in a showdown, the committee might uphold the tradition of deferring to a well-regarded senior subcommittee chairman rather than the tradition of allowing the committee chair to run the hearing. Not wanting to risk being overruled by his own committee, an outcome he thought likely in Simpson's final year, he asked Abraham to defer to Simpson and postpone the vote. Abraham resisted, but Simpson pressed on. "I have been here 17 years," he pointed out, "and at each and every mark-up ... the Chairman ... deferred to the chairman of the subcommittee." Hatch forced Abraham to back down, and Abraham had to wait for a later session of the mark-up.[20]

Pistone went to all of the mark-up sessions, looking for opportunities to talk with staff members after each session ended and assessing when the thirty-day rule would come up for a vote. But she still did not have a Republican sponsor.

At the end of one mark-up session, she again chatted with David Miller from Brown's staff. Miller said that he hadn't yet had a response from Brown. He also told Pistone that he'd heard that Kennedy was working on a compromise, to impose a deadline, but to apply it only to defensive asylum cases, in which an alien applied for asylum after being apprehended.

Pistone was astonished. Just when she could see a complete victory at hand, a lurking compromise might make it impossible. She called Patty First, one of Kennedy's assistants.

"That wasn't supposed to get out!" First said. "We haven't even drafted it yet. It's something we have been thinking about as a fallback in case we saw the motion to strike going down."

"How did it get out?" Pistone asked.

"I mentioned it when I was on the phone with DeSanctis last night, talking about the possibility of co-sponsorship," she said. "But I had no idea he'd tell Miller. We'll get out the word right away that all we're thinking about is a straight motion to strike."

Pistone was worried that any rumor of a fallback position would impair the CPA's effort to stop deadlines altogether. She was also worried that, while Kennedy might be right to think that a fallback would eventually be necessary, his office might draft a fallback that was more generous to Simpson than we would want. She therefore offered to send First some proposed fallback language. Based on the work that Jean Koh Peters and David Fry had done in New Haven, she sent First a draft in which the deadline would be two years, it would apply only to defensive cases, and the INS could waive the deadline for "good cause," a term used in dozens of federal laws to justify exceptions, including late filing of documents. First accepted her structure but said that she had to change the deadline to one year to make it more reasonable.

A few minutes later, Pistone heard a terrible rumor. Senator Paul Simon, the influential Illinois Democrat whom we had counted as a certain supporter, had been rethinking his position and now thought that some deadline was necessary, though thirty days was too short. Now the CPA would not only have to win over Republicans, but shore up its support among Democrats. Calls quickly went out to the CPA's grass-roots supporters in Chicago, to find everyone we knew who had a personal connection to Simon.

By March 4, DeSanctis had drafted a motion to strike for his boss to make. He sent the amendment to us. However, he cautioned, while he was "certain" that DeWine would offer it, he still hadn't had a chance to discuss it with him. He hoped to meet with him within a few days.

We spent the next week waiting for a call from DeSanctis, but no call came. We also barraged Simon with calls and letters from people he knew well. I had campaigned for Simon when he ran for president in 1988, so I wrote him my own letter, too, explaining my small connection to him and the hardship that an asylum deadline would cause. Finally, I received a letter from him. The typed portion said that "I believe that the asylum application should not be open-ended." But at the bottom of the letter, he had written by hand that "I am now convinced—since dictating this—that INS is effectively moving on this serious problem, and no legislative change is necessary."[21] That particular crisis had been averted.

But the next one was just beginning. The following day, Brown studied Miller's recommendation that he sponsor the motion to strike the time limit. He came out of his office and told his assistants, "draft me something with sixty days." His staff members were disappointed, but they had no choice. Still, they did not know whether Brown wanted a fallback in case a motion to strike failed, or whether he wanted to use a sixty-day compromise to derail the CPA's strategy. The answer soon became clear. Brown really wanted a deadline, though a somewhat longer one than Simpson's proposal. He may even have come up with a sixty-day plan at the request of Simpson, who knew that we were getting a good reception.

By the time of the March 13 mark-up session, DeWine had formally agreed to co-sponsor, with Kennedy, the motion to strike. When senators arrived at the meeting, they found that Brown had placed a copy of his sixty-day proposal on their chairs, but the time limit was so short that the idea did not attract any interest, even from senators looking for a middle ground. If Hatch had reached the issue that day, First later reported, we would have killed the deadline on the spot, for she was able to count at least ten votes for the DeWine-Kennedy motion. But the mark-up did not get to our section, and although sixty days was too short, Brown perceived that he might get somewhere with a more generous compromise.

The next morning, on her way to the mark-up, Pistone saw Senator Thompson on the street. "Senator," she called out. He approached her. She explained that later in the morning, he'd have to vote on the DeWine amendment, and she explained why he should support it. He told her he'd consider it, but it was plain to her that despite the hours that CPA members and refugees had spent with his staff members, he'd never heard anything about this issue. "That's when I realized how important it was to get contact with the senators themselves," Pistone recalls.[22]

A few hours later, most of the focus was on Abraham's split-the-bill amendment, which was finally scheduled for a vote. By this time, however, much of the drama had gone out of that struggle. Several senators on the committee, including DeWine and Specter, had publicly declared that legal and illegal immigration should not be combined in one bill. Simpson knew he would lose, and that he would not be able to get enough Senate floor time to bring up two major bills before he retired. He blamed his impending defeat on "the [split-the-bill] cry of the media in one of their bone-headed rituals." Abraham's amendment carried, twelve to six.[23]

Behind the scenes, another drama was under way. Brown brought to the mark-up still another asylum compromise, a one-year deadline. Democratic staff members watched the reactions of senators as they read Brown's new draft, and they could tell that this time, there was real interest in a possible compromise. But Brown's compromise wasn't nearly as good as the one Pistone had drafted, which some Democratic staffers still had under wraps. One of them sought out Pistone in the audience section of the hearing room and asked her whether the time had come to share the draft with DeSanctis, to find out whether DeWine could accept that fallback plan if it later became clear that DeWine's original amendment would fail. Pistone assented.

The staff member then attempted to give the draft to DeSanctis. But the staffer mistook Miller for DeSanctis, and gave it to Miller instead. Miller immediately showed it to Brown. Brown directed Miller to tell Kennedy that Brown could agree to the Democrats' one-year defensive-only fallback, provided that they delete the "good cause" exception. Simpson's own exception for changed conditions in the applicant's country could remain.

Now the CPA and the Democrats had a problem. Kennedy quickly made it clear that the "good cause" exception was essential. But the Republicans knew that the Democrats could tolerate a compromise very similar to one that Brown also found acceptable.

Once again, the mark-up adjourned without reaching the issue. The committee was certain to get there during its next meeting, however. For six frantic days, CPA members pushed hard on the senators in the middle, many of whom were now telling their staffs that having killed the curb on legal immigration, they did not want to hand Simpson another defeat in his final year, and that some sort of face-saving compromise was necessary. The good news was that a simple deadline of thirty or sixty days was unlikely to pass. The bad news was that the proposal to kill a deadline altogether may have peaked too soon. Pistone had to develop arguments against her own fallback position. She rewrote all of the CPA's literature to focus the criticism on the concept of a deadline, even for defensive cases, rather than on Simpson's thirty-day proposal. From the INS, Commissioner Meissner called nine senators, stressing the waste of INS resources that adjudicating any deadline would entail. DeWine and Kennedy sent a letter to all of the other Judiciary Committee members. To appeal to the committee's conservatives, they included the hard-line claim that because arguments about whether an applicant's claim of changed circumstances would take time, "the DeWine-Kennedy amendment will result in faster deportation than the Brown amendment." The letter also reminded their colleagues about the doctors' letters they'd received in the book from Physicians for Human Rights.[24]

On the eve of the vote, DeSanctis and Miller discussed which senator's motion would be made first. Brown wanted to go first, because approval of his amendment would essentially kill DeWine's motion to strike. DeWine wanted to go first, on the hope that a resounding victory for his motion would persuade Brown to withdraw his compromise. Miller said that Brown would allow DeWine to make the first motion, but Brown was determined to offer his amendment, even if DeWine's motion to strike was approved.

When the mark-up reconvened, Brown had retyped his compromise, using every word of Pistone's own language, except that her two-year period had been reduced to one year, and Brown had replaced the "good cause" exception with one of his own making, another small step in the direction of the Democrats. In this iteration, Brown applied the deadline only to defensive cases, and he allowed an exception for "extraordinary circumstances" that prevented the applicant from filing on time. Brown's acceptance of the "defensive only" clause was a great victory for the CPA, because it exempted from the deadline at least three-quarters of all asylum applicants. The departure from Pistone's "good cause" language seemed significant, however. We knew from experience that many refugees who were unlucky enough to be picked up by the INS in raids on restaurants would be people who had already been in the United States for more than a year. For them, the opportunity to show some reason why they had waited, such as traumatization by torture in their countries, would be important. And many asylum officers and judges might be more lenient in applying a "good cause" than an "extraordinary circumstances" standard to the exception.

I watched the mark-up from the audience, elbow to elbow with lobbyists from corporations, law firms, and business associations. I'd seen Senate floor debates, both from the Senate gallery and on C-SPAN, but this was unlike anything I'd ever seen before. More than a dozen senators were working at a square of long, baize-covered tables just a few feet away, and this was real work, not just a performance for cameras or the making of a record for constituents. Except for a couple of opening statements, they were extemporizing, not reading speeches written by aides, and they were really grappling with each others' ideas, and negotiating the text of laws. This was the real meat of legislating, I realized, and in our amazing political system, although much of the persuading went on behind closed doors, the final but far from unimportant act was played out in the open.

DeWine led off the debate.[25] The INS had solved the asylum abuse problem by changing its regulation, he said, and it opposed the deadline because of the burdens it would impose. But the most compelling argument against Simpson's provision, he said, was that "the most deserving people, the most egregious cases, the most heart-wrenching cases, these individuals need the most time to file." He gave two examples. First, he described a Nigerian whose father had chaired an opposition political party. While he was imprisoned for eight months, guards carved the initials of the ruling general into his stomach and then sprayed pepper onto the wounds. They hit him with horsewhips and forced him to drink urine mixed with pepper spray.

After he was released, he fled to the United States. He was afraid to seek asylum because he knew that if he lost, he'd be forced to return to Nigeria. Five years after entering the United States, he was caught and put into deportation proceedings. At that point, he applied for asylum, and he won.

DeWine's second case study turned out to be Joseph, the Zairian student for whom my clinic had won asylum a few months earlier. He had been included in the CPA's collection of case studies that had been sent to every senator.

After Kennedy supported DeWine, Simpson replied that "for every one of those very compelling stories, there are other compelling stories of people who have certainly distorted the asylum process. . . . I just do not think it unreasonable to require a person who claims they have come here to escape persecution . . . to make that claim known rather than living in an illegal status."

Feinstein added that "there should be some cut-off on asylum."

Hatch then stated his own position. "I am going to vote for the DeWine amendment," he said. "And immediately thereafter, I will call up the Brown amendment which will limit it to a year. I am going to vote yes on both of them. Somebody might think that might be a little inconsistent. On the other hand, that is the nature of this beast around here sometimes."

We had stumbled into creating one of those situations that legislators most love, a chance to vote on both sides of an issue. They could please the refugee advocates by voting for DeWine, and then please Simpson and his allies by voting for Brown. Paul Simon announced, however, that "I am going to vote for the DeWine amendment, and I am going to vote against the Brown amendment."

Hatch instructed the clerk to call the roll. The vote was fifteen to one.[26] Only Simpson voted for his own provision.

We had no time at all, not even a minute, to celebrate the fruits of six months of hard work. The Brown amendment was put up for discussion, and we knew that some version of it would pass. The only question was whether some of the senators might get it amended to make Brown's "extraordinary circumstances" exception more lenient.

Arizona's Jon Kyl argued on Brown's behalf. "It seems to me that it really does have to be a very special case where that kind of point would go beyond the one year."

DeWine took issue with him. Brown's standard was "a horrible, horrible wall to have to climb." And, he asked, "what does 'prevented' mean? You know, no one puts a gun to the head of a refugee and prevents him or her from applying for asylum."

Senator Russell Feingold, a Democratic freshman from Wisconsin, put forward our "good cause" fallback as a substitute. Hatch asked whether DeWine could accept it. To our surprise but his credit, DeWine had staked out a position of principle. "I don't feel it is right to support anything where there is a time limit," he said. "It is just wrong." Pistone and I exchanged amazed glances. We now didn't know whether we wanted the senators to compromise on our fallback language or have a roll-call vote on accepting the Brown amendment. DeWine felt so strongly that perhaps he could command the votes to beat Brown as well as Simpson. Because DeWine's attack on the Simpson provision had come first, before Brown's motion was put forward, we now needed only nine votes, not ten, to defeat the Brown amendment; on a tie vote, Brown's effort to amend the bill would fail.

But mustering even nine votes, at this point, seemed unlikely, in view of how many senators, including a few of the Democrats, wanted to give Simpson some face-saving language. In any event, the committee was now in full motion, and there was no way for us to influence the outcome even if we'd had a clear idea about what to do.

The person who did know what to do was Edward Kennedy. Even in the small committee room, he drew on his superb oratorical skill to make his point. "It is really ordinary circumstances, not extraordinary circumstances, that are the rule of the day," he said. "That the person didn't know for example, that there was asylum, or that they weren't able to speak English, or that they weren't able to get a Legal Services attorney." His voice rose and rolled, as if he were addressing a rally. "It is these ordinary circumstances that will work the great injustice. Not the extraordinary. The ordinary." His voice fell again. "I am looking around the room, and I know where the votes are. And I wonder whether we could consider a good-cause exception." He tried to signal DeWine.

"Quite frankly, I think it would be preferable to the alternative which I see coming down the road."

Hatch strongly wanted a compromise rather than a contentious resolution. "Could you accept 'good cause,'" he asked Brown.

Who would determine whether good cause existed, Brown asked.

Kennedy assured him that it would be the Justice Department, not the applicant.

"It seems to me that is reasonable," Brown said quietly.

Feingold had also raised a question about whether Simpson's original exception, for changed circumstances in the asylum-seeker's country, was subsumed within the new "good cause" exception, or whether an additional exception for changed circumstances was necessary. DeWine came back to this issue and proposed it as a second exception.

"That is an example of a good cause," Kyl said. "I don't know whether you have to add it."

Kennedy saw both the risk that the compromise would unravel in further discussion and an opening to improve his position further in another way. "Why don't we try and work it out in the language of the [committee's] report?" he asked.

Hatch was eager to move on to other amendments. "Why don't we take the Brown amendment and work it [the exact language, and what the Committee report would say] in good faith? Is there any objection?"

There was none. The fight in the Senate committee was over. Pistone turned to me, wide-eyed. "Is that all there is?" she asked. "Aren't they even going to vote?"

"I was very disappointed," Pistone reported later. Because there was no vote on the Brown amendment, "you never really knew whether Feinstein, for instance, [voted against the Simpson provision because she] was really voting for no filing deadline or [because she planned to] undo it the next minute." But although she didn't have the satisfaction of seeing a decisive, confrontational formal vote, she realized that we'd won a 95 percent victory. We had not eliminated a deadline altogether in the Senate's bill. But by confining its application to the small fraction of cases in which refugees were arrested after more than a year in the United States, we had reduced it to a minor change in American law. And then, with the "good cause" exception, we'd given the Justice Department the power to grant asylum to almost anyone with a genuinely good excuse for filing late.

We had one further job to do immediately, but at the time I had no idea how significant it would later become. As Kennedy had indicated, the committee would have to write a formal report explaining what its bill meant. Part of that report would interpret the new "good cause" exception, and this explanation would become part of the official legislative history of the law. The Justice Department might rely on it when it wrote regulations interpreting the law, and advocates could cite it when they argued cases before asylum officers and immigration judges. I therefore sought out DeSanctis and suggested to him some language for the committee's report, with as many common types of excuses as I could think of, and permission for the Justice Department to think of additional exceptions, either in regulations or in individual cases:

> This exception is intended to permit allowances for circumstances that justifiably accounted for the applicant's not having filed an application within one year. Such circumstances include (but are not necessarily limited to) an applicant's physical or mental disability; changed circumstances, after the applicant entered the United States, that bear upon the applicant's eligibility for asylum or ability to substantiate an application for asylum; infancy; threats of retribution against the applicant's relatives abroad; attempts to file affirmatively that were unsuccessful because of technical defects; efforts to seek asylum that were delayed by the temporary unavailability of professional assistance; the illness or death of the applicant's legal representative; or other extenuating circumstances as determined by the Attorney General. The Attorney General may promulgate regulations illustrating examples of good cause including those identified in this report.

DeSanctis took my proposed language to Miller, who accepted it on Brown's behalf. But to have it printed as part of the committee's report, he also needed the approval of Richard Day, Simpson's chief counsel. Day balked. He included several of the proposed illustrative exceptions, such as changed circumstances after the alien's entry, disability, and threats against relatives. But he omitted new circumstances bearing on the applicant's ability to substantiate an asylum case, the applicant's infancy, technical defects in a prior application, and problems with obtaining legal assistance. Furthermore, he described the exceptions only as examples that the "good cause" language "could" include.[27] DeSanctis told me about these omissions, but at the time, I didn't pay much attention to them, because the more important issue had been making the deadline apply only to defensive cases. DeWine, on the other hand, thought the omissions were serious. He published his separate views in the committee report, arguing that "good cause" should be "broadly defined to include all reasonable circumstances that could prevent a deserving asylum seeker from applying for asylum."[28] And without any prodding from the CPA, he began to draft an amendment to the bill, which he could propose on the Senate floor, to restore the exceptions that Day had denied him in the committee's report. A few months earlier, DeWine was a conservative freshman senator who had known nothing about the problems of asylum applicants. But in a very short time he had become one of the Senate's most ardent advocates for the victims of human rights abuses.

# 8

# The House

## *January–March 1996*

These people should be required, the moment they appear at the airport, to say, "I am claiming asylum." How did they get on the airplane in the first place?

—Representative Anthony Beilenson,
member of the Committee on Rules
of the House of Representatives[1]

Through nearly the entire winter of 1995–96, until about a month before Smith's immigration bill was due to be debated on the floor, the Committee to Preserve Asylum lavished attention on the members of the Senate Judiciary Committee, but expended much less effort on the House of Representatives. Five reasons account for the difference in its approaches to the two houses of Congress. First, it had pitifully few organizational resources. The Lawyers Committee allowed Pistone to spend most of her time working on the legislation, but for everyone else, effort to affect the bill was a part-time addition to other work. Second, the task of organizing for a House debate seemed daunting. The committee could do a thorough job of keeping in touch with eighteen Senate offices, and it could barely imagine a campaign directed at all 100 senators if that became necessary. But trying to educate 435 congressional offices was probably more than the CPA could undertake. It didn't have enough people or contacts to identify potential advocates across the entire country. Third, Schumer had been a forceful defender of the thirty-day provision in the Judiciary Committee. Many House Democrats would follow his lead, just as Republicans would follow Smith and McCollum, so finding 218 votes to strike the provision, even if more resources had been available, seemed politically impossible.

Fourth, the advocates opposing an overseas-refugee cap had won their battle in the Senate subcommittee, leaving a relatively clear field in the Senate Judiciary Committee for the CPA and its mission of opposing asylum restrictions. In the House, by contrast, the CPA would have to compete for attention with overseas-refugee advocates, including some CPA members, who were trying to reverse the defeat of the Schiff amendment, and with the family coalition, whose principal mission was to split the bill. Finally, some CPA members, including myself, who had focused primarily on the thirty-day provision, believed that an unsuccessful House floor fight would leave us worse off than losing by default. Differences between the final House bill and the final Senate bill would be resolved, eventually, by delegates from the House and Senate to a Conference Committee of the two bodies. Assuming that we won in the Senate Judiciary Committee and that outcome was not challenged on the floor, the Conference Committee would decide the final outcome on our issue. But in the Conference Committee, Smith would certainly cite any overwhelming vote against us on the House floor as evidence that the House was firmly behind a thirty-day deadline. It might be better to run than fight.

These constraints did not affect either the family coalition or the smaller group of overseas-refugee advocates. They actively prepared for floor fights on splitting the bill and defeating the refugee cap, reaching out as much as possible to Republicans. One of their key moves was to hire a conservative advocate with congressional experience. The Lutheran Immigration and Refugee Service recruited Bronwyn Lance, a former legislative assistant for Republican representatives Charles Taylor of North Carolina and then Enid Waldholtz of Utah.[2] At first, the liberal advocates who formed the backbone of the family coalition were standoffish to Lance. "I was known as a token Republican conservative," she recalls. "But gradually they realized that they needed the conservatives to win."[3]

As soon as she began work, in December 1995, Lance helped to connect the immigration advocacy community to House Republican staffers. She already knew some likely allies, such as Paul Ryan, a pro-immigration staff member for freshman Sam Brownback of Kansas. Along with Jeanne Butterfield of the American Immigration Lawyers Association, Micheal Hill of the U.S. Catholic Conference, Carol Wolchok of the American Bar Association, Angela Kelley of NIF, and others, Lance began meeting with Republican staffers whose members were not on the Judiciary Committee and had not formed firm opinions on the issues in the immigration bill. Whenever possible, she included in meetings with conservative members' offices two advocates from conservative organizations, Stuart Anderson of the CATO Institute and Scott Hoffman of Americans for Tax Reform. "This was a good way to branch out to conservatives," Lance recalls. "There were a lot of liberals in our group, who had to realize that these people don't have horns and that we needed them to win the vote."[4]

The CPA did have one hope for success in the House, however. Smith had organized his bill in a more logical way than Simpson had. Most of Smith's bill dealt with control of unauthorized aliens. Most of the provisions affecting other would-be immigrants, including family members, business-sponsored immigrants, refugees, asylum-seekers, and beneficiaries of humanitarian parole, were clumped together in Title V.[5] Title V had four parts: family immigration restrictions (in Subtitle A), business restrictions (in Subtitle B), the refugee cap and new limitations on the attorney general's power to parole aliens into the United States (in Subtitle C), and the asylum deadline (in Subtitle D).[6] If the split-the-bill motion were drafted so as to sever all of Title V from the main bill, the refugee cap and the asylum deadline would be blown away along with the limits on family and business immigration. But would the split-the-bill advocates in the House select this logical fault line, or would they try to carve away only the first two sub-parts? And would the House split the bill?

The issue of piggybacking onto the split-the-bill effort was raised as early as the CPA's second meeting in the fall of 1995. A member who had been through mark-up hell in the House Judiciary Committee recalled that when Berman wrote his split-the-bill motion there, he'd left the asylum restrictions in Smith's "illegal" alien bill, rather than the "legal" bill that Berman was trying to split off for burial. But the House Judiciary Committee had been a peculiarly conservative forum, and asylum advocates hadn't been organized then. Perhaps the amendment would be framed more broadly on the House floor.

Whatever floor strategy might be adopted, it seemed clear that a necessary, but not sufficient, condition for eliminating the thirty-day limit in the House would be to convince Schumer to part company with McCollum on this issue. Schumer knew more about the asylum issue than any other House Democrat. So long as Schumer supported McCollum, it would be impossible to build the kind of coalition that we were simultaneously trying to forge in the Senate Judiciary Committee.

Early in January, I met with Bill McGeveran, Schumer's assistant. I understood Schumer's feeling that people should not be allowed to claim asylum and prolong their U.S. residence after being caught by the authorities, but I wanted to learn more about why McCollum thought a deadline should be applied to affirmative asylum applicants. McGeveran explained that Schumer was more concerned about defensive asylum cases, but he believed that some limit on affirmative cases was also needed, lest Congress appear to be "winking" at the long-term presence in the United States of undocumented aliens who might one day apply for asylum. I gave McGeveran some case studies of refugees, such as the Asian dissident we'd been touring through Senate offices, who had good reasons for waiting a long time before applying. He did not imply that cases like those I presented would budge Schumer.

I told Pistone about our meeting, and she decided that if we could not persuade Schumer with facts, we had little alternative but to try to influence him politically. Unlike McCollum and Smith, who represented Republican districts with relatively few human rights advocates, Schumer came from New York City, which teemed with social activists, and he was proud of his generally progressive record. Furthermore, Schumer was exploring a run for the 1998 Democratic nomination for governor of New York.[7] He would need large numbers of donations from liberals. Public awareness that he was a leader of an effort that would send political refugees to their graves would not be an asset. We decided to try to feature Schumer's role in the asylum debate in the New York Times.

We did not know anyone at the Times, so I just called the Times' immigration reporter. Her paper had not yet covered the thirty-day issue at all, and she asked me to send her material about it. I mailed her the CPA's packet of materials and hoped she would write a story.

At about the same time, members of the board of the Lawyers Committee for Human Rights, which has its principal office in New York City, asked Schumer to meet with them when he was in New York. He held the meeting, but he defended his position, and he pointed out to the Lawyers Committee that we had only individual case studies, not real statistical evidence, to show that deserving asylum applicants didn't file within thirty days after arrival.

A legislator asking for social science data rather than anecdotes or sound bites! How refreshing! The Lawyers Committee board members were disappointed that they had not persuaded Schumer, but they followed his suggestion. The committee's staff pulled the files of its legal volunteers' most recent two hundred closed cases, 80 percent of which had resulted in grants of asylum. It recorded the dates of entry and the filing dates for each case. Analyzing these records was tedious work, requiring several weeks.

When the project was nearly completed, the *New York Times* story appeared. Prominently placed, it began with the story of a man from Mauritania whom the reporter had interviewed. His asylum claim was based on retribution because his father had opposed the military-dominated government. He claimed to have been hung upside down and burned with a heated hammer, while in the next cell, his father was tortured and killed. He'd fled to New York, but he did not apply for asylum promptly because he spoke no English, had no money, and was terrified that if he revealed his presence to the authorities, he'd be sent home. The reporter had interviewed Schumer for her article, and she quoted his defense of the thirty-day deadline: "If you believe enough in America to claim asylum, you ought to come forward and not wait till someone says, 'Gotcha.'"[8] Three days later, the *Times* followed its story with an op-ed by Dr. Douglas Shenson, the director of the Human Rights Clinic at Montefiore Medical Center in the Bronx. Shenson treated refugees who were victims of torture. He said that if the thirty-day rule were approved, "many of my potential patients will be hustled back to their torturers, maybe for the last time."[9]

A few days later, the Lawyers Committee completed its statistical study. It turned out that only one-half of one percent of these very successful asylum applicants had applied within thirty days of arrival, and only 9 percent applied within six months. The following table provides a more detailed breakdown:

### Lawyers Committee for Human Rights
### Time within Which Former Clients Applied for Asylum
### (80 Percent of These Clients Were Granted Asylum)

| Within this period after arrival | This is the percentage of applicants who had applied |
|---|---|
| 30 days | .5 |
| 3 months | 1.5 |
| 6 months | 9.0 |
| 9 months | 21.5 |
| 12 months | 37.5 |
| 24 months | 71.0 |

The results surprised even the CPA. The Lawyers Committee sent them to Schumer,[10] along with a letter it had obtained from President Clinton stating that he "oppose[d] provisions that would require applications for asylum to be filed within 30 days."[11] The CPA also sent the statistics to members of the Senate Judiciary Committee, one week before that committee's mark-up began.

A few days later, another *New York Times* reporter called Schumer again, because the *Times* was about to run still another story on the issue, a feature story about clinics for torture victims like the one that Shenson directed. The CPA learned of Schumer's switch by reading it in the newspaper: "There are signs that Congressional supporters of the thirty-day rule may be breaking ranks. A key figure is Representative Charles E. Schumer, the Brooklyn Democrat, who said he would now agree to no deadline in 'affirmative' cases if a tougher line was taken on 'defensive' asylum."[12]

CPA members had passed the first hurdle toward getting the House to adopt a rule similar to the fallback they were prepared to accept in the Senate Judiciary Committee. But Schumer's support did not solve the problem. If McCollum went along with Schumer, the two legislators could easily change their own provision on the House floor, through a "manager's amendment" that Lamar Smith would propose at their behest. But if McCollum did not go along, Schumer and others would have to win a floor fight, either on behalf of a split-the-bill amendment that included the deadline, or in support of a separate amendment to apply a deadline only to defensive cases. Both of these scenarios would be exceedingly difficult to arrange.

The first approach would be to try to change McCollum's mind. That task might be far easier than finding at least 218 House supporters. Pistone and I took a refugee to meet with McCollum's staffer, Karl Kaufmann. Kaufmann listened politely to the man's story, and to our suggestion of a deadline only for defensive cases. He said he'd talk to McCollum, but later he told us that McCollum was not persuaded.

But the day after Schumer announced his change of heart in the *Times* story, Kaufmann and Pistone appeared on a university panel to talk about immigration policy. After his talk, Kaufmann told Pistone that McCollum was working on a manager's amendment to lengthen the deadline to sixty or ninety days.

Tom Bernstein, the chairman of the board of the Lawyers Committee, and Michael Posner, its executive director, had met with Schumer in New York. After he announced his change of heart, the Lawyers Committee officials asked for a second meeting, in Washington. Schumer offered to greet them in his office and then walk them down the hall to see McCollum. They took Pistone and me with them.

The meeting with McCollum was brief and, it seemed to me, pro forma. McCollum spent half of the time telling the Lawyers Committee representatives that he had arranged for American pharmaceutical companies to donate drugs to needy people in Latin America.[13] Then Schumer told McCollum that he had changed his mind and favored a deadline only for defensive cases. Bernstein tried to paint a realistic portrait of asylum applicants for McCollum, describing an asylum case he'd handled years earlier, as an associate at a New York law firm, on behalf of a Filipino refugee. Posner gave McCollum the Lawyers Committee's statistical data. McCollum did not engage with anyone on the issue, and he did not explain why he might have doubts about Schumer's plan. He said only that he would talk again with Schumer over the following weekend. I left the meeting hoping that the promise of a more private conference meant that some sort of bargain might be in the works. I do not know whether Schumer and McCollum in fact connected. We never heard of any follow-up by either congressman.

The next best bet was piggybacking. A few hours after the Lawyers Committee's meeting with Schumer and McCollum, some immigration advocates and the staffers for their congressional supporters met to discuss the content of the split-the-bill amendment.[14] No one invited Pistone or the CPA. The splitting effort had been gathering steam all winter, as had its Senate counterpart. With Lance's help, the family coalition had found two enthusiastic conservative sponsors, Dick Chrysler of Michigan and Sam Brownback of Kansas.[15] Swartz had persuaded the administration that splitting the bill was "good politics" and that it should lend the effort its very discreet support.[16] The NIF called on its supporters to contact approximately 150 representatives it thought could be persuaded to support a split.[17] Grover Norquist, director of the conservative Americans for Tax Reform and a personal friend of Speaker Gingrich, was working to persuade the Christian Coalition to join the effort.[18]

But the splitters were hardly confident of victory. They did not have a good vote count. They worried about including in their amendment any changes that Smith could say would facilitate "illegal" immigration. They anticipated that attacking the asylum restrictions in the split-the-bill amendment would bring McCollum into strong opposition to the amendment, that he would talk on the House floor about horrors at Kennedy Airport and cloud the issues about immigration by family members.[19] The taint administered to asylum by *60 Minutes* persisted. Carol Wolchok argued that the advocates should fight against asylum restrictions as well as curbs on legal immigration.[20] As a behind-the-scenes debate over just how to split the bill intensified, Joel Najar, Berman's staff assistant, drafted three different versions of what could become the split-the-bill amendment. One version protected only the legal immigration quotas and overseas refugees. The second version would have struck all of Title V, including the asylum deadlines. The third and most generous version would also have protected welfare benefits for legal aliens.[21] But only one congressional staff member argued for more than the minimum. The other staff members, from both parties, favored including in the amendment an attack on the refugee cap—but throwing asylum overboard. Because they were to be the sponsors of the amendment, Brownback and Chrysler made the final decision.[22] If successful, their amendment would remove from Smith's bill everything in Title V except asylum deadlines and the new restrictions on humanitarian parole. Accordingly, as Kate Balian, deputy U.S. representative for the United Nations High Commissioner for Refugees drily commented, "splitting the bill did not help on the asylum issues."[23]

The CPA's final hope for a favorable House outcome was to bring the asylum deadline issue to the floor on its own, a risky endeavor in view of the general perception of asylum as a way in which aliens circumvented the immigration system. Schumer encouraged the CPA to make the effort, and so did Joseph Rees. His boss, Christopher Smith, had already been approached by the overseas-refugee advocates to serve as their champion. He was highly respected and deeply committed to preserving the United States as a haven for victims of persecution. He might be willing to fight for asylum applicants as well.

It did not escape Rees's attention that Chrysler, Brownback, and their allies had jettisoned humanitarian parole along with asylum. Rees felt strongly that the humanitarian parole restrictions should be attacked as well. Parole had been used before 1980 to admit to the U.S., without regard to the legislated quotas, large numbers of refugees who fled during a crisis, such as the Hungarians who escaped when the Soviet Union crushed the 1956 anti-Communist uprising. After 1980, U.S. administrations had continued to use parole during migration emergencies, and they had also used parole to bring high-profile dissidents quickly to the United States, to apply for asylum.[24] Paroles were supposedly temporary admissions, not leading to immigration, but parolees often could not return home and, in many cases, became Americans through unusual routes, such as special acts of Congress. Congress had tried to end mass paroles when it set up the overseas-refugee program in 1980, but presidents had continued to parole aliens into the United States when it suited their foreign policies to do so.[25] Lamar Smith was particularly outraged by President Clinton's use of the parole power to admit up to twenty thousand Cubans annually under an agreement negotiated with Cuba.[26] When presidents used this power, they usually invoked a provision in the 1980 law, under which a president could parole aliens for "emergent reasons." However, aliens who were also refugees could be paroled only if "compelling reasons in the public interest with respect to that particular alien" required the president to use the parole power rather than allowing the person to immigrate within the refugee quota.[27] Presidents did not want to require Cubans to use the overseas refugee system because refugee processing typically took a long time. They resorted to the idea that people fleeing from Cuba were immigrating as family members or in some other category, and used parole to speed the process.

Lamar Smith's bill proposed to allow parole only on a "case-by-case basis" and only for very specific reasons: a life-threatening medical emergency for which the alien could not get treatment at home, an organ transplant to a close family member in the United States, a visit to the deathbed of a close family member, or a trip to the United States at the government's request to testify in a criminal proceeding.[28] Christopher Smith was willing to accept the case-by-case approach, but he wanted to knock out the limitations, believing that many other kinds of situations would warrant parole. He thought that if he accepted the case-by-case approach, either Lamar Smith would agree to broaden the grounds, or else the House would follow his lead.

Christopher Smith had agreed to become the main sponsor of the overseas-refugee cap amendment, but he didn't want to be the main spokesperson for more than one such challenge. At his urging, his colleague Benjamin Gilman, chairman of the full International Relations Committee, agreed to sponsor an amendment to soften the bill's asylum deadlines and its restrictions on parole. He and Schumer would be co-sponsors. Gilman's sponsorship seemed helpful because as a full committee chair, he carried considerable weight among Republicans.

But before the House could vote on Gilman's proposal, his amendment would have to be ruled "in order" by that body's Rules Committee. And defending his bill well, Lamar Smith sought to prevent the Rules Committee from allowing the House to vote on amendments he particularly disliked. In reality, this meant that Lamar Smith sought the help of Speaker Newt Gingrich and his staff, because in the 104th Congress, Gingrich had personally appointed all nine Republican members, and the committee only had four Democrats. Porter Goss, a Republican member, had recently commented, "How much is the Rules Committee the handmaiden of the Speaker? The answer is, totally."[29]

Gilman, Smith, and Schumer submitted their asylum amendment to the Rules Committee. It provided for a six-month deadline applicable only to defensive asylum applications, with an exception for cases where late consideration would be "clearly in the interest of justice." It also eliminated the categorical restrictions on the use of humanitarian parole.[30] The next day, Ed Grant, one of Hyde's staffers, took Rees and Christopher Smith aside. He said that Lamar Smith might be able to accept a House vote on a six-month deadline for asylum applications, but that he could not agree to let the House vote on an amendment that included removing the restrictions on parole. "Parole is pretty important," Rees said. "Then we'll fight you tooth and nail," Grant replied. Rees suggested that Hyde allow the Rules Committee to approve the amendment for a House vote, so that they could have that fight on the floor. Grant was unwilling to go that far.[31]

A day or two before the Rules Committee met,[32] its chairman, Gerald Solomon, held his usual closed-door meeting with Leonard Swinehart from the Speaker's office, David Hobbs from Majority Leader Richard Armey's office, and the counsel of Hyde's Judiciary Committee, from which the bill was being reported. The purpose of the meeting was to go through the large number of amendments that had been proposed and to decide which of them the Republican majority on the Rules Committee would be permitted to approve. The staff members from the leadership's offices were not immigration experts; they were not in a position to make decisions based on the merits of the proposed legislation.[33] As is their routine, therefore, they deferred to the Judiciary

Committee. That deference devolved to Lamar Smith, the author of the bill and subcommittee chair, so the result was to disallow a vote on Gilman's amendment. "It would have been Smith's call," the Speaker's aide later reported. "We [leadership staff members] don't have the depth of knowledge."[34]

Joseph Rees called staffers for three members of the Rules Committee in a last attempt to save the Gilman amendment from premature burial. All of them said that their bosses agreed with him on the merits of the amendment. If Rees had called them two days earlier, he learned, he could have arranged for the amendment to be allowed, because the Rules Committee had a tradition enabling each Republican member to insist that one or two particular amendments be sent to the floor for a vote, even if the Republican leadership opposed them strongly. But that privilege could be exercised only before the office of the Speaker had become involved. It was too late, because the leadership's staff members had already told Solomon that the Rules Committee should defer to Lamar Smith and bury Gilman's amendment.

Gilman, too, might have been able to forestall or reverse the decision made in the closed-door leadership meeting. Had he spoken to Solomon, a fellow New York Republican, expressing his personal concern about his amendment, he might have been able to persuade Solomon to do him a legislative favor by allowing a vote on his amendment. But Gilman was tied up with business involving his own International Relations Committee all week, and he did not find time to speak to Solomon.[35] Solomon and the staff members for the Speaker and the majority leader might even have thought that Gilman did not regard his amendment as a high priority. Often members sponsor amendments, and even write letters threatening to vote against a proposed rule if those amendments are not allowed to be voted on, in order to tell certain constituents or interest groups that they had done so, expecting that the amendments will nevertheless die in the Rules Committee.[36]

On the morning of the Rules Committee's meeting, therefore, a drama played itself out, but the insiders present could guess from the beginning how it would end. Gilman was occupied elsewhere and sent a statement supporting his amendment; by the time he arrived at the Rules Committee hearing on proposed amendments, it had already adjourned.[37] Smith spoke for the Gilman amendment, but Schumer did most of the heavy work. He reminded the committee that he'd been an original sponsor of the thirty-day limit, but "a number of groups brought to my attention the fact that people who deserve asylum, who are fleeing persecution from dictatorships never ... come forward within 30 days. They are bruised, they are scared, they are disoriented, and they just don't come forward." He cited the Lawyers Committee statistics. And he ran into a buzz saw of impressions based on the *60 Minutes* show.

Porter Goss, the Florida Republican who had commented on the committee's subservience to Gingrich, said that "95% of the Haitians coming in were economic refugees who had been taught two words in English, which was something like, 'political asylee,' which they mumbled and then disappeared into the countryside." Goss did not seem to grasp the idea that the people he was talking about were virtually the only ones who actually did apply for asylum within thirty days. Anthony Beilenson, a California Democrat, continued the assault. "These people should be required, the moment they appear at the airport, to say, 'I am claiming asylum.' ... How did they get on the airplane in the first place?"

Just before a voice vote, Representative David Dreier, the Republican vice chair of the committee, said that Lamar Smith had resolved the issue raised by Gilman's amendment in the manager's amendment. It would not have been possible for any member of the committee to know what that meant, because the text of the manager's amendment had not been circulated. Nevertheless, although the committee allowed the House to vote on thirty-two other amendments, it voted against allowing a floor vote on Gilman's change. The effort to eliminate a deadline on affirmative applications in the House bill had failed.

There was, however, a small but pleasant surprise. When the manager's amendment was published, it included, as Kaufmann had hinted and Dreier had said, a small liberalization of the deadline rule. It still applied to affirmative as well as defensive cases, and the exceptions had not been expanded, but the deadline had been increased to 180 days, long enough to encompass 9 percent of the Lawyers Committee's clients.

The Rules Committee also disallowed a vote to moderate summary exclusion,[38] but it did approve for House debate the overseas-refugee cap amendment sponsored by Christopher Smith and Steven Schiff, and the Chrysler-Brownback split-the-bill amendment. Between the two, the overseas-refugee cap amendment would be voted on first. Some members of the family coalition worried that the Rules Committee had deliberately set the order of voting to weaken Chrysler-Brownback; if the overseas-refugee cap was eliminated, a few members who cared deeply about refugees but were less concerned with family and business immigration might desert the larger effort.[39] However, they had no control over the sequence of votes.

The refugee groups had been very eager to have Christopher Smith lead their charge. They were very grateful to Schiff for having tried to carry their issue through the Judiciary Committee, but Smith was more senior, chaired a relevant subcommittee, knew the issue very well, and had a following as one of the House's most vocal pro-life leaders. They chose well. Using his connections with conservative pro-family organizations, Smith was able to get the Family Research Council to back his amendment.[40] Rees worked harder on the refugee amendment than he'd ever worked on any issue in Congress. But as the vote approached, he had no idea whether the amendment would carry.[41]

A few days before the vote, Lamar Smith offered the refugee organizations a deal. If they would forswear further opposition to a statutory ceiling on refugees, he would amend the bill so that the ceiling would be set at fifty thousand refugees exclusive of the Jewish emigrants from the former Soviet Union under the Lautenberg amendment. Thus, Jews would be able to complete their exodus, and then the statutory cap would settle down to the fifty thousand level that Smith and Simpson had desired. In essence, Smith's offer forced the refugee organizations to decide whether to abandon their principled opposition to a congressional refugee ceiling in order to obtain relatively high levels of refugee immigration while Jewish emigration from the former Soviet Union continued. They agonized over the offer. And they rejected it, hoping that it represented a sign of desperation on the part of Smith.[42] "I thought that going for broke was the best thing to do," Lance recalls. "We might lose it all, but we had high hopes that we could win it because . . . there were vestiges of the Cold War in the refugee issue. The gamble was worth taking."[43]

On the day of the vote, Joseph Rees walked to the House floor and saw Lamar Smith and Cordia Strom talking with his boss. Lamar Smith had just told Christopher Smith that he would allow the issue to be decided by a voice vote, making defeat of the overseas-refugee cap more likely because members could vote to kill it without being attacked for their vote by their next election opponent. Rees assumed that Lamar Smith had decided to let the amendment pass in order to siphon votes away from the split-the-bill amendment. But Ed Grant told him later that Lamar Smith had concluded that in a roll call, Christopher Smith would beat him three to one.[44]

The promise of a voice vote virtually assured the outcome of this battle of the Smiths. Christopher Smith opened the debate by recalling that during World War II, it "became clear that we had effectively sentenced hundreds of Jewish refugees to death" by forcing the *St. Louis* back to Europe. He argued that Lamar Smith's cap could doom Russian Jews and evangelical Christians, force the repatriation of Vietnamese who were still in the refugee pipeline, and result in the death of Bosnians. Lamar Smith countered that the refugee level set in the bill was "generous," and that Congress, rather than the administration, should set the annual levels. Schiff replied that there was no "serious allegation" that the administration had abused the process of consulting with Congress before setting an annual refugee level. Five other Representatives spoke briefly. True to his word, Lamar Smith allowed a voice vote, and the proposed refugee cap suffered an instant death.[45] This time, its demise was final, because the Senate subcommittee had killed it months earlier.

The split-the-bill amendment hit the floor the next day. It had nothing in it for victims of human rights abuses. The refugee cap had already been killed by Christopher Smith's amendment, and Chrysler and Brownback had opted to maximize their votes by drafting the amendment to delete from the bill all the restrictions on legal immigration except those on asylum-seekers and parolees. But the amendment was nevertheless of potentially great political importance to refugee advocates. If it passed, several major immigration advocacy organizations, such as the American Immigration Lawyers Association and some of the large religious groups, would be much more free to devote their time and attention, at subsequent stages of the legislative process, to the remaining issues, such as summary exclusion and asylum deadlines. If it failed, however, they would have to devote nearly all of their effort to preserving as much legal immigration as possible in the House-Senate Conference Committee that would eventually reconcile the two houses' immigration bills.

Those large organizations, along with the conservative organizations that Swartz had organized, had been working for weeks toward this critical vote. Three days before the vote, they thought they would need about 60 Republicans and 157 Democrats to make their majority, but anti-immigrant sentiment in the country was still strong, and they could count as allies only 40 Republicans and 104 firm Democrats.[46] The NIF faxed around the country its target list of House members who should be called.[47] The day before the vote, the NIF circulated another target list and asked for another round of calls.[48] The high-tech firms that had helped Abraham to split the bill in the Senate Judiciary Committee a few days earlier could not be as visible in the House, having earlier made their deal with Lamar Smith, but they "quietly" let it be known that they favored the same outcome in the larger body.

The White House now made a crucial change in its policy. Abandoning the Jordan Commission's recommendations to slash legal immigration, White House strategists and INS Commissioner Doris Meissner let it be known that the administration wanted Democrats to vote for the Chrysler-Brownback amendment.[49] Then, at the last minute, Grover Norquist succeeded in persuading Speaker Gingrich that legal immigration should be preserved. Gingrich's private endorsement was enough to bring the Christian Coalition into the fray.[50] The Christian Coalition seized on a provision in the bill making it harder for legal immigrants to bring their siblings to join them in the United States. The day before the vote, it issued a letter to all representatives warning that if the bill passed without the amendment, "brothers and sisters [of immigrants] would cease to be a part of the 'federal government approved' family."[51] As soon as the letter was issued, the National Immigration Forum "blast-faxed it to every House and Senate office," and as representatives were going into the House chamber to vote, Brownback's staff leafleted them with this one-page letter.[52]

Chrysler led off the debate, declaiming that "in a country of 260 million people, 700,000 legal immigrants is not an exorbitant amount." Lamar Smith argued that "37% of recent immigrants lack a high school education, compared to just 11% of those who are native born." He also claimed that the Bureau of Labor Statistics had estimated that low-skilled immigration accounted for up to 50% of the decline in real wages among high-school dropouts (a study later cited repeatedly by his supporters), but Chrysler countered that the Bureau's report had been done by a "graduate student" and had a "BLS disclaimer." Following the custom of the House, representatives alternated in speeches for and against the amendment. When his turn came, Gilman took issue with "immigrant bashers" who really wanted a moratorium on immigration; the 1920s, he said, had ushered in "a policy based on xenophobia and racism." He also expressed his dismay at the "anti-immigration forces who [through the Rules Committee] have denied us a chance to address the restrictive asylum and humanitarian parole provisions." McCollum called Smith's bill "very generous" and called the existing system for legal immigration "broken."[53]

Lamar Smith made the final speech. He began by quoting Mark Twain: "First you get your facts straight, then you can distort them all you want." Taking Twain's advice literally, he said that "this amendment ignores the wishes of the vast majority of the American people: 83 percent want us to control immigration."[54] Smith did not say what portion favored cutbacks in legal immigration.

The vote was taken. When the dust cleared, the bill had been split, by a vote of 238–183.[55] The margin was much greater than immigration advocates had expected. Quite possibly, a split-the-bill amendment that had attacked the asylum restrictions could also have passed, but the clock could not be turned back to try it out.[56]

Representatives who wanted the immigration bill to be more generous were not the only members to have amendments approved by the Rules Committee for votes on the floor. California's Elton Gallegly offered what would turn out to be the most controversial amendment in the entire immigration debate. He proposed to permit states to exclude the children of unauthorized aliens from their public school systems.[57]

Since 1986, the year he delivered a primary defeat to Bob Hope's son, Tony Hope, Gallegly had represented Ventura County, a solidly conservative bastion that now houses the Ronald Reagan Library. Mirroring his district, Gallegly had earned a 95 percent rating from the American Conservative Union in 1994, and he had made reducing illegal immigration one of his major policy objectives.[58] Gallegly was sympathetic to those taxpayers in California and Texas who for years had resented having to pay to educate the children of unauthorized aliens.

Twenty years earlier, Texas had tried to exclude such children from its public schools. In *Plyler v. Doe*, the Supreme Court had declared the Texas law an unconstitutional violation of the equal protection clause of the Fourteenth Amendment. The Court had noted that the children who would be thrown out of school had little control over their parents' immigration status, and that the Texas law "imposes ... a lifetime hardship on ... children not accountable for their disabling status." The Court concluded that "it is difficult to understand what the State hopes to achieve by promoting the creation and perpetuation of a subclass of illiterates within our boundaries, surely adding to the problems and costs of unemployment, welfare and crime. It is thus clear that whatever savings might be achieved ... they are wholly insubstantial in light of the costs involved to these children, the State, and the Nation."[59]

These arguments apparently failed to persuade Representative Gallegly and his supporters, nor were they daunted by the fact that *Plyler* had been a constitutional decision. For two reasons, they thought that the Court might now uphold a federal law denying unauthorized aliens the right to go to school. First, the Court had knocked down the Texas law by the narrow margin of five to four, and subsequent changes in Court personnel, particularly the retirement of Justice William Brennan, who had written the majority opinion, might bring about a new result. Second, Brennan himself had noted in his opinion, as an additional reason for striking down the state law, that the Constitution gave the federal Congress, not the states, the power to control the nation's borders. "The exercise of congressional power might well affect the State's prerogatives to afford differential treatment to a particular class of aliens," Brennan had written. Gallegly naturally drew the conclusion that if Congress expressly authorized states to deny schooling to the children of unauthorized aliens, the Court might uphold such restrictions.

Gallegly's opening remarks were full of oratorical bombast. "When illegal immigrants sit down in public school classrooms, the desk, textbooks, blackboards in effect become stolen property, stolen from the students rightfully entitled to those resources," he said. "Just because someone has busted through the front door, that does not entitle them to the contents of your home."

Democrats who were conservative on immigration issues and had supported Smith instantly recognized that the Gallegly amendment could torpedo the entire legislation, either by making it unacceptable to the Senate or by giving the president a justification for a veto. John Bryant, himself a Texan who had stood side-by-side with Smith when Smith's bill was first introduced, said that passage of the amendment would be a "tragedy." Anthony Beilenson, the California Democrat who had been so out of sympathy with asylum applicants during the Rules Committee debate, argued that people crossed the U.S. border illegally for jobs, and brought their children only incidentally, not to give them the advantage of a U.S. public education. He called the amendment "inhumane" and said that its passage would make it difficult for some of Smith's supporters to remain behind the bill.

Other opponents were even more direct. One called the amendment lacking in "moral currency," while another called it a "mean-spirited attempt that will hold children responsible for their parents' actions." The debate continued for a while, sometimes focusing on the constitutionality of the amendment, sometimes on its fairness to the children or to the adults they would eventually become, and sometimes on the cost to the states, either of providing the education or of the increased police services that opponents claimed would be needed to cope with the crimes caused by children who could not be schooled.[60]

Then, an unusual event occurred. Toward the end of the time that had been allowed for debate, Speaker Gingrich descended from the rostrum to give his own views on the amendment. Speakers of the House rarely participate in floor debates, choosing to intervene only when by speaking they may influence a crucial vote.[61] But in this case, Gingrich took pains to advertise the leadership's stance on the amendment, an action that would also make the Gallegly amendment a prominent national issue in an election year. Imposing on the states the financial burden of the federal government's inability to identify and deport all unauthorized aliens, he said, was an "unfunded mandate," a practice the

Contract with America, and subsequently the Congress, had vowed to end. "If this amendment goes down," Gingrich said, he would move to have the federal government absorb the two-to-three-billion-dollar educational cost currently being borne by a few border states. "It is wrong for us to be the welfare capital of the world," he thundered. "I hope every Member will vote yes for Gallegly, because that is the right thing to do, to send the right signal around the world."

Bryant was horrified. For months, he had been running for the Democratic nomination for senator. He had been expected to win the nomination, or at least win a first-round plurality and enter the runoff as the leading candidate. But a week before the immigration bill that Bryant had co-sponsored hit the House floor, a virtually unknown Mexican-American high school teacher, Victor Morales, had pulled off a surprising upset, besting Bryant and threatening to beat him a month later in the runoff.[62] The Gallegly amendment could not be good for Bryant's prospects. If it passed, he would have two bad choices. He could walk away from a popular bill with which he'd been identified, but that strategy could hurt him in the general election against Senator Phil Gramm. Alternatively, he could endorse the bill despite the amendment, but Morales could then try to use Bryant's support of the Gallegly provision against him in the Democratic runoff.[63]

Bryant's best hope was to try to defeat the Gallegly amendment by making it an even more visible issue than it already was, and his best chance of doing that was to take issue not only with Gallegly, but with the Speaker's intervention. "Every American should despair of our ability as a Congress to act in any significant way in a bipartisan fashion after that speech by Mr. Gingrich," he said. In his speech, Gingrich had argued that the nation, not the border states, should pay the costs associated with the federal government's inability to prevent illegal immigration. Bryant charged, "Mr. Gingrich, if you really believe what you said, you would not have instructed your Committee on Rules to forbid the offering of an amendment that would do exactly that. It is an outrage that the Speaker of the House would come down and seize upon this bill to make partisan gain.... Shame on you, Mr. Speaker. [This] smacks of nothing more than raw political opportunism." He asked the House "to repudiate a total failure of leadership by the Speaker of the House himself."[64]

A Republican loyalist made a modest attempt to inquire whether Bryant's "attempt to impugn the integrity of the Speaker" violated House rules, but the effort went nowhere in the rush to vote.[65] The count on Gallegly's amendment wasn't even close. It was approved 257 to 163.[66] The *Washington Post* noted that this vote marked "the first time that a key component of [California's] Proposition 187 had been accepted at the congressional level."[67]

The vote presented an immediate strategic problem for immigration advocates. The prospects for passage of a similar amendment in the Senate were "murky."[68] If the Senate also passed it, the president might veto the bill, eliminating all of the immigration restrictions that Congress was in the process of passing. However, the NIF recognized that "in the event that [a Gallegly] provision is passed [in the Senate], we would hope for a presidential veto, but we cannot rely on it in an election year."[69] Therefore, the NIF decided to work to prevent the Senate from approving a similar provision, passing the word that "it is critical that advocates send a strong message that it is unwise federal policy to kick kids out of school."[70]

Months later, the amendment that Representative Gallegly had injected on the House floor would become the bill's principal question of public debate, eclipsing asylum procedures and virtually all other issues. Meanwhile, however, the House passed the entire bill by a vote of 333–87,[71] the action moved to the Senate, and refugee advocates geared up for floor debate there on the issue they had left for last.

# 9

# The Senate
## *February–May 1996*

It's like allowing toll collectors to authorize the death penalty.
> —Frank Sharry, executive director of the
> National Immigration Forum, describing
> provisions for the summary exclusion of
> immigrants who lacked visas.[1]

At its first meeting, the Committee to Preserve Asylum had decided to concentrate on defeating asylum application deadlines, deferring, perhaps permanently, an effort to attack the more complicated and politically challenging issue of summary exclusion. As the CPA began to make some headway on deadlines with members of the Senate Judiciary Committee, one of its most active members, Carol Wolchok, began urging it to take on summary exclusion as well.

Wolchok was the staff member of the American Bar Association who worked on immigration policy. For many years, she had opposed earlier versions of summary exclusion in successive Congresses, a much easier task when a Democratic committee chairman could hold up a disfavored bill. Wolchok was personally a strong advocate of fair procedures for aliens as well as citizens; in addition, the American Bar Association had two interests in defeating summary exclusion.

First, the procedure short-circuited the familiar model of "due process" that was common to virtually all official American adjudication. Normally, the government may not deprive any person of liberty or property without telling that person the reasons for the proposed deprivation and giving the person a chance to dispute the charges before a neutral judge. The traditional model of due process also assures that the person may present witnesses and other evidence, may challenge the government's evidence, and may cross-examine the government's witnesses. A person who loses in such a hearing is usually allowed at least one court appeal. Summary exclusion threatened to eliminate the judge, the witnesses, the other evidence, the opportunity for cross-examination, and the appeal. It was therefore at odds with a central feature of the rule of law, the concept of neutral adjudication rationally based on carefully developed

145

evidence. The American Bar Association's membership consisted of lawyers with many specialties, relatively few of which involved immigration issues. But most lawyers, regardless of specialty, believed in maintaining the principle of fair hearings.

Second, the association operated a small refugee project of its own, called ProBar, in Harlingen, Texas. Private lawyers working under the auspices of ProBar helped Latin American refugees to win asylum.[2] Unlike the affirmative asylum applicants in the caseload of the Lawyers Committee for Human Rights, most of ProBar's clients were people who had been apprehended at or near the Mexican border. ProBar sought asylum for them defensively, during deportation or exclusion proceedings brought against them by the INS. If the law passed, many of these clients (at the very least, those who were stopped at the border without valid entry papers) could be deported summarily, and the ProBar lawyers wouldn't be able to present their cases to a judge.

Shortly before the Senate mark-up of the bill began, Wolchok persuaded Senator Kennedy's staff to reserve a room in the Senate office building for a briefing of Senate Judiciary Committee staff members by refugees' advocates. She recruited several CPA members to participate. I described refugees' rights under the current law, Pistone reiterated why a thirty-day deadline would destroy asylum, and Wolchok herself took on the most difficult task: describing the complicated changes that the summary exclusion provisions of the bill would make, and the ill effects that they would cause.

The briefing went well enough. Staff members from approximately ten of the eighteen senators on the committee attended, and many asked skeptical, probing questions, an encouraging sign that they did not regard learning about these issues as a waste of time. But no concrete results seemed to emerge either from the briefing or from follow-up calls or visits, and in particular, even as the mark-up began, no senator seemed willing to sponsor an amendment to challenge the bill's summary exclusion provisions.

Wolchok persevered. Kennedy's staff was sympathetic to her concerns, but Kennedy was managing so many fights with Simpson on other parts of the bill that he could not accept the leadership on summary exclusion. Unable to find even one staff member of the Senate Judiciary Committee's Democratic minority who would take up her cause, Wolchok turned to Tim Rieser, Senator Patrick Leahy's staff member on the Appropriations Subcommittee for Foreign Operations. In previous years, she'd worked with Rieser on other refugee issues.

Rieser heard her out and called Bruce Cohen, Leahy's counsel on the Judiciary Committee.[3] Wolchok, he told Cohen, was a good person who was raising an important issue. Cohen appreciated the degree to which Simpson's bill undercut fair legal process, but he didn't know whether attacking it would have any political salience. He called the senator's Vermont office, and he learned that a large number of Vermonters, many of them people who years earlier had founded the non-profit group Vermont Refugee Assistance, were deeply troubled about summary exclusion and had been in touch with the senator's local staff.

Cohen raised the issue with Leahy and found that the senator was willing to take on the battle. A former prosecutor, Leahy was the only Democrat who had ever been elected from Vermont to the United States Senate. He had won the office in the anti-Watergate backlash of 1974 and had been able to hold onto his seat in a string of subsequent elections. He had joined the Judiciary Committee in 1979, and while the Democrats were in the majority from 1987 to 1995, he had become a solid member of the committee's core of liberals. He had helped to lead the opposition to the Supreme Court nomination of Robert Bork, though he had voted to confirm other conservative nominees.[4]

Leahy had already decided to vote against the proposed thirty-day asylum deadline, but he had left to DeWine and Kennedy the job of lining up votes against Simpson on that issue. Unlike Kennedy, who had spent decades on the Immigration Subcommittee, Leahy had not yet become a spokesman on any of the issues touched by Simpson's bill.

Leahy was a very careful lawyer. As a state's attorney, he had personally prosecuted all of the felony cases in his county. He cared about issues of procedure that drew yawns from most of his colleagues. As the immigration bill worked its way through the Judiciary Committee mark-up, Leahy and Cohen studied how the bill would curtail the procedural protections afforded refugees fleeing to the United States.

The existing immigration law that Simpson planned to replace allowed a hearing before an immigration judge to all aliens who were apprehended at American borders or airports without proper travel documents. By contrast, Simpson's bill, as approved by the Immigration Subcommittee, allowed INS inspectors at airports to send aliens home on the next plane if they did not have proper U.S. visas. Of course many refugees in trouble with their home countries' governments could not get passports and therefore could not get U.S. visas stamped into them. Even refugees who did happen to have valid passports could not get visas from most U.S. consuls, who would normally tell them to wait for the months or years that it would take to obtain certification as refugees from overseas. But for political opponents of oppressive governments, waiting was often dangerous, and going to a U.S. embassy to apply for a visa or to ask for refugee status was still more risky.

The Simpson bill provided that four categories of people would no longer get the chance to have immigration judges decide their asylum claims, and they would lose their appeal rights as well. The categories included people caught at airports with false, forged, or stolen passports or visas, or with no documents at all; people who entered the U.S. illegally and were caught within two years thereafter; people (such as the Haitians and Cubans who had fled in earlier years) who were intercepted at sea by the Coast Guard; and anyone else if the attorney general had determined the existence of an "extraordinary migration situation" (that is, if a large number of refugees swamped the INS's ability to cope with them using its normal procedures). Also, a person couldn't win asylum at all, even with truncated procedures, unless he had traveled from his home country "directly" to the United States.[5] Like many of Simpson's bills in earlier years, the subcommittee's bill provided that a person who fit into one of the four categories could apply for asylum, but it did not direct the INS to ask whether the alien in question wanted this relief. If the alien asked for asylum, an INS official would interview him, but the interview could take place by video rather than in person. The alien would then be deported forthwith, unless he could persuade the officer that he had a "credible fear" of persecution. "Credible fear" was defined as a "substantial likelihood" that the alien's statements were true and a "significant possibility" that the alien could eventually win asylum.[6] An alien who passed these hurdles would not be deported immediately but would be jailed pending a hearing before an immigration judge.

Wolchok did not know that Leahy had slowly reached a decision to challenge summary exclusion. Two weeks into the mark-up, Cohen called her and asked for more detailed information on the effects of summary exclusion. Wolchok enlisted Pistone's help, and within hours, the two women compiled materials, some of which had been collected for the earlier briefing, and delivered them to Cohen's office.[7] The next day, in the Judiciary Committee mark-up, Leahy proposed an amendment to strike from the bill all of the summary exclusion provisions. "There are ... some countries [from which] the only way you're going to get here if you're being oppressed or if you're in danger of your life is escaping with false papers," he argued.

But Simpson parried with his favorite television broadcast. "Many of us saw the dramatically depicted 'Sixty Minutes' program where the alien, without any documents whatsoever and a pretty nice looking set of luggage gave the magic words, which is 'I want to claim asylum,' and shazam, the golden door opened."[8]

Simpson saw the issue through the lens of massive fraud. Leahy and his supporters viewed it through the eyes of a persecuted refugee. As a result, the two groups of senators at the mark-up barely spoke the same language. "I can't imagine someone thinking that they're going to be able to ... get the correct papers in order to be able to come here, when we find that most of the persecutions are the result of government action," Senator Kennedy said. "We can't take in everybody in the world," replied Arizona's John Kyl.

Most of the senators' votes could be predicted, and the outcome would therefore turn on a few swing votes: the conservative Democrat Howell Heflin, the moderate Democrat Dianne Feinstein, the moderate Republican Arlen Specter, the conservative Republicans Mike DeWine and Spencer Abraham, who seemed willing to break with Simpson on other provisions of the bill, and the chairman, Orrin Hatch, who was usually a conservative voice but had occasionally sided with Kennedy on issues other than immigration.

Sitting in the audience, Pistone was therefore thrilled to hear DeWine announce that he intended to vote with Leahy. He particularly took issue with the provision of Simpson's bill that would deny asylum to a person who stopped in another free country en route to the United States. "People can travel through two, three, or four countries and have good, legitimate reasons why they can't stay in those particular countries.... To say you have to jump directly—it's almost like a board game."

Feinstein, on the other hand, defended Simpson's provision, arguing that his "credible fear" language provided sufficient procedural protection for refugees. And speaking just before the vote, Hatch said that he would support Simpson. But, he said, "I have some concerns ... and I'm hopeful that [members of the Committee] will work to try and modify it [on the Senate floor]. Many asylum applicants fleeing persecution have to destroy their documents for various reasons, and many may not be able to travel directly to the United States.... I'd like to challenge the two of you [Simpson and Leahy] to work on the language between here and the floor."

"I have to work with Senator Simpson?" Leahy joked.

"I wouldn't work with a bald headed guy," said Simpson, whose head was as shiny as Leahy's.

"As you can see, we're making lots of headway here," Hatch added.

The roll was about to be called. Pistone could see that Senators Specter and Heflin were absent, and that Specter's aide was frantically trying to reach him so that his proxy could be given to one side or the other. But he seemed unable to get his senator to come to the phone.

The nine present Republicans voted first, in order of decreasing seniority. As a bloc, they voted with Simpson, until they reached their two most junior members, DeWine and Abraham, who voted for the Leahy amendment. When their turn came, all seven of the present Democrats voted with Leahy, except Feinstein, who voted with Simpson. Heflin and Specter remained absent and did not supply proxies. The Leahy amendment failed on an eight-to-eight tie vote, so summary exclusion would be included in the bill that went to the Senate floor.[9]

The closeness of the vote signaled the possibility that some version of the Leahy amendment might yet succeed on the Senate floor, but refugee advocates would have to face two new obstacles. First, it would be much more difficult to educate and persuade a majority of all one hundred senators than to work with the eighteen-member Judiciary Committee. It was far from clear that the CPA would have the organizational capacity for such a big campaign. Second, the ground suddenly shifted under everyone's feet.

On the very day that Leahy's amendment was defeated in the Senate, the House passed an anti-terrorism bill. Responding to the Oklahoma City bombing, the Senate had also passed an anti-terrorism bill late in 1995. The Senate's bill did not affect asylum or refugees. The anti-terrorism bill introduced in the House, however, included summary exclusion provisions very similar to those in Smith and Simpson's immigration bills, and these provisions were not limited to suspected terrorists.[10] Indeed, the House anti-terrorism bill was even more severe than the immigration bills; it applied summary exclusion not only to aliens apprehended at airports without proper papers, or who had entered the United States illegally within the past two years, but also to any alien caught in the United States who had crossed the border without permission. A person who had been living in the United States for thirty years, who had raised a family and become well integrated into the community, could therefore be summarily deported by an immigration inspector without even being given a hearing.[11]

The House bill hadn't been given much chance of passing, however. It included, in addition to the summary exclusion provisions that had little or nothing to do with terrorism, provisions restricting the appeals that could be taken by death-penalty inmates; expanding the federal government's power to use illegally obtained wiretap evidence; and permitting the federal government to study armor-piercing ammunition. The wiretap and ammunition provisions were so strongly opposed by the National Rifle Association that the House bill seemed doomed.

Suddenly, however, conservative House members formed a coalition with their liberal colleagues to kill the wiretap provision and reduce the impact of the weapon studies. On the floor, the bill was changed and passed rather than being killed.[12] Among the few provisions that survived were those restricting the rights of death penalty inmates—and of aliens without visas. The House and Senate appointed conferees (delegates) to reconcile their different anti-terrorism bills, but time was short. In less than a month, the first anniversary of the Oklahoma City bombing would occur. Congressional leaders were eager to pass something they could call an anti-terrorism law by then. Because so little was left in the House bill, Senate conferees might accept the House summary exclusion provisions. In that case, summary exclusion would become law even if Leahy succeeded in knocking out those provisions in the immigration bill.

A week later, the Committee to Preserve Asylum succeeded in killing the thirty-day deadline in the Senate Judiciary Committee, freeing it to work on the summary exclusion issue it had deferred at its first meeting. The task seemed more daunting, but the CPA was now vastly more experienced. It also didn't have to start from the very beginning. It could immediately circulate a new sign-on letter to the nearly one hundred local and national organizations that had joined in the fight against deadlines. And people in those organizations knew how to organize letters and calls to senators. Furthermore, many of the organizations that had signed the original letter were located in states not represented on the Judiciary Committee. Those groups had been forced to sit on the sidelines during the effort to beat the Senate's thirty-day rule, and because the House Rules Committee hadn't allowed a floor vote on the rule, they'd been equally unable to try to influence the House on asylum. Now they were free to try to persuade their own senators.

As a first step, the CPA had to decide what to fight for. The Leahy amendment had failed in the Judiciary Committee partly because it attempted to eliminate summary exclusion outright. Hatch, who would be influential in any floor vote, had indicated that he might favor a more modest limitation of summary exclusion. The Clinton administration was bound by the president's 1993 endorsement of the concept, so even if Commissioner Meissner preferred making no change in existing law, she could not endorse the strong version of his amendment that Leahy had offered in the committee. And for the moment at least, the administration was sticking with its preferred solution: to give discretionary, standby authority to the attorney general to use summary exclusion rather than provide hearings when it interdicted boats at sea, or when its normal processing facilities were swamped by sudden, large numbers of would-be immigrants.[13]

The administration did not want to have to use summary exclusion at all airports, docks, and border crossing stations on a regular, permanent basis. Nor did it want to apply summary exclusion to everyone who arrived without passports and visas. But the CPA could not simply make common cause with the administration, because the administration's bill accepted the tough definition of "credible fear" used by Simpson and provided for no judicial review under any circumstances.[14]

Wolchok and Pistone therefore began to develop their own compromise version of summary exclusion, hoping eventually to persuade Senator Leahy to accept it as his new proposal on the Senate floor. They also enlisted another CPA member, Micheal Hill, the immigration lobbyist for the United States Catholic Conference. A former congressional staff member himself, Hill was an experienced legislative drafter. Wolchok, Pistone, and Hill planned to give the administration what they thought it really needed, the ability in mass boatlift situations to bring people to United States ports, and to screen them summarily there, rather than having to perform cursory refugee screening on Coast Guard or navy vessels on the high seas in order to circumvent the more elaborate hearing requirements of the immigration law. But their idea of summary screening included many more procedural safeguards than either Simpson or the administration desired.

The CPA found a highly respected ally, the United Nations High Commissioner for Refugees. The Office of the Commissioner had already written a series of letters to key members of Congress, opposing asylum deadlines and summary exclusion.[15] Now it moved into a higher gear. Within days after the Senate Judiciary Committee rejected the Leahy amendment, Anne Willem Bijleveld, the UNHCR's Washington representative, wrote to Leahy thanking him for his efforts and noting UNHCR's objections to the bill approved by the committee. Bijleveld argued that the broad bar to asylum for people who had not traveled "directly" from an oppressor country would put the U.S. in violation of the Refugee Convention, and that the bill's definition of "credible fear" imposed too high a burden on refugees. The UNHCR hoped that Leahy could persuade the Senate to give all asylum-seekers real hearings, unless their claims were "manifestly unfounded."[16] A few days later, the UNHCR sent New Zealander Dennis McNamara, the head of the agency's refugee protection division, from Geneva to Washington to "lobby at the highest levels" against Simpson's proposals.[17]

While Wolchok and Hill drafted a new compromise to show to Bruce Cohen, and Dennis McNamara visited senators and administration officials, Pistone cranked up the CPA's national campaign. Hill made an elaborate chart showing how each senator had voted on immigration legislation over the years. On the basis of their records, senators were deemed likely, unlikely, or uncertain in their attitude toward a Leahy compromise. The CPA worked on every Senate office, both in Washington and through supportive organizations around the country, but to conserve its resources, it focused hardest on the senators it considered in the middle. For each senator, the CPA tried to develop the approach most likely to succeed. For example, Pistone thought that Senator Olympia Snowe, a freshman Republican, might be more open to the Leahy amendment if she were lobbied by a women's organization. She found that the Women's Committee on Refugee Women and Children had signed one of the CPA's letters, tracked it down, and asked the group to send its letter directly to Snowe.[18]

The larger family coalition supported the CPA's efforts, but the family coalition had to focus on other issues as well. The bill had been split in the Judiciary Committee, but the family coalition thought that Simpson would probably try again to cut legal immigration by offering a floor amendment of his own. Furthermore, the family coalition was deeply concerned about proposed cuts in welfare benefits for legal immigrants. Therefore, fighting summary exclusion was only part of its agenda.

For the inside-the-Beltway part of the summary exclusion campaign, Pistone, Wolchok, and Hill assigned each member of the CPA's steering committee in Washington to be responsible for educating the staffs of several senators. Pistone was assigned Virginia's John Warner, because she lived in Virginia and could make that call with the added credibility of a constituent. She didn't make much headway with Warner's staffer, but he did tell her that he had received more than a hundred calls on the summary exclusion issue, and he'd never seen a small provision so heavily lobbied. Feedback like that made her feel that the organizational efforts were working, and she threw herself into the work.

Two weeks before the Senate's immigration floor debate opened, after several days of secret negotiations, the House-Senate conference committee on the anti-terrorism bill completed its work. To the shock of the refugee advocates, the Senate delegates had agreed to accept the summary exclusion provisions passed by the House.[19] Majority Leader Robert Dole scheduled floor debate on the agreed bill within three days, on the eve of the anniversary of the Oklahoma City bombing.

The timing of this development was disastrous. Leahy was willing to try to attack summary exclusion in the anti-terrorism bill as well as in the immigration bill, but even though the Senate hadn't previously voted for those provisions in the anti-terrorism bill, his chances were very poor for two reasons. First, when a House-Senate conference committee reports a compromise to the floors of both houses, it arrives with a strong presumption of passage, and with the strong support of the majority party. It would therefore be even more difficult for Leahy to change the anti-terrorism bill than to change Simpson's immigration bill on the floor. Second, a conference report cannot be amended by the Senate,[20] and the Senate surely would not reject a bill against terrorism. Leahy's only hope was to persuade his colleagues to recommit the report to the conference committee with instructions to delete the summary exclusion provisions. But if he succeeded, the Senate would probably be unable to complete action before the anniversary of the bombing, and most senators wanted the press stories on that occasion to report that they had taken responsive measures.

Leahy addressed the problem of timing directly. "I understand the symbolism of trying to have this conference report adopted ... on the one-year anniversary.... but here we are talking about a very significant piece of legislation," he said, adding that after the Senate passed the bill, the House took ten months to pass its version and then expected the Senate to endorse the final conference report within days. "And, I dare suggest, there are not five Senators in here who have even read the conference report or have the foggiest notion of what it is they are voting on."

Leahy argued that the provisions to which he objected had nothing to do with terrorism, and that they should be debated in the immigration bill, not grafted onto the anti-terrorism legislation. He also attacked the wisdom of summary exclusion for those with false documents. "[V]ictims of the Holocaust [used] false identification provided by the brave diplomats Raoul Wallenberg and Chiune Sugihara during World War II.... There are times when the use of false documentation is not something that we would want to punish." He quoted from the Committee to Preserve Asylum's sign-on letter and inserted it into the *Congressional Record*. He cited the UNHCR's opposition to the "credible fear" standard. He objected to the bill's omission of judicial review. He argued that the INS would have to post a "phalanx" of new officers in the nation's international airports.

Only Senator Hatch replied, and he did not address the merits of Leahy's arguments. "Now, look, this bill is a tough bipartisan measure," he said. "Stated simply, it is a landmark piece of legislation.... We have crafted a bill that puts the Nation's interests above partisan politics [but Senator Leahy's motion] will scuttle the antiterrorism bill."

"I am not in any way trying to derail this bill," Leahy replied. "I am just saying that this is something that was tucked into it in the middle of the night. Nobody ever had a chance to debate it."

This bill "is desired by almost everybody who wants to do anything against terrorism," Hatch responded. "If this motion or any motion to recommit passes, this bill is dead, it will be killed. So we simply have to defeat any and all motions to recommit."

Senator Joseph Biden, the Judiciary Committee's ranking Democrat, took issue with Hatch's prediction. "That is not true," he said. "Every major bill we had, including the crime bill, we sent back to conference with instructions—at least on three occasions. This will not kill the bill."

The senators knew that technically, Biden was right. Congress would not adjourn for months, leaving plenty of time for the Conference Committee to revise its bill if necessary. But the all-important anniversary date loomed. The symbolic pressure to prove that Congress could respond to terrorism within a year pushed hard against any delay. When the roll was called, Leahy's motion lost, sixty-one to thirty-eight.[21]

The failure of Leahy's motion assured that summary exclusion would become law, because President Clinton had criticized the anti-terrorism bill for not being tough enough; he certainly would not veto it.[22] The prognosis for avoiding summary exclusion was bleak. But CPA members saw two small glimmers of hope. Perhaps they could persuade the president, in formal remarks on signing the anti-terrorism law, to call for repeal of the summary exclusion provisions. And when Simpson's immigration bill got to the Senate floor, perhaps Leahy could not only soften its summary exclusion provisions but also repeal the summary exclusion provisions that Congress had just enacted.

Pistone drafted a paragraph she hoped to have included in the president's signing statement. She sent it, along with a memorandum explaining its purpose, to the staff member of the National Security Council responsible for monitoring refugee policy. She wanted the president to say that he was concerned about the provisions "restricting the ability of people fleeing political and religious persecution to apply for asylum," and that he feared that "genuine refugees may be returned to persecution." Under her proposal, the president would add that summary exclusion would "present the INS with extraordinary administrative and financial burdens at a time they have successfully reformed and improved the asylum process."[23] She did succeed in provoking the White House to say something, but the message was considerably more obscure. "This bill also makes a number of major, ill-advised changes in our immigration laws having nothing to do with fighting terrorism," the president wrote. "These provisions eliminate most remedial relief for long-term legal residents.... The provisions will produce extraordinary administrative burdens on the Immigration and Naturalization Service."[24] The phrase "extraordinary administrative burdens" survived in the president's rhetoric, but any comprehensible reference to asylum was gone.

The CPA did get one lucky break, however. A refugee story burst into national visibility, enabling immigration advocates to put a human face on the abstract procedural issue of summary exclusion.

Fauziya Kassindja[25] grew up in the small village of Kpalime, Togo. Her father owned a small trucking business that had made him wealthy by local standards. He used his wealth for the benefit of his five daughters and two sons. Though he was illiterate, he arranged for his children to be educated. Recalling the screams of his sister when she had undergone the tribal practice of clitorectomy, and the tetanus infection she had contracted as result of the genital cutting, he shielded his daughters from his extended family's pressure to force the ritual on them. Kassindja's older sisters married without being cut, but in 1993, when she was sixteen, her father died and she lost his protection.

Her mother was forced by local tradition to leave her husband's home, and her uncle moved in and arranged for her to become the fourth wife of a man who insisted that her clitoris be removed, as had been done to all his other wives. Kassindja's objections to the marriage and the procedure did not move her aunt. But her mother gave her $3,500 that she'd been allowed to inherit from her late husband. On what would have been her wedding day, when the women who were to hold her down and cut her genitals were already in the house, Kassindja escaped, took a taxi to the Ghanaian border, walked across, took another taxi to the Accra airport, and paid a fixer to get her on a flight to Germany, without a passport.

A German woman at the Düsseldorf airport allowed her to stay in her house for two months in exchange for chores, but Kassindja spoke no German and wanted to go to America, where she had relatives. Using a phony passport, she flew to Newark Airport and told immigration officials that her travel documents were false and that she wanted asylum.[26]

INS officials handcuffed her and sent her to jail to await a hearing. At the jail, which was run by a private company under contract with the INS, she was put in a large, cold, windowless room and told to remove her clothes. She asked to keep her underwear because she was menstruating, but the guard refused. As she shivered on a toilet, she saw a male guard watching her through the door. When she asked for a waste can for her sanitary napkin, another guard suggested that she eat it.[27]

She was astonished by her treatment in an American jail, particularly because she hadn't been accused of any crime.[28] She was given two right-footed sandals, and stained underwear that fell down if not tucked under a belt. She was put into isolation because she broke prison rules by washing her hands to pray before sunrise. When other prisoners rioted, she was tear-gassed and beaten. Then she was transferred to another jail where she was strip-searched and locked in a maximum security cell with an American convict.[29]

Meanwhile, her cousin had paid a Washington lawyer five hundred dollars to represent her at her asylum hearing. The lawyer fobbed the case off on Layli Miller Bashir, an American University law student working in his office. She was sent to Philadelphia to meet Kassindja for the first time just four hours before she had to present the case to Immigration Judge Donald V. Ferlise.

"The judge refused to allow me to make an opening argument," Bashir recalled. "He immediately interrupted and took over the direct examination. The judge was remarkably insensitive and impatient and he frequently, angrily interrupted me and Fauziya. He demanded to know whether or not it was really important or relevant to have her go into the details [of female genital mutilation], he insisted that I do not go into the details [and] twenty minutes after [her] interrupted and disjointed testimony, the judge issued an oral decision denying Fauziya asylum because he found her to be unbelievable. His decision didn't surprise me. He knew nothing about her culture ... and knew little about her story."[30]

Kassindja was returned to jail pending appeal, and Bashir persuaded her teacher Karen Musalo to take the case. Musalo, who taught asylum and refugee law at the University of California's Hastings College of Law, was just moving to Washington, D.C., for a one-year assignment as director of American University's international human rights clinic.

Most asylum cases are conducted quietly and privately, in part because most of them have little news value, and in part because most asylum applicants are afraid that if their home governments found that they were charging them with human rights abuses, they would retaliate against relatives who had been left behind. But Kassindja's case was different. She was charging that her country's custom, not particular government officials, threatened to persecute her. And to win, she would have to overcome not only Judge Ferlise's doubts about her credibility, but also make new legal precedent. The Justice Department's Board of Immigration Appeals, to which the case would now have to go, had never ruled that threatened genital mutilation was a valid basis for a claim of asylum. Therefore, as Musalo prepared the appeal, she also worked to make the name Kassindja a household word.

The snowball started with a small grain. Musalo explained the case to Keith Donoghue, a legal reporter for the *Recorder*, a West Coast legal newspaper.[31] She was also able to persuade columnist Judy Mann to write about it in the *Washington Post*.[32] Then the story got stuck for three months, but early in April 1996, just before Senate debate on the immigration bill began, Ellen Goodman wrote about the case in the *Boston Globe* and in syndicated papers.[33] A few days later, A. M. Rosenthal wrote on the editorial page of the *New York Times* that it had been hard for Kassindja to believe that "her determination not to surrender to torture and humiliation brought her shackles and cells."[34] Two days later, the *Times* ran a long front-page article that brought the details of Kassindja's escape and the horror of her detention conditions to the attention of readers and editors throughout the country, creating significant embarrassment at the INS.[35]

Musalo was not only Kassindja's lawyer but a core member of the Committee to Preserve Asylum. She was keenly aware of the impending vote on the Leahy amendment. As she fielded the growing number of press inquiries that each story generated, she pointed out that if the Simpson bill were not amended, future asylum-seekers might not even get a chance to present a case to an immigration judge, much less the kind of appeal to which her client was entitled. Indeed, an INS interviewer at the airport would certainly have deported Kassindja to be mutilated in Togo, because even if he believed her, the Board of Immigration Appeals had not yet declared that the threat of genital mutilation was a valid ground for asylum.

At 5:00 A.M. on the morning that the *Times* story appeared, Musalo was awakened in California by a telephone call from Wendy Japhet. Japhet's boss, the actress Sally Field, was outraged by what had happened to Kassindja and wanted to know how she could help. During the following two weeks, Musalo educated Japhet, and through her, Field, about the relationship between the Kassindja case and the ongoing policy debate over summary exclusion procedures.[36]

Musalo was equally successful in helping the press make the connection. "If some members of Congress had their way, Ms. Kassindja would have been returned to Togo long ago," editorialized the *Times*. "Denial of an asylum claim would be subject to review by a supervisor, but not by any other administrative or judicial body.... Senator Patrick Leahy ... would override the harsh exclusion provisions in the immigration bill but also supersede the same provisions in the anti-terrorism bill. Congress should follow his lead."[37]

Meanwhile, Wolchok and Hill were still drafting the Leahy amendment that the *Times* and other papers had endorsed. Their task was to accept summary exclusion in some form, so that Leahy would challenge only the unfair scope and procedures of the Simpson bill, not its concept; to make the new procedures as fair as possible for aliens; to avoid making them so fair that the amendment would fail to get the fifty-one votes it needed in the Senate; and to repeal most of the damage that had been done to the process by the anti-terrorism bill. They cut back most severely the circumstances under which summary rather than full hearing procedures could be used, and in the one situation in which they allowed summary exclusion, they created procedural protections that neither the anti-terrorism law nor the Simpson bill allowed. Consistent with the UNHCR recommendation, they also lowered the standard that an alien would have to meet in order to move from summary to full procedures. When they finished their work, they submitted it to the senator, who accepted most of their proposals. This table compares the Leahy amendment to the Simpson bill:[38]

| Issue | Judiciary Committee's bill and anti-terrorism law (cumulative effect) | Leahy amendment (changing both the bill and the anti-terrorism law) |
|---|---|---|
| Aliens who would get summary procedures rather than full hearings | 1. Anyone arriving at an airport or border without proper travel documents, or with false documents<br>2. Anyone without a visa who was escorted to the U.S. by a Coast Guard or navy vessel<br>3. Anyone found in the U.S., having entered, however long ago, without proper documents<br>4. Anyone arriving during a boatlift when INS's facilities are swamped | Anyone arriving without proper travel documents during a boatlift when the INS's facilities are swamped |

| | | |
|---|---|---|
| The official who would do the initial airport screening to determine whether the alien fears persecution and should therefore see any asylum officer for a "credible fear" determination | An INS official (but not one who was trained in asylum) | Same |
| If the alien is sent to the next stage (rather than deported) as a result of the first screening, the person who would do a second screening to determine whether the alien would get a full hearing | A person with training in asylum law | An asylum officer with both training and at least one year of previous experience in the adjudication of asylum cases |
| Legal counsel available to the alien at a second screening | The alien may "consult with" a lawyer (or another person of his or her choosing) before the screening interview (not at government expense) | The alien may be "represented by" a lawyer or another person (not at government expense) |
| Consequences if the second screening officer decides that the alien does have a credible fear of persecution | The alien is to be jailed pending a full hearing[39] | The alien will have a hearing (jail neither required nor prohibited) |
| Allowable appeals if the second screening officer decides that the alien does not have a credible fear of persecution | Prompt review by a supervisor, but this is not an appeal, so the alien does not have the right to participate<br><br>No court review (except of whether the person is in fact an alien)<br><br>Unless the supervisor disagrees, the alien is deported forthwith | The alien may have administrative appellate review before being deported<br><br>... |

| Criterion for an alien to demonstrate "credible fear" and avoid immediate deportation | A substantial likelihood that the alien's statements are true, plus a significant possibility that the alien could establish eligibility as a refugee | In light of the statements and evidence the alien offers, his or her claim for asylum is not manifestly unfounded |
|---|---|---|
| Lawsuits allowed to challenge the legality of the summary exclusion law itself, or the regulations or procedures implementing it | No | Yes |
| Full hearings rather than summary exclusion provided at the government's discretion to any aliens otherwise covered by the new law | No | Yes, at the attorney general's discretion, if the person fled a country that engaged in torture, prolonged arbitrary detention without trial, abductions, or certain other acts |
| Aliens barred from even seeking asylum | Yes—those who present false documents, unless those documents were needed to depart from a persecuting country and the alien traveled directly from that country to the U.S.[40] | No |

The Senate might have disposed of the immigration bill shortly after its debate opened on April 15, before the Kassindja story peaked and before the CPA and other opponents of the immigration bill had time to bring their public campaigns to a crescendo. But Senator Kennedy moved to add an amendment that would increase the minimum wage, a popular measure that put Republicans on the spot. In response, Majority Leader Bob Dole was forced to take the bill off the Senate calendar for two weeks, during which the CPA intensified its lobbying campaign,[41] focusing on senators who had voted against Leahy's motion to recommit the anti-terrorism bill.

In the final days before the bill came up for a vote, advocacy for the Leahy amendment reached new heights. CPA members distributed to their supporters, as they had on several prior occasions, a set of "talking points" to use when they telephoned senators' offices (a copy of this set of talking points is reproduced as appendix D). Senator DeWine agreed to co-sponsor the amendment, making it a bipartisan proposal. The CPA faxed across the country "One More Emergency Appeal," asking organizations to find members of their boards of directors who could call senators directly.[42]

Major newspapers picked up the theme. Anthony Lewis wrote of the anti-terrorism law's summary exclusion provisions that "I have seen a good deal of nastiness in the work of Congress over the years, but I do not remember such detailed and gratuitous cruelty.... Why should senators as decent as Orrin Hatch ... stand still for such harshness?"[43] Leahy and DeWine sent all of the senators, including Hatch, a "Dear Colleague" letter, asking them to support their amendment, and they included a copy of Lewis's New York Times column (a copy of their letter is reproduced as appendix E). Other newspapers joined the chorus. The conservative Washington Times editorialized that "in their rush to pass an anti-terrorism bill, lawmakers perhaps unwittingly and unnecessarily restricted the present rights of persons seeking asylum.... Lawmakers should restore procedural protections for asylum-seekers."[44] Each time a new story appeared, CPA members faxed copies of it to senators' aides and to the groups with which they were working around the country. The Kassindja story remained particularly visible, and the INS was hard pressed to explain to reporters why Kassindja should be kept in jail while the appeal board contemplated her case. Nine days after the Times' front-page story on Kassindja appeared, the INS suddenly reversed itself and freed her from prison.[45] This prompted a new round of press accounts. Kassindja appeared on Nightline, CNN, and CBS. Delacorte Press bought her life story for six hundred thousand dollars.[46]

For Karen Musalo and the CPA, the timing of that week couldn't have been better. For months, Richard Boswell, Musalo's husband and also a law professor, along with Equality Now, a women's human rights organization, had helped Musalo with publicity on the case. With Kassindja free, they hired a hotel room in Washington and invited the national press to meet her. The date was April 29, 1996. The Senate would begin to debate amendments to the immigration the following morning, although in fact it did not reach the Leahy amendment until the second day of debate. The press turned out to see and hear Kassindja, but Musalo also spoke. "As distressing as the current situation of asylum-seekers is, if Congress has its way, things will become far worse," she told the reporters. "If they can't convince a low-level INS employee that they have what is called a credible claim for asylum, they will be put right back on the airplane and returned to the country of persecution. Bona fide refugees who arrive in the U.S. traumatized and exhausted will not be able to make their case in this type of kangaroo court." She noted that the Leahy amendment could help to provide asylum seekers with "our protection and not our punishment."[47]

Leahy held his own press conference the following day, and the NIF provided two more living examples of refugees who might have been sent back to tyranny under a summary exclusion regime. Alan Baban, an Iraqi Kurd, had been arrested by Saddam Hussein's forces in 1989. During two weeks of inter-rogation, he was stripped, hung upside-down from the ceiling, whipped, and shocked. Then he was imprisoned without charges for two years. He was freed after Iraq lost the Gulf War, but he was arrested four months later and escaped only by bribing a guard. He fled through Turkey and flew to Boston. Like Kassindja, he was imprisoned immediately because he did not have valid travel documents, and he spent more than a year in prison. The immigration judge who heard his case denied him asylum, however, speculating that the scars on Baban's back might have come from corporal punishment that he said was common in Muslim societies, and Baban was released and granted asylum only after an appeal.[48] Under the anti-terrorism law, if an INS official hadn't believed him, he would not have had a hearing before an immigration judge, much less the appeal that led to his freedom in America.

A month after being released from prison, Baban stood next to Senator Patrick Leahy in the United States Capitol.[49] With him was Anna, a Peruvian woman whose last name was withheld from the press. She too had arrived without proper papers, after fleeing from a guerrilla movement. "I asked her to tell about her experience," Leahy told the Senate the next day. "Less than two sentences into her story, as the memories of what she had put up with 2 years ago played back, she broke down crying.... Two years later, the memories are so strong that, emotionally, she was unable to talk with us about it. Can you image if [at] the border, an INS officer had said, 'Quick, tell me why you should stay here?' "[50]

If senators hadn't heard from their staffs about a large volume of telephone calls supporting the Leahy amendment, they could hardly have avoided the press accounts of the Kassindja and Leahy press conferences, or the editorials and columns that they spawned. ABC-TV featured Kassindja on ABC's *World News Tonight*.[51] The French press agency made Kassindja a story around the world.[52] The *Washington Post* took the trouble to obtain the INS's comment not only about Kassindja's case, but about the impending Leahy amendment. In its story on Kassindja's press conference it reported that an INS spokesman said that "the Clinton administration supports such revisions."[53] The *Post* followed up with an editorial stating that "Sen. Leahy's effort, which has the backing of the people charged with enforcing the immigration laws, should be supported."[54]

Cohen made sure that the most important stories and editorials were on every senator's desk when the debate opened on the Leahy amendment on the morning of May 1. In his opening speech, Leahy referred to the editorials, columns, and national organizations supporting him, and he told the stories of Kassindja and the refugees he'd met at his press conference. His amendment was long and technical, in part because sections of it repealed new law that had been on the books only a few days. No senator proposed to change parts of it or craft a new compromise on the floor, as Brown and Kennedy had in essence done to the time-limit provision in committee. Rather, Simpson opposed the entire amendment, and it became clear that everything would turn on an up-or-down vote.

"The American people suffer compassion fatigue," Simpson argued. They have good reason for it, because would-be immigrants get false documents from smugglers and "flush them down the toilet of the aircraft. Some have eaten them." Then they claim asylum; "many of us saw this so dramatically in the 'Sixty Minutes' presentation."

"We ought to be looking at what the current condition is," replied Kennedy, "not what the conditions were . . . three years ago. . . . That whole spigot, in terms of jobs [attracting false asylum-seekers] has been closed down by the INS."

"The most worthy cases for asylum would be excluded if we impose this new summary exclusion procedure," DeWine added. "Among those excluded would be cases of victims of politically motivated torture and rape, the very people who are most likely to use false documents to flee." He also recalled a friend of his father who had escaped from Nazi German with false documents. "The few times in our history when we have turned our back on people who are persecuted, and there are examples of this, the Nazi Germany situation, we have lived to regret it."[55]

Although senators gave their speeches on the Leahy amendment in the morning, the Senate was not scheduled to vote on it until late afternoon, when senators could enter the chamber to cast several votes in succession on the various amendments that had been offered. CPA members took advantage of this final delay to continue bombarding senators' offices with phone calls. Alan Keller, a New York physician and human rights activist who had appeared with Leahy the previous day at his press conference, returned to Washington for the vote, calling senators' offices from the Metroliner as he traveled. "Carol [Wolchok] and I showed up at Bruce [Cohen]'s office and we spent the entire day there," recalls Pistone. "We basically took over the place, got a phone each and a chair and a little part of someone's desk and we got out our lists of organizations that had been working on the legislation. We spent the entire day on the phone calling offices in the Senate and calling people around the country and telling them to call."[56] In California, Musalo placed one final call to Wendy Japhet, to ask that Sally Field, who knew Senator Feinstein, call her immediately and, with the Kassindja case as background, request that she change her vote on the Leahy amendment, which she had opposed in the Judiciary Committee. Japhet agreed, and Field made the call.[57]

The human rights advocates knew that some of the sixty-one senators who had voted against Leahy on the anti-terrorism bill would vote for him now, when terrorism was not in the name of the law on the floor. But how many? They could tell that the vote would be very close, and several swing senators' aides could or would not predict which way their bosses would vote. In some cases, the aides themselves did not know, because the senators were being cajoled personally throughout the day by Leahy, Kennedy, Simpson, and others.

At midday, a letter from the White House arrived. Kennedy and Leahy had long sought such a letter, hoping that they could cite it on the floor to support their position. But although the administration did not want to have to undertake summary exclusion at all of the nation's ports of entry, and very much wanted to repeal the section of the anti-terrorism bill that would soon require it to do just that, it had not been able to bring itself to send the unequivocal endorsement of the Leahy amendment that its legislative allies had hoped for. Instead, the administration declined to endorse the amendment's "unless manifestly unfounded" standard for what would constitute "credible fear:" "We appreciate your efforts, and those of Senators Leahy and DeWine," wrote a special assistant to the president, but went on to say:

> While the Administration disagrees with provisions in the amendment regarding the standard an alien would be required to meet to demonstrate a credible fear of persecution and regarding judicial review under the expedited exclusion procedures, we welcome efforts to limit more sweeping changes in this area which ... could compromise our world leadership on refugee protection issues.[58]

Somehow, this equivocal administration letter never became public. Therefore the INS spokesperson's comment to the *Washington Post* that the Clinton administration "supports such revisions" became, for all practical purposes, the administration's last word on the Leahy amendment.

A consequence of the letter, however, was that if Vice President Gore had to vote to break a tie, Leahy could not assume that he would vote in favor of the amendment. Kennedy and Leahy did not call his office to ask him to stand by to vote, and in fact he was not in the Capitol building when the vote was held. To prevail, we would have to win the votes of fifty-one senators, not just fifty.

As Pistone and Wolchok made their calls, they could watch the Senate session on C-SPAN's cable television broadcast. Early in the afternoon, Pistone saw Hatch's aide Mark Disler approach Bruce Cohen on the Senate floor. She thought that might mean that Hatch would support the Leahy amendment on the Senate floor. A few minutes later, Hatch went to the floor, where he gave a short speech in favor of the Leahy amendment on grounds of both economy (summary exclusion would "require INS officers ... to make threshold determinations of how an alien traveled to the United States.... This would present a burden to our INS officers at borders who ... would have to perform additional bureaucratic functions") and accuracy (asylum applicants may not "have the necessary proof of their claim with them"). He added, perhaps stung by Anthony Lewis's criticism of him by name, that the summary exclusion provision in the terrorism bill had been "primarily driven by some House Members and ... I knew that we would deal with this here on the immigration bill. [So] I do not think it is inconsistent for those who supported the terrorism bill to support the Leahy asylum amendment. [Also] I like the changes he made [so] even though I voted against the amendment in committee, I [will vote for it today]."[59]

Wolchok and Pistone had already been telephoning for six hours, but they immediately began an entirely new round of calls to other members of the CPA as well as to Senate offices, particularly Republican offices, to spread the word about Hatch's statement. "There were times when everyone thought it was a lost cause," Pistone said. "And I heard [Wolchok] on the phone saying, 'Make those calls, you never know.'"[60]

I was one of Wolchok's many callers, pressing a dozen senators' offices from my office at Georgetown University. My senators were mostly in what we considered the "undecided" column. Many of the staff members to whom I spoke were non-committal, and I could not pin them down. But I kept calling, and faxing them more editorials and more information, throughout the day, right up to the moment when I could see, from C-SPAN, that the vote was about to be held.

I watched the very end of the debate and the roll call on a television set in a law school lounge. Each side was allowed two minutes, just before the vote, to make a final summation. Leahy's and Simpson's last comments were predictable statements: fair hearings for those escaping persecution, versus *60 Minutes*. But Simpson had a final surprise. He yielded his last "two seconds," when the Senate floor had filled with those coming to vote, to New York's Senator Alphonse D'Amato, who, in fact, spoke for an important half minute. D'Amato had never spoken on this issue, and because he represented a progressive state with many immigrants, we had strenuously sought his vote, although he hadn't indicated what he would do. Now we knew, and so did his many Republican colleagues.

"If we say pass this amendment, what you are saying is let people come in with illegal documents, just claim political persecution and set them loose," D'Amato said. "You do not have the facilities to hold them in, nor the facilities to have hearings. You will be gutting the bill."[61]

D'Amato had the last word. I thought his brief diatribe had cost us some votes, because for a few senators, it might be all they'd heard on the issue. But I had no way to measure its impact.

The clerk of the Senate called the roll. Senators could enter the chamber and vote at any time within a fifteen-minute period. As the votes were announced, they seemed nearly evenly balanced; we would win or lose by just a vote or two. Many of the votes were predictable, but there were a few surprises. Arlen Specter voted against the amendment, a bad sign. Robert Bennett, a conservative Republican, voted on our side, probably influenced by his fellow senator from Utah, Orrin Hatch. The two liberal Democratic senators from North Dakota, Kent Conrad and Byron Dorgan, were expected to vote for the Leahy amendment.[62] They shocked us by voting against it, and only years afterward, when I was writing this book, did I learn that disappointment with Senator Leahy's vote on an unrelated agriculture bill may have cost their support.[63]

Late in the roll call, Dianne Feinstein entered the room, approached the front desk, and studied the way others had voted. She waited a few minutes, and then voted for the amendment.

Immediately, from a corner of the C-SPAN screen, Simpson entered the picture and approached Feinstein, perhaps trying to persuade her to change her vote. Under Senate rules, a senator can change a vote at any time before the result is announced, and the majority leader (in this case, Senator Robert Dole) could even extend the fifteen-minute voting period while senators consider vote changes.[64]

Finally, the time was up, or so I thought. C-SPAN usually mutes its microphones during roll calls, but someone's hand must have slipped off the mute button; Senator James Exon hadn't yet cast what we expected to be his vote against Leahy, and I heard someone say under his breath that the count stood at fifty-one to forty-eight in favor of the amendment.

And then everything just stopped. No further sound could be heard, but the C-SPAN picture showed, in the midst of general senatorial milling, Simpson still talking to Feinstein. But Leahy also approached Feinstein. Now the two men stood on each side of her, apparently engaged in the last debate of this long effort. Leahy left the picture, but Michael Myers, Kennedy's chief assistant for immigration issues, took his place. Senator Dole watched, holding the vote count open while the apparent struggle continued over whether Senator Feinstein would change her vote.[65]

A long seven minutes passed. At last the clerk announced that Senator Exon had voted no, and that the final count was fifty-one to forty-nine.[66] Feinstein had held. Every ounce of Wolchok's perseverance, every public relations effort by Musalo and Kassindja, and every hour of cajoling by activists across the country, had been well invested (appendix F shows the votes of each senator).

For the human rights and refugee community, the struggle over the Leahy amendment was the most visible battle of the Senate's immigration debate, but the final vote on the bill was still a day away, and meanwhile, what turned out to be an equally important issue was being resolved behind the scenes. After the Judiciary Committee's compromise on asylum filing deadlines, DeWine had wanted Simpson to include in the Judiciary Committee's report a fairly extensive description of the types of circumstances that would constitute "good cause" for seeking asylum more than a year after entering the United States. He'd been incensed when Richard Day, Simpson's staff member, had refused. In addition to writing his own separate views to accompany the committee's report, DeWine had quietly drafted an amendment to graft the exceptions onto the bill, and he'd threatened Simpson with a floor fight.

Simpson had his hands full with what were, for him, more important issues. In addition to trying to beat the Leahy amendment, he was trying—without ultimate success—to get the full Senate to cut legal immigration levels, despite the Judiciary Committee's rejection of that proposal when it had split the bill.[67] Also, Simpson had proposed federal standards for state-issued birth certificates, and that the government begin to create a federal system through which prospective employers could check whether their workers were unauthorized aliens. Senator Abraham opposed him not only on cutting legal immigration but also on these worker identification issues, which Simpson regarded as "the critical test of the legislation" to deter future illegal immigration.[68] Simpson could ill afford to pick a public fight with still another conservative Republican.

Simpson therefore ended up giving DeWine more than what DeWine had originally asked for. Simpson agreed to embody DeWine's proposed language, not in a mere committee report, but in the immigration law itself, in the manager's amendment that Simpson himself would sponsor.

The day after the vote on the Leahy amendment, therefore, Simpson offered a manager's amendment that he had cleared with both Hatch and Kennedy to assure that there would be no opposition from either Republicans or Democrats. Quickly accepted by unanimous consent, it included DeWine's definition of "good cause" to excuse a late asylum application:

> [G]ood cause may include, but is not limited to, circumstances that changed after the applicant entered the U.S. and that are relevant to the applicant's eligibility for asylum; physical or mental disability; threats of retribution against the applicant's relatives abroad; attempts to file affirmatively that were unsuccessful because of technical defects; efforts to seek asylum that were delayed by the temporary unavailability of professional assistance; the illness or death of the applicant's legal representative; or other extenuating circumstances as determined by the Attorney General.[69]

Soon thereafter, the Senate passed the immigration bill. In the form in which the Senate passed the bill, refugee advocates could rejoice at their success. They had killed the statutory numerical cap on overseas refugees in the Senate subcommittee, and it had never made another appearance. In the Judiciary Committee, they had increased from thirty days to one year the time in which refugees could apply for asylum, and more important, the deadline would apply only to the small number of refugees who did not apply for asylum affirmatively, who lived in the United States for more than a year, and who were then apprehended by the authorities. On the floor, the bill had been amended to provide six explicit categories of excuses even for the few would-be asylum applicants to whom the deadline would apply, and the INS, which hadn't wanted to impose a deadline to begin with, was authorized to permit additional types of exemptions. Finally, the Senate bill repealed the far-reaching summary exclusion provisions of the anti-terrorism law, and the Senate had also rejected the nearly as draconian summary exclusion provisions that its Judiciary Committee had approved. In their place, the bill would apply summary exclusion only when the government determined that its normal immigration facilities were swamped. Even then, the Senate bill gave asylum-seekers procedural rights far beyond those that Simpson would have allowed.

In the House, however, only the overseas-refugee cap had been killed. With very limited exceptions, the House bill would apply a six-month deadline to affirmative as well as defensive asylum applicants. It would impose summary exclusion, with virtually no procedural protections, to large numbers of arriving aliens, and it would leave the anti-terrorism provisions on the books as well, denying hearings not only to arriving aliens, but also to those who had entered the United States illegally many years earlier.

Reconciling the two bills would be the task of the delegates from the House and Senate to still another Conference Committee. Even before the Senate passed its bill, immigration and refugee advocates began to ponder how they could influence that ultimate legislative body.

# 10

# The Conference
## May–September 1996

No aspect of our immigration policy is more closely tied to the history and founding principles of our nation than the practice of offering refuge to those suffering political or religious persecution abroad.

—Representative Lamar Smith[1]

No one dared take a break. On the very day on which the Senate passed its bill, the immigration organizations began to try to influence the House-Senate Conference Committee that would merge the two versions of the law. The House and Senate leaders had not yet selected their delegates to the Conference Committee, but the NIF knew from the outset that Smith was likely to be the leader of the House delegation, that he would take a strong stand in favor of the more restrictive House bill, and that the other House Republicans might all follow his lead. Its opening move, therefore, was to try to involve the more moderate Henry Hyde in the work of the Conference Committee. Hours after the Senate voted ninety-seven to three to pass the bill, the NIF faxed its activists, urging them to ask their own representatives to put pressure on Hyde to accept the Leahy amendment.[2]

Micheal Hill, who as the advocate for the Catholic Conference could speak directly to Hyde, went further. He met with Hyde, urging him to ask the Speaker to appoint himself, rather than Smith, as the leader of the House delegation. Hill hoped that Hyde would bring to the table at least one moderate vote from the House Republican delegation, and that as the delegation's leader he might exercise an even greater influence in the direction of reasonable compromises with the Senate. But Hyde was disinclined to participate in the Conference Committee, expecting to be burdened by duties he'd accepted as the chair of the Republican National Convention's platform committee.

While wooing Hyde, the immigration advocates also assessed the damage and ranked their lobbying objectives. One issue had gone away; the statutory cap on overseas refugees had been killed in both houses and could not be revived by the Conference Committee. But nearly all of the other problems persisted. New quota limitations on legal immigration had also been defeated in each house, but Congress was on the verge of restricting legal immigration in a different way, by limiting sponsorship of immigrant relatives to relatively wealthy Americans. A provision in each bill barred Americans from sponsoring their family members for legal immigration unless the sponsor earned at least a certain amount of money. The Senate bill set the amount at 125 percent of the poverty level, while the House figure was 200 percent. The median income of all full-time wage and salary workers in the U.S. was only 163 percent of the poverty level for a family of four; the House bill, had it been law in 1995, would have precluded 44 percent of the American sponsors of immigrant parents, adult children, or siblings. The NIF termed this clause in the bill a "back door" cut in legal immigration,[3] and keeping the final percentage as low as possible became one of its objectives for Conference Committee lobbying.

Organizations within the non-profit community detested dozens of other provisions in one or both bills, but as in early phases of lobbying, each organization prioritized its desires and then coordinated its strategy with others. In principle, it might have been best for all of the non-profit organizations to negotiate among themselves and agree on a single, common set of priorities. In practice, however, that would not have been possible, because each organization had a somewhat different membership or constituency. Some were primarily concerned, for example, with serving families that wanted to help relatives to immigrate legally. Others represented immigrants who were already in the United States as permanent residents; their primary mission was to prevent cutbacks in social benefits. Some were particularly concerned about procedural fairness, and the bill's provisions curtailing judicial review. A few, including the Committee to Preserve Asylum, perceived their mission as advocacy for asylum applicants. They reasoned that if they subordinated this goal in favor of what others saw as more important immigration issues, such as the sponsorship requirement, refugees' voices would not be heard in the final stages of the legislative process. Accordingly, the groups did not devise a single coalition strategy. Each emphasized what it saw as the most critical issues, although serious efforts were made to keep other groups informed of ongoing lobbying efforts.

The NIF listed eight issues of "priority concern." Defeating the Gallegly amendment topped the list, followed by preserving the Leahy amendment and adopting the Senate's resolution of the asylum application deadline issue. Keeping the sponsorship percentage low was sixth on its list, and most of its other priorities involved avoiding new welfare restrictions on legal immigrants.[4] The American Immigration Lawyers Association listed seven priorities. First on its list was to overturn or shorten the bills' re-entry bars, provisions that for extended periods, some as long as ten years, would prevent people who had overstayed temporary visas from again visiting the United States. Retaining the Leahy amendment was the third item on AILA's list, and defeating the 200 percent sponsorship requirement was fifth. Killing the House's six-month time limit on affirmative asylum applications was not among AILA's "priority" issues.[5]

Pistone recognized that with so many issues still in contention, it would be difficult to keep the non-profit community focused even in significant part on the refugee issues. Beating the House's more restrictive version on the issue of deadlines might be even more difficult than winning on summary exclusion. Because the Committee to Preserve Asylum had won a satisfactory outcome on the deadlines issue in committee, without a floor fight, this issue had never received the attention from the press and the public that had been lavished on the Leahy amendment. Indeed, a few days after the Senate acted, the *New York Times* proclaimed editorially that the "Senate's version is superior to the harshly punitive bill the House passed in March." The *Times* mentioned the Gallegly amendment and devoted a paragraph of praise to Senator Leahy. But although it praised the Leahy amendment because it "keeps asylum accessible," the editorial did not mention the danger that the House bill posed to affirmative asylum applicants.[6]

Pistone therefore began to re-mobilize the CPA. Borrowing several organizations' fax trees, she urged groups to use any connections their board members might have to persuade Hyde to chair the House delegation. She also asked them to send conferees stories of successful asylum-seekers who had applied more than six months after arriving, and of refugees who had arrived so distraught that they could not have related their experiences accurately to airport interviewers.[7]

Generating large volumes of calls and letters had been a staple of the CPA and its sister organizations throughout the efforts to influence the House and Senate. But now, even telling supporters to whom they should call or write was problematic. The Senate quickly appointed its delegates to the Conference Committee.[8] But the House hesitated. The reason for the delay was a House rule under which, twenty days after conferees are appointed, the Democratic minority could make motions to "instruct" the House delegates to adopt certain positions. The Republican majority could vote down the motions, and even if such a motion passed, the instructions would not be binding.[9] But the motions would require the House to divide on contentious issues, possibly forcing some Republicans into difficult pre-election votes. The immigration bill was long, and resolving the issues between the House and Senate would take more than twenty days. Delaying the appointment of conferees would keep motions to instruct from being in order, and thereby avoid embarrassing some Republican members.[10] It also had the effect of keeping at least some of the eventual House delegates out of the line of lobbying fire, though obviously Smith, McCollum, and John Bryant, the ranking Democrat on the Immigration Subcommittee, would be among the members of the House delegation.

Senate Majority Leader Trent Lott appointed Hatch to lead the Senate's delegation. This was fortunate, both because Hatch had supported the Leahy amendment, and because it would put some pressure on his House counterpart, Hyde, to lead the House's delegates. The other Senate Republicans were Simpson, Thurmond, Grassley, Kyl, and Specter. The Democrats were Leahy (to whom Joseph Biden, the ranking minority member of the Judiciary, yielded his presumptive place while he ran for reelection), Kennedy, Simon, Feinstein, and Kohl.

With respect to each provision as to which the House and Senate had differed, the conferees could adopt either body's outcome or rewrite the provision to compromise between the two bodies. Congressional rules provided that the final bill written by the Conference Committee (called a conference report) could not be official unless signed by a majority of the delegates from each body.[11] The arithmetic of lobbying therefore seemed clear, at least as to the Senate. Kennedy, Leahy, Simon, and Kohl could be counted on to support the generally more liberal provisions of the Senate bill. If Hatch and Feinstein stuck with them, they could block the Senate delegates from supporting a retrograde bill. Those six senators could insist on anything they wanted, and prevent issuance of a conference report until Lamar Smith accepted their demands. But Hatch and Feinstein wanted to produce a bill before the Senate adjourned for the fall election campaign. Just how tough would they hang?

For insurance against a Feinstein defection, Pistone and others tried to enlist Arlen Specter, even though he hadn't actively helped to defeat asylum deadlines, had been absent for the Judiciary Committee vote on summary exclusion, and had voted against the Leahy amendment on the floor. He was reputed to be one of the most moderate of Republican senators, and his vote on Leahy seemed inexplicable. One of his staff members told me that he'd been puzzled by Specter's vote, and that we shouldn't regard his boss as a lost cause. But he also warned that Specter made up his own mind on issues, rather than relying on staff, and that getting a meeting with Specter himself would be extremely difficult.

On the House side, the arithmetic was even more daunting. The difference between the number of Republicans and Democrats on the House delegation might be more than one. And John Bryant, who was certain to be a delegate, had co-sponsored the bill with Smith, although he strongly opposed the Gallegly amendment. Even if the numerical difference between the parties was only one, the pro-immigrant lobbyists would have to persuade both Hyde and John Bryant to support Senate resolutions of highly contested issues. If the numerical difference was more than one, they would have to find at least one more Republican supporter on the House delegation.

Shortly after the Senate named its delegates, we heard two reports that threw all of our arithmetic into question. First, one of my former students, who worked in Congress, told me that the Republican leadership had decided not to appoint its delegates until after Smith had already worked out all of the issues with Hatch and Simpson. Congressional rules required that all members of a Conference Committee be permitted to participate in voting on the conference report, but the rules did not preclude some members of the Conference Committee from writing the final bill behind closed doors and then presenting a virtual fait accompli to the other members. In this case, I was told, the senior

Republicans had decided that they would privately and unofficially negotiate the differences between the House and Senate bills. The actual Conference Committee would eventually have one brief, official meeting, but that meeting would be a sham. It would merely rubber-stamp the hundreds of decisions to which the senior Republicans had already agreed. That scenario didn't make sense to me, because whenever the Conference Committee meeting took place, Hatch could undo any particular decision by siding with the Democrats from the Senate's delegation. But the second report explained the apparent paradox. By chance, I was seated at a lunch next to a former congressman who was following the situation closely. Hatch and the other Republicans, he told me, had already made a pact with each other that none of them would defect from pre-agreed Republican positions when the formal Conference Committee meeting took place. Thus the Republican senators and the Republican representatives would decide the final outcomes by themselves, and even if Hatch didn't like the outcome, he would not try to change it when the meeting took place.

This Republican plan, if true, would negate any Democratic influence on the result, and it would preclude the usual close cooperation between the committee and the government (in this case, the INS) that typically characterized the conference process. But it would not eliminate Hatch's clout, for he could still threaten, during the Republican senators' caucuses, not to sign the conference report unless he was satisfied, and that would prevent the bill from going forward. Furthermore, it was still necessary to keep Senator Feinstein and Representative Bryant from supporting the Republicans, because Feinstein could supply the missing signature if Hatch were holding out, and Bryant might do the same if Hyde chaired his delegation and held out for a more moderate bill.

With coordination more critical than ever, the CPA became part of the larger coalition of non-governmental organizations opposed to the more radical changes of the House bill. It met almost every week to exchange information and assign tasks. One of my jobs was to try to pull John Bryant away from the six-month deadline in the House bill. Fortunately, one of his close friends was a human rights activist who went to see him and took me along.

Bryant proved cordial but extremely unreceptive. "Six months is a long time," he said. "Why can't a person apply for asylum in six months if he knows that's the rule?" I explained that people traumatized by torture and violence often can't talk about their experiences for a long time afterward. "But that's how you work through these life traumas," he replied, "by talking about what happened with people who love you." He seemed to overlook the fact that INS asylum officers, or even the applicants' own lawyers, were not loving family members. Mary Rawson came with me when I returned to see Bryant a second time. She told Bryant how she had been so frightened of the authorities, even U.S. authorities, after fleeing from her country that she'd hid in her brother's apartment for months, not even venturing into the streets. Bryant seemed to think that fears like hers should not interfere with prompt asylum applications. "If I'm running away from someone and I'm in danger," he said, "I'd run up to a house and tell someone what the problem was. The United States is that house."

By this time, after months of working with staff members from many offices on Capitol Hill, we had pretty good working relationships with a large number of people, and information flowed pretty easily. We began to get more reports about how the Republicans were organizing their work. Cordia Strom and Richard Day, respectively Smith's and Simpson's chief staff lawyers, were meeting regularly, sometimes with other Republicans' staff members as well. They were making the decisions about what would be in the final bill, except that they would leave to the Republican senators and representatives themselves any issue that any Republican lawmaker wanted the principals themselves to decide. Quickly, Pistone called a member of Hatch's staff, who said that Hatch would flag the deadline and summary exclusion issues for decisions by principals. We also learned that the staffs had decided to use the "architecture" of the House bill as the basis for the final draft, plugging some of the Senate's policy decisions into the House-passed bill. Unfortunately, this approach would make the provisions of the House bill into the default position and give that body some additional clout.

Assured that the refugee issues would be "members'" issues, we knew that the fate of these provisions would lie with half a dozen senators, and that of the six Republican senators in the Conference Committee, only Hatch had voted for the Leahy amendment. To help persuade them to stick with the Senate provisions despite their own predilections, Senators DeWine and Abraham sent them a letter about ten issues, which asked them to adopt the Senate positions on summary exclusion and asylum time limits.[12] Similarly, Republican representative Lincoln Diaz-Balart, who represented many Miami Cubans, wrote a letter to conferees saying that the House bill "inadequately recognizes the terrible choices faced by those who, living under a brutally repressive regime, can only escape oppression by using false documents."[13] Christopher Smith followed it with a letter from nineteen House members urging support for the Senate version on both refugee issues.[14]

The Clinton administration might have made lobbying somewhat easier for us by endorsing the Senate's version of summary exclusion, but it saw in the division between House and Senate an opportunity to obtain more discretionary authority, with fewer possibilities for judicial review of its decisions, than the Leahy amendment permitted. INS General Counsel David Martin had all along wanted a summary exclusion provision that would give the agency complete discretion about when to use the procedure (rather than requiring its use at all airports and border crossings) but once invoked, would prevent courts from slowing down the exclusion process by reviewing agency decisions. Through such a law, he hoped to encourage future presidents to let refugees fleeing by boat come to the United States for quick, final asylum adjudications, rather than give in to the temptation (to which both Bush and Clinton had

succumbed) to interdict them at sea in order to keep them away from American shores and courts.[15] The Leahy amendment foiled this plan. After the
Senate vote, Martin met with Democratic staffers in the office of Michael
Meyers, Senator Kennedy's senior immigration staff member, seeking a compromise between his desired outcome and the Senate's bill. During the meeting, he came up with idea of allowing a single court challenge to summary
exclusion procedures, shortly after the law was enacted, but excluding any judicial review of individual summary exclusion.

This new idea was controversial both within the administration and among
the Democratic staff members, so although INS officials told us that they
would not back the Leahy amendment, they deflected our repeated requests,
over a period of weeks, to tell us any details of what they would support as an
outcome of the House-Senate Conference Committee.

Finally, Martin attended a conference of immigration law teachers in
Boulder, Colorado, where he distributed copies of the administration's new
proposal. Martin was himself a renowned immigration law teacher, well posi-
tioned to serve as a bridge between the administration and the academic community and through it, the larger world of immigration advocates.

Like the Leahy amendment, the new INS plan deleted the requirement that
summary exclusion procedures be used against every alien arriving without
proper travel documents at a U.S. airport. But although the Leahy amendment
gave the administration authority to use summary exclusion only when the
attorney general declared a migration emergency, the administration also
wanted to use this power whenever unauthorized aliens arrived in the United
States by sea, whether escorted (during boatlifts) or unescorted (as in the case
of smugglers' vessels, such as the *Golden Venture*, that were not detected until
they reached the United States). Predictably, the administration also rejected
the Senate's definition of "credible fear" sufficient to entitle an alien to a full
hearing. The Leahy amendment provided that credible fear was present whenever "in light of statements and evidence" the alien produced, her claim "would
not be manifestly unfounded." At last, the administration accepted the "manifestly unfounded" language, but it added that there had to be "a substantial
likelihood" that the alien's statements were true. The administration advocated
allowing an immigration judge to review an asylum officer's conclusion that an
alien lacked credible fear, but it provided that the initial negative conclusion
couldn't be overturned by the judge unless it were "clearly erroneous." In addition, the administration's version would preclude any further review by the
regular federal courts of individual cases, and it permitted only very limited
federal court challenges even to the generic policies and procedures that the
INS would eventually set up to administer the system. It allowed suits to challenge "any regulations" implementing summary exclusion or "any policy directive or other written instruction" which under other provisions of U.S. law
would have to be published in the *Federal Register* for public comment before it

could be promulgated.[16] But it barred court challenges to unwritten administrative practices.

This new INS plan was not as terrible as I feared it might be. At least the administration had finally accepted a screening standard lower than "credible fear." But clearly, the plan was capable of improvement. For example, it could be modified to allow a broader array of court challenges to unlawful government procedures. The refugee organizations didn't seem to have much influence with the administration, but I thought that our Senate allies might do better. As soon as I returned to Washington from Boulder, I faxed a copy of the administration's new plan, along with my critique, to several refugee organizations and to staffers for several Democratic senators. I suggested, for example, that the administration be urged to change its phrase "substantial likelihood" to "significant possibility," so that in determining the threshold judgment for whether an alien should get a hearing when corroborating evidence was not yet available, no one could think that the alien would have to prove that it was more "likely" than not that she was telling the truth.

I didn't hear from any Senate offices, but the director of one of the organizations told me that I'd made a mistake in sending my memo only to Democrats. This had been a bipartisan effort all along, the director reminded me, and to avoid seeming partisan, I should send the memo to our Republican supporters as well. This seemed like sensible advice, so I faxed a copy to the staffers for Senators DeWine and Hatch as well.

The next afternoon, I received a blistering telephone call from a Democratic staff member, livid because I had sent the administration's draft to Republicans. I learned that on the day Martin circulated the draft in Boulder, the administration had sent to Capitol Hill a letter describing it only in the most general terms, without details of the restrictions it was proposing.[17] Some Democratic staffers had received the draft legislative language, but they had understood that it was being kept confidential until they'd had time to ask the administration to make changes. The staffer was furious with me because my transmission of the draft to Republican offices was tantamount to releasing it to Simpson and Smith; it would become a "live alternative" to the Leahy amendment. But, I protested, I was hardly revealing any deep secrets; Martin had given out fifty copies of the draft to law professors from all over the country. "Then he's an idiot," the staffer screamed at me, "and you are too." I sheepishly promised him that I wouldn't give out any more copies, and when Simpson's staff called me to ask for a copy, I knew that the information actually hadn't gone too far. Years later, I learned that while I was being chastised for having giving out copies of Martin's draft to Republicans, Martin was being criticized by White House staffers for sharing his draft with members of the public in Boulder, and he was divested of further authority to negotiate a resolution of the summary exclusion issue.[18]

Meanwhile, two other issues in the bill were becoming much more prominent than refugee concerns in the pages of the nation's newspapers and, therefore, in the awareness of the public. The first of these issues was the Gallegly amendment, which loomed large for several reasons. It was one of the most easily understood and starkest differences between the House and Senate bills. By speaking for it on the House floor, Speaker Gingrich had put his personal prestige behind it, and Democrats were almost unanimously opposed to it, so it was a good partisan story. It offered a national version of California's noisy Proposition 187 debate, another good angle for journalism. The outcome could affect the contest for California's electoral votes in the 1996 presidential election. And if children of unauthorized aliens were forced out of school, the fiscal consequences, and perhaps the crime consequences as well, could be very significant, particularly in California and Texas.

More than anything else, the election campaign kept the Gallegly amendment on the front pages. Senator Robert Dole, who had locked up the Republican presidential nomination, was far behind Clinton in California. Dole had voted to kill a similar amendment in 1982, but he endorsed the Gallegly amendment, hoping to make the immigration bill so unpalatable to Clinton supporters that Clinton would have to veto it, a move that would be particularly unpopular in California because of that state's large influx of unauthorized aliens. A veto "would send a signal by Bill Clinton that he is unequivocal about his desire for California citizens to continue to fund education for illegal immigrant children," said Kenneth Khachigian, who headed Dole's California campaign. Governor Pete Wilson added that if Clinton vetoed the bill "he'd get killed here."[19] At a meeting of immigration advocates, one expert on California suggested that the politics of Gallegly were even more complicated: Dole knew he couldn't win in California even if Clinton vetoed the bill, but the outcome would be a lot closer there, forcing Clinton to spend millions of dollars on television advertising in the state. Those millions would then be unavailable for use in the Midwest, where the election was much more competitive. After Dole announced his support for the amendment, Hatch predicted, correctly, that the Gallegly amendment would be "the biggest issue" in the Conference Committee.[20]

Welfare benefits for legal aliens also became a more prominent issue after both Houses had passed their bills. "Provisions on Legal Immigrants Jeopardize Bill," screamed a front-page *New York Times* headline, alerting editors across the country to a story they might have missed.[21] As with Gallegly, the press smelled a good political story, and the very first paragraph of the *Times'* article predicted that "a battle with the White House is looming" over this aspect of the bill. Legal aliens included family members of citizens, certain skilled employees, and people qualifying within a few other categories, who had been admitted under quotas and given permanent lawful status and "green cards" entitling them to work. They paid U.S. taxes, but because they were not citizens, they could not vote. Until 1996, they were entitled to social benefits like citizens, but even before the immigration bills got to the conference stage, welfare reform bills moving quickly through Congress promised to cut their eligibility drastically and to make the cuts retroactive to lawful aliens already in the United States. Specifically, the welfare bills barred a lawful alien from receiving food stamps or supplemental security income, such as disability assistance to the poor. For the first five years of an alien's residence, he could not receive needs-based benefits, such as Medicaid, and after five years, eligibility for those benefits would be up to the legislatures of their states. Even if the states allowed benefits, most sponsored family members would remain ineligible, because their sponsors' incomes would be "deemed" available to them.[22]

The immigration bills threatened to go even further and in some respects, for a change, the Senate bill was more restrictive. The provisions of the Senate bill deeming sponsors' income as available to legal immigrants would have made such people ineligible for nearly all needs-based benefits (including programs for treating communicable diseases), but the House bill exempted emergency Medicaid, immunizations, emergency disaster relief, Head Start, family violence services and, for future applicants, student loans. Under the Senate bill, the government could sue sponsors for not supporting the aliens for whom they had promised to provide. And although lawful immigrants could use certain government benefits during their first years in the United States, their availment would render them deportable. The House immigration bill rendered an alien deportable only if he used more than twelve months of aid to families with dependent children, food stamps, Medicaid, or state welfare benefits within seven years. The Senate bill shortened the seven-year period to five years and expanded the list to virtually all low-income programs. However, under the Senate bill, an immigrant's excessive use of a welfare program would be forgiven after five years, while the House bill rendered the alien deportable forever, and barred such a person from ever becoming a citizen.[23]

The publicity surrounding the Gallegly amendment and the welfare restrictions was instigated, in part, by our colleagues from other parts of the nonprofit advocacy community, such as the National Immigration Law Center. We in the contingent concerned with refugees wished them well, of course, but we had to intensify the pressure on our own issues to keep them in the limelight. Following the model that had worked for us before, we wrote op-ed pieces, but now that only a few key members of Congress held all the cards, we targeted particular districts and states. Some of them were not accepted for publication, but the rate of acceptance was high enough to make the effort worthwhile.[24] Alan Keller, the doctor who directed the torture victims' clinic in New York, published a column in the *Salt Lake Tribune,* in Hatch's home state of Utah, describing the difficulty that his patients would have had trying to persuade airport inspectors that they were genuine refugees. He praised Hatch for his vote for the Leahy amendment and noted the "pivotal role" he would play in the Conference Committee.[25] To try to educate Lamar Smith, who listed himself in the *Congressional Directory* as a Christian Scientist, I wrote an article for the *Christian Science Monitor* on the inadequacy of a six-month deadline.[26] Trying to get McCollum's attention, I wrote a piece for the *Miami Herald,* arguing that if he would accept the Senate's refugee provisions, "people who flee communist and other totalitarian regimes or who face death for practicing their religions will have a much better chance to begin new lives in freedom."[27] (I did get McCollum's attention, but instead of changing his mind, he wrote a letter to the *Herald* saying that under his law every "asylum applicant" would have the opportunity to talk to a trained asylum officer, not a "low level" immigration officer as I'd claimed.[28] The *Herald* did not print my reply.) Of course we faxed reprints of all the news stories, columns, and editorials to each of the conferees.

All of our lobbying and press efforts had an air of unreality, however. The legislative process had become secretive. No one seemed to know who the House conferees would be, whether even the House Republicans other than Smith and McCollum would have any influence over the bill, when the formal conference would take place, or what was going on in the informal negotiations among the Republicans who were meeting. To its surprise, the Clinton administration, like the non-governmental advocates, was largely excluded from the decision-making process. Officials tried to compensate by visiting members that they thought would be conferees and talking about provisions that they guessed might be on the table.[29]

In addition, day by day the Gallegly amendment was becoming the only immigration story. Forty-seven senators, including five Republicans, wrote a letter to Dole opposing the Gallegly amendment; this large number of signatories signaled that a filibuster on the issue would succeed, preventing passage of any bill.[30] Hyde and Hatch let it be known that, despite Dole's support for the amendment, they would try to modify or kill it.[31] House Majority Leader Richard Armey predicted that the amendment would survive.[32] The two Republican senators from Texas wrote Hatch that "permitting any child to grow up in the United States idle and illiterate is an unacceptable national policy,"[33] provoking Speaker Gingrich to reply the following day that "every state should have the right to decide whether its limited budget should be spent to provide benefits to illegal aliens."[34] The press settled in to watch what promised to be an entertaining power struggle within the Republican Party.

Despite their noisy public disagreement about Gallegly, behind the scenes the Republicans were quietly resolving nearly all the other differences between the House and Senate bills. We advocates heard increasingly concerned reports from staff members that only Hatch and his staffers were arguing for the Senate's more tolerant outcomes on asylum deadlines and summary exclusion. If the Republicans ever resolved their Gallegly impasse, there would be tremendous pressure on Hatch, from all or nearly all of the other Republican conferees, to concede on the refugee issues. He needed an ally.

The most promising candidate was still Arlen Specter. The advocacy community did everything it could to educate him, but with little success. When he met with the Philadelphia chapter of the American Jewish Committee, he was asked about his vote against the Leahy amendment, but he answered the question in a muddled way, as if he'd thought that if he had voted for the amendment he would have toughened the anti-terrorism bill's restrictions on civil liberties. He declined to meet personally with refugee advocates. He wouldn't even meet with INS officials.[35] The advocates lobbied friends of Specter who had known him for years, and although they said they'd try to persuade him, there was no signal that anyone was getting through. His staff members attended many of the meetings of the Republicans hammering out the final bill, but having no instructions from their senator, they remained mute on the refugee issues.

Congress' impending mid-summer recess for the two parties' national nominating conventions seemed to bring everything to a head in late July. Immigration advocates had hoped that the internal Republican split over the Gallegly amendment would delay the conference report until just before Congress adjourned for the year, giving liberal senators and the president more leverage by threatening a filibuster or a veto. But Specter brokered what he called a "compromise" between Gallegly and at least some of the Senate opponents of Gallegly.[36] Children of newly arriving unauthorized aliens could be barred from attending school. Children currently in elementary schools could remain enrolled through sixth grade, but upon reaching seventh grade, they would have to pay tuition in excess of five thousand dollars per year. Critics immediately pointed out that parents unable to pay the money would have to withdraw their children from school, and this act would flag them for deportation.[37]

Some aspects of the Republicans' resolution of the refugee issues were also leaked, though no legislative language had emerged. Lacking support from any other Republican, Hatch had agreed to accept most of the more stringent features of the House bill's system of summary exclusion, including the new name for the procedure, "expedited removal." That procedure would be imposed on all aliens arriving without proper documents, as the House bill had provided. Hatch had, however, salvaged a modicum of appellate process from the Leahy amendment. According to the *New York Times,* an alien who was found by an asylum officer to lack "credible fear" could get a "hearing" before an immigration judge, with a "reasonable time" to prepare for it.[38] Pistone soon learned, however, that an alien would have only seven days to prepare. She also learned that the Republican conferees had decided to impose a deadline on applications by affirmative as well as defensive asylum applicants, but the House had again agreed to increase the time limit, this time from six months to a year.[39] While the increase in the period in which applications could be filed was welcome, it was more than offset by the conferees' decision to apply the deadline to affirmative cases. Furthermore, the conferees had refused to accept either the Senate's broad "good cause" exception or the specific examples that DeWine had persuaded Simpson to include in his manager's amendment. Instead, the conferees included exceptions only for "changed circumstances" materially affecting asylum eligibility or "extraordinary circumstances" relating to the applicant's delay.

To Pistone, these resolutions were "pretty terrible news,"[40] preserving more of the House bill than what we'd won in the Senate. But they were still tentative;

the entire agreement could later unravel if it were not enacted in the week before Congress took its August recess. Trent Lott had been elected Senate majority leader after Dole resigned from the Senate on June 6 to spend the fall running for president.[41] Lott wanted to drive the report quickly through his body, but Representative Barney Frank stopped the bill in the House. The House Republican leadership had earlier promised him that Democrats would have a chance at least to talk about the bill before it was passed, and he particularly wanted discussion of the "provisions affecting refugees and asylum seekers."[42] This was impossible on the Republicans' schedule, as the Republicans' new bill hadn't even yet been printed. And just as Congress recessed, the president made the Republicans' political equation still more complicated by promising to veto any bill that included either the original Gallegly provision or the Specter compromise.[43]

When Congress returned from the party conventions after Labor Day, it had less than a month in which to complete its work before adjourning to run for election. Gallegly had said that "all deals were off" if Congress recessed in July without passing the bill, and although he later reconsidered, Specter now distanced himself from the package. Pistone and others continued to try to persuade members to liberalize the refugee provisions (or even to find out exactly what they said), but they had little success, and it began to appear that the Republicans' outcome could be improved only by self-destruction of the entire bill. This might still happen if the Republicans kept the Gallegly amendment in the bill, provoking a filibuster or veto.

Indeed, now that the president had promised a veto, some activists began hoping privately that the Gallegly amendment would remain in the legislation, but all of them continued to lobby vigorously for its removal.[44] They recognized that the Gallegly amendment was a "drag on the entire immigration bill,"[45] and that a presidential veto over the issue offered one of the few strands of hope for defeating the bill altogether. But having urged the president to threaten a veto, they didn't dare risk a strategy of tepid or mere pro forma opposition. "The president was on a limb and he had to feel confident that [the immigration community] would back him up," said one advocate. "If we hadn't folowed through on our promise to do so, it would have been a long-term disaster for us. And he could always have backed down from his veto threat."[46] The advocates also opened a new front, urging Clinton to threaten to veto the bill not only because of the Gallegly amendment, but also because of restrictions on welfare benefits for legal aliens.[47]

In mid-September, the House leadership finally named its conferees, and Lamar Smith simultaneously released the Republicans' three-hundred-page bill. The composition of the House delegation reflected both the Republicans' dominance of the process[48] and the strong influence that members from three states exert over immigration law. Sixty-four percent of the House Republican conferees, and 63 percent of all of the House conferees, were from California, Texas, or Florida.[49] The bill included Specter's version of the Gallegly amendment, although rumors persisted that the Republican leadership was still debating whether to drop it (to pass a bill) or keep it (so that Dole could deny Clinton credit for signing the bill and could run for election in California against his veto).[50] Simpson and Smith met with Scott Reed, Dole's campaign manager, to plead that they be allowed to drop Gallegly. Reed refused.[51] But Dole's campaign wasn't yet competitive in the polls, slowly diminishing his influence. Furthermore, half of the California Republican candidates for Congress who were in tight races preferred having a bill rather than a veto.[52] Simpson, frustrated, went public, accusing Dole's advisors in a floor speech of the type of cynicism of which Dole accused Clinton.[53] Simpson termed Dole's pro-Gallegly, anti-legislative strategy as "Machiavelliean mumbo jumbo."[54]

The Democrats who had been shut out of the conference process were even more frustrated than Simpson. They tried once again to suggest comments on what was now the draft of the final bill, but they were again rebuffed. "We were told that we had to wait to talk to them until they had a final product," said the legislative assistant of a Democrat on the Judiciary Committee. "But by the time they did, it was [supposedly] such a delicate compromise that we were told we couldn't touch it and there could only be an up or down vote."

By this time, the Gallegly amendment had attracted so much attention that all other issues were lost in the noise. Senator Feinstein announced that if the Gallegly amendment were removed, she would support the bill "as is." A *New York Times* story about the politics of the bill relegated Democrats' objections to all of the other provisions, including the refugee sections, to the last of twenty paragraphs.[55] Kennedy and Leahy held a press conference to talk about the many issues on which they disagreed with the Republicans, but their protest received scant press coverage.[56]

The bill was very harsh. By choosing the most, rather than the least, restrictive provisions from the House and Senate bills, the Republicans had crafted a final bill that was "even more extreme than House or Senate versions."[57]

With but a week to go until Congress adjourned, the Republican leadership could wait no longer to resolve the Gallegly issue. It decided to jettison the amendment altogether,[58] allowing Dole only the face-saving appearance of having made the call himself.[59] Then they quickly scheduled the pro forma Conference Committee meeting. Although the session was supposedly "public," they arranged for it to be held in Room H-137 of the Capitol, a room barely large enough to hold the conferees, their staff members, and a few reporters. The executive associate commissioner of immigration was allowed to be present on behalf of the INS, but only for fifteen minutes.[60] Along with dozens of other advocates, I stood on line in the hallway, hoping for a chance to observe the meeting, but only one member of the public was admitted to the room. The Conference Committee meeting wasn't broadcast on C-SPAN or even the Capitol's closed-circuit TV system. All we knew at the time was that whatever was happening inside wasn't pleasant; through the door, Senator Kennedy could be heard screaming at the Republicans.

We soon learned why. The Democrats had arrived in the room with their proposed amendments. Leahy had brought with him an amendment to apply the one-year deadline only to affirmative applicants, and another to restore most of the Senate-passed expedited removal protections.[61] The Democrats did not expect to prevail, because the Republicans including Hatch had committed themselves to support the Republican bill. But when they took their seats, the Democratic conferees were presented with a new version of the bill. The Gallegly amendment had been removed, but that wasn't the only change in the bill that had been released several days earlier. The Republicans had put twenty other new changes on the Democrats' chairs.[62] Smith announced that "to save time," only those Republican amendments would be in order; the Democrats would not be allowed even to offer their amendments for consideration.[63] Leahy protested about his "summary exclusion" from the real negotiations on the bill.[64] "Silly me," quipped Barney Frank, "I though we were legislating."[65] Even John Bryant called the bill an outrage.[66] But there was nothing the Democrats could do. Every Republican signed the conference report, as did Senator Feinstein, while all of the other Democrats refused.[67]

Senator Kennedy and Minority Leader Tom Daschle hoped that a Senate filibuster against the conference report could yet prompt changes or kill the legislation, and Daschle bravely announced that "it's either going to be done our way or it won't be done at all."[68] But with many Democrats eager to show that they were taking a tough stand against illegal immigration in an election year, Kennedy wasn't sure that he could find enough Democrats to sustain a filibuster, particularly if Lott held Congress in session until a bill passed.[69]

The House passed the bill the next day.[70] We advocates spent that day calling Senate offices to find out who would join Kennedy in a filibuster, or at least speak out against the bill to demonstrate that a presidential veto would be sustained.[71] But we weren't getting many takers. The bill seemed headed for Senate passage the following day. Along with many other advocates, I was unaware that enactment of the law was in fact not assured, and that one last drama was being played out quietly behind closed doors.

# 11

# The President

## *September 25–28, 1996*

Nobody knew what cards were underneath.

> —Joshua Bernstein, senior policy analyst,
> National Immigration Law Center[1]

Bill Clinton had campaigned for president in 1992 promising to "end welfare as we know it."[2] In the summer of 1996, his first term was coming to a close. Not only were the welfare laws he had criticized still in place, but he had twice vetoed welfare reform bills that Congress had passed. He had been able to justify those vetoes, despite his campaign rhetoric and his virtual silence about what kind of welfare reform he wanted Congress to pass, because on both occasions, Congress included in the bills severe cutbacks in food stamps and aid for disabled children. In late spring, 1996, it looked as though the Republicans running Congress would give Clinton still another bill he could veto easily, a bill that included cutbacks in the immensely popular Medicaid program. But Clinton wanted to sign a welfare bill, and congressional leaders wanted to show that they could compromise enough to pass an important law, even though Senator Daniel Patrick Moynihan described the impact on children of this particular statute as "the most brutal act of social policy since Reconstruction."[3] Congress eliminated the Medicaid cuts, and in "the most sweeping reversal of domestic social policy since the New Deal,"[4] Clinton signed the bill.[5]

Congress saved Medicaid but savaged legal immigrants. The bill was intended both to create work incentives for some recipients of government benefits and to save money; in fact, twenty-two billion dollars, 40 percent of the money that the bill was expected to save in its first six years, represented cutbacks in benefits for legal immigrants.[6] The bill denied food stamps, federal disability benefits, and many other types of welfare to most legal immigrants, including elderly and disabled immigrants who had come to the United States many years before the law was passed. Most of them would be cut off within months of the bill's enactment. Officials estimated that eight hundred thousand elderly and disabled legal immigrants would soon lose Supplemental Security Income benefits and would, as a result, be "thrown out of their homes or out of nursing homes ... that are no longer reimbursed for their care."[7] A million legal immigrants would lose the food stamps they needed for daily nutrition.[8]

The president was aware of the bill's anti-immigrant provisions. Even as he signed the bill, he acknowledged "that the congressional leadership insisted on cuts in programs for legal immigrants that are far too deep."[9] In separate statements, he added that "legal immigrants and their children ... should not be penalized if they become disabled and require medical assistance through no fault of their own,"[10] and that "I am convinced this [set of provisions] would never have passed alone [without the accompanying sections requiring welfare recipients to work] and I am convinced when we send legislation to Congress to correct it, it will be corrected."[11]

Clinton's core Democratic supporters were not mollified by a vague promise to correct a bad law at some later time. Clinton was severely chastised by the press and by members of his own party. The *Washington Post* editorialized that "only the terminally gullible" could believe that his decision to sign the bill had anything to do with principle; it was about "political expediency and opportunism" and particularly unbecoming a president who was ahead of his electoral opponent by twenty points in the polls.[12] The National Organization for Women held a protest rally in front of the White House,[13] former governor Mario Cuomo and the Reverend Jesse Jackson criticized the president in speeches at his own nominating convention,[14] and a senior welfare official of the Department of Health and Human Services resigned in protest.[15]

Between early August, when the president announced that he would sign the welfare bill, and mid-September, when Republicans finally released the conference report on the immigration bill, criticism of the president mounted. Democratic political strategists began to worry that if Clinton agreed to an immigration bill containing still another strike against recent legal immigrants, some of his liberal core supporters would not bother to vote on election day.[16] Immigrant advocacy organizations began to see an opportunity either to roll back the welfare cutbacks when the immigration bill was passed, or to kill the immigration bill because its title on welfare benefits made matters even worse.

Late in August, the National Immigration Forum asked its supporters to find well-known Americans "that may be readily recognized as potential Clinton supporters" to sign a letter urging that he veto the immigration bill "if it is not changed to correct the harm legal immigrants will undoubtedly suffer" as a result of the welfare bill.[17] In fact when the Republicans unveiled the conference report a month later, it was evident that, far from reducing the pain that the new welfare law would cause, the immigration bill included several additional cutbacks for immigrants. The bill required Americans who wanted to sponsor members of their family to immigrate into the United States to earn at least twice the federal poverty level (or 140 percent if the immigrant were the sponsor's spouse or minor child), a provision that "would for the first time in American history make class a significant feature in determining who gets to immigrate to the United States."[18] The National Immigration Forum concluded that more than a third of U.S. citizens who sponsored their minor children in 1994 would have been barred from doing so under the new law.[19] The bill approved by the Conference Committee decreed deportation for legal immigrants who evaded its ban on using food stamps or other public services. It also prevented such persons from becoming citizens of the United States. And it barred citizenship for legal immigrants whose sponsors had unpaid bills.[20]

The president had threatened to veto the immigration bill if it included the Gallegly amendment, but he had never suggested that he would veto the bill for any other reason. His silence on other issues was so profound that Senator Tom Daschle, the Democratic Minority Leader, had stated publicly that he believed that Clinton would sign the bill if the Gallegly provision were dropped.[21]

Smith and Simpson expected that even after dropping the Gallegly amendment, they might have to muster sixty votes to force cloture of a Senate filibuster against the conference report. But because the president had been silent on other issues, they doubted that they would also meet with resistance from the White House.

While the Republicans were pushing their bill through the hastily convened Conference Committee and trying to fend of Democratic criticism of the closed conference process, groups that advocated on behalf of legal immigrants became more active than ever before. They worked hard to persuade White House staff members to object to Title V, which contained the provisions of the bill affecting sponsorship of and benefits for legal immigrants.

The leader of this group of advocacy organizations was Joshua Bernstein, senior policy analyst at the Washington office of the National Immigration Law Center. The Center is based in Los Angeles, where it maintains a staff of five lawyers who provide advice and litigation assistance to legal aid agencies, pro bono lawyers, and community groups working for immigrants. But it also had two Washington policy experts, including Bernstein, who worked on legislation and administrative advocacy.[22]

In July, when the welfare bill was passed, "there had been a battle within the administration between the political people, who said Clinton had to sign the bill, and the policy people, who would have preferred a third veto," Bernstein later recalled. "But by the middle of September, after the press criticism of the cutbacks for immigrants, restricting immigration had become a political loser. The White House staff could hear us when we said that the immigration bill would only make things worse, and at that point, the political and policy people started pushing in the same direction, against any further restrictions."[23]

Bernstein wrote a memorandum describing the many ways in which Title V would hurt legal immigrants. He and his colleagues circulated it widely, making certain that it reached the press as well as the White House staff. To attract even more attention, Senators Kennedy, Leahy, and Simon joined several labor unions and religious organizations in a press conference at which they called on the president to veto the bill despite the removal of the Gallegly amendment.[24] As the nation's newspapers focused editorial criticism on Title V,[25] White House officials offered House Speaker Newt Gingrich and Senate Majority Leader Trent Lott a simple deal: remove Title V from the bill, and the president would sign it. There was a procedural problem, because by this time, September was nearly over. The bill had already been passed by the House 305–123,[26] it was awaiting action by the Senate, and members of Congress were eager to end the session and go home to run for re-election. It would have been difficult, and perhaps too time-consuming, to get both Houses to agree to recommit the bill to the Conference Committee to take out Title V. However, Congress had not yet passed the omnibus appropriation bill for fiscal year 1997, and because the 1996 appropriation would expire on September 30, the appropriation bill had to be enacted before Congress could adjourn. On Thursday, September 26, White House legislative liaison John Hilley therefore proposed that Congress let the immigration bill die, but make all of its provisions, except Title V, a rider to the appropriation bill, which the president would sign. Gingrich and Lott were not pleased to hear about eleventh-hour objections from the White House even after they had agreed to remove the provision that had seemed to be the sticking point. "Gallegly had been used as a mask to cover the opposition of the administration to any real illegal immigration reform legislation," Lott said.[27] But they quickly agreed in principle to this arrangement.[28]

The Republican leaders were not themselves experts on immigration law or on the details of the 1996 legislation. They had to rely on Smith and Simpson to turn the agreement in principle into actual changes to the bill. Neither Smith nor Simpson was willing to delete all of Title V, and as afternoon turned to evening, they learned that many House Republicans also objected to their leaders' willingness to delete the Title.[29] One House Republican source complained that Gingrich "didn't tell anyone [about his deal with the White House] so you couldn't object.... In Gingrich's mind, it was his decision alone and that's all that mattered—that you could cave entirely and give away the candy store and the entire shopping mall and just announce that."[30]

At 9:30 Thursday evening, Smith and Simpson began negotiating with Senator Kennedy and Representative Howard Berman, a prominent Democratic opponent of the bill and a member of Smith's Immigration Subcommittee.[31] The Republicans were determined to save as much as possible of Title V, notwithstanding the arrangement to which Gingrich and Lott had agreed. Smith began by making it clear that the congressional leaders had directed him to discuss Title V, but that no other issues, such as expedited removal procedures, were open for negotiation. At about 11:00 P.M., Smith suggested that all staff members, including those from his own staff and the White House staff, be excluded from the room, and that the talks include only senators and representatives. Perhaps out of consideration for their staff members, the Democrats agreed to the suggestion, much to those staff members' dismay.[32]

As the night progressed, "all four legislators had to negotiate in the dark," Bernstein recalled. "Berman and Kennedy didn't know how much leverage they had, because the White House staff had been excluded from the room. Smith and Simpson didn't know how much Gingrich would back them up. Nobody knew what cards were underneath."

Although nobody was certain about political backing, Smith knew the intricacies of the bill better than anyone else, particularly because the Conference Committee had agreed to use the House bill, which he and Cordia Strom had drafted, as the basic structure of the legislation. Smith continued what a Republican source termed his "salvage operation ... to preserve as much of Title V as we can."[33] By 1:00 A.M., he and Simpson had persuaded Berman and Kennedy to accept a deal that retained Title V, but "sliced away limited portions of it."[34]

On Friday morning, the advocacy organizations learned the shape of the deal. Some of them thought that it was the best that could be achieved, and Representative Berman agreed with that opinion. Others were horrified; they thought that the agreement between the White House, Gingrich, and Lott had driven a stake through Title V, which was now rising from its grave. The believed that the Democratic negotiators should have been able to win more concessions.[35]

At this point, the deal was still tentative, because the White House negotiators had been excluded from the talks and hadn't yet blessed the result, though Berman and Kennedy had intimated that since they themselves were on board, White House agreement was likely. To hedge against a breakdown in the agreement, however, Lott filed a cloture petition in the Senate. If no final agreement was reached, there would be a vote at 2:00 Monday afternoon to stop any filibuster against the immigration bill.[36]

If they were going to have any influence at all, the advocates would have to act quickly. There wasn't time for a large meeting, so they conferred in small groups and by telephone. What worried them most about asking the White House to kill the deal was the possibility that the Republicans would then just close debate and pass the bill that the Conference Committee had approved, with all of its Title V provisions, even those that Berman and Kennedy had been able to delete. Clinton might then retreat and sign the bill rather than facing an electorate, especially in California, angry about the illegal immigration that several other titles of the bill attempted to address.

On the other hand, the White House had a lot of leverage, too, even if the Republicans could find sixty votes for cloture in the Senate. So long as Congress was in session, the Republican freshman representatives elected in 1994 could not go home to campaign, and their Democratic challengers were busily attacking them in their home districts. GOP leaders believed that their chance of continuing to control the House diminished with each day that members were unable to campaign. And even after the cloture vote that could not be held sooner than the afternoon of September 30, Democrats would be entitled to debate for thirty hours more, pushing a vote on the immigration bill over until the following Wednesday.[37] Furthermore, Democrats could also slow down the fiscal year appropriation, forcing Republicans to stay in town to pass short extensions of the budget or, if they refused to do that, to shut down the government, a tactic that had backfired on them when they'd tried it late in 1995. Because Republicans had taken so long to resolve their internal disagreement over the Gallegly amendment, the immigration bill had reached the Senate floor in the last days of the session, a time when opponents of any measure have special procedural opportunities that give them leverage over its content.

Meanwhile, Senator Lott did all he could to wed the White House to the deal that had been cooked up during the night. "I have the impression from Senator Simpson that he and Senator Kennedy and Congressman Berman and Congressman Smith ... feel that they have some modifications of Title V that are significant and they all can live with," he told the press. "You know, if it's a Kennedy-Berman-Simpson bill, looks like maybe we could go with that ... if everybody will just say, yes, we accept this."[38]

By the middle of the afternoon, Berman himself was beginning to change his mind about the deal. Cordia Strom had spent the morning reducing the night's agreement to statutory language, and a close reading of the text persuaded him that it was "not reflective of the talks."[39] In addition, Janet Murguia, a senior White House legislative advisor, urged him to back away from the agreement because, in the view of the White House staff, it conflicted with the deal the White House believed it had made with Gingrich and Lott to delete all of the restrictions in Title V. A Democratic source later explained that the negotiations involving Berman and Smith had occurred "in a vacuum," with at least some of the negotiators unaware "of what was going on between the White House and Lott."[40]

Still, Berman agonized, worried both because the Republicans might have the firepower to pass the conference bill and because he might have led Smith to believe that they had an agreement. Murguia urged him to call Smith and tell him that because of the discrepancies between the text and his understanding of the agreement, and White House objections, the deal was off. Still, Berman hesitated; he didn't see how he could back out. "Dammit," she said, "just pick up the phone right now and tell him the deal is off." And he did.[41]

Meanwhile, many of us who had been advocating for asylum-seekers knew nothing of these Title V negotiations. We knew only that Senator Kennedy was organizing a filibuster, which offered a slim chance of killing the whole immigration bill, particularly if things got stretched out a few days longer and Congress couldn't resist the pressure to go home. A major immigration bill had died just that way in the final days of the legislative session before the 1984 election.[42] The death of the bill would leave in place the harsh expedited removal provisions of the anti-terrorism bill (which unlike the immigration bill applied those provisions to thousands of unauthorized aliens who had been living in the United States for many years). But other provisions of the immigration bill seemed so bad that many immigration advocates would have liked to let it die, and would have preferred to try to repeal parts of the anti-terrorism law in the next congress, after the heat of the presidential election had died down.

Like many others, I was glued to my telephone, calling staff members to find out how many senators would join Kennedy, if necessary, to vote against cloture. If we couldn't find forty-one senators to filibuster, our minimum objective was to locate thirty-four senators who would vote to uphold a presidential veto. We were certain that the president would not veto the bill unless he were sure that his veto would stick. But despite calls, e-mails, and faxes to our supporters around the country and on Capitol Hill, we were having trouble finding even thirty-four senators who would commit to opposing the bill. Many still seemed undecided, waiting for signals from the White House.

While we were making our calls, C-SPAN was bringing us (and the staffers we were calling) live coverage from the Senate floor. Suddenly, Simpson entered the Senate chamber, and he was angry. "Let me tell you what happened yesterday," he told his colleagues. "Get it down." He said that he had sat down with Smith, Berman, and Kennedy to "give a little" on Title V, but nobody had ever agreed to "give up Title V—not Orrin Hatch, the chairman, not Senator Kyl, not Senator Feinstein." (Simpson did not mention his majority leader). He'd had to negotiate, he said, because Clinton had unfairly changed the terms of debate. Republicans had agreed to delete the Gallegly amendment, to which the White House had objected, but "within the last day or so" the president had "moved the goal posts.... I have never seen anything like it in 31 years of legislating.... He got flak and he wants to change some of it. But he isn't going to do it on this watch."[43]

Then he told the senators what he planned to do. "Monday at 2 o'clock ... cloture will carry.... After the hours of postcloture debate are over, we will do that on through the night, we will vote [and send the bill that was approved by the Conference to] the President's desk.... It was not crafted by people who ... do something different than they said they would do before. And I am sick of it."[44] A few minutes later, on the House side, Majority Leader Richard Armey revealed that "the White House has indicated that they are not willing to accept an agreement reached last night" by the four negotiators.[45] Berman replied that "before we all get too high and mighty about what is happening, remember the Republican Conference Committee, where no one was allowed to offer an amendment, where the bipartisan relationships ... were totally violated, where months went by without a Conference Committee."[46]

I was delighted to learn that there had been negotiations, and that they had broken down. Suddenly, the possibility of filibusters and vetoes had new vitality. Briefly, the advocacy community was re-energized in its efforts to stop the bill.

Across town, Joshua Bernstein and his allies, who were willing to accept an immigration bill if Title V could be removed, despaired. "When Simpson made his speech, I thought we'd blown it," he recalled. "I thought we'd get the bill as passed by the Conference."[47] Another benefits advocate told me, "I began to worry that after having been awake for two days straight, I'd made a terrible misjudgment [by urging Berman to back away from the deal] and that I'd be responsible for the greatest possible loss in benefits for immigrants. I went home dejected."

What none of the advocates knew, however, was that despite Simpson's bluster, the Republicans had run out of time. It was already late in the day on Friday, September 27. Kennedy didn't have the votes to prevent cloture on Monday, but a post-cloture debate on the immigration bill would tie up the Senate past Monday evening, when the fiscal year would end and the government would have to shut down. Clinton also threatened to let the government shut down for lack of funds, and to blame the Republicans, unless Title V was removed.[48] "Republicans feared that they would take most of the blame," as they had a year earlier.[49]

The Republican leadership therefore opened a second night of negotiations, this time between Gingrich, Lott, the chairmen of the congressional Appropriations Committees, and the White House staff; Smith and Simpson did not arrive until the negotiation had nearly ended at 4:30 A.M. on Saturday.[50] In their absence, nearly all the restrictions in Title V disappeared from the bill. The negotiators eliminated the section blocking naturalization of immigrants who used public benefits and providing for their deportation, the section denying AIDS treatment to illegal immigrants, and the section that would have increased the period of time that sponsors, rather than the public, would be responsible for needy legal immigrants. It reduced from 140 percent to 125 percent of the poverty level the income required to sponsor a minor child. It cut a provision that would have denied unemployment compensation to refugees. It also reprieved immigrants who under the new welfare law were due to lose food stamps within days; under the amended immigration bill, they could remain as beneficiaries of the program until at least April 1997.[51]

Early Saturday morning, Joshua Bernstein and his allies gathered at the office of the American Civil Liberties Union to read the final agreement. "We had mixed feelings," he recalled. "Within a few days we'd gone from no deal to a bad deal, then no deal again, and then we'd removed all these terrible provisions, a huge victory. But at the same time, we knew how harmful the rest of the bill was. We knew that advocates who had worked on other parts of the bill would be disappointed that the last hope of derailing the bill altogether had just ended. How you felt about the ending depended on the issue on which you had worked."[52]

Bernstein was exactly right. As I drove my son home from a soccer game that morning, I heard on the radio that the legislative struggle was over. I felt as though I'd been punched in the stomach. The deadline for asylum-seekers and the expedited removal procedures for aliens without proper papers would now enter into law. But refugee advocates had known since early August that this ending, while not inevitable, was likely. As a result, the next phase of battle had already begun.

*Part III*

# Parting Shots

# 12

# The Regulations
## *1997-1999*

Making a decision in Washington usually kicks off the campaign to reverse it.
—Paul C. Warnke, former director,
U.S. Arms Control and Disarmament Agency[1]

From early August 1996, when Pistone learned how the Republicans were planning to craft the refugee provisions of the conference report, until mid-September, when the report was published, we could describe the coming train wreck, but we couldn't yet see the train. By late September, when Smith and Hatch refused to allow Democrats even to offer amendments at the Conference Committee meeting, we could count the boxcars and hear the whistle. Our attempt to stop the train by asking Senators to filibuster the bill was aborted by the successful last-minute White House negotiations that ameliorated the social welfare provisions but did nothing for refugees.

We knew, however, that after the bill was passed, another struggle would begin. The INS would have to write extensive regulations to implement the new law, and these regulations would fill in many of the details where Congress had painted with a broad brush. When it wrote the regulations, the INS might be influenced by any interpretations that the new law's sponsors had articulated during congressional consideration of the bill. And because the Senate would still have to vote on the conference report (or, more accurately, on the omnibus budget resolution embodying the conference report), there would be one more opportunity for senatorial speeches.

Individuals and organizations that lobby for legislation often ask their congressional supporters to make speeches or engage in colloquys (dialogues) to record formally the legislators' contemporaneous interpretations of a bill that is likely to pass. Sometimes they submit proposals for the legislators to consider. In the closing days of the Congress, Pistone and I sent Senator Hatch such a proposal. Hatch seemed like the right person to ask, because he'd supported the Senate versions of both asylum-related issues, and he spoke authoritatively as a Republican co-chair of the Conference Committee that had written the final compromise.

193

Hatch didn't accept all of our suggestions, because he didn't want to trigger a counter-colloquy by senators whose interpretation of the new law might be less generous than his own. But he and Senator Abraham were willing to try to put a decent face on some bad provisions in the law.

On September 30, shortly before the Senate voted on the appropriation bill that incorporated the new immigration law, Abraham took the floor to "ask the Chairman of the Judiciary Committee a few questions to clarify the changes made in the asylum provisions." He noted the exceptions to the one-year deadline. "Would the Chairman explain the meaning of these exceptions?" he asked.

Hatch was eager to oblige his colleague. The exceptions for changed circumstances and extraordinary circumstances, he said, were "intended to provide adequate protections to those with legitimate claims of asylum." Trying to save as much as possible from the manager's amendment that DeWine had extracted from Simpson, he added, "I expect that circumstances covered by the Senate's good cause exception will likely be covered by either the changed circumstances exception or the extraordinary circumstances exception contained in the conference report language."

Abraham asked him to elaborate on the changed circumstances exception. That provision, Hatch explained, "will deal with situations like those in which the situation in the alien's home country may have changed, the applicant obtains more information about likely retribution he or she might face if the applicant returned home, and other situations that Congress may not be able to anticipate at this time."

Abraham, playing his part as Hatch's straight man for this occasion, asked him about the other exception. "Extraordinary circumstances," Hatch explained, "could include, for instance, physical or mental disability, unsuccessful efforts to seek asylum that failed due to technical defects or errors for which the alien was not responsible, and other extenuating circumstances."[2]

In a separate floor speech, Hatch elaborated further on his interpretation. The changed circumstances exception, he said, would apply "where the applicant may have become aware through reports from home or the news media just how dangerous it would be for the alien to return home." He also said more about the meaning of the "credible fear" standard that the INS should apply during expedited removal. "The Senate bill," Hatch recalled, had provided for a determination of whether the asylum claim was "manifestly unfounded," while the House would have imposed "a 'significant possibility' standard coupled with an inquiry into whether there was a substantial likelihood that the alien's statements were true. The conference report struck a compromise by rejecting the higher standard of credibility included in the House bill." The new standard, he said, is intended to be a "low screening standard for admission into the usual full asylum process."[3]

These statements during the final hours of congressional consideration of the bill marked the end of the congressional battle and the beginning of the struggle to influence administrative implementation of the law. Within days after the bill passed, Pistone and I surveyed the damage, calculated what we might try to recoup through the administrative process, and began to plan a new campaign.

With respect to the deadline, Congress had dealt refugees a severe blow by applying a one-year limit to people applying for asylum affirmatively as well as to those who had been apprehended. But Congress had also left several issues unresolved. First, for affirmative applicants who filed after the deadline, what level of INS official would apply and interpret the exceptions? Approximately two-thirds of the people who apply affirmatively do so on their own (*pro se*), without professional representation.[4] About a third of the *pro se* applicants leave blank one or more questions on the application form, such as those asking their race and religion, the place they entered the United States, or their immigration status when they entered. When these questions go unanswered, clerks in the INS's regional "Service Centers" reject the applications summarily and return them, unfiled, to the applicants.[5] We worried that the same fate would await applicants who filed after a year; they would never even see a trained asylum officer who could elicit an explanation that would qualify under one of the statutory exceptions. In addition, the clerks' returns of the incomplete applications could cause the applicants to miss the new deadline.

Second, even if the INS were to agree that asylum officers rather than clerks would evaluate claims of exception, would the applicants have to make those claims in writing, or could they explain their situations orally? The resolution of this question could make a huge difference for applicants who did not write English well, or whose justifications involved complex facts or close interpretations of the exceptions. Even sophisticated applicants might not be able to explain their tardiness adequately until an official described to them what the INS meant when it asked them about changed or extraordinary circumstances.

Third, to what extent might the INS be willing to import into its regulations some of the exceptions that DeWine had been able to write into the Senate version of the bill? An explicit statement of the types of circumstances that would qualify as exceptions would enable asylum officers to feel themselves on safe ground (that is, safe from criticism by superiors or by Congress) when they allowed late-filing applicants to win asylum. Such regulations would also put applicants at less risk of losing asylum as a result of the whim or crabbed interpretation of a particular INS official. On the other hand, getting the INS to list particular types of exceptional circumstances was risky. Some asylum officers or immigration judges might think that any type of circumstance that wasn't on the list should not qualify for exceptional treatment. This risk could be minimized if the INS were willing to state that the list was not exclusive. But if we persuaded the INS to write such a list and the agency failed to include a nonexclusivity statement, at least some refugees might be worse off than if no list were written at all. For this reason, some of the advocates with whom we'd been working advised us not to urge the INS to write a regulatory list of exceptions. They considered it safer to let each asylum officer interpret the congressional language freshly in every case. Pistone and I understood their fear, but we thought that if we could persuade the INS to list exceptions, we could also persuade it to make the necessary statement of non-exclusivity. We had to gulp hard on this tactical choice, though, because we could actually do some harm.

With respect to expedited removal, even more issues were left open by the statute. The law provided that aliens who arrived at U.S. ports of entry were to be pre-screened by immigration officers to determine whether they feared persecution. This part of the law would be administered primarily by two kinds of INS inspectors. Every person who arrives from another country at a United States port of entry, such as an airport, is initially pre-screened at an immigration booth by a "primary inspector" of the INS. If this officer detects any documentary irregularities, the alien is escorted to a government office elsewhere in the airport, where a more searching examination is conducted by a "secondary inspector." Asylum-seekers constitute only a minute fraction of all arriving aliens, and even of all aliens as to whom documentary questions arise. Therefore, this "secondary inspector," who is not a human rights specialist, would have to do the pre-screening to determine which aliens arriving without proper papers expressed fear of persecution and, therefore, should be referred to asylum experts. Thousands of times a year, these relatively untrained secondary inspectors would exercise a power previously given only to highly trained immigration judges: to return people to the land from which they came. In fact, they would be exercising much more power than judges had wielded, because the consequence of being deported was no longer merely a flight home, but a prohibition on entering the United States, even as a visitor, for five years.[6] And although judicial deportations are subject to court review, Congress had foreclosed such review of secondary inspectors' deportation decisions.

The new statute addressed "credible fear" interviews—the second stage in the process—in some detail, but by contrast it said very little about how the secondary inspectors were to conduct airport screening interviews, which if imperfectly carried out could result in the return of genuine refugees to countries where they would be persecuted. How soon after a primary inspector flagged a problem would an alien have to meet with a secondary inspector? What information, if any, would aliens be given about the pre-screening process, and about their right to seek asylum, before they spoke with the secondary inspector? How would language barriers be surmounted? How could aliens be put enough at ease to discuss issues such as rape and torture with these inspectors? How would the inspectors identify refugees suffering from such severe trauma that they could not articulate their fears immediately? And in the absence of a review process, how could human rights organizations or, for that matter, even senior INS officials know that the inspectors were making life-and-death decisions competently?

For aliens not immediately deported because the secondary inspectors decided that they did, indeed, fear persecution, another set of issues arose. The statute left it to the government to determine whether the asylum officers would conduct their "credible fear" interviews at the airports, immediately after the secondary inspectors had passed the aliens along, or several days or weeks later at INS offices or detention facilities. An interval would make it much more likely that an alien could obtain professional advice and representation, even if he or she were jailed in the interim. How much information, including information about the availability of representatives, would aliens get at this stage? How would interpretation be handled at this stage of the process? What training would the asylum officers receive, particularly with regard to applying the "credible fear" test? To what extent would the INS make it possible for representatives to investigate facts and present their clients' stories to the asylum officers?

As a result of adoption of the Leahy amendment and the subsequent House-Senate compromise, the new law allowed an alien who lost in a credible fear interview to appeal, within a week, to an immigration judge. The judge could not grant asylum at this stage. But he or she could reverse the negative credible fear determination. Then the alien, like one who had received a positive credible fear determination from an asylum officer, would eventually get a full asylum hearing before an immigration judge. How meaningful would this review be? What procedural rights would the alien have? To what extent would lawyers or other representatives be able to help aliens in this "last chance" effort to avoid deportation?

We knew that the INS would try to write regulations quickly, because under the federal Administrative Procedure Act, it had to give the public a chance to comment on any proposed regulations. In order to write the proposed regulations, give the public a month to comment on them, take account of the comments, and put the new regulations into effect by April 1, 1997, when expedited removal would begin, the INS would have to finish drafting them by the end of December. The main focus of our efforts would be to stimulate official comments by members and supporters of the Committee to Preserve Asylum. But we decided that we would first launch a pre-emptive strike by publishing an article while the INS was still drafting its proposals. The article would tell the INS drafters what to do, and it would also disseminate our opinions widely, so that non-governmental organizations would be able to start writing their formal comments as soon as the INS's draft was published in the *Federal Register*. The perfect vehicle was a trade publication called *Interpreter Releases*. Unlike law reviews, it was published every week, so our article, if accepted, could be printed days after we completed it. And *Interpreter Releases* was read by most immigration practitioners and widely distributed within the INS.

We started writing within days after the statute passed Congress. A month later, we had completed the article. We argued that Service Center personnel, who had no human rights training, would be unable to evaluate justifications for late filing, and that, therefore, every apparently late affirmative application should be forwarded to an asylum officer for evaluation during an oral interview. Quoting from the Abraham-Hatch colloquy, we argued that the exception for "changed circumstances" should apply, not only to cases in which conditions had actually changed in the applicant's country, but also to situations in which the refugee received fresh information about deteriorations in human rights that had actually occurred before the deadline expired.

Hatch's statement to the effect that the exceptions in the final bill encompassed "most" of the circumstances that had been spelled out by DeWine's list in the Senate version prompted us to argue that everything in DeWine's list should now find its way into the administration's regulation interpreting the statutory term "extraordinary circumstances." Of course we argued that the INS could not anticipate all such circumstances, so any list approximating the one written by Senator DeWine should further specify that it was not intended to be exclusive.

In an effort to go beyond DeWine's list, we also quoted from the transcript of Representative McCollum's response to my question in our televised debate a year earlier. McCollum had said that he expected that the INS "would be required to tell people who came in that they could apply for asylum." We knew that the INS would not be able to meet this expectation, and we argued that if the INS could not actually tell aliens about their right to apply for asylum, ignorance of the existence of this process should excuse compliance with the deadline.

Turning to the expedited removal process, we spelled out a process that, within the requirements of the new law, would best protect refugees. Before being interviewed by secondary inspectors, we wrote, aliens arriving at airports should be permitted to eat and to rest from their transoceanic flights. They should be given written and videotaped materials describing the removal process and their right to seek asylum. They should be permitted to telephone family members or friends in the United States and have their assistance while being quizzed by officers who could deport them on the spot. Those who did not speak English fluently should have competent interpreters when speaking to inspectors.

The secondary inspectors, we urged, should look for any sign, verbal or nonverbal, that an alien was afraid to go home. They should take symptoms of depression as possible signs of a post-torture stress disorder. They should also send on to asylum officers any person, even one expressing no fear, from a country known to be a serious human-rights violator. We also suggested that the inspectors ask an alien who had no fear, and who therefore would be deported immediately, to sign a statement saying that the alien was not afraid to go home. Refusal to sign the statement, we argued, should itself be regarded as a sign of fear.

We recommended that aliens sent onward for credible-fear interviews should not be re-interviewed immediately at the airports where they had arrived. Jet lag and fear would make it very difficult for them to explain the details of their persecution immediately. They should be given time to rest and to prepare for the interviews. The government should enable them to make telephone calls to find lawyers or other representatives to assist them.

The interviews themselves, like the screening interviews with inspectors, should be conducted in private and with the help of able interpreters who themselves were sworn to secrecy. The asylum officer, the alien, and the interpreter should be in one room together, so that the interpreter could see the alien's body language, even though it might be less expensive for the INS to put an interpreter on a speaker phone. Although not required by the law to do so, the INS should assign, as interviewers, asylum officers who had already had at least one year of experience interviewing affirmative asylum applicants. These officers should be trained to apply what Senator Hatch had called a "low screening standard"; the result of finding that the alien had a "credible fear" would only be to permit the alien to have a full hearing before an immigration judge, not to grant the alien asylum.

Aliens found not to have a credible fear should be given fair procedures for their last chance to claim asylum, the prompt review by an immigration judge of that credible-fear determination. The review before the judge should be held in person, and if the alien had a lawyer or other representative, the representative should be permitted to present the issues to the judge.[7]

As soon as our article was printed, we sent copies of it to several INS officials, hoping that it would guide their policy-making. A month later, these officials (including the general counsel and the director of the Office of International Affairs) invited us, along with a large number of other representatives of non-governmental organizations, to meet with them about the impending publication of regulations. The meeting, it turned out, raised many questions and answered few.

The officials had decided, they told us, to write regulations in two stages. The agency would propose an "interim" regulation early in January. After considering public comments, the interim regulation would go into effect in April, 1997, when the expedited-removal provisions of the new statute became effective, but at that time a new period for comments would begin. The public's comments on the interim regulation would be considered before a final regulation was issued several months later.

The officials said that they had accepted the idea that the Service Centers would pass all affirmative applications to asylum officers and would not themselves deny applications because they seemed to be late. But it had not yet decided whether to write a non-exclusive list of circumstances that would constitute exceptions to the deadline. "We're leaning toward a middle ground," one official said mysteriously.

The officials also announced that at least initially, expedited removal would be applied only to aliens who were apprehended at airports or other official ports of entry into the United States. The statute allowed but did not require the INS to use expedited removal to deport aliens who had entered the United States without permission and evaded detection for less than two years, but the

INS wanted first to "get some experience" at ports of entry. This decision greatly simplified the work of the INS, but it equally simplified the task of the humanitarian organizations, which would now be able to concentrate resources on new arrivals in the United States.

Although the INS's announcements were received well, the atmosphere in the meeting became more chilly when dialogue began. The officials were unwilling to show us a draft of the proposed regulations, so we had to express our concerns with no idea of how close the officials might be to our own thinking.

Representatives from some of the organizations stated their fear that frightened aliens would not receive fair and sympathetic treatment from secondary inspectors who initiated the expedited removal process. They urged that the secondary inspectors tell arriving aliens that if they feared returning home, they could ask for asylum. Ominously, the INS officials would make no commitment about what the aliens would be told.

Some advocates echoed the call that Pistone and I had made for a "problem list" of countries from which people would be assumed to be escaping. A senior INS official dismissed this suggestion, saying that if there were such a list, the inspectors would immediately deport anyone who was not from a country on the list. I suggested that they could be trained to use better judgment than that, but the official said that I was "bucking human nature."

Another advocate urged that arriving aliens who came with phone numbers of lawyers to help them should be able to contact those lawyers on arrival and to have them present when they met with the secondary inspectors. "I don't think there is anything in [our draft] regulation" on that, we were told. But if a person asked to have a lawyer present, "we would say no."

The officials said that they had not yet decided where interviews with asylum officers would be held for the minority of aliens who were not deported by secondary inspectors. They were thinking, however, of holding the interviews in the detention centers to which the aliens would be sent.

An expert on victims of torture protested that torture survivors "clamp down and have panic attacks" when interviewed in detention centers, and the interviews should be moved away from prisons. The INS officials responded that INS detention centers had been renamed "service processing centers."

An advocate urged that at least at the asylum-officer interview, in-person rather than speaker-phone interpretation should be provided. But the officials said that they were thinking of using an AT&T service that provides interpreters by telephone.[8]

We left the meeting with little idea of the all-important details that the proposed regulation would contain. But we didn't have long to wait. Two weeks later, the proposed interim regulation was published.[9]

We were not pleasantly surprised. The INS had incorporated virtually none of the suggestions from the meeting, or from our *Interpreter Releases* article, into its regulation. There was no list of circumstances that would automatically qualify applicants for relief from the deadline. The agency explained its rejection of our recommendation in a note accompanying the proposed regulation. It had "considered having the regulation identify specific examples of extraordinary circumstances," but "the proposed rule opts in favor of a provision that generally defines the term as events or factors beyond the alien's control that caused the failure to meet the one year deadline." The INS believed that "such a general definition provides guidance to decision makers while offering more flexibility than a definition by example would. Nevertheless, we can imagine several examples that would likely satisfy this definition." There followed the briefest statement of examples: where the applicant had a physical, mental, or legal disability, or had received ineffective assistance of counsel "as that concept has been interpreted by the Board of Immigration Appeals."[10] The list did not approximate the one DeWine had written, but even if the list had been longer, it had no binding effect on decision-makers because it appeared only in the explanatory note, not in the regulation itself. Furthermore, the agency's oral assurance that Service Center personnel wouldn't adjudicate deadline issues wasn't mirrored either in the text of the regulation or in the explanatory note.

The INS also seemed to have made a careless error in a related portion of the proposed regulation on asylum applications. The new proposal permitted asylum officers to deny applications whenever the alien could be removed to a safe third country that had offered resettlement. This provision would overturn one of the few asylum-related victories that the Senate conferees had wrung from their House counterparts during the Conference Committee. The law that had passed Congress, like the Senate bill, had authorized the INS to deny asylum to refugees who could be resettled in a safe third country when the third country and the United States had signed an agreement to that effect.[11]

The regulation's provisions on the procedures to be followed in expedited removal provided few safeguards. The proposal did not give arriving aliens any chance to eat or rest before being examined by a secondary inspector, nor did it give them the opportunity to consult with family or professional advisors, even if such people were waiting at the airport. There were no assurances that the process, or the dire consequences of withholding information, would be described clearly to the alien. Nothing was said about interpretation.

For aliens detained for credible-fear determinations, the regulation was silent about the time or place of the interview, even though we had been told orally that the agency had ruled out instant interviews at airports. Although the statute allowed the detainees to consult with lawyers before credible-fear interviews, the regulation did not assure indigent aliens that they could use prison phones to seek or confer with lawyers. Here, too, the regulation did not mention interpretation.

The regulation did not require that the officials who conducted credible-fear interviews be experienced, or even that they be asylum officers, though in the explanatory note, the INS said that it would "attempt" to assign asylum officers to this task. It did not direct the decision-makers to apply only a low screening standard. It did not even instruct an interviewer to explain to the alien, after the encounter, the officer's understanding of the facts, or to give the alien a chance to correct any misimpressions before ordering the alien deported.

Although an alien had a right under a remnant of the Leahy amendment to have an immigration judge review a negative credible-fear decision, the regulation did not require anyone to notify the alien of this opportunity. If the alien did request review, the regulation provided that it could be held "through a telephone conference without the consent of the alien." And although it specified that the alien could consult with a person of his or her choosing (e.g., a lawyer) "prior to" the review, it did not specify that the alien would be allowed to have a lawyer make an argument to the judge.

The INS gave the public only thirty days to comment on the interim regulation.[12] But because we had already written the *Interpreter Releases* article, Pistone and I were able to convert it quickly into a critique of the regulation. We filed our formal comments two weeks after the regulation was published,[13] simultaneously posting it on the World Wide Web and sending notice of the website address by fax tree to supporters of the Committee to Preserve Asylum. We also sent copies to legislators who had supported us in the congressional battle. Our hope, of course, was to help our allies to write and submit their own comments, a difficult job with only two weeks left in the permitted period.

The public interest community rallied. Within the thirty-day period, the INS received one hundred twenty-four comments on its proposal.[14] Eighty-eight of them came from human rights and religious organizations and teachers of immigration or human rights law.[15] The commenters included the United Nations High Commissioner for Refugees, the U.S. Catholic Conference, Amnesty International, the Lawyers Committee for Human Rights, the American Bar Association, the American Jewish Committee, the Center for Victims of Torture, and dozens of other national and local organizations with which the CPA had worked for a year. Many of the comments supported the arguments we had made in the article.

Unfortunately, not all the comments came from non-profit organizations. Representative Lamar Smith filed sixteen single-spaced pages of comments, to try to influence the INS to be as restrictive as possible. He recommended that expedited removal procedures be used not only for aliens apprehended at airports and border crossings but also for those who crossed a border furtively and were apprehended within a day thereafter. He urged the INS to prohibit aliens' lawyers from being present at credible-fear interviews. And, in a comment pushing exactly in the opposite direction from ours, he urged that the agency's standard for "extraordinary circumstances" should be more narrowly defined.[16] But Smith's letter was not the only congressional comment. Spencer Abraham had succeeded Simpson as chair of the Senate Immigration Subcommittee, and he advised the agency to write a "non-exclusive list of examples of circumstances that will excuse filing beyond the one-year asylum deadline." He also reminded the agency of his eleventh-hour dialogue with Senator Hatch, and urged the INS in the regulations to set a "low screening standard" for credible fear.[17] Senators Edward M. Kennedy and Paul Wellstone chimed in as well, echoing the request for a non-exclusive list of examples and requesting that asylum-seekers be allowed to have lawyers in any situation that could result in deportation.[18]

The day after the comment period closed, officials from the INS's Office of International Affairs (which included its Asylum Bureau) convened the first in a series of meetings with non-governmental organizations to discuss implementation of expedited removal. The agency was principally interested in the groups' comments on the forms that the INS planned to use in secondary inspection and credible-fear interviews. For the organizations, the meetings also served as a window into INS officials' thinking about the implementation problems the INS faced and the procedures it wanted to follow.

For the INS, the main problem was that more than twelve million people arrived at airports or border crossings each year with passports or visas that raised the suspicions of primary inspectors and triggered secondary inspections. Eleven of the twelve million were then passed into the United States by the secondary inspectors. Of the million who were denied entry, only about six thousand were asylum-seekers. Any procedures or protections for the benefit of the six thousand refugees that had to be administered *before* secondary inspection took place would have to be given, as well, to the twelve million other people diverted to secondary inspection. Therefore, some of the concepts we had proposed, such as giving an arriving alien the opportunity to rest up after a transoceanic flight, and to have a meal, or to contact friends or legal representatives before being interviewed by secondary inspectors, struck INS officials as completely impractical. Similarly, the INS was reluctant to provide written notice of the credible-fear process to everyone subjected to secondary inspection, most of whom would turn out to have proper documents and therefore never be subjected to that process.

So the INS would simply apply its existing operating procedures, with minimum deviation to take into account the new law affecting aliens who arrived without proper documents. They would be taken from arriving flights to an interview by a secondary inspector in the airport. Unless they told the secondary inspector that they feared being returned, they would be detained for at most a day or two, while travel arrangements were made, and returned forthwith to their countries. Those who did express or demonstrate a fear would be taken to detention centers where they would be interviewed, a minimum of two days later, by asylum officers.

Human rights advocates noted that some of these aliens would have family members waiting for them at the airport, on the other side of the customs barrier. In some cases, those family members might be able to supply facts that would help persuade a secondary inspector that the alien's travel documents were in order, or that the alien was at risk of persecution if returned. They asked whether the alien would be able to summon such a relative to assist in the interview with the inspector.[19]

This suggestion, like the idea of giving aliens a period of rest, was too greatly at odds with the INS's existing procedures for the millions of non-refugees who had to undergo secondary inspection. "We'll take note of this but it will be a very hard sell," said one official. Similarly, the officials turned aside a suggestion that female aliens who did not want to discuss having been raped with male immigration inspectors should be able to elect a female inspector. ""We'll note your concern, but you are in a law enforcement posture [in secondary inspection], not an asylum interview," they said. "In our dialogue with the inspectors [in this agency], even to get this [the procedures we came up with] we had to press."

Some of the human rights advocates suggested that for aliens who demonstrated a fear, two days was too little time in which to try to find a professional representative and prepare for an asylum interview. Two days was a particularly short period for an alien, jailed in a foreign country, perhaps speaking no English, and having very limited access to prison telephones, to get ready for a proceeding that could result in rapid deportation. The officials responded that getting a two-day delay of the interview had been a "major victory" within the agency. "People on [Capitol] Hill would like expedited exclusion to be done at the airport within an hour after the person arrives [but] we think we can sell forty-eight hours on the Hill."

At a follow-up meeting two weeks later, officials budged infinitesimally on one issue. Within the agency, they had raised the issue of whether waiting relatives could help aliens during secondary inspection, and they reported that although "as a rule, this won't happen, if a grandmother is out there with the key documents proving that the person being held at the airport is really a resident alien, it might happen."

The International Affairs Office personnel, at least, seemed to understand the concerns of the human rights advocates, and they thought that they could avoid injustice by providing proper "sensitivity training" to the secondary inspectors and by encouraging them to refer all close cases to asylum officers for a more careful determination of credible fear. "The general direction of our guidance is 'when in doubt, bump.'" However, although inspector training seemed to be a process within their control, changes that would require other INS offices to take action, or to spend money, seemed beyond the realm of the possible. For example, in response to our concerns about proper interpretation during the airport interviews, they said that the inspectors "deal with this all the time. They use INS staff and airline staff ... coming off the planes." But when the Lutherans' John Fredriksson pointed out that employees of the national airlines of undeveloped countries are usually well-connected people who could land prized government jobs, the International Affairs officials replied that hiring new interpreters "is not our prerogative. 'Inspections' has been up and running a lot longer than we have. . . . It's not our prerogative to tell the airport inspectors not to ever use airline personnel."

A few days later, the INS issued its proposed final regulation. Unlike the proposed interim regulation, this version would have legal status, as a binding interim regulation, for more than two years, until the final regulation was actually promulgated.[20] Human rights advocates eagerly highlighted eighty-three pages of fine print in the *Federal Register* to see whether the agency had improved the proposed regulation in response to their comments. In fact, the INS had made some improvements, particularly with respect to issues about the deadline—though its effort had been more a partial, halting effort than a real solution to the problems.

First, the agency had interpreted the law to allow anyone to apply for asylum during the year after the statute's April 1997 effective date. This generous, non-retroactive construction was by no means required by the statute, and it was very important. Refugees who had fled to the United States before March 1996 would not be barred by failure to apply at once, because they would have another thirteen months, not just one month, in which to seek asylum. This interpretation also implied that imperfections in the deadline provisions of the interim regulation could be corrected, in the final regulation, before the deadline took effect in April 1998 and began to affect refugees adversely. Unfortunately, the INS took more than two years to issue the final regulation, so, in the end, this hope was not mirrored by reality.

Second, the agency had responded quite positively, if not thoroughly, to our suggestion that the regulation should include a list of types of circumstances that would qualify as exceptions to the deadline. Noting that "a large number of commenters" had requested such a list, it reversed the position it had taken when it published the proposed regulation and published such a list in the regulation itself. But the INS's list was not as inclusive as we had recommended, and its text included a small, but potentially significant, ambiguity. Furthermore, although the agency made a strong statement about the non-inclusivity of the list, it once again printed this statement in the wrong place.

The agency's definition of "changed" circumstances included, appropriately, changes in conditions in the alien's home country. Beyond that, the agency proposed to include changes in "objective circumstances" relating to the applicant in the United States. The word "objective" seemed problematic, for two reasons. First, this term was not used in the statute, so the regulation seemed, in this instance, to be even more limiting than the language the House had written. Second, it might be interpreted to exclude the very type of exception that Hatch and Abraham had discussed in their floor colloquy: the case in which the only thing that changed, after a year, was the refugee's awareness that human rights conditions at home had deteriorated seriously.

When it addressed "extraordinary" circumstances, the INS had moved considerably in our direction. Its list included serious illness or mental or physical disability of significant duration; legal disability; a very restricted form of "ineffective assistance of counsel";[21] the maintenance of "Temporary Protected Status"; and the fact that the applicant had filed before the deadline expired, but the application had been returned to the applicant for corrections. This list included several, but not all, of the excuses we'd urged the agency to list, though it gave us a foot in the door to ask for expansions in the final regulation. For example, it was significant that the agency recognized that a person with "Temporary Protected Status" (a type of temporary asylum for very limited groups of refugees) would not ordinarily apply for asylum, since such a person had a legal immigration status and would not think of seeking asylum until it expired. The justification for this exception would also apply to other late filers who previously enjoyed a legal status, such as people fleeing persecution who also had student or work visas.

The textual ambiguity was that for each set of exceptions, the interim regulation specified that the circumstances justifying an exception "may" include those on the list. This term made us worry that asylum officers and judges might think that they were not required to grant an exception, even if the applicant's circumstances were of the listed type.

Finally, the INS again buried in its preamble, rather than in the regulation itself, its important statement that "the list is not all-inclusive, and it is recognized that there are many other circumstances that might apply if the applicant is able to show that but for such circumstances the application would have been filed within the first year of the alien's arrival in the United States."[22] What could the agency be thinking, we wondered? Was it trying to please both the human rights community and Lamar Smith by making an excellent policy statement but not printing it in the *Code of Federal Regulations,* the official rulebook that asylum officers, judges, and lawyers would consult whenever the issue arose?

The human rights community had prevailed on some related issues. The proposed regulation had not specified whether ministerial personnel in the INS's regional Service Centers would be able to reject applications summarily if they appeared to have been filed late and no excuse was stated. We'd asked that they not be given that authority. In the interim regulation, the INS agreed that "[b]ecause of the importance of a decision to deny an alien the right to apply for asylum, the Department has chosen to adopt the suggestion that only asylum officers, immigration judges, and the BIA [the administrative appeal board]" be allowed to make deadline decisions.[23] And the INS had accepted our complaint that its proposed rule had improperly required aliens to prove "by clear and convincing evidence" that they qualified for an exception; the statute required proof only "to the satisfaction" of the adjudicator.[24]

On the other hand, the INS seemed to have dug itself in on the issue of allowing itself to deny asylum to people who could be deported to third countries (such as Israel) that would accept them. In our comments, we had called to the agency's attention what we thought was its inadvertent oversight in not limiting the scope of that provision to accepting countries with which the U.S. had negotiated removal agreements. But the interim regulation included the offending provision, and the agency did not even explain why it had not changed a provision that, in our judgment, was inconsistent with the law.[25]

The provisions on summary exclusion included very few surprises for the human rights advocates, because the INS's decisions had been forecast at the meetings we'd had with officials. As expected, the regulation provided for arriving aliens to be taken into secondary inspection without rest, information about the procedural system for determining asylum claims, or the opportunity to talk to waiting relatives or to lawyers, although for the first time the agency said in writing that "occasionally, family members or persons waiting to meet the arriving alien may be allowed to assist in translation of the [secondary inspection] interview."[26] It confirmed that credible-fear interviews would take place at detention centers, rejecting as too expensive our recommendation that they take place in the INS's asylum offices. It also rejected our recommendation that totally indigent aliens who were in jail awaiting credible-fear interviews be given small change so that they could use prison telephones to seek professional representation. "[T]he statute," the INS recalled stuffily, "that provides for [legal] consultation specifically states that the consultation shall be at no expense to the Government."[27] The government thereby stated its intention to carry out a process that would lead to the deportation, to persecution and death, of some refugees because they could not obtain quarters for phone calls to lawyers. This prompted us, in subsequent criticism, to recall the scene in Stanley Kubrick's *Dr. Strangelove*, in which a British army officer who didn't have a dime in his pocket was unable, for a time, to telephone the Pentagon and thereby prevent nuclear destruction of the world.[28] But what happened a year later is even more peculiar. The INS retreated from refusing to let indigents in expedited removal proceedings to call lawyers at government expense, issuing a directive permitting them to make *local* calls to lawyers on prison phones.[29] However, it jailed most of its detainees in facilities that were located at some distance from major cities. From these facilities, inmates would have to make toll calls, not local calls, to get in touch with lawyers.

In the interim regulation, the INS declined to put in writing what Senator Hatch and INS officials had reiterated orally, to the effect that the credible-fear standard was a "low screening standard."[30] As it had done in our meetings, it relied on forthcoming "extensive training" of employees to "encourage flexibility and a broad application of the statutory standard."[31] But the INS did accept two other procedural suggestions we had made for credible-fear interviews. At the end of each interview, the asylum officer would be required to review with the alien the written summary that the officer had made and give the alien an opportunity to correct errors. This procedure would reduce the chance that errors of understanding or interpretation would lead to erroneous deportations. Also, whenever the asylum officer found that the alien did not have a credible fear of persecution, he or she was directed to inform the alien, both orally and in writing, about the alien's right to appeal the finding to an immigration judge, and the alien could exercise that right by telling the asylum officer, on the spot, that an appeal was desired. This procedure would make it much less likely that aliens would inadvertently lose the appeal opportunity that had been retained from the Leahy amendment.[32]

Although the regulation specified that asylum officers were required to allow the aliens' lawyers to attend credible-fear interviews and could allow them to make statements,[33] it was curiously silent about analogous rights for such lawyers during appeals to immigration judges. We had thought that the judges, even more than asylum officers, would want lawyers to participate, both because judges of all kinds usually feel more satisfied that their hearings afford fair process when participants are represented, and because the hearings themselves tend to be more orderly and restrained when lawyers represent and speak for their clients. But the regulation only echoed the statute's minimum guarantee that the alien could consult a lawyer "prior to" the review.[34] The regulation did not preclude attorney participation in the judges' reviews of credible fear determinations, and refugee advocates, who had for more than a decade appeared routinely before the immigration judges in ordinary asylum cases, assumed that they would be allowed full participation in these new proceedings as well. But a few days later, Chief Immigration Judge Michael J. Creppy sent a memorandum to all immigration judges stating that although an alien could consult a lawyer before the judge's review "there is no right to *representation* prior to or during the review, either in the statute or the regulation." In a footnote, he added that "nothing in the statute, regulations, or [this memorandum] entitles an attorney to make an opening statement, call and question witnesses, cross examine, object to written evidence, or make a closing argument."[35] Perhaps for the first time in American history, lawyers were routinely barred from speaking to judges who could determine the fates of their clients.[36]

The interim regulation had improved the INS's original proposal in several respects, but as the INS itself had recognized by promulgating it only as a temporary provision and providing four months for further public comment, it could still be made better. Starting the day it was published, therefore, Pistone and I set out to write a new critique, this time in the form of one of the world's most rapidly written law review articles. We reasoned that we had already reached immigration practitioners through their main newsletter, and by publishing our new critique in a scholarly journal we could achieve another wide dissemination to a different audience. Publication in a journal would also enable us to buy reprints that we could mail to legislators, administrators, and other advocates.

Within a few weeks, therefore, we had completed a manuscript arguing that the INS was moving in the right direction but hadn't yet written as fair a regulation as it could issue consistently with an essentially unfair statute. Six weeks later, still well in time for others to use it to inform their own comments, it was published.[37] We filed the article with the INS as our own official comments on the interim and proposed final regulation,[38] distributed reprints widely, and again posted the text on the World Wide Web. Forty-one other organizations and individuals filed comments.[39] These commenters included, of course, Representative Lamar Smith, who complained that the INS had left open the possibility that aliens found to have a credible fear of persecution might be released from detention, temporarily, until they could have full hearings before immigration judges.[40]

Human rights activists hoped for an ongoing dialogue as INS officials digested the public comments and prepared to revise its regulation. But for months, not much happened. INS representatives did meet periodically with the advocates, but most of the meetings did not concern the proposed regulatory reforms. Rather, these meetings had two other functions.

The INS used the meetings to offer informal statistical reports, based on the first few months of experience with expedited removal, to show that the system was working well and that human rights were being respected. INS officials revealed that during the first three months of the law's application, about 95 percent of the people stopped at ports of entry because they lacked valid entry documents were deported immediately; the other 5 percent who expressed a fear of returning were imprisoned to await credible-fear interviews by asylum officers. The percentage who were not summarily deported increased to 20 percent if only airports, and not land border crossings, were considered, because most of the people apprehended with false papers at the Mexican or Canadian border did not claim any fear of persecution.[41] The asylum officers were finding that aliens had credible fear in about 80 percent of the cases referred to them, suggesting to the INS that its officials actually were applying an appropriately low screening standard to allow would-be refugees to obtain full hearings.[42] The statistics reinforced the advocates' view, however, that if the expedited-removal process was infected by systemic error, the problems lay at the stage of secondary inspection rather than in the credible-fear interviews. How could anyone outside of the INS know whether the secondary inspectors were effectively ferreting out refugees who were so bruised or frightened, so well defended against expressing any emotion, that they did not reveal fear of persecution to the secondary inspector? The advocates wanted to be able to observe some secondary inspections, at least to spot-check the process. The INS steadfastly refused to allow them to do so,[43] noting candidly in the briefings that the American Civil Liberties Union had sued the agency immediately after the law went into effect, to enjoin its implementation, and that the suit was at that time still pending.[44] The ACLU had been forced to sue quickly because Congress had barred all suits filed more than thirty days after the regulations were issued, but that fact did not make agency officials feel any more warmly about the legal challenge to their authority.

For their part, the advocates tried to convey to the INS their concerns about how the interim regulation was being implemented. For example, Pistone complained that people who were waiting to be interviewed by a secondary inspector should be given some information to read about the process before they were asked questions. Others complained that a few asylum officers were not applying a low screening standard, but were in fact cross-examining the aliens for hours. At every meeting, Carol Wolchok raised a basic concern on behalf of the 95 percent of aliens in expedited removal who did not express fear of persecution, as well as the 5 percent who did. She pointed out that low-level inspectors were now exercising a power to expel aliens that could previously be exercised only by judges after full hearings.[45] Yet the inspectors were not required to inform the aliens of the basis for their belief that their papers were not in order, or to give the aliens the opportunity to have a lawyer prove that the papers were in fact in order. The INS consistently replied that the issue was in litigation.

The meetings between the INS and the advocates to discuss expedited removal tended to be relatively tense. Large numbers of advocates and many INS officials attended, often producing meetings of fifty or more people at which the officials were eager to hear first-hand reports from the field, even if they demonstrated deviations from official policy, but reluctant to make promises about implementation, much less about any requested regulatory changes, such as fairer rules about legal representation or interpretation. Both the size of the meetings and the pending litigation limited how much could be accomplished.

By contrast, the INS was much more able and willing to discuss the asylum deadline issues with the advocates. Several factors accounted for this: the INS had more clearly opposed the deadlines in Congress, putting them on the same side as the advocates who were now asking them to ameliorate them, to the extent possible, through regulations. The agency was not yet implementing the deadline, because its interim regulation had postponed its effective date by one year until April 1998, and it therefore had no bureaucratic stake in maintaining existing operating procedures.[46] No litigation was pending on this issue. And the number of advocates interested in discussing details of how the deadline would be administered was much smaller, usually fewer than a dozen, so meetings could be more informal.

In October 1997, I and other advocates attended what we believed was a particularly good meeting with INS officials to discuss the pending regulations. All of these officials were involved in writing the regulations.[47] Although they cautioned that none of their recommendations had yet been approved by the "higher-ups," they shared with us the good news that they had suggested that many of our proposals should be adopted. They would support moving from the preamble to the regulation itself the statement that the list of exceptional circumstances was only illustrative, not all-inclusive. They agreed that the exception for "changed" conditions should include the situation in which human rights conditions had not changed in the year before an alien applied, but the alien was only recently able to learn of a worsened threat of persecution. Although most of them were unwilling to implement our suggestion on this point by deleting the word "objective" from the description of the exception, one whispered to us that she would try to get it removed. They agreed to consider deleting words in the regulation that seemed even tougher than the statute in requiring aliens to prove that exceptional circumstances had caused a delay.[48]

We reminded the officials that we wanted the INS to list three more types of situations as "exceptional" circumstances, excusing a late application. They said that they would probably add the exception we wanted for lateness as a result of threats to relatives who were still at the mercy of the countries that refugees had fled. They were very skeptical about our request for an exemption for those who could not afford legal representation and had sought, but not obtained, free legal services. They seemed to fear that this exemption could be easily abused by people who had not genuinely sought help within a year. They were slightly warmer to our suggestion that aliens with student or work visas be excused from applying for asylum until a reasonable period of time after those visas had expired. This proposal, they told us, had been "very controversial" within the agency, some officials believing that Congress could have enacted an exception for aliens lawfully in the United States but had not done so. We argued that nothing could be inferred from legislative silence, since there had been no explicit vote in either house on this particular issue and the exception could be authorized under the general language that Congress had enacted. They said that at the moment, the exception we wanted was in the regulatory draft, in part because the law would be easier to administer if the agency could process the many applications from such aliens without having to make case-by-case determinations of their eligibility under the deadline. But they warned that because of the controversy, it might not remain in the regulation.

Finally, we took issue with the provision in the interim regulation allowing deportation of asylum-seekers to safe third countries even in the absence of a relevant international agreement. The officials told us that they were reviewing this issue and would "probably" change it to require a pre-existing agreement.

We were thrilled that the INS appeared responsive to our concerns, but we were very aware that more senior officials still needed to review the recommendations that the regulation-writers were making. At the end of the meeting, we asked for another meeting with the officials, and we were told that we would be able to meet with them on December 3. But just before the December 3 meeting was to be held, the INS abruptly canceled it. Shortly thereafter, an INS representative telephoned to say that senior officials had decided that there would be no more meetings on this subject.

Given how well our meeting in October had gone, we were disappointed to be cut out of the regulatory process, and we feared that this decision might mean that the same senior officials who had closed down the process had also overruled the more junior staff on many of the policy issues we'd discussed. Of course the INS was within its rights not to talk to us. Federal law required only that it consider the written comments that we had filed, so we were fortunate that the INS had been willing to meet with us at all. On the other hand, the law did not preclude the INS from meeting with us either,[49] and the INS probably had as much to gain from such meetings as we did. A very open process, with many such meetings, had enabled the non-profit organizations to understand the logic of David Martin's regulations in 1994, and the INS's willingness to discuss and negotiate with the organizations at that time had undoubtedly contributed to the fact that no organization had sued the agency to challenge that set of regulatory reforms.

We decided on a three-pronged approach to try to reassert our role in the process or to influence the outcome in other ways. First, we wanted to know what we were up against inside the agency, so we sought sources who would tell us something about the discussions that had taken place within the INS. We did not learn who had decided to cancel our meeting, but we did learn why the statement of non-exclusivity of the listed exceptions had been written only in the preamble and not in the regulation itself: this was simply a compromise between liberals in the INS who agreed with us and "hard-liners" on the staff who didn't want to make such a statement at all. We also learned why the regulation had not guaranteed that lawyers could speak in court when they were representing aliens in appeals from negative credible-fear determinations, and why Chief Judge Creppy's memorandum, building on the regulation, had denied them this right. The INS, it turned out, had been unable to estimate how often such appeals would take place. (The frequency turned out to be quite low because asylum officers found credible fear as a result of 80 percent of their interviews). It had therefore been unsure about its ability to provide government lawyers to argue against a credible-fear finding in these appeals, and Judge Creppy had not wanted judges to hear cases in which only the alien, and not the INS, was represented by counsel.

As the second element of our strategy, we alerted Senator DeWine, who had spearheaded the Senate's effort to include in the statute half a dozen broad, explicit exceptions to the deadline. DeWine wrote a letter to INS Commissioner Doris Meissner, praising her for including some of the Senate's exceptions in the interim regulation and urging her to include the rest of them (concern about relatives at risk, delays in obtaining legal help, lawful immigration status before the deadline ran, and illness of the applicant's representative). He also asked that she move from the preamble to the rule the statement that the listed exceptions weren't exclusive, and to state clearly that listed exceptions "shall" (rather than "may") excuse late filings. DeWine recruited two of his fellow senators to co-sign his letter.[50]

Third, we decided to try to reverse the INS's decision to refrain from consulting with us again as it drafted the deadline regulation. Since we did not know who had made this decision, our only hope was to assume that it had not been the commissioner herself, and to appeal to her to permit us back into the process. Accordingly, the Lawyers Committee for Human Rights requested her to meet with a small group of us.[51] Happily for us, she agreed to a meeting.

We thought we might see only the commissioner, or that she might invite one or two staff members, but when we arrived, she ushered us into a conference room with six other senior INS officials, a good omen, suggesting that we were being taken very seriously. Among them was Paul Virtue, who had succeeded David Martin as general counsel when Martin returned to his teaching job at the University of Virginia. Virtue was certain to have a major voice in the content of the final regulation. We gave the commissioner a memorandum describing the nine most important outstanding regulatory issues, and what we wanted the agency to do about them.[52] We also brought her a copy of the unanswered letter that the three senators had sent her two months earlier, for we suspected that it had been intercepted for reply by her congressional relations staff and had never actually reached her.[53]

We told the commissioner about the excellent meeting we'd had in October, 1997, and of our distress at having been frozen out of the regulation-writing process thereafter. The commissioner instantly agreed with us that the agency should continue to consult us, and the next substantive meeting was put on all of our calendars. Since we had time remaining, we also raised the most important item on the memorandum we'd given her, hoping to pin down one issue, and not have to argue later about it with more junior staff. So we explained the importance of specifying in the regulation that the list of exceptions wasn't exclusive.

The commissioner turned to Mr. Virtue for a response.

"We don't have any problem putting that into the regulation itself," he said. We had obtained in less than two minutes of meeting time one of the major changes that we had been trying to achieve through months of writing articles and formal regulatory comments.

At the promised meeting that followed, INS officials turned out in force; five of us represented the advocacy community, but seventeen INS officials came to hear and respond to our proposals and arguments. We passed around a list of outstanding issues, our recommendations, and in several cases, proposed text to improve on the language of the interim regulation.

The officials told us that the agency had agreed to add one of the exceptions for which we'd advocated (aliens who did not apply promptly for asylum because they were in the United States in a different lawful immigration status). On most of the other issues we raised, they were less categorical, but they hinted that, while formal agreement within the agency wasn't yet final, the trend was in the direction we proposed. For example, there was likely to be an exception for threats to relatives, and the INS would amend the regulation to deny asylum to people who could be placed in "safe third countries" only when there was a prior agreement between the United States and those countries. On a few issues, including our proposal of an exception for aliens who were wait-listed for legal help, the officials took issue with us, and although we argued for our point of view, we seemed unlikely to prevail. They seemed unwilling to create the lawyers' wait-list exception, for example, not so much because of fear of fraud (an objection we thought we could help them overcome by proposing standards to document wait-list status) but because they didn't want to imply that an alien who lacked legal help couldn't file an asylum application.[54]

After this meeting, we waited for months, unable to learn more about the debates within the agency. The interim regulation, with its utterly inadequate provisions for exceptions to the deadline, went into effect. The government had hurried us to comment on its proposed interim regulation and then on its proposed final regulation, but after it received all the comments, it seemed to take forever to issue the final regulation. While we waited, we learned something about deeper levels of the law.

# 13

# The Deeper Levels of the Law
## *February 1997–May 1998*

> The person who designs forms . . . may be hard to find. . . . The person may
> be interested in working with you to cut unnecessary paperwork, or he
> may not have the power to make changes on his own. If not, you should
> bring to bear other pressures for change.
>
> —United States Commission on Federal Paperwork[1]

More than thirty-five years ago, I took a law school course called "the legal
process." Using a brilliant 1,400-page set of materials by the late Harvard Law
School professors Henry M. Hart Jr. and Albert M. Sacks,[2] this immensely rich
course explored basic questions about which legal institutions should regulate
which kinds of human conduct. I emerged from the course dazzled by its complex themes but deeply impressed by a powerful idea that to the authors of the
materials was probably only a minor revelation.

This is the powerful idea: "Law" isn't merely the Constitution of the United
States, the public laws that Congress and the states have enacted, and the decisions of courts. Law is made through many other processes, and embodied in
many other forms, including agency regulations, tariffs written by utility companies and approved by government agencies, private contracts (which become
law for the parties that sign them), the fine print on the back of airline tickets,
collective bargaining agreements, government agencies' formal opinions, those
agencies' adjudicative decisions, and even the customs built into every human culture.

One important element of law, in this sense of the word, is the language
used and the demands made by forms, particularly government forms. Forms
are one of the most important tools that governments use to guide and control
behavior, both of the government's own employees and of the general public.
The forms that police officers must complete after arrests, for example, help to
remind officers of the procedures they must follow when arresting a suspect
and also help ensure that the officers actually follow those procedures. Tax
return forms used by the public are an important element for coercing tax payments; the forms help taxpayers compute their liabilities, but they also make
cheating less likely by requiring detailed disclosures that may later be checked

for accuracy. In a sense, the battle over much public legislation is a battle over what will eventually appear on forms. Whenever Congress passes legislation, many policy issues fall between the cracks of the new law's explicit provisions. In the aftermath of legislation, while some of the interstitial policy-making turns on the wording of the implementing regulations, other important policy issues are resolved only when text is drafted for the government forms that will strongly influence the conduct of officials and the public.

Forms are not the only important, low-level variety of barely visible "law." Government operating manuals (which tell officials exactly what they should do in various on-the-job situations), training manuals (used by government personnel to train lower-level officials about how to perform their work), informal letters and memoranda from headquarters, press releases and speeches by senior agency personnel, and even the work styles, ideas, ideologies, or prejudices of individual officials have enormous impact on the public. All of these elements of law are the subject of continuing post-legislative advocacy by affected constituencies, day in and day out, particularly in the formative period after a new law or regulation is promulgated.

So it was with the refugee provisions in the new immigration law. In the year after it was passed, most of the advocacy organizations' efforts went into trying to influence the regulations and toward training their own staffs to cope with the new rules and institutions that the law created. But these groups did not lose sight of the importance of trying to influence the new forms and manuals that the INS would soon begin to use.

Because expedited removal was scheduled to be implemented a full year before the asylum deadline would take effect, drafting the forms to give effect to this change in the law took priority. For expedited removal, the INS would not need to distribute forms for use by the general public, but it would need to change the forms that secondary inspectors used to record the results of their interviews with arriving aliens suspected of not having valid travel documents. For the first time, these inspectors would be making final decisions to expel most of these aliens, and they would also have to determine which aliens to refer for possible credible-fear interviews.

It was not obvious that the advocacy groups would be able to have any role whatever in the development of the inspectors' forms. No law requires a government agency to allow public participation in the development of forms that only its own officials will complete. However, the INS apparently saw some advantage, or at least an opportunity to engage in more open government, by sharing an early draft with the human rights community.

Therefore, two months before it had to start administering expedited removal, the INS convened a meeting with non-governmental organizations to ask for their comments. Even though the INS faxed the draft forms to the organizations only the night before the meeting, and some of the representatives hadn't seen them yet, about forty-five advocates packed into a small conference room behind an INS cafeteria to talk with officials about the new "I-867" form, which a secondary inspector would have to fill out during an interview with each arriving alien subject to expedited removal.[3]

What the INS proposed, after "a lot of hard compromises" within the agency, was a secondary inspection form that aliens would not see until they were required to sign it at the end of an interview. At the beginning of that interview, the inspector would read to them, from the first page of the form, sixteen sentences explaining the purpose and possible consequences of the encounter. The inspector would try to find, somewhere in the airport, a person who could interpret this section of the form into the alien's language and assist in the interpretation of the interview. The text seemed to be have been written for a person with at least a college education. For example, the inspector would say, "Any statement you make may be used against you in this or any subsequent administrative proceeding. You appear to be inadmissible to the United States.... If you give misinformation, you may be subject to criminal or civil penalties, or barred from receiving certain immigration benefits or relief."[4]

The statement would include the following disclosure about the protection that the United States offered to refugees:

> U.S. law provides protection to certain persons who face persecution or harm upon return to their country. If you fear or have a concern about being sent home, you should tell me so. You will have the opportunity to speak privately and confidentially to another officer about your fear or concern. That officer will determine if you should not be removed from the United States because of that fear.[5]

After reading the statement, the inspector would ask questions about the alien's lack of documentation or apparently false documentation, and other questions unrelated to possible persecution. Then, the final page of the form would require the inspector to ask these two questions and record the alien's answers to them:

> Do you have any fear or concern about being removed from the United States or of being sent home?
> If so, what is the nature of that fear or concern?

Replies that persuaded the inspector that the alien was afraid would trigger a credible-fear interview. INS officials assured the advocates that they were well aware that the inspectors would not be trained in the nuances of asylum law (e.g., the requirement that only five specified grounds for feared persecution, such as persecution on account of religion, qualified an alien for asylum). Therefore, the form did not prompt inspectors to ask further questions about the nature of the alien's fear, and they would not do so.

In comments offered during the meeting, and by mail and fax afterward, human rights advocates took issue with many aspects of the form.[6] They complained that even if comprehension were not degraded by imprecise interpretation, the language of the initial disclosure was too complex for refugees with limited educations. They said that the INS should have hired an educational expert to assess the grade level below which the vocabulary chosen by the INS might be inappropriate. They agreed that the inspectors should ask about "fear" but expressed dismay that neither the disclosure statement nor the questions on the form directed an inspector also to mention "asylum" by name, because that term might be familiar to some refugees fleeing persecution. They argued that the second question, asking the refugee to state the "nature" of a fear of return, was inconsistent with the INS's acknowledgment that the inspectors lacked training that would enable them to distinguish between qualifying and non-qualifying types of fears. Instead, they proposed, the inspector should ask the question about "fear" a second time, using somewhat different words, in case the alien had not understood the first question. They proposed that if the INS were unwilling to use the word "asylum," this second question should ask, "Would you be harmed if you are returned to your home country or country?" Finally, they suggested that to make still more certain that aliens would not be removed erroneously, an alien should be required to write, in hand, in the alien's own language, a statement that he or she was not afraid of being returned, and that refusal to write this sentence should be interpreted as an indication of fear, triggering the next review.

To its credit, the INS did revise the form, although it did not accept every suggestion. In a second meeting with advocates two weeks later, an official explained that to make even some of the changes that the advocates had desired, they "shook the roots of this institution" and had produced "a litany of questions [on the form] beyond our wildest dreams, and we have inspectors' buy-in [acquiescence]." The INS had simplified the initial disclosure somewhat, though the agency had neither the time nor appropriate authorization to hire an educational consultant. The disclosure now stated, for the first time, that the United States protects people who would face torture if returned. And the INS had removed the question about the "nature" of the alien's fear, and had replaced it with the question the advocates had proposed, which asked whether the alien expected to be harmed if returned. A positive answer to either the "fear" question or the "harm" question would warrant a referral for an asylum officer interview.[7]

On the other hand, the agency steadfastly refused to direct inspectors to use the word "asylum." Officials first said that "we were trying to move away from legalese," but they also acknowledged that the blows the agency had received in the 1993 *60 Minutes* show were still reverberating. "Some people see this as a magic word that would invite false claims," one official said. "It was soundly rejected by the other elements [not the International Affairs Office] in the Service." The agency also rejected the proposed requirement of a handwritten statement on the form.

Once the language of the expedited removal form had been settled, the advocates turned their attention to the revisions that the INS planned to make to the affirmative asylum application form. Ironically, members of the public had a greater right to comment on this form than on the inspector's form for expedited removal, but in practice, the agency was far less consultative.

The public's right to participate by commenting on the application form arose from the Paperwork Reduction Act that Congress had passed in 1980 and had most recently revised in 1995.[8] Under this law, forms meant to be filled out by the public are "information collection requests." Before an agency can print such a form, it must publish certain information in the *Federal Register,* sixty days in advance, "and otherwise consult with members of the public."[9] A draft of the form itself does not have to be published, but the agency must at least provide, in the *Federal Register,* a summary of the form and a brief description of why it needs to print it. After the agency has considered any public comments, the federal Office of Management and Budget (OMB) may allow the agency to use the form.

When it published its proposed asylum regulation early in January 1997, the INS did not simultaneously publish a revised application form. The advocates anticipated that the agency would eventually revise the form to deal with the new deadline and its exceptions, and they wrote to the INS to suggest that the agency "seek public input on the actual revisions to the form and its instructions, as it did when [the form] was last revised [in 1995]."[10] A month later, the agency did publish a notice in the *Federal Register* stating that it intended to revise the form.[11] But in contrast to the consultations it initiated regarding the expedited removal form, it did not notify the advocates or call a meeting to discuss the revisions. Furthermore, although the notice gave members of the public until April 14 to submit comments, it did not reprint the form itself or describe the changes that the INS planned to make. Caught up in the flurry of having to comment on the pending proposed regulation (for which public input was due in early March) and preparing to represent clients in expedited removal proceedings, the advocates missed the notice. They did see a draft of the revised form that an agency official gave to a staff member of the American Immigration Law Foundation, and because this draft included what seemed to be a badly worded question about the deadline and its exceptions, they wrote a letter to an agency official to protest its possible use.[12] But neither side followed up. The advocates did not realize that the INS was on the verge of using the form, and the INS was so caught up in preparing to administer expedited removal and other legal changes imposed by the new legislation that the letter went unanswered.

The advocates also missed a second *Federal Register* notice, two weeks later, that could have alerted them to the imminence of the form's use. In this second notice, the INS abrogated the public's right to comment. It said that it "cannot wait for the 60-day comment period to close since the effective date for implementation of the revised Form ... is April 1."[13] The abrogation was permitted under an emergency exception in the Paperwork Reduction Act, but as a result, the OMB could only allow the revised form to be used for six months.[14]

The OMB granted the temporary permission, and the INS began using the revised application form in the spring of 1997. The key question on the revised form read as follows:

> Are you filing this application more than one year after your last arrival in the United States? If YES, you must attach an explanation of why you did not file within the first year after your arrival. Describe any change(s) in circumstances since your arrival which resulted in your decision to apply for asylum at this time or any extraordinary circumstances which prevented you from applying earlier. Failure to adequately explain such changed or extraordinary circumstances may result in ineligibility to apply for asylum.[15]

This question was flawed in many ways. It was not unreasonable for the INS to ask applicants whether they were filing more than a year after arrival; even though this information could be deduced from the answers to two other questions on the form, it was more convenient for the agency to have the applicant make this determination. However, the wisdom of requiring that late applicants justify their lateness under one of the statutory exceptions, in writing, was quite dubious. First, the fact that two-thirds of the people who applied affirmatively for asylum lacked legal or other professional representation was critical. Many of these uncounseled applicants had a poor command of the English language, and even if they knew the meaning of the term "extraordinary circumstances," they might have a hard time writing a narrative explanation to show that their circumstances were "extraordinary." Second, the term "extraordinary" would not convey to someone who answered the question all the types of circumstances that would qualify for exceptional treatment. A person who had become ill during her eleventh month of U.S. residence might think that illness was "ordinary" and therefore abandon her claim for asylum. The term was actually a legal shorthand for a long list of exceptions that would eventually be explicated through INS regulations, immigration judges' decisions, and opinions of the Board of Immigration Appeals. No one could be expected to know its full meaning without consulting a law library. Third, some applicants who thought they knew enough to answer the question might impair their applications by explaining only some of the several reasons for their lateness, focusing an adjudicator's attention on a weak claim when a stronger one might be available.

Therefore, it would have been better if the INS had simply asked whether the application was being filed more than a year after entry, and instructed its asylum officers in all such cases to ask a series of questions in the applicant's oral interview to ascertain whether any recognized exception might possibly apply. Asylum officers and immigration judges would be in a much better position than applicants to know what constituted a valid changed or extraordinary circumstance. But the advocates did not make these arguments to the INS before the agency started using the form. They did not discover either of the notices in the *Federal Register,* and despite their request, the INS did not consult them before revising the form.

There was, in addition, a fourth reason why the INS should not have revised its form in the spring of 1997 to include a question about late filing. The question itself, and its accompanying warnings that an applicant who didn't complete it could thereby be denied asylum, was illegal. On February 26, a week before the INS published its *Federal Register* notice abrogating the public comment period and asking emergency approval of the revised form, Attorney General Janet Reno had approved the agency's interim and proposed final asylum regulation.[16] This regulation had specified that the time limit would not start to run for anyone until April 1, 1997;[17] therefore, no one who filed during the next year could be regarding as having filed too late. The INS had needed to revise the asylum application form in any event, because, among other things, the new statute had changed some terminology.[18] But under its own regulation, the INS had jumped the gun when it included the deadline question on this revised form.

Four months passed before the advocates realized that the INS was using an illegal form.[19] When they discovered the problem, they were furious. Noting that the form's statement requiring an explanation of lateness "gives false and misleading information to people who may be considering applying," they demanded a meeting with INS officials. "[I]f the form is not recalled immediately," they suggested, "INS could be enjoined in a lawsuit brought to restrain the agency from continuing to distribute this form."[20]

The INS quickly agreed to a meeting, and it candidly admitted that it had made a mistake. But it had printed vast quantities of the revised form and had distributed them to its field offices and its forms distribution center. Not only would the cost of reprinting be high, but the INS would need to publish a new *Federal Register* notice and to obtain new permission from the OMB to revise the form again, an effort out of proportion to the problem at hand, because the agency planned to revise the form yet again in the spring of 1998.

The advocates had a fallback position, and INS officials readily accepted it. The agency was willing to print and send to its field offices thousands of correction notices, which officials would staple to the front page of every copy of the asylum application form. This "clarifying instruction" would explain that "applicants who file prior to April 2, 1998 are not required to seek asylum within one year" so "you do not have to answer" the question about the timeliness of the application. "Leaving this answer blank will not make your application incomplete," the instruction added.[21]

The problem of the offending question had been solved, but only temporarily, because in April 1998 the INS would begin asking it again. Fortunately, the OMB's emergency six-month authorization for the INS to use its revised form was about to expire, and even though the INS would be able to obtain a short extension,[22] it would have to fulfill the consultation requirements of the Paperwork Reduction Act for a long-term renewal of the form.

When it reapplied for long-term renewal, the INS published the actual proposed form in the *Federal Register*.[23] This version asked essentially the same question that had been printed in the April 1 revision.[24] As in the previous version, nothing on the form or its instructions gave late filers any explanation of what might constitute changed or extraordinary circumstances (even though by this time the INS had issued its interim regulation listing at least a few types of circumstances that would be regarded as exceptional), and the form did not alert such filers that it would be helpful to obtain professional assistance in dealing with such technical issues.

Invoking their rights under the Paperwork Reduction Act, Amnesty International, the American Immigration Lawyers Association, the Lawyers Committee for Human Rights, and others responded. They objected both to the question about the deadline and to the opaque accompanying instruction that merely repeated the question.[25] They explained why unrepresented applicants from other cultures would have a hard time giving a narrative response to justify an exception, why the instructions for answering the question were utterly inadequate, and in what ways the form continued to mislead those to whom it was addressed.[26] They suggested allowing aliens to explain lateness orally rather than in writing. In addition, as a fallback, they made several suggestions for revising the instructions for answering the question, so that if the INS insisted on a written answer, unrepresented aliens would have some ideas about the kinds of explanations that would excuse a late filing, and so that they would be alerted to the desirability of getting legal help.

The agency accepted the fallback. It rewrote the instructions for the new form to say that:

> If you need, or would like, help in completing this form and preparing your written statements, assistance from pro bono attorneys and/or voluntary agencies may be available. They may help you at no cost or for a reduced fee. If you have not already received from INS a list of attorneys and accredited representatives, you may obtain a list by calling [an 800 number].
>
> The government will accept as an explanation [of late filing] certain changes in the conditions in your country, certain changes in your own circumstances, and certain other events that may have prevented you from applying earlier. For example, some of the events the government might consider as valid explanations include, but are not limited to, the following:
>
>> You have learned that human rights conditions in your country have worsened since you left;
>> Because of your health, you were not able to submit this application within a year after you arrived;
>> You submitted an application, but it was returned to you because it was not complete. . . .

Federal regulations specify some of the other types of events that may also qualify as valid explanations for why you filed late. These regulations are found at Title 8, Section 208.4 of the Code of Federal Regulations. The list in the Code of Federal Regulations is not all inclusive, and the government recognizes that there are many other circumstances that might be acceptable reasons for filing after one year of arrival. . . . If . . . your explanation is not accepted by the government . . . you could still be eligible for withholding of deportation.[27]

The deadline question itself still asked applicants to explain why they "did not file within the first year," but it no longer used technical terminology of any kind. It simply added that "for guidance in answering this question, see [the detailed instructions above]."[28]

This was a huge improvement over the April edition. Not only was it less intimidating, but it gave late applicants some idea of what might enable them to qualify, and where to go for more help. We didn't expect that many unrepresented applicants would try to find Title 8 of the Code of Federal Regulations, but we did think that the citation might send them running for legal help, and the instructions started them down the track of finding such assistance at no cost. In addition, the illustration that "you have learned that" human rights conditions had worsened helped to point the INS in the direction of accepting changes in the applicant's awareness, and not only changes in objective human rights conditions, as a basis for late filing.

On the other hand, we were disappointed that the INS continued to insist on written explanations, and we could pursue one more protest, because the OMB would accept public comments for thirty days before approving the form. Each group that had asked the INS to delete the question was torn between its appreciation for the lengths to which the agency had gone to accommodate the advocates' concerns, and its awareness that asylum officers could do a much better job than the asylum applicants in identifying possible exceptions. Ultimately, we resolved this ambivalence by asking the OMB to reject the question, and we repeated to the OMB the arguments that we had previously made to the INS about how the requirement might deter valid applicants.[29]

The OMB asked the INS to respond to our comments.[30] The INS responded that other questions on the application form required written rather than oral responses, and "to make any one question on the [form] optional . . . represents an inconsistent approach to the other elements of the . . . form." Also, an applicant's omission of written reasons for lateness on the form would prevent asylum officers (and INS lawyers contesting cases before immigration judges) from "developing important lines of questions during the asylum proceedings."[31]

The OMB apparently accepted these arguments, but it suggested that the INS make two changes in the question. It asked the INS to require applicants to explain only "briefly" why they did not file within a year, and to alert applicants, in the question, that they should "also be prepared to explain at your interview or hearing why you did not file it within the first year."[32] Thus the OMB proposed what it saw as a compromise between our position and that of the INS: to require a writing *and* forecast a further oral explanation. The INS replied that the word "briefly" would mislead applicants because "applicants are encouraged throughout the instructions . . . to provide detailed responses to the questions." It did accept the OMB's suggestion to forecast the additional oral explanation.[33] There the matter ended. The OMB accepted the form, although "due to the extensive public comments" it approved the agency's use of the new form only through the end of January 2000, a shorter period of time than the INS had requested, and it refused the agency's request not to display the form's expiration date.[34] The advocacy groups would have yet another opportunity to complain, if the form seemed to be deterring late filers from attempting to seek asylum.

The battles over the forms was not the advocates' only effort to influence the deeper levels of the new "law" of asylum. The INS continued to hold regular meetings with the advocacy organizations at which officials distributed copies of internal policy directives[35] and made notes of the advocates' grievances about how expedited removal or the adjudication of the new deadline was being administered.[36] Like arguments over the wording of the regulations or the forms, negotiations with the INS on these issues lacked the sweep and drama of congressional committee votes and floor fights. But their resolution created law, just as Congress had made law when it passed the new statute.

In particular, human rights advocates were frustrated that on April 1, 1998, the INS had begun to apply the new one-year asylum deadline, but it hadn't yet issued the final regulation describing the exceptions. We hoped, based on the comments that officials had made during the meetings with Paul Virtue and others, that the INS would probably incorporate into that final regulation several of the improvements that we had advocated in our formal comments. But because the government's clearance process for the final regulation seemed interminable, the INS had to find some different vehicle for interpreting the statute (and the interim regulation), and communicating its policies to the hundreds of asylum officers who would have to make daily decisions about whether late-filing applicants qualified for a "changed" or "extraordinary circumstances" exception. The vehicle, it turned out, would be a "training module," a manual on how to apply the new rules and exceptions, written by INS headquarters in Washington, and distributed during group training sessions to every asylum officer.

INS officials realized that they could write a better training module, and have fewer conflicts with the non-governmental advocates, if they showed us a draft and allowed us to make suggestions.[37] Most of our suggestions for this manual tracked the recommendations that we had already made for improving the interim regulation.

We were very relieved when we saw the manual that the INS issued. It did not give us everything we wanted,[38] but it did implement many of the changes that we had been seeking in the final regulation. The interim regulation had created a "changed circumstances" exception for aliens applying within a reasonable time after "temporary protected status" expired. The manual expanded this to cover applicants who applied within a reasonable period of time after the expiration of *any* legal status, such as a tourist, student, or temporary work visa.[39] The regulation did not specify that threats to a refugee's relatives who were still abroad would constitute a "changed circumstance," but the manual included this exception.[40] The manual specified, as the regulation had not, that the list of extraordinary circumstances published in the interim regulation "is not all inclusive, however, and there are many other circumstances that might apply."[41] An illustrative example in the manual made it clear that an applicant could benefit by a "changed" circumstance in her country even if she didn't know of the change,[42] implying that the exception would also apply, as we had urged, if she did know of the change but had learned about it after being in the United States for more than a year. Furthermore, the manual continued to evolve. In April 1998, changed circumstances "could be," but were not limited to, the types listed in the manual, but by November, such circumstances "include[d]" and were not limited to the listed types.[43]

So by 1998, Congress had receded into the background, and the regulations were mired in bureaucratic machinery, but law continued to be made, through the publication of forms and the printing of operating manuals. The "law" that enables students to apply for asylum within a reasonable time after their student visas expire, even if more than a year after they entered the United States, was written not by Congress, or even by the attorney general, but by the drafters of a training manual. But the low level of visibility of this little scrap of law does not make it any less important than an act of the national legislature. For any particular refugee, the words on a form, the examples and guidance used in an agency training "module," or the details of an INS field directive[44] can be as important as the immigration statute itself in determining whether, ultimately, the refugee is returned to persecution or allowed to begin the long, hard path toward security and freedom in America.

# 14

# The Wave

Nothing ever dies. It always will come back.
—Senator Alan K. Simpson[1]

Congress passed the "Illegal Immigration Reform and Immigrant Responsibility Act of 1996," and related provisions unfavorable to immigrants in the anti-terrorism and welfare laws, just as a wave of postwar anti-immigrant sentiment spread across the United States. The enactment of the immigration restrictions in these three statutes might have been possible only in the brief two-year life span of the 104th Congress.[2] In 1993, 65 percent of Americans thought that immigration to the United States should be decreased; by 1997, even though Congress did not cut immigration quotas, that figure had fallen to 36 percent.[3] What may have been a temporary spike in public distress about immigration coincided with the advent of the first Republican House of Representatives in forty years, a newly Republican Senate, the first term of a Democratic president elected by plurality who favored, or was at least reluctant to oppose, a "tough" immigration bill while running for reelection, and the last months in office of a popular Senate Immigration Subcommittee chairman whose state included few immigrants and who had made a career of trying to limit immigration. A month after Simpson left the Senate, he was replaced as chairman by Spencer Abraham, who had led the fight against Simpson's effort to cut immigration quotas and had supported DeWine's efforts to protect refugees.[4] Had Abraham held the Senate subcommittee chairmanship during the 104th Congress, he would have been a member, and in fact a particularly influential member, of the Conference Committee. The bill that emerged would almost surely have been much more limited, at least with respect to its impact on potential asylum applicants.

Some of the provisions of the new immigration law, such as those providing better policing of American borders, were relatively uncontroversial.[5] But the three 1996 laws also imposed harsh new rules on particular groups of immigrants. Its restrictions on procedural rights for asylum-seekers, summarized below, marked a real retreat from the system of adjudication, including judicial review, that had been in place under the 1980 Refugee Act. Certain other immigrants who were not asylum-seekers fared even worse.[6]

225

## Legal Immigrants in Families with Low Incomes

The immigration bill did not directly cut authorized levels for legal immigration, but the new sponsorship requirements attacked legal immigration indirectly by making it more difficult for families who are not wealthy to help their relatives immigrate into the United States. The law requires a sponsor (or a co-sponsor) to be able to support the sponsor's own family and the immigrant's family at 125 percent of the poverty level, and it makes sponsors legally liable to the government for support of the new immigrants, if they become unable to support themselves. A study by the Urban Institute concluded that 41 percent of all households headed by immigrants would be unable to qualify for sponsorship, a figure that rose to 57 percent for Mexican and Central American families.[7] Some experts predicted that the sponsorship requirement would not cause any reduction in overall immigration, but that fewer people would be able to immigrate from Mexico, Central America, and Haiti, and that the United States would take in a correspondingly larger number of wealthier immigrants from other countries.[8]

At the same time that the immigration law made it more difficult for low-income immigrant families to become reunited with close relatives who were still abroad, the welfare law removed the social safety net from sponsored family members who did immigrate. It denied food stamps and Supplemental Security Income (financial assistance for low-income people who are blind, aged, or disabled) to nearly all legal immigrants.[9] For their first five years in the United States, future new immigrants were also barred from receiving assistance under several other federal programs, and after five years, they could remain ineligible until they became citizens, because their sponsors' income would be deemed available to them for purpose of establishing their income-based qualification for assistance.[10]

### Legal Aliens with Old, Minor Criminal Records

Until the 1996 immigration law was passed, legal aliens who had committed certain criminal offenses were deportable, but the attorney general (who delegated his or her authority to the immigration judges) could balance the equities in most individual cases and grant a waiver to allow such aliens to remain in the United States.[11] The anti-terrorism act and the immigration act denied waivers to anyone guilty of an "aggravated felony," while simultaneously vastly expanding the list of felonies that were "aggravated." A term that in 1988 had meant only murder and certain drug and weapons trafficking crimes was expanded to include any crime of violence or theft for which a sentence of one year was imposed, even if the sentence was suspended in favor of probation and the alien never served time in jail. With the disappearance of the waiver authority, legal aliens who long ago had committed infractions could no longer visit their homelands and expect to be able to return, and many who were arrested for minor offenses in the United States, such as shoplifting, were deported.[12] As interpreted by the attorney general, the anti-terrorism act's elimination of waiver authority was retroactive to convictions before the law was passed and to aliens who had lived in the United States for years or even decades after the sentence had been completed.[13]

This combination of changes resulted almost immediately in severe and surprising hardship for some immigrants who had been living in the United States for a long time. Although many others were also affected,[14] the case of Jesus Collado attracted the greatest press attention. Collado was a forty-three-year old legal immigrant from the Dominican Republic who managed a restaurant in New York. In the spring of 1997, when he returned via Kennedy Airport from a vacation in the Dominican Republic, he was arrested and jailed by immigration officials. Twenty-three years earlier, when he was nineteen, he had been convicted of sexual misconduct and sentenced to a year's probation because he'd had a sexual relationship with his fifteen-year-old girlfriend. His crime had recently been re-defined as an "aggravated felony" within the meaning of the new immigration law, which retroactively reached back into his past. The INS believed that it had no choice but to deport him, because its authority to grant waivers had been repealed, and until late in 1997 it also believed that the new law required jailing Collado and others like him until the agency could deport them. While Collado was in jail, his eighteen-year-old daughter nearly died in a car accident.[15]

## Immigrants On Line for Legal Status

For years before Congress passed the 1996 law, aliens who had filed applications for immigrant visas (either as relatives of U.S. citizens or certain permanent residents, or as business-sponsored employees) often entered the United States without authorization and remained here for several years until their visa number was reached. In 1994, Congress passed a law specifying that in order to get a "green card," such a person had to pay a one-thousand-dollar fine for jumping the gun on immigration. The law was due to expire in 1997. In the 1996 law, Congress declined to extend this provision. At the time, a million immigrants were waiting in the United States for the visas that they would eventually receive; now, they could no longer stay in the United States. The new law also barred anyone who remained in the United States without authorization for six months from entering the United States for several years thereafter. As a result of the expiration of the 1994 law, this group of a million people was put in the position of having to leave their homes, families, and jobs to return to their homelands.[16]

## Central Americans and Others Who Were Waiting for Their Cases to Be Heard

Through the 1980s, civil wars ravaged El Salvador, Guatemala, and Nicaragua. Approximately 350,000 people from these countries overstayed tourist visas or entered the United States without permission and began new lives. Some applied for asylum and waited in what were at the time multi-year adjudication backlogs; others never applied. Some were granted temporary permission to remain in the United States, without asylum, under special provisions of the immigration law. The group included about 250,000 Guatemalans and Salvadorans who were denied asylum, only to have the denials vacated and their cases queued for re-adjudication many years later as a result of the "ABC" settlement of a class action lawsuit in which the INS had been charged with discriminatory enforcement of the asylum law.[17] Another 60,000 immigrants in the pipeline were Nicaraguans who had fled the Sandinista regime and had been covered by a special program for their protection. Most of these immigrants had put down roots and found employment in the United States. Many had children. Before 1997, such a person would occasionally be apprehended by the INS and ordered to appear before an immigration judge in a deportation proceeding. Under the law, even if the immigrant did not qualify for asylum, the judge could grant her a "suspension of deportation" and allow her to remain in the United States if the judge was convinced that she had lived in the United States for seven years, that she had good moral character, and that her deportation would cause "extreme hardship" either to herself or to a spouse, parent, or child who was a U.S. citizen or lawful permanent resident.

The 1996 law changed the name of the "suspension" process, terming it "cancellation of removal." It also made the standard for granting this relief much tougher. Applicants had to have been in the United States for ten years, not seven; the deportation would have to cause "exceptional and extremely unusual hardship" rather than merely "extreme" hardship; and even this very severe hardship would not qualify if it fell only upon the applicant herself. Furthermore, only 4,000 people per year could qualify for this relief from deportation. To make matters worse, a decision of the Board of Immigration Appeals a few months after the law was passed interpreted the statute to stop the running of the clock as soon as immigration court proceedings had begun, so that time waiting for the court to reach the case did not count toward qualifying the immigrant for relief, and it applied this timing rule retroactively to people who had been waiting in line for court hearings for many years.[18] Thus the new standards and numerical cap were made applicable to many who had already been in the United States for part or all of the former seven-year waiting period. The law and the decision was a forecast of deportation for hundreds of thousands of people who had patiently waited for years under special programs and court settlements agreed to by prior presidential administrations.[19]

### People Wrongly Deported Because of Justice Department Errors

A more amorphous group of immigrants were those in many miscellaneous categories who found themselves in deportation proceedings and who believed that their immigration judges had erroneously ordered them deported. Under the law as it existed before 1997, virtually all immigration court decisions could be appealed to a regular federal court and decided by judges who, unlike immigration judges, were independent of the Department of Justice and had life tenure. Yale Law School professor Peter Schuck found that immigrants won 25 percent to 40 percent of such appeals, suggesting "a lot of errors, a lot of procedural errors and a lot of substantive errors."[20] But aliens subjected to expedited removal (most of whom are not asylum applicants, but may in some cases be charged erroneously with having false documents) are allowed no federal court review of their deportations.[21] Congress may also have eliminated federal court review of deportation decisions based on denials of so-called "discretionary" relief, such as refusals to allow people to remain in the United States under the "exceptional and extremely unusual hardship" standard.[22]

The law on refugees was also made more restrictive, but as this book has shown, the act that Congress passed was not nearly as tough on refugees as Smith and Simpson had wanted it to be. A summary comparison of the starting and ending points of the legislation, as interpreted through its regulations and implemented through its forms and operating manuals, shows that the human rights and refugee organizations succeeded significantly, though not totally, in their efforts to kill or moderate the provisions they most feared.

### Admissions through the Overseas–Refugee Program

Representative Smith and Senator Simpson sought to impose a statutory ceiling, at fifty thousand, on the number of people who could be admitted annually through the overseas-refugee program. The statutory limit was eliminated altogether. However, perhaps out of fear that key members of Congress continued to regard the recent level of refugee admissions as excessively high, the administration announced its own 13 percent administrative reduction in the maximum number of refugees who could be admitted from overseas, from ninety thousand in fiscal year 1996 to seventy-eight thousand in fiscal year 1997.[23] Senators Hatch, DeWine, and Abraham protested, to no avail, that "in evaluating whether this reduction is appropriate, it may be helpful to recall that both the Senate and the House rejected attempts to impose a statutory cap on refugee admissions."[24]

### Expedited Removal

Smith and Simpson's version of expedited removal, as introduced in their own bills and then embellished by provisions of the anti-terrorism bill that almost became law,[25] would have applied expedited removal procedures retroactively to all aliens who were apprehended in the United States and thought by the INS to have arrived without visas, or with falsified papers. Immigration inspectors would have ordered them removed, and then physically removed them, without giving them any further opportunity to explain their circumstances. If they claimed fear of persecution, they would have been given asylum interviews, but aliens apprehended at airports or border crossings would have been interviewed immediately, at those ports of entry. The interviewing officials would not necessarily have had training in asylum law or human rights conditions in the alien's country. Even an alien who claimed a fear of persecution would have been removed without a hearing before a judge unless the alien convinced the inspector that it was "more probable than not" that his or her statements were true. Nor would the alien have had an opportunity to appeal an adverse decision to an immigration judge, much less a federal judge with life tenure. The federal courts would also have been prohibited from considering any challenge to the legality of these procedures.

Virtually all of these standards and procedures were eventually moderated, though not as extensively as the Leahy amendment would have changed them. By law, unauthorized aliens who have lived in the United States for at least two years are exempted from these procedures. By regulation, the expedited system is applied only to aliens without proper documents who are caught at ports of entry, not aliens who cross into the United States between ports of entry or those whose entry is approved by an immigration inspector. The inspectors are required to use forms that direct them to ask arriving aliens in several different ways whether they fear returning to their countries. Affirmative answers result in interviews, after at least two days and away from the airport, by trained asylum officers. The screening standard was reduced, so that in fact the officers send to full hearings, before immigration judges, about 80 percent of the aliens they interview. Negative decisions by the asylum officers can be appealed to immigration judges, who apply the same low screening standard to determine whether to schedule full hearings. Judicial review is denied with respect to individual deportation orders, but Congress allowed judicial review of the basic elements of the procedural scheme of the statute and of its implementing regulations.[26]

## Asylum Deadlines and Exceptions

Simpson and Smith (after Smith accepted the McCollum amendment) would have denied asylum summarily to anyone who sought to apply for it more than thirty days after entering the United States. They would have permitted only one exception, where an applicant could prove recently changed circumstances in the applicant's country. The bill that passed the House subcommittee also would have made it more difficult to win asylum by requiring applicants to prove that more probably than not they would be persecuted if returned.

In the end, the deadline was extended to one year, and exceptions were created not only for changed conditions in the applicant's country, but also for other types of "changed" circumstances and for "extraordinary" circumstances, a term that was expanded first through regulations and then through INS manuals and practices. Many new types of exceptions were thus explicitly created in the wake of the statute's enactment, and the list of extraordinary exceptions was made open-ended, inviting applicants and their representatives to advocate for additional exemptions. A set of instructions on the official asylum application form now helps applicants to claim exemptions and advises them to seek free legal assistance to obtain relief from the deadline. As a result of the statutory and administrative changes, INS asylum officers grant exceptions to two-thirds of the applicants for asylum who apply more than a year after entering the United States.[27]

Nevertheless, both of the "reforms" to asylum procedure that Congress enacted in 1996 should now be revisited. They should be revised if not repealed altogether. The deadline for affirmative applicants is a good target for early repeal because it causes great harm to individuals who deserve protection, the harm that it causes is easy to understand, and the requirement of a deadline for affirmative applicants was imposed as a result of a peculiarly closed Conference Committee procedure. Knowledge of the deadline in some parts of the immigrant community may have increased the percentage of those who file within a year to more than the 37.5 percent who applied that quickly before the law was passed.[28] But this is cold comfort, because the percentage who filed within their first year in the United States was so low to begin with. The fact that asylum officers grant exceptions to most late filers is not as encouraging as it might seem, either. First, notwithstanding reasonable INS interpretations of the exceptions, more than a thousand people who applied late during the last eight months of 1998 were denied asylum without regard to the strength of their claims, simply because they missed the deadline.[29] Second, many would-be affirmative asylum applicants who miss the deadline probably do not apply for protection, either because they are unaware of the exceptions or do not believe that they could qualify for one of them. Finally, the technical complexity of many of the exceptions may favor represented applicants compared to those who are interviewed without the assistance of lawyers or other professionals, making justice depend on wealth or luck rather than the merits of a claim.[30]

Expedited removal is a more complex situation. It has been in effect since April 1997, and some statistical information about its impact is available, but critical information is missing. We know that expedited removal procedures were applied to a large number of people apprehended at ports of entry without proper papers—about fifty-five thousand during the first year of the operation of the new law, 5 percent of whom were identified as having a fear of persecution and sent to asylum officers for credible-fear interviews.[31] Seventy-nine percent of the 5 percent were found by the officers to have credible fear and were sent on for full hearings before immigration judges.[32]

The 79 percent statistic tends to suggest that at the asylum officer stage, the process may work fairly well, providing the vast majority of aliens with the opportunity to have a hearing. But human rights advocates always believed that errors were more likely to be made by the INS's secondary inspectors than by its trained asylum officers.[33] Was the 5 percent statistic good enough? Were the secondary inspectors summarily deporting any significant fraction of aliens for whom asylum officers might have found credible fear? The INS thought not; 87 percent of the aliens to whom expedited removal was applied were Mexican nationals,[34] whose rate of success in affirmative asylum cases was less than 1 percent.[35] However, the only way in which human rights advocates could be confident that secondary inspectors were following proper procedures and not making egregious errors would be to observe at least a random sample of secondary-inspection interviews.[36] Independent observers could determine, for example, whether the inspectors were rushing their interviews in order to put people who were not putative refugees on planes that were refueling for return trips,[37] whether they were actually asking the questions about "fear" required by INS procedures, whether they were appropriately attentive to non-verbal indications of fear, whether they were subtly prompting some aliens not to express a fear, whether male inspectors interviewed female aliens in a way that would make it likely that the women would reveal rape or other sexual abuse, and whether inspectors were passing all apparently fearful applicants to the next stage of the process, without making subtle judgments about the applicants' eligibility for asylum.

Unfortunately, although it cooperated in a brief internal Government Accounting Office (GAO) review of secondary inspection,[38] the INS refused to allow observation by independent non-governmental observers. The Ford Foundation and the Joyce Mertz-Gilmore Foundation sponsored an independent review by a study group whose board of advisors included Richard Day, who had been chief counsel to the Senate Judiciary Committee under Senator Simpson, and T. Alexander Aleinikoff, who had been INS general counsel and executive associate commissioner. But the Department of Justice denied the group's request for access to secondary inspections because it "believe[d] it is not possible ... without compromising our law enforcement mission and the interests of individuals involved in the process."[39]

In the absence of a solid independent study validating the accuracy of the expedited removal process, Congress should give serious attention to reports of errors and abuses, such as these:

—Mohamoud Farah, a Somalian refugee, arrived from Egypt at Kennedy airport on October 31, 1997. When an INS official at the airport discovered that he lacked a visa, the officer "insulted me, cursed at me ... pushed me backwards, and I fell down. Before I knew what was happening, three or four INS officers were putting shackles on my arms and legs. They bound my wrists and ankles to the legs of a chair ... and cursed at me.... I remained shackled for fourteen and a half hours. During that time, despite my requests, I was not given any food or water, nor was I allowed to use the restroom.... They eventually sent me to another office where someone from INS began to take a statement.... I was expected to discuss very painful experiences with the same people who were being abusive to me.... After they took the statement, I had to wait in that office for three more hours. I still was not allowed water or given permission to use the restroom. Finally I was transported to the detention facility.... At that point I was finally able to have some water and use the restroom, but received no food until lunch the next day.... After 101 days in detention, on February 9, 1998, I was granted political asylum."[40]

—Two Ecuadorian men who allegedly received death threats after complaining of police corruption arrived in the United States on July 15, 1997. The inspectors at the airport listened to their stories, "just smiled and said, 'that's a lie,'" handcuffed the men to a hotel bed overnight, and returned them to Ecuador the next day, with no credible-fear interview.[41]

—An Albanian woman who said she had been gang-raped in retaliation for her husband's refusal to fight for the government arrived in the United States in May 1997. Inspectors at Logan Airport in Boston gave her a document that she could not read because she did not speak English. It was translated for her over the telephone. She got past the inspectors and was given a credible-fear interview, but she had no lawyer. She explained her fear that she would be tortured but did not reveal that she had been raped. "The translator was a male and on top of that an Albanian," she later told a reporter. "I was afraid to say anything about the rape in case he talked." The officer found that she had no credible fear. She appealed to an immigration judge. The judge would not let her lawyer speak during the hearing, and the INS supplied another male Albanian interpreter. This time, she did talk about being raped, but the judge didn't believe her because she hadn't told the asylum officer about the rape. Although the judge ordered her deported to Albania immediately, her lawyer quickly contacted the American Civil Liberties Union, which moved to allow her to become a plaintiff in its pending class action suit to challenge the expedited removal law. The woman was deported, but she dared not return to her home. An Albanian family "found her, disheveled and forlorn, on a street near the airport in Tirana."[42] After the *New York Times* printed a long story about her treatment under the expedited removal law, and the Civil Liberties Union reported to the INS that a man from her native village was trying to contact the Albanian family that was hiding her, the INS invoked the humanitarian parole provision of the immigration law to allow her to return to the United States to pursue an asylum claim. The INS argued that this development showed that expedited removal was working well. "This shows that we very carefully consider all the cases brought before us and that if new and additional information is presented to us, we can respond appropriately," an INS official said.[43]

—A Sudanese Christian couple, fleeing religious persecution, crossed the border without proper documentation from Mexico into Brownsville, Texas. The husband was apprehended, placed into expedited removal, found to have credible fear, and detained for a hearing. His wife, however, crossed the border undetected, only to be apprehended shortly thereafter by the border patrol in downtown Brownsville. She told INS agents she was afraid that she would be persecuted, but they ordered her deported and she would have been sent home. Because she was Sudanese, she could not simply be sent back across the Mexican border. The INS had to detain her while it arranged to fly her to Sudan. Luckily, her husband saw her in the detention facility and demanded a credible-fear interview for her, which she passed.[44]

—Even a person who arrives with a visa may be handled arbitrarily if an airport inspector believes that the passenger doesn't plan to comply with the terms of the visa. Zdenek Geres, a tourist from the Czech Republic, reported being questioned at the Atlanta airport by an INS officer whose badge gave his name as "Clinton." Geres said that Clinton claimed to be the president's brother and that he could jail Geres if Geres lied to him. The officer didn't believe that Geres had come to visit his friend Donald Oliver and refused to call Oliver for confirmation. He said that he believed that Geres had come to find a job and he put Geres on the next plane home. Because Geres did not claim and could not have claimed to be a refugee, he did not have any opportunity to talk to a different INS official.[45]

—Some airport inspectors reportedly attack arriving aliens with derogatory language (such as "you f___ing Somalis"), interview aliens at a counter within earshot of other interviewees, try to interview non-English speaking aliens with gestures, provide inadequate interpretation, and fail to translate statements they require aliens to sign.[46] Of course, in keeping with INS regulations, aliens are prohibited from consulting lawyers before secondary inspection interviews. One journalist, a "victim of very severe torture, requested—after affirmatively volunteering that he wished to apply for asylum and that the passport he had used to flee to the United States was not his own—to speak with a lawyer, because he believed that in the United States people have a right to counsel [but] he was refused."[47]

Congress should particularly address issues involving detention of people who have been found to have credible fear.[48] Detention, "in windowless cells on dimly lit corridors," in which asylum applicants are denied food and water every day between 3:30 P.M. and 3:30 A.M.,[49] is not merely unpleasant and degrading for people who have committed no crime. The practice also impairs their ability to win their asylum cases. It prevents them from maintaining effective contact with representatives, and it prevents them from finding the witnesses and documents that they will need at their asylum interviews and immigration court hearings.[50] INS policy permits the release, pending hearings, of asylum-seekers who have been found to meet the credible-fear standard, have a place to live, and are not potentially barred (e.g, by being possible terrorists) from winning asylum.[51] Some are released, and many of those are then able to collect evidence and win asylum. But the INS allows its individual district directors unbridled discretion to decide who is to be released and who should be kept detained, even permitting them to vitiate the agency's pre-trial release policy. The New York director evidently decided not to release anyone.[52] Apparently the impetus within some circles in the INS for detaining asylum-seekers who have been found to have credible fear results, not from a belief that they will abscond instead of appearing at their hearings, but from the availability of special funds, derived from a seven-dollar tax on international airline tickets sold in the United States, that are earmarked for the detention of aliens without proper documents who are apprehended at airports. These funds enable the INS to house such aliens in "1,100 'user fee' beds" and cannot be spent for other purposes such as detaining unauthorized aliens who overstay their visas after entering the United States lawfully.[53] Human rights advocates respond that "arbitrary detention based solely on the temporary availability of detention space subverts [the] basic governmental responsibility [to make] intelligent choices about scarce detention resources."[54]

Repeal or amendment of the deadline and expedited removal provisions seems politically feasible in view of the fact that Congress repealed several of its other 1996 immigration restrictions within two years after it passed them. With Simpson gone, Abraham heading the Senate Immigration Subcommittee, and the Republican Party smarting from an Hispanic voter backlash in California that helped Clinton win his battle for re-election there, Congress backpedaled rapidly. First it restored Supplemental Security Income benefits worth nine billion dollars to half a million people who had become legal immigrants before the 1996 law was passed.[55] It followed up by restoring food stamps to about 250,000 legal immigrants who were children, elderly, or disabled when the law was enacted.[56] A 1997 law granted amnesty to 150,000 Nicaraguans and 5,000 Cubans who had arrived in the United States before December 1995, and it allowed 250,000 Salvadorans and 50,000 Guatemalans to apply to remain in the United States under a hardship standard even less demanding than the standard in place before the 1996 law was passed.[57] A year later, Congress also granted amnesty to 50,000 unauthorized Haitians who had applied for asylum, but were not granted it, before 1996.[58] Congress even repealed its retroactive application of the 1996 provision requiring aliens on line for green cards to return home while they waited their turn.[59] Meanwhile, outside Congress, other moderating changes occurred. Courts declared unconstitutional the 1996 act's bar on judicial review of deportation orders against aliens convicted of crimes[60] and reversed the attorney general's interpretation of the 1996 act as barring herself from granting waivers to unauthorized aliens who had committed minor crimes but who had met the standards for waiver prior to enactment of the new law.[61] The INS itself changed its regulations on detention pending deportation of aliens who had committed minor offenses and released Jesus Collado from prison.[62] In 1998, a leading authority on immigration law could write that "even after the recent changes by Congress [and despite new legal provisions that are arbitrary toward asylum-seekers and deportation hardship cases], American immigration policy is more generous, less racist, and (if we are careful) more politically sustainable than ever before."[63] In essence, FAIR's Dan Stein agreed. "We're in a period of immigration pandering," he said. "It's like trying to stop a freight train."[64]

Following this liberalizing trend, Congress might also repeal the asylum deadline, and in view of the 79 percent approval rate, it could eliminate the credible-fear screening interviews for arriving aliens who express a fear of return or a desire to apply for asylum. Although Representative Lamar Smith seems determined to maintain the restrictions enacted in 1996,[65] his Senate counterpart, Immigration Subcommittee chairman Spencer Abraham, voted for the Leahy amendment and to limit the one-year deadline to defensive asylum cases. Of course both houses of Congress would have to support a repeal, but in a future Conference Committee, the House might trade asylum liberalization for some other legal change it wanted from the Senate.

Indeed only two months after expedited removal went into effect, the Commission on Immigration Reform recommended repeal of the requirement that aliens found by airport inspectors to have a fear of return should have to undergo credible-fear interviews before they can have hearings. It reasoned that the 3,600 people sent for credible-fear interviews "can be handled through the normal removal proceedings that provide greater protection to asylum seekers."[66] It suggested that credible-fear reviews should be used only to determine which asylum applicants should be released from detention pending hearings.[67] The following year, the commission implied that even with respect to arriving aliens who are not asylum-seekers, the expedited removal system may not discourage recidivism as well as the old system, because although the legal effect might be the same, deportation as a result of a judicial hearing carries a more effective message than summary deportation by an official at an airport or border crossing. "What is gained in expediting by the new statutory process may be lost in increased recidivism."[68]

The new expedited removal system is unlikely to be repealed in its entirety, however, because INS officials talk about it as a "law enforcement bonanza" at the land border crossings, where only a very tiny fraction of aliens are asylum applicants (at least in this period of relatively greater respect for human rights in Central America).[69] If the system is not entirely replaced, Congress should at least restore basic elements of fairness and accuracy to the process. Aliens arriving at airports should be permitted to request and receive assistance in their airport interviews, if such assistance would not delay the interviews by more than a few hours. Those who have had long flights should be allowed a reasonable period of rest, the opportunity to have some food and water, and the opportunity to use restrooms, before being interviewed. The airport interviews should be conducted in complete privacy, and the interpreters should be both competent and legally required to respect the confidentiality of the communication. The INS should be required to allow independent monitoring of a sample of secondary interviews, under the supervision of qualified sociologists; the GAO study involved much too small a sample to be reliable, and the GAO observers apparently did not apparently study whether the inspectors were exceeding their instructions by asking too many questions. Lawyers and other advocates accredited by the INS should be permitted to provide their traditional representational services in both credible-fear interviews and immigration judge reviews of those interviews. The current prohibition on the expenditure of federal funds for the representation of asylum-seekers should be replaced by a small appropriation for the Justice Department to contract with non-profit organizations to offer free representation to indigent asylum-seekers whose removal is being sought by the INS.[70] Pre-hearing detention of aliens who have been found to have a credible fear of persecution should be reserved for exceptional circumstances, such as when aliens are thought by the INS to be potential terrorists.[71]

In addition, if expedited removal remains part of the landscape, Congress or the attorney general should revise the system to apply the procedure only to aliens who lack a visa or whose travel documents appear to be false or to have been altered. At present, inspectors also apply expedited removal procedures to anyone who they think has lied to obtain a facially valid visa; e.g., a person who claimed to be a tourist but is suspected by an inspector of harboring an intention to work in the United States and therefore of having obtained a visa by fraudulent means. These people, unlike those who claim a fear of being returned home, are sent back at once; they do not have the opportunity for a credible-fear interview by another official. The power to exclude a person from the country, and simultaneously bar the alien from attempting another re-entry by any means for the next five years, should not be delegated to inspectors who rely on guesses.

In the longer run, the asylum system and the overseas-refugee resettlement program must be considered together, as an integrated response to the responsibilities of the United States to a worldwide problem of human rights deprivations. Three factors may prompt changes in the overseas program that could reduce the number of refugees seeking asylum after traveling to the United States. First, the United States has gradually been training foreign airport officials to recognize passengers who may be trying to come to the United States without proper travel documents, and to intercept them before they board their aircraft. The process of intercepting refugees before they can reach the United States to claim asylum will be accelerated by a provision in the 1996 act, inspired by Representative Schumer, requiring the U.S. government to set up "preinspection stations" staffed by INS officials in five major foreign airports.[72] To the extent that preinspection by airline personnel or government officials is effective, fewer persecuted aliens will be able to seek asylum. The overseas-refugee program will be their only hope of obtaining resettlement in the United States. The procedures for access to this program should take account of the increasing obstacles to travel to the United States for the purpose of seeking asylum.[73] Second, eventually the Lautenberg amendment will have run its course because to the extent that the eligible populations of people in the former Soviet Union and Southeast Asia want to emigrate to the United States, they will have done so.[74] As ex-Soviet Jews and Southeast Asian refugees apply in smaller numbers for refugee status,[75] Congress and the administration will face a choice: they could continue to authorize the admission of seventy-eight thousand or more refugees, as in fiscal years 1998 and 1999,[76] drawing refugees from a more diverse group of countries, or they could reduce refugee admissions on the theory that fewer people need or want resettlement in the United States.[77] Having to make this choice should compel fresh thinking about refugee policy. Third, as it rethinks its policy, the U.S. will recognize that the overseas-refugee program is, in principle, better for refugees than the availability of asylum processing. Overseas determinations can avoid the waste of effort and money that occurs whenever an alien traverses an ocean only to be denied asylum and deported, hardship is reduced because beneficiaries of the overseas program are subsidized during the resettlement process, and the overseas-refugee program is more popular politically than asylum, because all overseas refugees arrive as legal aliens.[78]

In view of recurring persecution in many parts of the world, it would be desirable, as fewer refugees arrive from the former Soviet Union and Southeast Asia, to maintain at least the current levels of refugee admissions and within those levels, to try to locate and accept as overseas refugees many of the people who now flee oppression and win asylum in the United States. To the extent possible, the U.S. should seek out and admit through the overseas refugee program people who are most at risk of persecution, are qualified for protection under the Refugee Convention, are unable to settle permanently and securely where they are presently located, and cannot come to the United States because they are unable to afford plane tickets (and false documents).[79] Accepting more refugees from regions other than the former Soviet Union and Southeast Asia will not eliminate the need for an asylum law, because even a more globally administered overseas-refugee program will not reach everyone eligible for its assistance, and some people who qualify for refugee treatment will continue to take flight on their own and seek refuge in the United States. In any year in which the overseas-refugee program does not meet its authorized ceiling, however, any unspent resettlement funds should be used to help resettle indigent people who win asylum, to better equalize the benefits between those who win refugee status overseas and those who obtain virtually the same status in the United States.

The U.S. government already gives top priority to admitting from overseas those refugees who face the highest risks to their personal security.[80] But the number of such people actually admitted who have fled from the countries ruled by the world's most oppressive leaders is small. Assuming that the people of the United States are willing to make the political commitment to maintain at least the current level of refugee admissions, Congress and the administration should eventually increase resources for the settlement of refugees who have fled countries in which systematic human rights violations are most prevalent.[81] These countries include several nations in Africa and the Near East.[82]

The neighboring countries to which human rights victims most often flee have large populations of displaced persons. Only a small fraction of those persons are refugees within the meaning of the Refugee Convention. Furthermore, resettlement is the best solution for only some of those who qualify for convention protection, and other developed countries should share with the United

States the responsibility of resettling those who cannot return home or be resettled in their own regions. Therefore, the United States will have to continue to rely to a large extent on offices of the United Nations High Commissioner for Refugees for recommendations regarding which refugees to accept for U.S. resettlement.[83] The UNHCR has a broader international refugee perspective than the U.S. government and has had very extensive experience with refugee populations across the world. In addition, independent U.S. refugee screening of large groups of refugees may not be practicable.[84]

In some recent years, reliance on the UNHCR has seemed problematic. UNHCR has its own resource limitations[85] and its own priorities, which may differ from those of the United States.[86] In the early 1990s resettlement became a low priority at UNHCR, particularly for refugees living in urban areas. UNHCR apparently feared that creation of a resettlement program in third-world cities would create a magnet, drawing rural refugees to the resettlement processing centers.[87] UNHCR referred fewer than five hundred African refugees to the U.S. program during the first ten months of fiscal year 1997, and human rights activists charged that UNHCR had become a "gate-keeper, turning refugees away from consideration by the U.S. program."[88]

In the years immediately after 1997, however, UNHCR markedly increased the number of African refugees that it referred to the United States for possible resettlement, and this positive trend could continue if the United States becomes willing to accept more refugees from regions where the need is great. If the number of possible U.S. resettlements of human rights victims from Africa and Asia increases by tens of thousands, and the UNHCR is willing to increase accordingly the number of refugees that it refers to the United States for resettlement, Congress should supplement UNHCR resources through modest additional appropriations. Already, the United States provides funds to support two UNHCR Junior Professional Officers who work on initial refugee screening in Africa.[89] This program, or one like it, could be expanded to fill an increasing need.

Reforming the most unfair procedures of expedited removal, applying a filing deadline only to defensive asylum cases, and making the overseas-refugee program more easily available to human rights victims in Africa and Asia are moderate, feasible measures that would improve the American response to persecution in other lands. Undertaking these measures would further demonstrate that the wave of fear that contributed to passage of the 1996 law attenuated during the late 1990s, and that the nation remains committed to the goals of its Refugee Act.

# 15

# Public Interest Advocacy
# in Congress

*Lobbying is additive. Lots of people do lots of things right, and you may win.*

– David Cohen[1]

The moderating changes in the refugee provisions, like the rescue of legal immigration and the elimination of additional restrictions on benefits for legal immigrants, resulted from the combined effort of legislators who opposed Smith and Simpson and of non-governmental organizations that organized constituents and lobbied both Congress and the administration for more than three years. It is, of course, risky to draw firm conclusions from a single case study. But based on the experience of advocacy by human rights and religious groups with respect to the immigration bill and its implementing regulations, I offer sixteen hypotheses that may be of use to public interest advocates and can be tested through future studies of efforts by non-profit organizations to affect public policy.[2]

## 1. Participation is possible

Congress is a large and very complex public institution, but even in its modern bureaucratic form, it is not so complicated or inaccessible as to render it beyond the influence of public interest organizations. In a way, the immigration bill put this first proposition to the test. The bill became a priority issue for Republican legislators who had been handed control of the congressional machinery for the first time in forty years. Organizations that traditionally had advocated for immigrants in Congress were disrupted by the fall from power of their principal legislative allies. Immigration was also a highly emotional subject, and the weight of public opinion favored restriction. Yet the organizations were able to rally. They helped their congressional supporters to defeat the threatened cutbacks in legal immigration and the overseas-refugee program. Although they could not knock out all of the bill's objectionable features, they were able to change many of them in important ways.

I have deliberately referred to organizations rather than individuals in this first suggestion. A single individual constituent may still be able to influence federal legislation, particularly if he or she knows a member of Congress personally. But the heavy lifting has to be done by organizations, for only they have the ability to mobilize large numbers of voters, in many parts of the country, on short notice. Furthermore, organizations that are already well established when a legislative crisis emerges are more likely to be effective than new ad hoc groups, because the established organizations already have the necessary infrastructure and interpersonal connections. Creation of a new Committee to Preserve Asylum was essential because no pre-existing organization was primarily focused on stopping the thirty-day deadline. But the Committee's effectiveness stemmed in significant part from the willingness of older organizations to share their fax trees and expertise.

## 2. Traditional methods of influencing legislation still matter

It may be fashionable to dismiss lobbying as a preserve of the wealthy and powerful, a way of influencing public policy that depends on making large campaign contributions, hosting members of Congress for golf weekends, or knowing senators personally. The ability to direct large sums of money and to purchase personal access to legislators may determine or strongly influence the outcome of bills, or provisions of bills, that transfer large sums of money to or from an industry or individual vitally affected by the change in law (e.g., a bill regulating cable television rates, allowing banks to own insurance companies, or creating a new tax loophole).[3] The immigration bill was not such a bill; the interests on each side were not primarily economic. At least when large transfers of money are not at stake, traditional methods of influencing legislation still matter. These are the methods that every secondary school student learns about: writing to and telephoning members of Congress, explaining the impact of proposed bills on one's own life, asking others in the community or the nation to write to members as well, writing letters to editors, and asking newspapers, columnists, and their radio and television counterparts to develop stories and editorials about important public issues. The success of the Leahy amendment in the Senate, in particular, resulted in large measure from the effective use of these tried and true techniques. A substantial volume of correspondence from citizens, particularly on issues that are not among the five most visible current controversies, registers with members of Congress because members rarely hear from their constituents about issues that aren't on the front page. As one member of Congress has noted, "most of the things we vote on, we don't hear from the people."[4]

Inside-the-Beltway advocates on the immigration bill did not try to garner support for their positions by generating or focusing campaign contributions. But the human rights and religious organizations did make heavy use of another instrument of effective advocacy: their national policy offices. These small professional advocacy staffs were critical to the organizations' successes. Advocates in the Washington offices of the Lawyers Committee on Human Rights, the United States Catholic Conference, the National Immigration

Forum, Amnesty International, the Lutheran Immigration and Refugee Service, the American Bar Association, the American Immigration Lawyers Association, and others spent thousands of hours briefing congressional staff members and preparing and distributing memoranda to explain the consequences of the Smith and Simpson bills. Only a few members of Congress made themselves personally available to these groups, but staff members from a very large number of congressional offices took seriously the arguments and briefings from the groups' Washington experts, particularly when the requests for meetings from the professional advocates were mirrored by a flood of telephone calls and faxes from constituents in the legislators' states.[5]

It would be naive to claim that money is irrelevant to the process of influencing non-economic legislation. The advocacy organizations could not have maintained Washington staffs without funds to pay for their salaries (however low) and such operational expenses as rent and telephone bills. Furthermore, although the organizations did not themselves make campaign contributions, they did occasionally speak through individuals who had done so in the past or who might do so in the future. Two dramatic examples emerge from the immigration advocacy. First, the religious organizations leading the fight against the refugee cap in the Senate subcommittee carefully solicited assistance from Iowans who knew Senator Grassley or who had contributed to his campaigns. "You have to find the person who knows the senator, and at this point, contributions are absolutely relevant," one Washington advocate told me. "The term 'grass roots' does not refer only to college students who are Amnesty International members and have participated in big demonstrations. Not all grass roots are equal."[6]

Second, Representative Charles Schumer may well have changed his position on applying a deadline to affirmative asylum applicants because he had decided to run for statewide office in New York and needed to reach out to liberals for campaign contributions. He could not afford a reputation as the Democrat who had most helped to destroy asylum.

The advocacy organizations, however, made very little use of politicians' insatiable need for campaign contributions, perhaps because these particular advocates had so few connections to major contributors. At one point, Pistone sent a research assistant to the Federal Election Commission to obtain copies of the names and addresses of contributors of five hundred dollars or more to the campaigns of key legislators, but she never used the information she collected. Perhaps a persuasive advocacy letter directed to a few hundred large contributors of a key member of Congress, urging them to communicate with their representative, would have been an effective adjunct to the overall lobbying effort, but it was not attempted in connection with the immigration bill.

### 3. Advocates should anticipate a staggering amount of work

Commensurate with its importance, national advocacy requires an unbelievable amount of time and effort, and the coordination of hundreds, or even thousands, of people. Each new stage of the process brought into play additional legislators, more districts and states to be organized, and ever-larger numbers of letters and faxes to be sent. The professional advocates often worked into the night and over weekends. They spent years of intermittent activity, before 1995, to keep expedited removal from becoming law, and two full years of extremely intense activity, in the 104th Congress, fighting the Smith and Simpson bills.

### 4. It's not over when it's over

It isn't possible to rest easy even when the legislative battle ends. Various administrative struggles often begin at that point, and their outcome can make the legislative result significantly better or worse. The regulations, forms, and manuals implementing the refugee provisions of the immigration bill became extremely important in shaping how the law actually affects immigrants. Existing statutes and agency practices provide for public participation in administrative law-making. In addition, legislation is always subject to amendment, repeal, or judicial interpretation, requiring further follow-up activity.

### 5. Public interest organizations play a significant role in agenda-setting

Public interest organizations cannot necessarily determine the outcome of a legislative fight, but like legislators themselves, they can play a very substantial role in establishing which issues will be fought about.[7] Through their ability to locate sponsors for amendments, organize grass-roots campaigns, and focus attention on their central issues, they help to decide which topics will be controversial and which proposals will pass Congress with little notice. For example, the organizations that serve beneficiaries of the overseas-refugee program made the proposed cap on refugees their top priority, and the Committee to Preserve Asylum focused first on the asylum deadline and then on expedited removal. Only as non-profit advocacy groups highlighted these issues did they become controversial; broad-based opposition to the Smith and Simpson proposals did not emerge spontaneously from within the Congress.[8] Similarly, the welfare provisions of the bill became controversial at the last minute because the National Immigration Law Center and its allies made them controversial. Conversely, because no groups made it a priority to advocate for the rights of aliens with minor criminal records, the provisions of the bill that later caused them great hardship never became a major issue.

### 6. The administration is a heavy hitter

Even when the administration's party controls neither house of Congress (and all the more so when it controls at least one house), the administration is a force to be reckoned with. Like Congress, the administration consists of many different officials who have to be contacted and persuaded during a campaign of legislative advocacy. The power of the administration derives from the expertise of the professionals who administer the law, the lack of strong party discipline within Congress, the Senate's filibuster rule (which gives extra influence to the minority party), the president's ability to rally public opinion, and the possibility of a presidential veto. To the Congress and the public, the White House and even the INS seemed merely reactive at many stages of the immigration debate. But they influenced the outcome at several critical junctures. The president's acceptance of the Jordan Commission report helped to embolden Smith and Simpson to try to cut legal immigration. The administration's sudden change of heart, and its support of splitting the bill just before the House vote, was one of the final blows ensuring that legal immigration would not be restricted further. Its steadfast opposition to the Gallegly amendment killed that measure. The president's overall support for the welfare bill enabled conservatives to enact cutbacks in benefits for immigrants in that legislation, but the administration's eleventh-hour intervention in negotiations on the immigration bill prevented further erosion in that area. With respect to the asylum issues, the non-governmental immigration advocates probably succeeded in killing the thirty-day and six-month versions of the deadline because the administration stood with them, and the administration's legislative stance later translated into a reasonably generous spirit when regulations, forms, and operating manuals had to be drafted. By contrast, the president's early endorsement of the concept of expedited removal virtually assured that some version of this new procedure would be enacted. The non-governmental advocates hated expedited removal as much as they disliked an asylum deadline, but without as much help from an administration that refused to accept the "manifestly unfounded" standard of the Leahy amendment, they did not fare as well on this issue, and the administration was later less willing to accommodate their concerns in the procedural regulations.

### 7. Packaging matters a lot

Packaging issues into bills is a particularly important type of setting the agenda. Putting an unpopular proposal into an otherwise popular bill can kill the popular bill or pass the unpopular one, particularly in the House of Representatives, where the Rules Committee can prevent consideration of floor amendments. In addition, including many proposed changes in a single bill can spread thin the resources of both proponents and opponents of legislation. This tactic can also divide a coalition opposed to the legislation. Legislators and advocacy organizations must therefore pay the closest attention to the strategic issues of how proposals are combined in a bill, whether it is one that they help to write or one that they fiercely oppose.

Smith and Simpson cleverly rolled into single immigration bills nearly every restrictionist idea that had been kicking around the Congress for years. Only in this way did they have a prayer of enacting limits on legal immigration or curbing the overseas-refugee program. Cutting back procedural protections for potential asylum-seekers would not have passed as a free-standing measure, but it could be approved by the House, and ultimately by the Senate as part of an unamendable conference package, when tied to an anti-terrorism bill or a bill providing for greater border enforcement. A bill eliminating welfare benefits for legal immigrants would have attracted a presidential veto, but the president dared not veto a popular welfare reform bill that included such a cutback as one of its titles. The omnibus bill strategy also impeded the ability of the immigration advocates to fight back, because they had to work on a vast number of issues simultaneously, and it was exceedingly difficult to persuade constituents, journalists, and editorial writers to pay attention to a dozen or more issues at once.

FAIR understood these principles well. It made the most of its ability to influence the two Immigration Subcommittee chairs who drafted the bills. "Our big advantage was that the original bill was gigantic," recalled Executive Director Dan Stein. "It was huge, and covered so many areas the opposition's resources were overwhelmed.... They were constrained to limit their resources to only a handful of key battles over key amendments."[9]

An omnibus packaging strategy is, of course, two-edged. Putting so many issues in one bill probably helped Smith and Simpson to pass most of them, but they and their allies were also kept busy by having to fight on many fronts. Perhaps Simpson would have been able to obtain one more vote against the Leahy amendment if he had not been working on other issues at the same time. And he may have needed so many allies on so many issues in the last days of the Senate's consideration of the bill that he could not resist Senator DeWine's request (backed by the threat of a floor fight) for a "manager's amendment" to inject statutory exceptions into the asylum deadline provision.

Agenda control worked for the Republican leadership in a more random way at a later stage of the process. Representative Gallegly was not able to make his public education amendment into law, but he was able to dominate the immigration agenda for months during the summer of 1996, so that other issues, like the fate of the Leahy amendment in the Conference Committee, were unable to break into most news stories. If the House had voted down the Gallegly amendment to begin with, Senator Specter or others might have had attention or political capital available for other conflicts, and other sections of the final bill might have become much more moderate.

### 8. Procedure is central

This proposition is true in two different senses. Regulation of procedure is often the means by which the government affects basic human affairs, as when legislatures, unable constitutionally to ban abortions, require women to travel twice to clinics (often over long distances and at considerable expense) before obtaining them.[10] In addition, sophisticated use of congressional procedures often affects or determines the fate of proposed legislation. The immigration law illustrates both of these principles.

Almost all of the problems that caused asylum to become controversial in the early 1990s resulted from poor procedures. The deficiencies included inadequate visa checks that resulted in the admission to the United States of terrorists like Sheik Rahman, an INS policy of granting work authorization to all affirmative asylum applicants without creating an adjudication staff large enough to interview the applicants promptly, and laws and regulations that provided scant preliminary asylum screening and inadequate detention space at ports of entry, particularly New York, which seemed swamped by aliens arriving with false documents. Clinton administration officials addressed these problems with several procedural changes, including eliminating the automatic employment authorization, doing away with time-consuming written explanations of why asylum officers were denying applicants' claims, adjudicating new asylum cases on a "fast track" ahead of older cases in the backlog, and training airline personnel to examine U.S. visas at several foreign airports. The congressional proponents of restrictions proposed their own, more drastic procedural reforms, though these innovations drew charges of being unfair to refugees: short statutes of limitation on asylum applications, summary adjudication at all airports and land border crossings, denial of access to counsel before deportation by an airport or border inspector, and curtailed judicial review. Similarly, those trying to protect refugees focused on procedural amendments to these procedural changes, including exceptions to the deadlines, required training for those administering the new system, and review by immigration judges, if not full federal court review.

The fight over fairness for potential refugees was mirrored by the fight over fairness for members of Congress who opposed the restrictionists. The Senate's long tradition of respect for every member helped to ensure a relatively open process, so that all amendments could be considered and voted on in committee and on the floor. But in the House, the process was much more closed. In the House Judiciary Committee, Smith and Hyde allowed their opponents to speak and offer amendments, but nearly all changes were summarily rejected in party-line votes. Then things got worse. The Rules Committee refused to allow the House to consider amendments to eliminate expedited removal and the asylum deadline. And although the Senate significantly modified expedited removal and all but eliminated the deadline, the Republicans steadfastly excluded the Democratic members of the Conference Committee from all of the real deliberations and refused even to allow them to offer amendments for consideration during the one brief official Conference Committee meeting. Finally, in the last days of the 104th Congress, a congressional quirk—the simultaneous pendency of a "must-pass" omnibus appropriation bill—enabled an "unamendable" immigration bill reported by the Conference Committee to be amended and folded into another law. At the same time, the possibility of delays during a post-cloture filibuster gave the president and the Democratic opponents of the bill the political clout to bring about the amendment.

## 9. Timing is also critical

Timing may not be everything, but it requires close attention. Legislative advocates are used to hearing that early contact with congressional offices is of little use, because members and their staffs are so busy that they cannot be bothered with, or even remember, issues that are not likely to be ripe within a few days. On the other hand, waiting until the last days before a vote is risky and often impossible, because even staff members may then be unavailable, and an advocate must usually discuss the issues with staff members of legislators in many different offices. Furthermore, the timing of legislative action is often unclear; we spent three months thinking that the Senate Judiciary Committee might, at any moment, take up the asylum provisions of the bill.

A more subtle question is whether, in the legislative sphere, one can win too soon. By defeating affirmative asylum deadlines in the Judiciary Committee, we avoided having to mount an uphill Senate floor fight and educate eighty additional senators about our issue. However, because we had won and we did not want to reopen a controversial issue, we did not bring further senatorial or press attention to this issue. We might have been dangerously vulnerable if Simpson had suddenly introduced an amendment to reverse the Judiciary Committee's decision, but we thought that scenario unlikely in view of the margin against him in the committee's only vote on the issue.[11] But one result of our early Senate victory was that, although the House bill still included a short deadline on affirmative applications, this issue disappeared from public view. As the immigration bill reached the Senate floor, the nation's newspapers carried many stories, columns, and editorials about expedited removal, which was the subject of a major fight. But scant public attention was paid to asylum deadlines. The full Senate did not focus explicit attention on that issue. Accordingly, when Republicans were privately reconciling the House and Senate bills in their unofficial version of a Conference Committee, they felt little pressure, either from a Senate vote or from public clamor, to accept the Senate's "defensive-only" position on asylum deadlines. This may have been a real cost of succeeding too easily, too soon.

On the other hand, if we had not killed a deadline on affirmative asylum applications in the Senate Judiciary Committee, we would have been tied up organizing a floor fight on that issue. If we had been forced to go to the floor to attack the deadline, we probably would not have had the will or the resources to mount a simultaneous challenge to Simpson's expedited-removal provisions. Indeed, such a fight might never have attracted a Senate sponsor. Senator Leahy was emboldened to attack summary exclusion, first in the Judiciary Committee and then on the floor, in part by the fact that refugee advocates' opposition to a short deadline was attracting support from most members of the committee. Therefore, postponing a fight over the proposed thirty-day rule until the bill got to the Senate floor could have given the issue greater public visibility. But the result in the larger body would have been more uncertain, and it would probably have precluded an attack on the expedited-removal procedures in Simpson's bill. The outcome would have been not only a less fair expedited-removal procedure for aliens newly arriving without proper documents. The expedited-removal provisions of the anti-terrorism law, which were repealed by the Leahy amendment and by the final immigration bill, would have gone into effect. Expedited-removal procedures would, therefore, have been applied to the large number of aliens who, during past decades, had entered the United States without presenting themselves to immigration inspectors.

### 10. A personal meeting is worth a dozen phone calls

Even in our modern, bureaucratic, electronic world, personal contact remains strikingly important. The advocates made the most impact on legislative offices to which they could bring refugees to tell their stories directly to members or staffers. They were also successful with offices where at least they themselves could develop personal relationships with members of the staff. A turning point in what became the floor fight on the Leahy amendment was the briefing that several of us offered to Senate staff members, at which we met some of those staffers for the first time. Senator Hatch's office had never returned phone calls from Pistone or me until we met his staff member during that briefing; after that, Hatch's office was extremely cordial and responsive to our arguments and helpful in keeping us abreast of legislative developments. In contrast, we made no impact on Representative Smith, who, after early 1995, walled himself off from contact with the immigration advocates and didn't respond to our requests for meetings, or on Senator Specter, who didn't attend the key mark-up votes and apparently didn't share his thinking even with his own assistant for immigration. Similarly, Smith's strategy of not naming House conferees until it was too late to influence the bill gave the more junior House Republican members of the Conference Committee a good excuse to avoid meeting with us. Such meetings might have provoked them to think independently about the issues on the table.

### 11. Coalitions are essential, but they also impose limits, and some organizations in coalitions have more weight than others

A single individual, or even a single organization, is unlikely to have much impact on the federal legislative process, at least when Congress is considering a large, important bill. One person or one group (at least one non-profit group) rarely has enough political power to turn the tide, or even sufficient staff personnel or constituents to inform or persuade a large number of relevant legislators. But coalitions of organizations can pool their expertise, their Rolodexes, and their other resources, dividing up legislators to be contacted and asking constituents to advocate for issues dear to the hearts of several coalition partners.

Opponents of asylum restrictions had no choice but to engage in coalition politics. All immigration advocates labored under the disability that their constituents didn't vote, because even lawful permanent U.S. residents don't receive that privilege until they become citizens. But advocates for future asylum applicants represented people who weren't even present in the United States. Much of the Committee to Preserve Asylum's initial success depended on making connections with and obtaining advice from larger, more established advocacy organizations, particularly the U.S. Catholic Conference and the National Immigration Forum.

Newcomers to the process quickly discovered, however, that coalition politics imposes compromise within a coalition, and weaker members of the coalition are more likely to have to do the compromising. The Committee to Preserve Asylum was concerned at first only with asylum deadlines, and later with expedited removal as well, but the larger, more experienced, and better established members of the coalition opposing the bill cared more about several issues affecting many more people: preserving current levels of family-based and employment-based immigration, holding the line on welfare benefits for legal aliens, avoiding severe restrictions on sponsorship, and preserving the overseas-refugee program. The larger organizations sympathized with and sometimes advocated for asylum-seekers, and they never asked asylum advocates, or any other group, to refrain from advocacy on any issue. But when critical moments for compromise arrived, the asylum advocates' proposals were left out of the package. This happened twice: when House Democrats, and moderate Republicans, in consultation with several of the advocacy groups, drafted the split-the-bill amendment to rescue all legal immigration *except* asylum and humanitarian parole, and when a last-minute fight was organized on behalf of legal aliens only, rather than for asylum-seekers as well.[12] One advocate later reflected that "judgments were being made every day about what we could realistically hope to impact. I think we actually had a good shot at the asylum issue [but] legal immigration was an issue that almost all the groups were behind, and for some groups it was by far the most important issue. Soon, all the energy was going behind that issue, and we were playing catchup to have other issues considered."[13]

The suggestion that some organizations have more clout than others invites an interesting comparison between the Committee to Preserve Asylum, which formed quickly to try to save asylum, and the group of about half a dozen much older organizations that advocated on behalf of a similar group of people, would-be future beneficiaries of the overseas-refugee program. In both cases, the ultimate constituents were non-voters, and both of these groups of refugees were threatened by the Smith and Simpson bills. Yet the overseas-refugee advocates won their legislative fight totally and early, while the asylum advocates won only partially and had to fight on through the last days of the 104th Congress.

The difference can be explained in some part, perhaps, by the relative appeal of the two issues. Overseas refugees wait abroad, on a virtual line, for permission to enter the United States legally. Asylum-seekers often have to leave their countries very quickly, sometimes escaping hours before assassins can catch up with them. Americans who know about both programs sometimes think of the asylum-seekers as line-jumpers. Political backing among voters also explains part of the difference. Thanks to historical circumstances and the Lautenberg amendment, Jews from the former Soviet Union and Southeast Asians have been major beneficiaries of the overseas-refugee program, and many voters, who themselves have come from those parts of the world, strongly support the program. Asylum-seekers, by contrast, come from all over the world, and few if any identifiable blocs of voters are concerned about them. In addition, opposition to a numerical cap on refugees (many of whom in 1995 still sought exit from a formerly Communist country) was easy to explain to busy members of Congress; asylum deadlines and particularly expedited removal procedures were much more complex.

But a fourth difference between the ease of lobbying successfully for overseas refugees and for asylum-seekers involves the advocacy organizations themselves. In contrast to the ad hoc nature of the Committee to Preserve Asylum, a "huge infrastructure" has sprung up to administer the overseas-refugee resettlement program.[14] Nine non-governmental agencies have cooperative agreements with and grants from the State Department to resettle in the United States those refugees who are identified and accepted through the overseas-refugee program. These agencies have local affiliates across the United States; the U.S. Catholic Conference alone has about 150 such affiliates. The affiliates distribute grants and other assistance to refugees for several months after their resettlement.

The Smith and Simpson legislation threatened not only the constituents of these organizations but the organizations themselves. Even before the bills were drafted in 1995, refugee quotas set by the administration had declined, and these programs had begun to cut their budgets and lay off staff. Many of the staff members being cut were themselves members of the ethnic communities whose future refugees were threatened by Smith and Simpson. The bills threatened further to decimate the relief organizations.

The nine organizations were directly threatened, and in addition, they were well organized politically. They had Washington offices, and for years, representatives from those offices had met every other week as the Washington Liaison Group of the Committee on Migration and Refugee Affairs of InterAction, an umbrella organization of more than a hundred relief and development organizations. Essentially, the Committee on Migration and Refugee Affairs was a trade organization; its members needed such an organization because they received federal funds and had common concerns about accounting for such funds and reporting properly to the federal government, which also periodically paid for representatives from the local affiliates to attend meetings in Washington that the government convened. The committee also had a full-time staff person, whose salary was paid from the dues that each agency paid to InterAction.

So when Smith and Simpson were drafting their bills, the Washington Liaison group was already mobilizing to defeat a statutory refugee limit. The members of the group knew each other well, they had instant contact with people who worked in and had been served by local organizations in hundreds of congressional districts, and they and their local affiliates had strong economic as well as ideological incentives to fight the cap. Several of these organizations became the backbone of the effort that defeated that proposal.[15]

## 12. Fallback positions are agonizing

For the advocates, the most difficult moments of the legislative battle involved the development, timing, and exposure of fallback positions. Part of the problem is the sense of stewardship that public interest advocates feel for the interests or constituents they represent, most of whom did not choose their representatives, even in the fictitious sense that stockholders choose their boards of directors and through them, the lobbyists on a corporation's payroll. Public interest advocates perpetually doubt their right to take less than an absolutist position, even when it is clear that advocating an absolutist position will result in worse legislation than seeking a compromise.

Another, less obvious source of agony is the pressure that fallback positions impose on advocacy organizations to create closed processes and webs of internal secrets. In principle, most public interest advocates believe in consensus politics and transparent decision-making. They do not want to exclude anyone from any decision process because exclusion can lead to hurt feelings and distrust within an organization or coalition. In practice, coalitions must be fairly large to be effective, but the larger they are, the greater the chance that the coalition's secrets will leak. And fallback positions on legislation must be kept secret until deliberately exposed, because even congressional supporters of an organization, eager for compromise, will immediately embrace the organization's fallback position, ignoring its preferred proposal.

Pressures arise, therefore, not to announce, or even discuss, fallback positions in meetings of organizations or coalitions. They tend to be tightly guarded by a few members of an advocacy organization. But public interest advocates are often concerned about legitimacy; if such proposals have not been discussed widely among the professional advocates within a coalition, much less a broader constituency, how can they legitimately be offered to members of Congress on behalf of the coalition? And if they are offered to coalition members or congressional staff in secret and at the last minute, coalition members who had not been informed may feel dismissed or betrayed. This is particularly a problem for loose-knit organizations (like the Committee to Preserve Asylum) that have no by-laws or formal decision-making mechanisms. It may help for such organizations to create formal executive committees that are authorized to develop fallback strategies and not discuss them with a larger group, but for public interest advocates, hierarchical solutions are rarely satisfactory.

## 13. Facts matter

Successful advocacy includes effective articulation, and catchy phrases have their place. But even in an age of slogans, generalities cannot be counted on to move legislators. The refugee advocates were much better off because they could offer legislators specific facts. Individual case studies, such as the story of Joseph, moved some legislators (such as DeWine). Valid statistics, such as the INS's report of the success of David Martin's reforms and the Lawyers Committee's study of its past asylum cases, made the anecdotes more important.

Marshaling these facts to appeal to the emotions of the public and its legislators was also necessary. Senator Simpson attributed the fifteen-to-one Judiciary Committee vote against the thirty-day deadline to the fact that the advocacy organizations' "lobbying was filled with emotion, fear, guilt, and racism. They could take any issue and pour the Statue of Liberty into it. They go right for the emotional gut. The violins and the choruses start, and shit, that's it."[16]

## 14. Legislative advocacy is itself a highly emotional activity

Public interest advocates who contemplate working on a bill in Congress should anticipate that they are likely to ride their own emotional roller coasters. They must work an astounding number of hours, and their work can result in a big victory, a compromise that leaves them wondering if they have sold out the interests they claimed to represent, or an utter defeat. Moreover, because the congressional process has so many stages, they may experience all of these emotions several times. The road to the end of the immigration bill was paved with suspense. Many members of the Committee to Preserve Asylum were thrilled to win most of what they had sought in the Senate Judiciary Committee; deeply depressed when the Rules Committee wouldn't allow the House to vote on asylum deadlines; excited throughout the day that ended with the fifty-one to forty-nine vote for the Leahy amendment on the Senate floor; depressed again by how little of the Leahy amendment was accepted by the Republicans on the Conference Committee; and sorely disappointed that the White House put up a last-minute fight to kill the welfare provisions of the bill, but didn't attempt at that time to kill the deadline or to give the attorney general discretion not to use expedited-removal procedures at airports. And at all times, we felt guilty because whatever we did, we weren't doing enough. It was hard to go home at night and have a semblance of a private life, because we could never know whether one more call, one more editorial, one more effort to expand the coalition, might not bring in the final vote necessary for a majority. Litigators constantly experience powerful emotions that arise from their advocacy; apparently, legislative advocates do so too.

## 15. Part of what happens is just dumb luck

In any very complex system like the congressional legislative process, some outcomes are just the result of good or bad luck, beyond the control of the competing forces. Carmel Fisk's temporary absence from Representative McCollum's office, as a result of which she was apparently unaware of the INS's 1994 regulatory reforms, may have been a piece of very bad luck that resulted in the transposition of the 1993 asylum deadline from the Mazzoli-McCollum-Schumer bill into McCollum's amendment to Smith's legislation. A Democratic staffer's mistake in the identity of one of his Republican counterparts may have prematurely disclosed a fallback position, making it inevitable that the Senate's bill would include a one-year deadline on defensive applications rather than no deadline at all. A dispute over an unrelated farm bill apparently lost the vote of at least one and maybe both of North Dakota's senators for the Leahy amendment. On the other hand, good luck showered on the refugee advocates when Fauziya Kassindja's release from jail, with its attendant publicity, happened to coincide with the imminently approaching Senate vote on the Leahy amendment, and when Sally Field, who had the ear of Senator Feinstein, read about the Kassindja case and offered her assistance. Public interest advocates, like their corporate counterparts, must be prepared to accept random disasters and should watch for serendipitous opportunities.

Ms. Field's offer (which may or may not have made the difference in persuading Senator Feinstein to cast a decisive vote for the Leahy amendment) illustrates an important distinction between having political clout and gaining the ability through organizational activity to obtain and wield such clout. By virtue of her talent and celebrity, Ms. Field had potential influence, or at least access to legislators, before the immigration reform bills were introduced. Members of Congress, like most people, are often pleased to accept telephone calls from people who are famous and well respected. Karen Musalo, who represented Ms. Kassindja, was not well known to legislators. But by working with the press and with several advocacy organizations, Ms. Musalo gradually acquired the ability to convey a message to a large audience, including Ms. Field. As a result, Ms. Field reached out to Ms. Musalo, and that connection further increased Ms. Musalo's ability to influence the legislation. The point is that public interest advocates often lack access and influence when they begin a project, but through hard work and an expanding network of connections, they may be able to acquire the leverage they need.

### 16. One's potential opponents are often central to a winning strategy, and it is important not to stereotype them

Perhaps this point needs no elaboration after the narrative related in this book, for it is obvious that without such Republican allies as Senators Mike DeWine, Spencer Abraham, and Orrin Hatch, and Representatives Christopher Smith, Sam Brownback, and Steven Schiff, legal immigration quotas would have been slashed, refugee immigration would have been capped, and the asylum deadline and expedited-removal provisions would have been even worse than what Congress passed. Some of the advocacy organizations were so used to working with liberals in Congress that months of precious time passed before they were able to seek and find Republicans who shared their outlook on immigration.

The immigration experience is likely to be replicated on other issues. Republicans may be somewhat less fractious than Democrats, but they are not monolithic, and the influx of libertarians into Republican ranks in Congress has created opportunities for new and unusual liberal-libertarian majorities. The importance of working with Republicans who think independently cannot be overstated, even in periods when Democrats control both houses of Congress. When Democrats held a majority in both houses of Congress, independent-thinking conservative Democrats often denied the party's leadership effective control over legislative outcomes in either body. In any event, the days of even a nominal, permanent Democratic hegemony are probably over.

Advocacy by non-profit organizations has become an important, constructive component of the national legislative process. Public interest advocates now speak for large numbers of people who, like future refugees, might otherwise have no voice in Congress. Drawing upon the precepts that emerge from non-profit organizations' legislative efforts to protect refugees, public interest advocates may be better able to help lawmakers to keep the nation's legislation consistent with its most cherished values.

# Epilogue

A year after winning asylum, Mary Rawson was eligible to change her immigration status and become a lawful permanent resident of the United States. To do this, she had to go with her lawyer for another interview with an officer of the Immigration and Naturalization Service.

Like the first immigration inspector whom Ms. Rawson had met at Kennedy Airport, this officer examined her passport with care. She too saw that Ms. Rawson's entry visa had been restricted to visits for professional purposes. She did not like the fact that Ms. Rawson had entered with the wrong visa, then won asylum.

"Have you ever been a prostitute?" she asked, a question often asked because prostitutes are barred from becoming permanent residents. Ms. Rawson thought she had been asked the same question she had by now answered many times, "Have you ever been persecuted?" She said she had. The INS official grew suspicious and asked many more questions.

"You've been granted asylum, so my hands are tied, and I will grant your request for permanent residence," the officer finally told Ms. Rawson. "But you should not have been allowed to enter the United States on this visa. If I had been the inspector at Kennedy Airport, I would have put you on the next plane back home."

Ms. Rawson's lawyer, Enid Gonzales Aleman, looked the INS examiner in the eye. "Then we thank God that you were not that inspector," she said. "If you had been the inspector on duty that day, Mary Rawson would now be dead."

# Glossary

**Affirmative asylum**—Asylum cases initiated by an application for asylum filed by persons who have not been apprehended and charged with being improperly in the United States. In other words, cases initiated by people who, at the time they filed applications, had not been threatened by the U.S. government with deportation from the United States.

**AILA**—The American Immigration Lawyers Association, the trade association of the nation's immigration lawyers.

**Asylum**—An immigration status granted by the Immigration and Naturalization Service, or by an immigration judge of the Justice Department's Executive Office for Immigration Review (EOIR). Under U.S. law, these agencies may grant asylum to a person in the United States or at its borders who meet several tests. Most important, the government must determine that they have been persecuted or have a well-founded fear of persecution in their own homeland.

**CPA**—The Committee to Preserve Asylum, the coalition created to oppose efforts to curtail procedural rights for asylum-seekers.

**EOIR**—The Justice Department's Executive Office for Immigration Review, the agency that includes the immigration judges and the appellate Board of Immigration.

**Exclusion**—The process of preventing a person who has no right to enter the United States from doing so. It contrasts with deportation, the name given before 1997 to the process of removing from the United States a person who had already entered the United States but had no right to remain.

**Expedited removal** (also called "summary exclusion")—A process through which aliens arriving in the United States without proper travel documents (particularly a visa or other permission to enter the United States) would be interviewed by an INS official at the border or airport and returned immediately, unless the alien was able to persuade INS officials that he or she had a "credible fear" of persecution. This process contrasted with full hearings before immigration judges, the procedure available to other people seeking asylum (e.g., asylum-seekers who arrived with proper documents but who did not leave the United States when their visas expired).

**FAIR**—The Federation for American Immigration Reform, the nation's leading anti-immigration lobby.

**INA**—Immigration and Nationality Act, the basic American immigration law, which has been amended many times since 1952.

**INS**—Immigration and Naturalization Service, the agency responsible for administering the U.S. immigration laws

**Lautenberg amendment**—Provision of law, beginning in 1989, permitting Soviet Jews and people in a small number of other designated groups to qualify as refugees without having to prove a well-founded fear of persecution on an individual basis.

**LPC**—"Likely to become a public charge." A basis for excluding would-be immigrants, used in the 1930s in many American consulates in Europe to deny visas to Jews.

**Mark-up**—The procedure through which a congressional committee or subcommittee allows its members to propose amendments to a pending bill, section by section, discusses and votes on the amendments, and then either kills the bill as amended or approves its consideration at the next stage of the legislative process.

**NIF**—The National Immigration Forum, one of the major advocacy organizations representing immigrants.

**OMB**—The Office of Management and Budget, a federal agency within the Executive Office of the President. It coordinates budgetary policy, but its duties also include approving certain government forms before they can be distributed to the public.

**Parole**—A process through which the U.S. government may allow certain aliens to enter the United States temporarily, subject to subsequent decisions about their immigration status.

**Removal**—A term adopted in the 1996 legislation to refer to the process of removing from the United States aliens who have no right to enter or remain. Previously, such people were removed in proceedings denominated "deportation" or "exclusion" cases, depending on whether or not the person had already entered the United States.

**Summary exclusion**—See "expedited removal." These terms have exactly the same meaning. The term "summary exclusion" was used during much of the congressional debate, particularly in the Senate, but the term "expedited removal" was the one finally embodied in the 1996 legislation.

**UCSJ**—Union of Councils for Soviet Jews, a nonprofit organization coordinating advocacy and services for Jews seeking to leave the former Soviet Union.

**UNHCR**—United Nations High Commissioner for Refugees, the United Nations official charged with coordinating international refugee policy.

**Withholding of removal** (before 1997, withholding of deportation)—A principle, based on the *non-refoulement* provision of the Refugee Convention and embodied in the U.S. Refugee Act, under which an alien may not be deported to a country in which the alien's life or freedom would be threatened because of his or her race, religion, nationality, membership in a particular social group, or political opinion. As a result of a case decided by the Supreme Court interpreting the asylum provisions of the Refugee Act, it is usually more difficult for an alien to prove eligibility for withholding than eligibility for asylum, even though withholding confers fewer benefits (it does not allow those who obtain it to become permanent residents and eventually citizens, or to bring their dependents to the United States).

# *Appendix A*

# Progress of the Immigration Bills through the 104th Congress

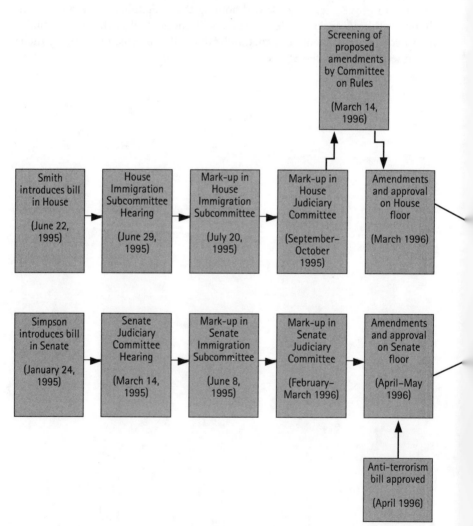

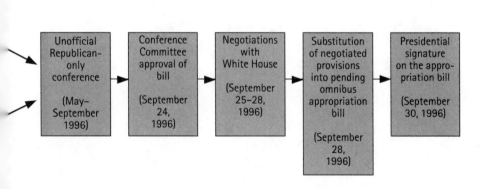

Unofficial
Republican-
only
conference

(May–
September
1996)

Conference
Committee
approval of
bill

(September
24,
1996)

Negotiations
with
White House

(September
25–28,
1996)

Substitution
of negotiated
provisions
into pending
omnibus
appropriation
bill

(September
28,
1996)

Presidential
signature
on the appro-
priation bill

(September
30, 1996)

# Appendix B

# The Committee to Preserve Asylum's First Mailing to Senators
## *(Case Studies Omitted)*

## Committee to Preserve Asylum
### 100 Maryland Avenue, NE, Suite 502
### Washington, DC 20002
### Phone: 202-547-5692
### Fax: 202-662-9409

December 21, 1995

Dear Member of the Senate Judiciary Committee:

We are an ad hoc coalition of religious groups, human rights organizations, concerned physicians, and immigration and civil rights advocates that have come together to oppose the current effort by some Senators that would effectively end asylum in the United States.

The right to seek asylum is an internationally recognized human right, incorporated into U.S. law by Congress in the 1980 Refugee Act. It protects individuals fleeing persecution on account of race, religion, nationality, political opinion, or membership in a particular social group. Each year the U.S. grants asylum to about 8,000 people, less than 1% of legal immigrants. The asylum provisions in S. 269, the Immigration Control and Financial Responsibility Act, would seriously undermine human rights protection for these bona fide refugees.

We are writing to express our opposition to one particular provision of the immigration reform bill that is soon to be marked up by the Senate Judiciary Committee — **Section 196.** This provision would bar granting asylum to virtually all refugees who apply more than 30 days after entering the United States. For reasons illustrated in the attached documents, **this section would effectively deny asylum to most worthy applicants while failing to deter frivolous claims and adding to the administrative burden of the asylum process.**

Thank you for your attention to our concerns.

Sincerely yours,

**Organizational Endorsements:**
American Friends Service Committee
American Immigration Law Foundation
American Immigration Lawyers Association
Amnesty International USA
American Jewish Committee
Asylum and Refugee Rights Law Project, Washington Lawyers' Committee for Civil
    Rights and Urban Affairs
Ayuda, Inc., Washington, DC
Cambridge-Somerville Legal Services, Massachusetts
Catholic Charities, Boston
Center for Immigrants Rights, New York
Center for Victims of Torture
Central American Resource Center - CARECEN of Washington, DC
Centro Mujeres de la Esperanza, El Paso
Church of the Brethren Washington Office
Church World Services Immigration and Refugee Program
Coalition for Immigrant and Refugee Rights and Services, San Francisco
Coalition for Humane Immigrant Rights of Los Angeles
Columban Fathers' Justice and Peace Office
Committee to Protect Journalists
D.C. Latino Civil Rights Task Force
Dialogue on Diversity, Washington, DC
Dominican Sisters of San Rafael, California
Emerald Isle Immigration Center, New York
Episcopal Migration Ministries
Exodus World Service, Illinois
Falls Church Immigration Clinic, Virginia
Florence Immigrant and Refugee Rights Project, Inc., Arizona
Foreign-born Information and Referral Network, Inc., Maryland
Freedom House, Detroit
Greater Boston Legal Services
Guatemala Human Rights Commission/USA

Heartland Alliance, Chicago
Hermandad Mexicana Nacional, Chicago
Hispanic Committee of Virginia
Hispanics United of Rockville, Maryland
Hogar Hispano, Catholic Charities, Diocese of Arlington, Virginia
Human Rights Watch
Illinois Coalition for Immigrant and Refugee Protection
Immigrant and Refugee Rights Clinic, City University of New York Law School
Immigrant Law Project, Legal Services of Eastern Missouri
Immigration and Refugee Services of America
Indian Law Resource Center
Institute for Women, Law and Development, Washington, DC
International Human Rights Law Group
International Institute of Boston
International Institute of Los Angeles
International Institute of New Jersey
International Institute of Rhode Island
Jewish Federation of Metropolitan Chicago
Jews for Racial and Economic Justice, New York
Jubilee Church, Washington, DC
Kentucky Interreligious Taskforce on Central America
Las Americas Refugee Asylum Project
Lawyers Committee for Human Rights
Lawyers' Committee for Civil Rights of the San Francisco Bay Area
Lutheran Immigration and Refugee Service
Marjorie Kovler Center for the Treatment of Survivors of Torture, Chicago
Maryknoll Justice and Peace Office, Washington, DC
Massachusetts Law Reform Institute
Massachusetts Immigrant and Refugee Advocacy Coalition
Mennonite Central Committee
Mexican American Legal Defense and Education Fund (MALDEF)
Minnesota Advocates for Human Rights
National Association of Korean Americans
National Committee Against Repressive Legislation
National Immigration Project of the National Lawyers Guild
National Jewish Community Relations Advisory Council
National Organization of Women, Massachusetts Chapter
National Spiritual Assembly of the Baha'is of the United States
Network: A National Catholic Social Justice Lobby
North Texas Immigration Coalition, Dallas
NW Immigrant Rights Project, Seattle
Office of Migration, Immigration Legal Services, Archdiocese of Detroit
Ola Raza, Inc., California
Physicians for Human Rights

Physicians for Social Responsibility
Political Asylum Immigration Representation Project, Boston
Proyecto San Pablo, Yuma, Arizona
Proyecto Libertad, Harlingen, Texas
Refugee/Immigrant Rights Coalition
Rio Grande Border Witness Program
Robert F. Kennedy Memorial Center for Human Rights
Sisters of St. Joseph of Carondelet, California
Sponsors Organized to Assist Refugees, Oregon
Tucson Ecumenical Council Legal Assistance
U.S. Committee for Refugees
Union of Councils for Soviet Jews
United Church Board for World Ministries, United Church of Christ
Vietnamese Association of Illinois
Vive, An Organization for World Refugees, Buffalo, New York

**Individual Endorsements:**
Rev. Patrick Delahanty
    Director of Migration and Refugee Services, Archdiocese of Louisville
Rev. Charles Demere
    Pax World Service
Rev. John Frizzell
    Commission on Peace, Episcopal Diocese of Washington
Michael W. Galligan
    Past Co-Chair of the American Immigration Lawyers Association Committee
    on Asylum and Refugees
Rev. Alan Geyer
    Commission on Peace, Episcopal Diocese of Washington
Robert E. Juceam
    President of the American Immigration Law Foundation
Sr. Elizabeth Kelliher
    Franciscan Sisters of the Atonement
Helen Lauffer
    Director of The Homeless and Immigration Division, Travelers Aid Services
Paul L. Locatelli, S.J.
    President, Santa Clara University
Rev. Joseph Lund
    Commission on Peace, Episcopal Diocese of Washington
Michael J. Meyer
    Presidential Professor of Ethics & the Common Good, Santa Clara University
Sr. Christine Mulready
    Intercommunity Center for Justice and Peace, New York

Prof. Karen Musalo
  Washington College of Law, The American University
John A. Privett, S.J.
  Provincial, California Province of Society of Jesus
Daniel M. Singer
  Trustee, Washington Lawyers' Committee for Civil Rights and Urban Affairs
Rev. Donald L. Smith
  Coordinator for Specialized Ministries Synod of Southern California &
  Hawaii, Presbyterian Church (organization listed for purposes of identification
  only)
Msgr. Bryan O. Walsh, P.S.
  Archdiocesan Director, Catholic Charities of the Archdiocese of Miami
Prof. Norman L. Zucker
  Political Science Department, The University of Rhode Island

# Congress Should Not Impose a Filing Deadline
# for Asylum Applications

**1.   A Short Filing Deadline Would Foreclose Most Legitimate Asylum
Claims.**

For a number of reasons, very few legitimate asylum seekers are able to apply for
asylum within a short time after arriving in the U.S.:

• In most cases, refugees fleeing persecution (even journalists, teachers and
  other professionals) leave their home countries with little more than the clothes
  on their backs. It is only after they obtain the basic necessities of life — food,
  shelter, and clothing — that they can think of applying for asylum.

• By definition, refugees who deserve asylum are persons who have fled situations of extreme danger and trauma. If they or close family members have been
  the victims of rape, torture, or other physical abuse, they need time to recover
  before they can even begin to think about applying for asylum. Even then,
  many legitimate applicants who fear persecution by repressive governments
  are reluctant to present claims until they gain confidence that their claims will
  be treated fairly and confidentially and not result in retaliation against them or
  their loved ones back home.

• Many refugees arrive without knowing anything about the process of applying
  for asylum. Once they become aware and are otherwise ready to apply, they

must find a human rights organization or pro-bono lawyer to help them (no easy task!).

• Refugees must fill out the asylum application in English and compile its attachments, often running to more than a hundred pages. To have a reasonable chance of success, they need to obtain affidavits and documentary support (often from overseas) and they must prepare certified English-language translations of all foreign-language documents. Simply collecting the supporting documents often takes more than 30 days.

• Some applicants for asylum do not make the agonizing decision to abandon their homeland and seek asylum until they have no viable alternative means to stay away temporarily. They are living in the United States in legal status hoping that dictators in their countries will be overthrown before they must return. They often wait in the U.S. for months or even a year or two before reluctantly concluding that asylum is their only alternative.

Attached are several representative case studies of people who have won asylum, none of whom would be eligible for asylum if the proposed legislation were in effect. These cases, and nearly all other meritorious claims for asylum, illustrate that *legitimate asylum applicants rarely make their first contacts with human rights organizations, much less file asylum applications, within their first months of entry into the U.S.*

**2.  A Filing Deadline of 30 Days, or of Any Other Period, Is Not Needed.**

Before 1995, the INS granted asylum applicants the rights to live and work in the U.S. while their applications were pending, often for a number of years. Consequently, asylum applications often were filed as a way to obtain work authorization during a lengthy application process. The 30-day rule was first proposed in 1993 as one way to weed out non-meritorious claims.

The INS overhauled its regulations in January 1995 to address this problem. Applying for asylum no longer confers the right to work, and the INS is adjudicating 90% of new claims within 60 days after their receipt — a fraction of the time the agency was taking in previous years. The new system has caused a dramatic decline in new applications, from 13,000 per month at the end of 1994 to 3,000 per month currently.

**A filing deadline will not reduce the administrative burden for the INS**

The Department of Justice said in a recent letter to Senator Simpson:

We strongly oppose this provision. It will require the INS to divert resources from adjudication of the merits of asylum applications to adjudication of the timeliness of filing. Since eligibility for withholding of deportation is not affected by this section, the Attorney General must still adjudicate the merits of a refugee claim.

### A filing deadline may not result in fewer non-meritorious asylum applications.

In fact, the enactment of a filing deadline might actually increase the number of non-meritorious cases, as people with borderline asylum claims who come to the U.S. on non-immigrant visas may file to meet the deadline rather than wait to see whether democratic forces in their countries succeed in overthrowing oppressive dictators. Before it imposes a remedy that may backfire, Congress should at least wait to see whether the 1995 reforms continue to keep down the number of non-meritorious cases.

### A filing deadline will not help the INS remove undocumented individuals who are not entitled to asylum.

When persons who are undocumented apply for asylum, they identify themselves to the INS and, if they lose their cases, are automatically put into deportation proceedings within 2-3 months. The filing deadline will have the unintended effect of making it more difficult to locate and deport undocumented persons, because once a person misses the deadline, he or she will lack any incentive to come forward and risk deportation.

### 3. An Exception for Changed Circumstances Will Not Relieve the Injustice of a Filing Deadline.

S. 269 presently contains an exception to the filing deadline, which permits later consideration of asylum claims when they are based on changed circumstances that arose after the applicant arrived in the United States. While this exception might help those few people from countries in which, for example, coups take place while they are in the United States, it does not address any of the problems more typically experienced by victims of persecution, which are described above.

# *Appendix C*

# Senate Judiciary Committee, 104th Congress

**Republicans**

Orrin G. Hatch—Utah
Strom Thurmond—South Carolina
Alan K. Simpson—Wyoming
Charles E. Grassley—Iowa
Arlen Specter—Pennsylvania
Hank Brown—Colorado
Fred Thompson—Tennessee
Jon Kyl—Arizona
Mike DeWine—Ohio
Spencer Abraham—Michigan

**Democrats**

Joseph R. Biden—Delaware
Edward M. Kennedy—Massachusetts
Patrick J. Leahy—Vermont
Howell Heflin—Alabama
Paul Simon—Illinois
Herb Kohl—Wisconsin
Dianne Feinstein—California
Russell Feingold—Wisconsin

# Appendix D

# Talking Points for the Leahy Amendment
## (April 1996)

This outline of arguments was used by human rights advocates when they talked to legislators and to their staff members, urging them to support the Leahy amendment.

## THE NEW BARS TO ASYLUM WOULD RETURN HUMAN RIGHTS VICTIMS TO FURTHER PERSECUTION

### Vote for the LEAHY amendment

The Anti-terrorism bill imposes new bars to applying for asylum. It gives low-level immigration officers the authority to deport back to their persecutors refugees (not terrorists) who were forced to flee persecution without valid travel documents. Similar provisions also appear in Sections 131, 132, 141, 142 and 193 of S. 1664, the Immigration Control and Financial Responsibility Act of 1996. The anti-terrorism summary exclusion provisions, which will soon become law, punish people whose only means of fleeing repressive governments is by using invalid travel documents.

**Many true refugees are forced to flee persecution without valid travel documents either because they do not have time to acquire them or because applying for them would threaten their lives.**

Under current law, a person who arrives in the United States without valid travel documents and fears persecution in his or her home country may go before an immigration judge and prove eligibility for asylum. The asylum seeker may be represented at the hearing at no cost to the government.

273

The new bars to asylum would preclude such a person from even applying for asylum unless he or she can first persuade a low-level government official that he or she has a "credible fear" of persecution <u>and</u> used the invalid travel documents to flee directly from a country where there is a "significant danger" of being returned to persecution. This all may have to be proven immediately after a stressful journey, and without the assistance of counsel or an interpreter, and without the involvement of any judicial or quasi-judicial officer.

### *The new bars and summary procedures are problematic for several reasons.*

#### A "false papers" rule would harm human rights victims.
By definition, asylum seekers frequently fear persecution by the government of their home country — the same government that issues travel documents and checks identity papers and exit permits at the airports and border crossings. It should be recalled that the United States has long honored Raoul Wallenberg, who saved countless lives during the Holocaust by issuing unofficial travel documents so that refugees could flee further persecution.

#### Meritorious asylum seekers would be returned to persecution.
The INS has made serious errors while trying to apply the "credible fear" test. Under current law, asylum seekers who arrive in the U.S. without valid travel documents are detained pending their hearing unless they prove a "credible fear" of persecution in their home country. Human rights organizations have documented many cases in which people were denied temporary release under this standard, but later were <u>granted</u> asylum at their hearing before an immigration judge. Under the new bars to asylum, they would have been summarily sent back to the country that was persecuting them.

#### The Department of Justice opposes the new bars to asylum.
Deputy Attorney General Jamie Gorelick wrote in her February 14 letter to Judiciary Committee Chairman Orrin G. Hatch that the Justice Department **opposes** sections 133/193, noting that "Absent smuggling or an extraordinary migration situation, we can handle asylum applications for excludable aliens under our regular procedures."

#### The new bars would deny protection to refugees who had to change planes on route to the United States.
Before being able to apply for asylum, a refugee who used false documents would have to prove that they were needed to leave her country or to transit through another country. This requirement would prejudice

both asylum seekers who flee countries that do not have direct carrier routes to the U.S. and those who must travel over land through countries that do not have asylum laws, that may be friendly with the government they are fleeing, or that are hostile to people of their background or nationality. Refugees from Asian and African countries in particular face this situation.

**The new bars to asylum are inconsistent with U.S. obligations under international law and will inevitably lead to errors.**

The new bars lack the minimal procedural safeguards to prevent the mistaken return of a genuine refugee to certain persecution. The UNHCR "fears that many bona fide refugees will be returned to countries where their lives or freedom will be threatened" if the new bars to asylum become law. (Letter from Anne Willen Bijleveld to Sen. Orrin Hatch, March 6, 1996).

# Vote for the LEAHY Amendment

The **LEAHY amendment** would again amend the Immigration and Nationality Act so that the Attorney General has summary exclusion authority only in extraordinary situations. Under this new authority, the Attorney General could exclude refugees whose claims for political asylum were manifestly unfounded. Such determinations would be subject to an administrative review and the refugee could be represented at the interview at no expense to the government. The LEAHY amendment would not require the refugee to prove that he or she traveled directly to the United States from the country of persecution, it would not apply to asylum seekers who are forced to travel without documents, and it is consistent with U.S. obligations under international law.

For more information, call the Lawyers Committee for Human Rights (202) 547-5692.

# Appendix E

# The Leahy-DeWine
# "Dear Colleague" Letter
## Urging a Vote for the Leahy Amendment

Senators Leahy and DeWine wrote this letter to their ninety-eight colleagues, asking them to vote for the Leahy amendment.

## United States Senate
### WASHINGTON, DC 20510

April 26, 1996

Dear Colleague:

We write to ask you to support an amendment to preserve our asylum process, which we intend to offer to S.1664, the Immigration Control and Fiscal Responsibility Act of 1996. This amendment has become essential in light of the unfortunate changes to general immigration law inserted at conference into the anti-terrorism law.

The United States should not abandon its traditional place in the world as a refuge from oppression and a beacon of hope and freedom, nor should we sacrifice our leadership role in protecting international human rights. Unfortunately, that is the impact of these provisions in the immigration bill and those inserted into the anti-terrorism law. They deny refugees the opportunity to claim asylum and, instead, summarily exclude them from the United States and send them back to their persecutors.

Our amendment would amend the new barriers to asylum petitioners proposed in sections 131, 132, 141, 142, and 193 of the immigration bill; establish a special exclusion procedure for extraordinary migration situations declared by the Attorney General, and amend the changes to asylum law inserted at conference into the anti-terrorism law.

The bill fails to take into account the unfortunate but all too

real circumstances that exist in repressive regimes around the
world. Refugees flee by all sorts of means, including using
false documents and escaping through third countries en route to
the United States. The bill would punish asylum seekers who are
afraid to apply to their government for proper travel documents
and identification papers and those who cannot travel "directly"
to the United States. Such refugees would be subject to screening at our border by low-level immigration officers who could
summarily exclude them and prevent them even from applying for
political asylum.

Had these provisions been in place, Fidel Castro's daughter
might not have been allowed to come here since she defected with
a phony passport and traveled through Spain. Had similar provisions been in place during World War II, those saved by Raoul
Wallenberg, Oskar Schindler and Chiune Sugihara could have been
summarily excluded because they used false documents to escape
the Holocaust.

The Department of Justice has opposed the extreme provisions of
the bill and suggests only that it be accorded standby authority
to utilize expedited procedures in case of a massive migration
situation. Our amendment will accommodate those concerns.

In fact, our asylum process was thoroughly reformed as recently
as 1995. Last year asylum applications declined significantly
and those that were filed were timely processed with only 20
percent being granted. There is no need for the drastic changes
being proposed in the bill nor justification for requiring the
INS to dedicate significant resources to establishing a
specially-trained phalanx of asylum officers to be stationed at
all airports, seaports and other ports of entry around the country to conduct such summary screenings of asylum applicants. In
fact, these changes are disruptive, burdensome and costly.

The majority report on the bill devotes very little attention to
this important matter, but it is discussed in the Minority Views
and in Senator Leahy's additional minority views. We urge you to
join with us, the United Nations High Commissioner on Refugees,
and with leading international human rights organizations and
support our amendment to the asylum provisions of the immigration bill.

We enclose copies of a recent column by Anthony Lewis and a
recent editorial from the New York Times on these matters.

Sincerely,


PATRICK J. LEAHY                    MIKE DeWINE
United States Senator               United States Senator

# Appendix F

# The Vote on the
# Leahy Amendment
## May 1, 1996

**Republicans for the amendment (12):**

| | |
|---|---|
| Abraham | Hatch |
| Bennett | Hatfield |
| Campbell | Jeffords |
| Chafee | Lugar |
| DeWine | Mack |
| Frist | Snowe |

**Democrats for the amendment (39):**

| | |
|---|---|
| Akaka | Kerry |
| Baucus | Kohl |
| Biden | Lautenberg |
| Bingaman | Leahy |
| Boxer | Levin |
| Bradley | Lieberman |
| Breaux | Mikulski |
| Bumpers | Mosley-Braun |
| Byrd | Moynihan |
| Daschle | Murray |
| Dodd | Nunn |
| Feingold | Pell |
| Feinstein | Pryor |
| Ford | Robb |
| Glenn | Rockefeller |
| Graham | Sarbanes |
| Harkin | Simon |
| Heflin | Wellstone |
| Inouye | Wyden |
| Kennedy | |

**Republicans against the amendment (41):**

| | |
|---|---|
| Ashcroft | Kassebaum |
| Bond | Kempthorne |
| Brown | Kyl |
| Burns | Lott |
| Coats | McCain |
| Cochran | McConnell |
| Cohen | Murkowski |
| Coverdell | Nickles |
| Craig | Pressler |
| D'Amato | Roth |
| Dole | Santorum |
| Domenici | Shelby |
| Faircloth | Simpson |
| Gorton | Smith |
| Gramm | Specter |
| Grams | Stevens |
| Grassley | Thomas |
| Gregg | Thompson |
| Helms | Thurmond |
| Hutchison | Warner |
| Inhofe | |

**Democrats against the amendment (8):**

| | |
|---|---|
| Bryan | Hollings |
| Conrad | Johnston |
| Dorgan | Kerrey |
| Exon | Reid |

# Notes

## Introduction

1. Dan Balz, "GOP 'Contract' Pledges 10 Tough Acts to Follow," *The Washington Post*, November 20, 1994.
2. The term "well-founded fear" appears in the definition of a "refugee," 8 U.S.C. Sec. 101 (a) (42).
3. For many years, students of legislative process read Eric Redman, *The Dance of Legislation* (New York: Simon and Schuster, 1973), a case study of the passage of the law creating the National Health Service Corps. The more recent classics are Jeffrey H. Birnbaum and Alan S. Murray, *Showdown at Gucci Gulch* (New York: Random House, 1987) (the tax reform act of 1986); Steven Waldman, *The Bill* (New York: Viking, 1995) (Clinton's National Service Corps); and Ronald D. Elving, *Conflict and Compromise* (New York: Simon and Schuster, 1995) (Family and Medical Leave Act of 1993).
4. The other accounts are "Bleak House 1968: A Report on Test Case Litigation," *New York University Law Review* 44 (1969): 115 (the perspective of a public interest advocate trying to achieve social change by bringing test cases before overworked, indifferent judges); *Counsel for the Deceived* (New York: Pantheon, 1972) (my efforts as the Consumer Advocate of the City of New York to obtain redress for the victims of consumer fraud); *Behind the Scenes: The Politics of a Constitutional Convention* (Washington, D.C.: Georgetown University Press, 1985) (my observations as a back-bench delegate to the District of Columbia's Statehood Constitutional Convention); *Reflections on Clinical Legal Education* (Boston: Northeastern University Press, 1998) (with Michael Meltsner) (reports on twenty-five years of supervising students in law-school-operated law offices for indigent clients).
5. Michael Pertschuk, *Giant Killers* (New York: W. W. Norton, 1986). See also Michael Pertschuk and Wendy Schaetzel, *The People Rising* (New York: Thunders Mouth Press, 1989) (public interest advocates help to defeat the nomination of Robert Bork to become an associate justice of the Supreme Court).
6. My two principal contributions were instigating a new coalition to fight the imposition of deadlines on asylum applications, related in chapter 5, and generating criticism of the Immigration and Naturalization Service's proposed regulations to implement the new law, described in chapter 12.
7. David Martin, who served as the general counsel of the Immigration and Naturalization Service during the congressional deliberations described in this book, read a draft of this manuscript and reported that he too knew of no deals or negotiations not described here. Memorandum to the author, Nov. 25, 1998.
8. Kevin R. Johnson, "The Social and Legal Construction of Nonpersons," *Inter-American Law Review* 28 (1996): 263.

9. Attempting to enter the United States without inspection by an immigration officer is a misdemeanor punishable by imprisonment for six months. Immigration and Nationality Act Sec. 275. It is rarely prosecuted. Interview with former INS General Counsel David Martin, November 24, 1998. Remaining in the United States after a valid visa expires is not a violation of any criminal law.

10. Lexis/Nexis has published some committee transcripts on its on-line database, but its coverage of mark-ups has been very spotty, and is apparently decreasing or ending

## Chapter 1: From Plymouth Rock to Kennebunkport

1. U.S. Commission on Immigration Reform, *U.S. Refugee Policy: Taking Leadership* (1997), 1.

2. Robert M. Bartlett, *The Faith of the Pilgrims: An American Heritage* (New York: United Church Press, 1978), 18–22, 311; Allen French, *Charles I and the Puritan Upheaval* (Boston: Houghton Mifflin, 1955), 239. Like many modern-day refugees, the Pilgrims may have had mixed religious and economic motivations for coming to America. Poverty and food shortages in Holland may have contributed to their decision to leave Holland and cross the Atlantic (Bartlett, 27), and Holland became less tolerant of refugees as their numbers increased. From Leiden, *Morning Edition*, National Public Radio, November 27, 1997, Transcript 97112712–210.

3. Everett Emerson, *Puritanism in America, 1620–1750* (Boston: Twayne Publishers, 1977), 15–19. Unlike the Pilgrims, the Puritans worshiped in parish churches and therefore were not considered a separate sect (French, 239). Puritan clergymen convinced entire congregations to migrate to America (Emerson, 32), and although "direct evidence on the subject [of the Puritans' motivations for coming to America] is meager" (French, 15), it has been said that "the body of New England immigrants were driven by the belief that in England religious conditions were unbearable" (French, 319). "Imprisonment was used deliberately to break the will of individual sufferers, and the threat of it overshadowed the Puritans as a class." Some of the Puritans "died from their treatment" in English prisons. Ibid.

4. D. W. Meinig, *The Shaping of America* (New Haven: Yale University Press, 1986), 152.

5. Meinig, 123.

6. Meinig, 124; Mario T. Bennett, *American Immigration Policies: A History* (Washington, D.C.: Public Affairs Press, 1963), 5; John F. Kennedy, *A Nation of Immigrants*, rev. ed. (New York: Harper and Row, 1968), 12.

7. Bennett, 4.

8. Bennett, 3.

9. Marcus Lee Hansen, *The Atlantic Migration* (New York: Harper and Row, 1951), 50.

10. Carl A. Brasseaux, *The Founding of New Acadia* (Baton Rouge: Louisiana State University Press, 1987), 13; Carl A. Brasseaux, *Acadian to Cajun* (Jackson: University Press of Mississippi, 1992), 4.

11. Hansen, 57–58.

12. Theodore C. Blegen, *Norwegian Migration to America, 1825–1860* (New York: Arno Press, 1969), 28.

13. Vernon M. Briggs, *Immigration Policy and the American Labor Force* (Baltimore: Johns Hopkins University Press, 1984), 19.

14. Select Commission on Immigration and Refugee Policy, *U.S. Immigration Policy and the National Interest* (1981), 92–93.

15. Gerald L. Neuman, "The Lost Century of American Immigration Law (1776–1875)," *Columbia Law Review* 93 (1993): 1833, 1842, 1849, 1867–68. A few of the state attempts to restrict immigration were halted by the courts. For example, Massachusetts and New York tried to tax certain arriving passengers, but the Supreme Court struck down the states' laws as invalid restrictions on the power of Congress to regulate international commerce. *Passenger Cases*, 48 U.S. 283 (1849). Occasionally states were able to circumvent the judicial restrictions. Neuman, 1855–59.

16. In the 1840s, in reaction to increased immigration by Germans and French Canadians, a secret society called the Order of the Star Spangled Banner was formed for the purpose of trying to restrict entry and political participation, particularly by Catholics. Because members were told to answer any questions by saying that "I know nothing" about such an organization, the political movement that arose from the secret society was known as the "Know Nothing" movement and by 1854 it had become the Know Nothing Party. It won control of the Massachusetts legislature and elected governors in seven states but it split over slavery and disappeared during the Civil War. During the antebellum period, nativism was only a minor political phenomenon. Briggs, 21–22; Bennett, 12.

17. For a work that lays out elegantly and in much greater depth than this chapter the history of Chinese exclusion from the 1860s to 1890, see Lucy E. Salyer, *Laws Harsh as Tigers* (Chapel Hill: University of North Carolina Press, 1995), 2–23.

18. Economic opportunity was the primary cause of Chinese immigration in the 1850s, but many Cantonese were also prompted to emigrate by the disruptions of the Taiping Rebellion of 1850–1864, the "most important political event in the Chinese Empire in the nineteenth century." Twenty million people died in this unsuccessful effort to create a more equitable society, and many Chinese sought to escape to California. Briggs, 22.

19. In 1870, a Reconstruction Congress was determined to amend the statute, dating from 1790, that permitted only white aliens to be naturalized as citizens. Thomas Alexander Aleinikoff, David A. Martin, and Hiroshi Motomura, *Immigration and Citizenship: Process and Policy,* 4th ed. (St. Paul, Minn.: West Group, 1998), 44. But even as Congress passed a law to permit the naturalization of people of African descent, the California legislators and their allies succeeded in blocking passage of an amendment that would also have allowed people born in Asia to become citizens. In 1879, as Field was preparing a bid for the 1880 Democratic presidential nomination, he publicly advocated amending a treaty with China to limit immigration. "We are alarmed upon this coast at the incursion of Chinese," Field said. "In the language of Senator Booth ... 'the practical issue is, whether the civilization of this coast, its society, morals, and industry, shall be of American or Asiatic type.' It is to us a question of property, civilization, and existence." Interview with Stephen J. Field in the *San Francisco Argonaut,* August 9, 1879, quoted in Carl Brent Swisher, *Stephen J. Field, Craftsman of the Law* (Washington, D.C.: The Brookings Institution, 1930), 221. Field's presidential bid failed, but he was apparently able to write into the Democratic Party's 1880 platform a plank advocating congressional restriction of Chinese immigration. See "The Restriction Bill in Congress," *Alta California,* Jan 14, 1884, p. 2; "Democratic Platform of 1880," clause 11, in Kirk H. Porter and Donald Bruce Johnson, *National Party Platforms 1840–1956* (Urbana: University of Illinois Press, 1956). The Republicans also favored restricting Chinese immigration. "Republican Platform," clause 6, ibid. The following year, Field lobbied senators to ratify a treaty with China permitting the United States to suspend immigration from that country. Swisher, 222–24. Field's biographer hints that Field's advocacy of immigration restrictions may have been motivated by a desire to shore up support from California voters who were angry that as a judge he had struck down the San Francisco "Queue Ordinance," a law that would have allowed corrections officials to cut the hair of prisoners. Many Chinese immigrants believed that the loss of their queues would bring them both disgrace on earth and penalties in the hereafter. See Swisher, 216, 220–21.

20. Act of May 6, 1882, 22 Stat. 58.

21. Act of September 13, 1888, 25 Stat. 476; Act of October 1, 1888, 25 Stat. 504.

22. *Chae Chan Ping v. United States* (The Chinese Exclusion Case), 130 U.S. 581 (1889).

23. *United States ex rel. Knauff v. Shaughnessy,* 338 U.S. 537 (1950); *Shaughnessy v. United States ex Rel. Mezei,* 245 U.S. 206 (1953). Discussions of the state of the plenary power doctrine after a hundred years include Hiroshi Motomura, "Immigration Law after a Century of Plenary Power: Phantom Constitutional Norms and Statutory Interpretation," *Yale Law Journal* 100 (1990): 545; Lenni B. Benson, "Back to the Future: Congress Attacks the Right

to Judicial Review of Immigration Proceedings," *Connecticut L. Rev.* 29 (1997): 1411, 1419–1438.

24. Act of March 3, 1891, 26 Stat. 1084.
25. Professor Alan Kraut, Department of History, American University, interview with author, Sept. 5, 1997.
26. *Statistical Abstracts of the United States* (editions from 1880 to 1924).
27. See Berta Esperanza Hernandez-Truyol, "Natives, Newcomers and Nativism: A Human Rights Model for the Twenty-First Century," *Fordham Urban Law Journal* 23 (1996): 1075, 1076.
28. Japanese immigration was curtailed not through an act of Congress, but by a "Gentlemen's Agreement" of 1907–8. Pursuant to negotiating authority embodied in a 1907 law (34 Stat. 898), President Theodore Roosevelt persuaded the Japanese government to agree to refrain from issuing laborers passports to come to the continental United States. Japan was willing to make this secret arrangement because it wanted to forestall the United States from passing a formal Japanese exclusion law. Hyung-chan Kim, *A Legal History of Asian Americans 1790–1990* (Westport, Conn.: Greenwood Press, 1994), 102–4; Bennett, 25–38.
29. E. P. Hutchinson, *Legislative History of American Immigration Policy, 1798–1965* (Philadelphia: University of Pennsylvania Press, 1981), 105–46. By 1896, the American Federation of Labor had adopted formal resolutions favoring restrictions on immigration. Briggs, 35.
30. 39 Stat. 874, February 5, 1917.
31. House Committee on Immigration and Naturalization, *Biological Aspects of Immigration, Hearings before the House Committee on Immigration and Naturalization,* 66th Cong., 2d sess., April 17, 1920, 23 (statement of Harry H. Laughlin, Secretary, Eugenics Research Association.)
32. House Committee on Immigration and Naturalization, *Europe as an Emigrant-Exporting Continent and the United States as an Immigrant-Receiving Nation, Hearings before the House Committee on Immigration and Naturalization,* 68th Cong., 1st sess., March 8, 1924, 1231.
33. 42 Stat. 5; Elliott Robert Barkan, *And Still They Come: Immigrants and American Society 1920 to the 1990s* (Wheeling, Ill.: H. Davidson, 1996), 11.
34. Salyer, 134.
35. Barkan, 12.
36. Immigration Act of 1924, 43 Stat. 153, May 26, 1924.
37. Salyer, 135.
38. Barkan, 14.
39. Between 1890 and 1919 a million and a half Christian Armenians living in the Muslim Ottoman Empire were killed because of their religious faith and their desire for political independence; another million fled to Europe or Russian Armenia. W. Gunther Plaut, *Asylum: A Moral Dilemma* (Westport, Conn.: Praeger, 1995), 12. Large numbers of White Russians also fled the dislocations of the Bolshevik revolution and sought protection in Europe and the United States. Norman L. Zucker and Naomi Flink Zucker, "From Immigration to Refugee Redefinition: A History of Refugee and Asylum Policy in the United States," in Gil Loescher, *Refugees and the Asylum Dilemma of the West* (University Park: Pennsylvania State University Press, 1992), 54–55.
40. The term "refugee" arose in the 16th century, when the French term "réfugié" was applied to the Huguenots, but it acquired legal meaning only in the 1920s. Plaut, 12; Eberhard Jahn, "Refugees," in *Encyclopedia of Public International Law* (Amsterdam: North Holland, 1985), 452.
41. Arrangements of July 5, 1922 (13 LNTS 237).
42. Richard Breitman and Alan M. Kraut, *American Refugee Policy and European Jewry, 1933–45* (Bloomington: Indiana University Press, 1987), 7–8. Hoover's personal attitude toward immigration, at least of those who were not from western and northern Europe, can be inferred from his reply to a criticism by then-Congressman Fiorello LaGuardia

whom he called "a little out of your class in presuming to criticize the President.... You should go back to where you belong and advise Mussolini on how to make good honest citizens in Italy. The Italians are predominately our murderers and bootleggers.... Like a lot of the foreign spawn, you do not appreciate the country which supports and tolerates you." Barkan, 14–15.

43. See Sanford J. Ungar, *Fresh Blood* (New York: Simon and Schuster, 1995), 352–57 (documenting the successful, restrictive efforts of the American Legion and The American Immigration Conference Board).

44. Barkan, 50–51.

45. Assistant Secretary of State Wilbur Carr, until 1937 in charge of the consuls who granted or denied visas, had earlier written that Russian and Polish Jewish emigrants from Rotterdam were "filthy, Un-American and often dangerous in their habits." Regarding Polish Jews, he had warned that "it is impossible to estimate the peril of the class of emigrants coming from this part of the world and every possible care and safeguard should be used to keep out the undesirables." Breitman and Kraut, 32. The reputation as an anti-Semite of another senior State Department official, Assistant Secretary Breckinridge Long, "is gradually being revised by historians" although whatever his motives, Long had a major role in excluding Jewish refugees in 1939 and 1940. Ibid., 126–35.

46. Memorandum to the secretary of state from George Messersmith, Nov. 13, 1936, quoted in Breitman and Kraut, 9, 48–49.

47. Barkan, 51; see Stephen Legomsky, *Immigration and Refugee Law and Policy*, 2d ed. (Westbury, N.Y.: Foundation Press, 1997), 753.

48. Early in 1939, 300,000 people applied to U.S. consuls in German for visas, and with "the streets of Vienna ... filled with people who needed to get out," U.S. consular personnel there were seeing 6,000 visa applicants per day, though the annual quota for Austria was only 1,413. Breitman and Kraut, 56, 66.

49. Barkan, 51.

50. Breitman and Kraut, 73. In the same year, the United States refused admission to the Jewish passengers aboard the refugee ship *St. Louis*, a development discussed in chapter 5.

51. Quoted and photographed in "America and the Holocaust," WGBH-TV (1994).

52. S. Adler-Rudel, "The Evian Conference on the Refugee Question," *Leo Baeck Institute Yearbook XIII* (New York: Secker and Warburg, 1968) 235, 242.

53. Ibid., 239.

54. Exhibit placard, U.S. Holocaust Memorial Museum, Washington, D.C. See also David S. Wyman, *Paper Walls: America and the Refugee Crisis 1938–1941* (Amherst: University of Massachusetts Press, 1968), 50.

55. "Refugees," in Edmund Jan Osmanczyk, *The Encyclopedia of the United Nations and International Relations* (New York: Taylor and Francis, 1990), 742.

56. Barkan, 74.

57. See Karen Musalo, Jennifer Moore, and Richard A. Boswell, *Refugee Law and Policy* (Durham, N.C.: Carolina Academic Press, 1997), 19–24.

58. James Hathaway, *The Law of Refugee Status* (Toronto: Butterworth, 1991), 5.

59. Statute of the Office of the United Nations High Commissioner for Refugees, chapter 2, article 6 (a) (ii) (1950). A different paragraph extended the authority of the commissioner to refugees without respect to the pre-1951 deadline, but this paragraph was not included in the definition of refugees used in the 1951 Convention.

60. Convention Relating to the Status of Refugees, 189 U.N.T.S. 150, chapter I, article 1 (a) (ii) (1951).

61. Convention Relating to the Status of Refugees, 189 U.N.T.S. 150, chapter I, article 1 (b) (i) (1951).

62. Hathaway, 8.

63. Convention Relating to the Status of Refugees, 189 U.N.T.S. 150, chapter I, articles 21, 22 and 23.

64. Convention Relating to the Status of Refugees, 189 U.N.T.S. 150, chapter I, article 33.
65. Aleinikoff et al., 998 (up to 200,000 admissions); Deborah E. Anker and Michael H. Posner, "The Forty Year Crisis: A Legislative History of the Refugee Act of 1980," *San Diego L. Rev.* 1 (1981): 9, 12 (limitations of the act).
66. P.L. 82–414, 66 Stat. 163 (January 27, 1952).
67. Anker and Posner, 13–14.
68. Sec. 212 (d) (5), 66 Stat. 188.
69. See Anker and Posner, 15–16. Eventually, 38,000 Hungarians were resettled in the United States through the parole power.
70. The text is reprinted in John F. Kennedy, *A Nation of Immigrants*, revised and enlarged edition (1986), Appendix D.
71. Michael Barone and Grant Ujifusa, "Management of the Immigration Act," *Almanac of American Politics* (Washington, D.C.: National Journal, 1996), 633; Hutchinson, "Subcommittee Service," *Legislative History of American Immigration Policy* (1981), 368.
72. Aleinikoff et al. 1998, 168–69.
73. P.L. 89–236, 79 Stat. 911. 973, 977. Immigrants were admitted in fiscal year 1991. Immigration and Naturalization Service, *Statistical Yearbook of the Immigration and Naturalization Service for Fiscal Year 1996* (1997), 25.
74. Anker and Posner, 17. This category was repealed and its subtotal reallocated when Congress passed a new Refugee Act in 1980.
75. Legomsky, 110.
76. Protocol Relating to the Status of Refugees, 606 U.N.T.S. 267 (1967).
77. Anker and Posner, 19.
78. Anker and Posner, 19–64.
79. Arthur C. Helton, *Political Asylum under the 1980 Refugee Act: An Unfulfilled Promise, J. of Law Reform* 17 (1984): 243.
80. Ibid., 248.
81. Legomsky, 769. By the late 1980s, most countries granted refugees a permanent residence. Rainer Hofmann, "Asylum and Refugee Law," in Jochen Abr. Frowein and Torsten Stein, *The Legal Position of Aliens in National and International Law* (Berlin: Springer-Verlag, 1987), 2045, 2058–59.
82. Wyman, 138–41.
83. See "Admission of Refugees Into the United States," *Hearings on H.R. 3056 Before the Subcommittee on Immigration, Citizenship and International Law of the House Committee on the Judiciary,* 95th Cong., 1st Sess. (1977), 126–30.
84. Anker and Posner, 30.
85. Anker and Posner, 32.
86. Kennedy succeeded James O. Eastland of Mississippi. Compare *Congressional Directory Supplement* (Washington, D.C.: GPO, 1978), 48 with *Congressional Staff Directory* (Indianapolis: Bobbs-Merrill, Co., 1979), 271.
87. See Anker and Posner, 20 *et seq.*
88. INA Sec. 212 (d).
89. Tahl Tyson, "The Refugee Act of 1980: Suggested Reforms in the Overseas Refugee Program to Safeguard Humanitarian Concerns from Competing Interests," *Wash. L. Rev.* 65 (1990): 921, 925.
90. Annual refugee admissions for fiscal year 1980–82 were 207,116, 159,252, and 97,355, respectively. Aleinikoff et al. 1998, 1005.
91. INA Sec. 207.
92. The 1980 law providing for withholding had some statutory and regulatory forerunners, but they did not provide for protection in as many circumstances as the international Convention seemed to require. They are summarized in Stephen H. Legomsky, 768–69. The removal provision was placed originally in Section 243(h) of the act. In 1996, the

name of this procedure was changed to a "restriction on removal" and it was moved to Section 241 of the act. As a result of language used in the implementing regulation, the procedure is now called "withholding of removal."

93. INA Sec. 208.
94. *Congressional Staff Directory* (1981), 261–62.
95. See U.S. Commission on Immigration Reform, *Legal Immigration: Setting Priorities* (1995), 122. For fiscal year 1984, for example, the U.S. allocated 62,000 of its 72,000 refugee slots to East Asia and the Soviet bloc countries. Musalo, Moore, and Boswell, 75.
96. Tyson, 927.
97. Tyson, 928.
98. Helton, 253.
99. Helton, 262.
100. U.S. Government Accounting Office, *Uniform Application of Standards Uncertain* (1987), 22.
101. Helton, 256.
102. Except as otherwise indicated, the biographical material on and quotations about Senator Simpson come from John Newhouse, "Taking it Personally," *The New Yorker,* March 16, 1992.
103. "Alan Simpson," *Current Biography,* October 1990, 552 (arrest for fighting).
104. Ward Sinclair, "Freshman Simpson: Western Breeze through Stuffy Senate," *The Washington Post,* January 22, 1980.
105. Neil A. Lewis, "Wyoming's Folksy Senate Orator, Sharp-Tongued Ally of the President," *The New York Times,* Oct. 24, 1990.
106. In 1980, Cuba temporarily relaxed emigration controls, allowing tens of thousands of Cubans to flee to the United States in small boats. In the early 1980s, 115,000 Cubans, who arrived during this "Mariel boatlift" and had been given a temporary immigration status, were also accepted for permanent resettlement
107. Helton, 261; Associated Press, "Backlog of 200,000 Hope for Asylum in U.S.," *The New York Times,* February 19, 1984 (1978 statistic).
108. Testimony of Doris Meissner, acting commissioner, Immigration and Naturalization Service, in Senate Subcommittee on Immigration and Refugee Policy, *Hearings before the Senate Subcommittee on Immigration and Refugee Policy,* October 14, 1981, 4.
109. Senate Judiciary Committee, *Immigration Reform and Control, Report of the Senate Judiciary Committee on S. 2222,* Rept. No. 97–485, 34.
110. Ibid., 61.
111. Ibid.
112. Ibid., 36.
113. S. 529, passed by Senate, *Congressional Record,* p. 12875, May 18, 1983; S. 529, passed by House of Representatives, *Congressional Record,* 17295, June 20, 1984; Robert Pear, "Amid Changes Immigration Bill Dies," *The New York Times,* Oct. 12, 1984.
114. After Representative Richard Ottinger's motion to delete the asylum restrictions failed, the House passed the bill by a margin of only five votes. *Congressional Record,* 17295, June 20, 1984.
115. *Congressional Record,* 13586, May 23, 1985 (remarks of Sen. Simpson).
116. P.L. 99–603, 100 Stat. 3359 (Nov. 6, 1986).
117. Aleinikoff, Martin and Motomura, 1030.
118. David A. Martin, "Making Asylum Policy: The 1994 Reforms," *Washington Law Review* 70 (1995): 725, 731.
119. Alexander T. Aleinikoff, David A. Martin, and Hiroshi Motomura, *Immigration Process and Policy,* 3d ed. (1995), 767.
120. *INS v. Cardoza-Fonseca,* 480 U.S. 421, 431 (1986).
121. Ibid., 452.

122. David Greenwald, "Judge Halts Deportation of 27,000," *The Orange County Register,* May 16, 1989.

123. It also agreed to adjudicate the cases of any additional Salvadorans and Guatemalans who were in the United States and could have filed for asylum but did not do so. Settlement of *American Baptist Churches v. Thornburgh,* 760 F. Supp. 796 (N.D. Cal. 1991). See 67 Interp. Rel. 1480 (1990).

124. Martin, 732.

125. Ashley Dunn, "Political Asylum Cases Swamp INS," *The Los Angeles Times,* April 10, 1992.

126. Al Kamen, "INS's Unofficial Open Door: Illegal Aliens Swamp N.Y. Holding Capacity," *The Washington Post,* January 27, 1992.

127. Ibid.

128. Grover Joseph Rees, quoted in Celia Dugger, "Immigrants: Separating the False and the True," *The New York Times,* July 8, 1996.

129. Kamen.

130. Court Robinson and Bill Frelick, "Lives in the Balance," *International Journal of Refugee Law* 2 (Special Issue, 1990): 293, 318.

131. *Congressional Record,* July 20, 1989, 15515–16 (Senator Lautenberg).

132. Pub. Law. 101–167, 103 Stat. 1262.

133. *Congressional Record,* July 20, 1989, 15530.

134. Ibid., 15527.

135. Senate Judiciary Committee, *U.S. Refugee Programs for 1991: Hearing before the Senate Judiciary Committee,* 102d Cong., 2d Sess., Oct. 3, 1990, 55.

136. P. L. 101–513, Title V, Sec. 598 (a), 104 Stat. 2063, Nov. 5, 1990; P. L. 102–391, Title V, Sec. 582, 106 Stat. 1686, Oct. 6, 1992.

137. The heartbreaking story of the American response to the Haitian refugees' flight is told in several law review articles. This very brief summary is drawn from one of the most lengthy and beautifully written accounts, told by three Yale law students who, along with dozens of others under the direction of Professor Harold Koh, worked literally night and day in the ultimately unsuccessful federal court litigation challenging the government's actions. Victoria Clawson, Elizabeth Detweiler, and Laura Ho, "Litigating as Law Students: An Inside Look at *Haitian Centers Council,*" Yale Law Journal 103 (1994): 2337, 2339.

138. The standard recalls the "credible basis for concern" test of the Lautenberg amendment, but former INS general counsel David Martin does not think that officials actually took it from that statute. David Martin, memorandum to the author, November 25, 1998.

139. A Yale law student member of the team representing Haitian refugees in ongoing litigation against the government coined the term "Kennebunkport Order" to emphasize the gap between the vacationing American president and the impoverished Haitians whose lives it risked. The term was picked up by the press and by the courts. Clawson et al., 2371.

140. Clawson et al., 2345, 2359.

141. See press stories collected in Clawson et al., 2371–73

## Chapter 2: Clinton's Turn

1. White House Press Conference announcing proposed immigration controls, including procedural restrictions on asylum claimants, July 27, 1993.

2. Statement by Governor Clinton on political refugees, May 27, 1992, *U.S. Newswire* (available on LEXIS/NEXIS).

3. Clinton Statement on Appeals Court Ruling on Haitian Repatriation, July 29, 1992, *U.S. Newswire* (available on LEXIS/NEXIS).

4. Steve Holland, "Large Protest at White House Against Haiti Policy," *Reuters North American Wire,* September 9, 1992.

5. "Excerpts from the President-Elect's News Conference in Arkansas," *The New York Times,* November 13, 1992.

6.  Victoria Clawson, Elizabeth Detweiler, and Laura Ho, "Litigating as Law Students: An Inside Look at *Haitian Centers Council*," *Yale Law Journal* 103 (1994): 2337, 2374.
7.  Howard French, "Haitians' Advocates Admit Some Feelings of Betrayal," *The New York Times,* January 15, 1993.
8.  Elaine Sciolino, "Clinton Aides Urge Freer Haiti Policy," *The New York Times,* January 6, 1993.
9.  Elaine Sciolino, "Clinton Says U.S. Will Continue Ban on Haitian Exodus," *The New York Times,* January 15, 1993.
10. Ruth Marcus and Al Kamen, "Aides Say Clinton Will Extend Policy on Returning Haitians," *The Washington Post,* January 14, 1993.
11. Harold Hongju Koh, "Reflections on *Refoulement* and *Haitian Centers Council*," *Harvard International Law Journal* 35 (1994): 1, 13.
12. Sciolino, January 15, 1993.
13. Clawson et al., 2374.
14. Sciolino, January 15, 1993.
15. French, January 15, 1993.
16. Ruth Marcus, "Clinton Besieged about Policy Shifts," *The Washington Post,* January 15, 1993.
17. Eric Schmitt, "Clinton Set to End Ban on Gay Troops," *The New York Times,* January 21, 1993.
18. Eric Schmitt, "Joint Chiefs Fighting Clinton Plan to Allow Homosexuals in Military," *The New York Times,* January 23, 1993.
19. Eric Schmitt, "Pentagon Chief Warns Clinton on Gay Policy," *The New York Times,* January 25, 1993.
20. Robert O'Harrow, Jr., "Suspect in CIA Slayings is Returned to U.S.," *The Washington Post,* June 18, 1997.
21. Robert O'Harrow, Jr., and Bill Miller, "CIA Suspect Left Trail of Conflicting Personal Data," *The Washington Post,* February 18, 1993.
22. O'Harrow, June 18, 1997. Kansi was tried under the name of Kasi, which he also used. He was originally indicted as Kansi, but the prosecutor changed the name to Kasi to reflect the version that the defendant used when he signed a statement he had given to the FBI. Brooke A. Masters and Wendy Melillo, "Trial Opens Today for Suspect in Slayings Outside CIA," *The Washington Post,* November 3, 1997.
23. Terrorism expert Brian Jenkins, quoted in Douglas Jehl, "Car Bombs: A Tool of Foreign Terror, Little Known in U.S.," *The New York Times,* January 27, 1993.
24. Christopher Wren, "Verdicts in Terror Trial," *The New York Times,* September 6, 1996.
25. Ralph Blumenthal et al., "The Bombing: Retracing the Steps," *The New York Times,* May 26, 1993.
26. Wren, September 6, 1996.
27. Blumenthal et al., May 26, 1993.
28. International Organizations and Human Rights Committee of the House Foreign Affairs Committee, *Hearing on U.S. Terrorism Policy of the International Security,* March 15, 1993 (Representative Tom Lantos); Alison Mitchell, "Specter of Terror," *The New York Times,* June 27, 1993; Patricia Hurtado, "Sheik, 9 Others Guilty of Plotting Jihad," *Newsday,* October 2, 1995.
29. Douglas Jehl, "C.I.A. Officers Played Role in Sheik Visas," *The New York Times,* July 22, 1993. The fact that the visa officials were actually CIA officers made implausible the State Department's initial explanation of the error, that "although there were various people in intelligence and in enforcement circles working closely with this case, the information was not communicated to the immigration side." House Hearing on Terrorism Policy (testimony of Acting Assistant Secretary of State James L. Ward).
30. Associated Press, "Bureaucratic Foulups, Mixups Let Fiery Sheik Get into U.S.," *The Chicago Tribune,* March 6, 1993.

31. Christopher Wren, "Verdicts in Terror Trial," *The New York Times*, September 6, 1996; Richard Bernstein, "Behind Arrest of Bomb Fugitive, Informer's Tip, Then Fast Action," *The New York Times*, February 10, 1995. He was arrested in Pakistan two years later and taken to the United States. In 1996, he was given a life sentence for trying to blow up American airliners, and a year later, he was convicted of masterminding the World Trade Center bombing. Benjamin Weiser, "'Mastermind' and Driver Found Guilty in 1993 Plot to Blow Up Trade Center," *The New York Times*, November 13, 1997.

32. In 1996, Rahman was sentenced to life in prison for his role in the bombing plot. Joseph P. Fried, "Sheik Sentenced to Life in Prison in Bombing Plot," *The New York Times*, January 18, 1996.

33. Vivienne Walt, "Aliens at the Gate; New York's INS Director Cracks Down," *Newsday*, November 29, 1993.

34. Al Kamen, "INS's Unofficial Open Door: Illegal Aliens Swamp N.Y. Holding Capacity," *The Washington Post*, January 27, 1992.

35. *60 Minutes*, CBS, March 14, 1993 (Lesley Stahl: "[Mr. Slattery's] bosses in Washington had told him that he could only give us a tour, he could not give us his opinion").

36. Willam Slattery, telephone interview with author, July 1, 1997.

37. Ira Mehlman, "The New Jet Set; How Questionable Political Asylum Claimants Enter the US at New York, New York's John F. Kennedy International Airport without Any Difficulty," *National Review*, March 15, 1993.

38. For a careful explanation of how various methods could address the high volume of asylum cases, and the advantages and disadvantages of each, see Stephen H. Legomsky, "The New Techniques for Managing High-Volume Asylum Systems," *Iowa L. Rev.* 81 (1996): 671.

39. In its Act of March 2, 1931, 46 Stat. 1467, Congress had provided that immigration inspectors should be paid for work between 5 P.M. and 8 A.M. at a rate of "one-half day's additional pay for each two hours or fraction thereof" but "not to exceed two and one-half days' pay for [a full night] and two additional days' pay for Sunday and holiday duty." Customs inspectors received similar overtime benefits under the Act of February 13, 1911, 36 Stat 899, 901. In 1991, the Congressional Research Service explained that in practice, a customs inspector "can earn eight or twelve hours of pay for one hour of work or sixteen hours of pay for three hours of work." Congressional Research Service, "Overtime and Premium Pay for U.S. Customs Service Inspectors," Report 91–473 GOV (June 11, 1991). The Research Service apparently did not write a similar report on overtime for immigration inspectors.

40. Slattery interview.

41. Ibid. The airlines, too, favored summary exclusion, presumably because compared to building more detention facilities, it would keep down the user fee. "Industry Pressures Congress to Support Immigration Measure," *Aviation Daily*, March 11, 1992.

42. Wendy Lin and Jack Sirica, "An Invitation to Terrorists? INS Admits It Can't Stop All Undesirables," *Newsday*, March 6, 1993.

43. Jim Mann, "Chinese Refugees Take to High Seas," *The Los Angeles Times*, March 16, 1993.

44. Tim Weiner, "Pleas for Asylum Inundate System for Immigration," *The New York Times*, April 25, 1993.

45. Susan Ferriss, "FAIR: Mounting Campaign to Keep Immigrants Out; Group's Stated Aim to Cap Population Walks Fine Line of Bigotry, Critics Say," *San Francisco Examiner*, December 12, 1993.

46. Ibid.

47. Ed Rogers, "Amnesty Plan for Illegal Aliens Opposed in Hearing," *United Press International*, October 29, 1981 (available on LEXIS/NEXIS).

48. Linda Chavez, "U.S. English Needs to Re-examine Its Purposes and Priorities," *The San Diego Union-Tribune*, December 4, 1988.

49. Ferriss, December 12, 1993.

50. James Crawford, "English-Only Movement is Bigger, and Worse, Than First Believed," *San Diego Union-Tribune,* October 30, 1988. Between 1983 and 1992, the Pioneer Fund contributed more than a million dollars to FAIR. Dan Stein, FAIR's executive director, noted however that the Fund's contributions never amounted to more than 5 percent of FAIR's revenues. He would not release to the press a list of donations to confirm his assertion. Ferriss, December 12, 1993.

51. Steven J. Rosenthal, "The Pioneer Fund," *American Behavioral Scientist* 39 (1995): 44, 50; Adam Miller, "Professors of Hate," *Rolling Stone,* October 20, 1994, 106, 111.

52. See Walt, November 29, 1993.

53. Weiner, April 25, 1993.

54. In fact, the Immigration and Naturalization Service had granted asylum to 34 percent of the asylum applicants in fiscal year 1992, the year before the broadcast. Immigration and Naturalization Service, *1996 Statistical Yearbook of the Immigration and Naturalization Service* 87 (1997). For the periods fiscal year 1986 to 1990 and 1991 to 1995, the rates at which the INS granted asylum applications were 24 percent and 23 percent, respectively. Ibid.

55. *60 Minutes,* CBS, March 14, 1993.

56. Legomsky, p. 693 n. 111.

57. "'60 Minutes' Segment Reveals Massive Asylum and Immigration Fraud; Fair Urges Immediate Action by Congress and the President," *PR Newswire,* March 15, 1993 (available on LEXIS/NEXIS).

58. Bill McGeveran, interview between author and Bill McGeveran, legislative assistant to Representative Charles Schumer, December 30, 1996.

59. International Organizations and Human Rights Committee of the House Foreign Affairs Committee, *Hearing on U.S. Terrorism Policy of the International Security,* March 15, 1993.

60. Michael Barone and Grant Ujifusa, *Almanac of American Politics* (Washington, D.C.: National Journal, 1995), 313; Mike Oliver, "Opponents: It's Time for McCollum to Go," *The Orlando Sentinal Tribune,* August 10, 1992.

61. News Conference, Introduction of a bill on immigration, *Federal News Service,* March 16, 1993 (available on LEXIS/NEXIS).

62. H.R. 1355 (103d Cong.) (McCollum bill); S. 667 (103d Cong.) (Simpson bill).

63. Gwen Ifill, "President Chooses an Expert to Halt Smuggling of Aliens," *The New York Times,* June 19, 1993.

64. Deborah Sontag, "Waiting for a Rudder at I.N.S.," *The New York Times,* June 13, 1993.

65. Ibid.

66. Ibid.

67. Ibid.

68. David Martin, "Making Asylum Policy: the 1994 Reforms," *Washington University Law Quarterly* 70 (1995): 725, 738.

69. Weiner, April 25, 1993.

70. Mary Benanti, "Administration 'Doesn't Have a Handle' on Smuggling Problem," *Gannett News Service,* May 28, 1993 (quoting Acting INS Commissioner Chris Sale) (available on LEXIS/NEXIS).

71. Senate Subcommittee on Immigration and Refugee Affairs, *Hearing on Terrorism, Asylum Issues and U.S. Immigration Policy (S. 667) before the Senate Subcommittee on Immigration and Refugee Affairs,* May 28, 1993, 24.

72. Martin, 739–40.

73. Mehlman (reporting Kennedy Airport visits of Jerry Tinker and Michael Meyers).

74. Senator Kennedy did not introduce a bill at this point, but he had circulated a written proposal that was discussed at the May 28 hearing of his subcommittee. *Hearing on Terrorism, Asylum Issues and U.S. Immigration Policy (S. 667) before the Senate Subcommittee on Immigration and Refugee Affairs,* May 28, 1993, 69.

75. Jane Fritsch, "The Immigrants—7 Die as Crowded Immigrant Ship Grounds off Queens,"

*The New York Times*, June 7, 1993; Ian Fisher, "The Scene: Waves of Panic Yield to Elation of Refugees," *The New York Times*, June 7, 1993; Tim Weiner, "Fixing Immigration," *The New York Times*, June 8, 1993; Celia W. Dugger, "Chinese Immigrants from Stranded Ship Are to Be Released," *The New York Times*, February 15, 1997 (revising to ten the number who died trying to reach shore).

76. Fritsch, June 7, 1993.
77. Dugger, February 15, 1997.
78. Weiner, June 8, 1993.
79. Michael S. Arnold, "Calls to Change Asylum System Gain Urgency," *The Washington Post*, June 13, 1993.
80. Michael Barone and Grant Ujifusa, *Almanac of American Politics* (1994) 885–887.
81. Ibid.
82. *1995 Current Biography Yearbook* (1995), 521.
83. "New Look at Immigration Policy After New York Bombing," *Morning Edition*, National Public Radio, March 10, 1993 (Transcript No. 1038–10) (interview of Schumer). Immigration and customs officials were already conducting pre-boarding inspections of passengers bound for the United States from the airport in Shannon, Ireland, and at some Canadian airports. But very few would-be asylum applicants used those airports to reach the United States.
84. Ibid.
85. Gene Pugliese, telephone interview between author and Immigration Judge Gene Pugliese, former legislative assistant to Charles Schumer, June 16, 1997.
86. Ibid.
87. H.R. 2602 (103d Cong.).
88. Carolyn Lochhead, "Push for Tougher Asylum Laws; Bipartisan Group Wants Would-be Refugees Screened at Airports," *The San Francisco Chronicle*, July 2, 1993.
89. Martin, 740.
90. Announcement by President Bill Clinton on Immigration Policy, July 27, 1993, *Federal News Service* (available on LEXIS/NEXIS).
91. White House Briefing on Illegal Immigration Policy and Initiatives, July 27, 1993, *Federal News Service* (available on LEXIS/NEXIS).
92. Slattery interview.
93. Martin, 740 and n. 37.
94. Devroy and Arnold.
95. "Churches Hit Clinton's refugee plan," *The Houston Chronicle*, August 7, 1993.
96. Knut Royce, "Plan to Bar Aliens," *Newsday*, July 27, 1993.
97. Press Release, "INS Proposal for Asylum Reform," *U.S. Newswire*, July 29, 1993 (available on LEXIS/NEXIS).
98. Frank Trejo, "Proposals Worry Refugee Advocates," *The Dallas Morning News*, August 10, 1993.
99. See Roberto Sanchez, "Peso Woes Not Linked to Soaring Border Crossings," *The Phoenix Gazette*, January 21, 1995.
100. See Charles R. Babcock, "Open Arms, Wary Eyes Greet Newest Refugees," *The Washington Post*, May 11, 1980; Association of American Law Schools, *The AALS Directory of Law Teachers 1988–89* (St. Paul, Minn.: West Group, 19888), 670.
101. David A. Martin and T. Alexander Aleinikoff, *Immigration: Process and Procedure*, 2d ed. (St. Paul, Min.: West Publishing Co., 1991); David A. Martin, "Reforming Asylum Adjudication: On Navigating the Coast of Bohemia," *Pennsylvania Law Review* 138 (1990), 1247.
102. S. 1333 (103d Cong.).
103. Marcus Stern, "Overhaul of Asylum Processing Is in Works," *The San Diego Union-Tribune*, November 6, 1993.
104. Francis X. Clines and Joe Sexton, "'What Are You, Rashid?'; Uncovering the Many Layers of

a Murder Suspect," *The New York Times*, March 14, 1994; Joe Sexton, "One Customer Wrecks a Life of Hard Work," *The New York Times*, July 30, 1995; Frank Lombardi, "Slay Victim's Mom Renews Deport Fight," *The New York Daily News*, March 11, 1997; George James, "Bridge Gunman Gets 141-Year Term," *The New York Times*, January 19, 1995.

105. James, January 19, 1995.
106. Lombardi, March 11, 1997; Frank Lombardi, "Judge Hit in Deport Case," *The New York Daily News*, March 5, 1997; Lisa Sandberg, "She Hits Asylum for Killer's Pal," *The New York Daily News*, October 31, 1996.
107. 59 Fed. Reg. 14779 (March 30, 1994).
108. Senate Judiciary Committee, *U.S. Refugee Program for 1993: Annual Refugee Consultations, Hearing before the Senate Judiciary Committee*, July 23, 1992, 57–63.
109. The Refugee Convention had been negotiated primarily to protect persons who had fled their countries of nationality and had a well-founded fear of persecution on one of the listed grounds, but the 1980 Refugee Act permitted the U.S. government also to accept as refugees a person who was still within her or her own country, provided that after congressional consultation, the president had specified the existence of "special circumstances." This provision of the law is now codified as Immigration and Nationality Act Sec. 101 (a) (42) (b).
110. *U.S. Refugee Programs for 1994: Annual Refugee Consultations, Hearing before the Senate Judiciary Committee*, September 23, 1993, 3, 52.
111. House Subcommittee on International Law, Immigration, and Refugees, *Hearing on Refugee Admissions Program for Fiscal Year 1994 before the House Subcommittee on International Law, Immigration and Refugees*, September 23, 1993, 2.
112. *Congressional Record*, S. 465 (February 1, 1994) (remarks of Sen. Lautenberg); S. 467 (remarks of Sen. Feinstein).
113. Ibid., S469–78.
114. Ann Devroy and Michael Arnold, "Clinton Escalates Fight on Illegal Immigration," *The Washington Post*, July 28, 1993 (Gallup Poll, 1993); Seth Mydans, "Poll Finds Tide of Immigration Brings Hostility," *The New York Times*, June 26, 1993 (other poll results).
115. Mydans, June 26, 1993.
116. Howard LaFranchi, "For U.S. Hispanics, Election '86 Brought Triumphs and Setbacks," *Christian Science Monitor*, November 10, 1986.
117. "The Message from California," *The Economist*, October 29, 1994, 27.
118. "Low Road," *Forbes*, September 13, 1993, 26.
119. James O. Goldsborough, "Don't Blame the Illegals for All Economic Woes," *The San Diego Union Tribune*, January 20, 1994 (citing Field Poll).
120. "To the Rescue," *The Economist*, September 3, 1994, 35.
121. Ed Mendel, "Prop. 187 Opponents Question FAIR Funding," *The San Diego Union-Tribune*, September 8, 1994; Jeffrey Miller, "Prop. 187 Linked to Controversial Group, Opponents Say," *The Orange County Register*, September 9, 1994.
122. Mark Horowitz, "It's Not Easy Being Brown," *The New York Times Magazine*, October 16, 1994.
123. Ken Chavez, "Gov. Wilson Backs SOS initiative," *The Orange County Register*, September 16, 1994.
124. Caroline J. Tolbert and Rodney E. Hero, "Race/Ethnicity and Direct Democracy: An Analysis of California's Illegal Immigration Initiative," *Journal of Politics* 58 (1996), 806, 808. For a careful statement of the policy arguments against the initiative, see "Proposition 187 and the Law of Unintended Consequences," *The Los Angeles Times*, October 2, 1994 (editorial).
125. Lisa Lapin, "Feinstein Opposes Prop. 187," *The Orange County Register*, October 22, 1994; Steve Proffitt, Dianne Feinstein, *The Los Angeles Times*, October 30, 1994.
126. Tolbert and Hero, 815. Eighty percent of California's voters at the time were white. Wendy J. Quinton, Gloria Cowan, and Brett D. Watson, "Personality and Attitudinal Predictions of

Support of Proposition 187—California's Anti-Illegal Alien Initiative," *Journal of Applied Social Psych.* 26 (1996): 2201, 2204.

127. Paul Clarke, "Valley Swam against GOP Tide," *The Los Angeles Times,* November 13, 1994.

128. Quinton et al., 2205.

129. The Mazzoli-McCollum-Schumer bill passed easily in Mazzoli's House Immigration Sub-committee, but after that, it bogged down. See Carolyn Lochhead, "House Panel Easily Approves Bill to Reduce Asylum Fraud," *The San Francisco Chronicle,* October 21, 1993.

130. See Haynes Johnson and David S. Broder, *The System: The American Way of Politics at the Breaking Point* (Boston: Little, Brown, 1996).

131. Martin, 741.

132. T. Alexander Aleinikoff, interview between author and T. Alexander Aleinikoff, former Executive Associate Commissioner, INS, July 11, 1997.

133. During the summer of 1994, the waters off Miami were again filled with boatloads of refugees from Haiti. Douglas Farah, "To Haitians Manning Small Boats, Cutters Still Mean a Ticket to U.S.," *The Washington Post,* July 9, 1994. In late July, Cubans tried to hijack three passenger ferries, seeking passage to the United States, and Cuban president Fidel Castro threatened to unleash a mass exodus of Cubans unless the U.S. tightened its control over its seacoast. William Booth, "U.S. Warns Cuba Over Refugees," *The Washington Post,* August 7, 1994. The INS asked Senator Kennedy to press forward with summary exclusion legislation. Kennedy acquiesced, and the bill (a substitute version of S. 1333) was approved by the Judiciary Committee on August 11, 1994. Memorandum to the author from Kathleen M. Sullivan, former counsel, Senate Subcomittee on Immigration and Refugee Affairs, Dec. 18, 1997. At that point, immigration advocates for the Lutheran Immigration and Refugee Service, the American Bar Association and the United States Catholic Conference sought a senator to put a "hold" on the bill, preventing rapid floor considera-tion. They approached Paul Wellstone of Minnesota, among other senators, because the Lutherans had a strong presence in his state and John Fredriksson, the Lutheran Immigration and Refugee Service's Washington representative, had a working relationship with his staff. Wellstone either put a formal hold on the bill or signaled that he wanted to take a long, hard look at it. This maneuver "gummed up the works at the end of the ses-sion"; by this time, it was too late in the life of the 103rd Congress for the bill's proponents, such as Senator Simpson, to overcome the delay that Wellstone imposed. John Fredriksson, telephone interview between author and John Fredriksson, former Washington represen-tative of the Lutheran Immigration and Refugee Service, July 1, 1998.

134. Aleinikoff interview.

135. Aleinikoff interview.

136. Most European countries make welfare payments to needy asylum applicants while their applications are pending, but even before restrictive welfare and immigration legislation passed in 1996, the United States did not do so. Martin, 733.

137. The INS backed down on the fee for another reason, too: adjudicating requests for fee waivers by indigent applicants would cost the INS more than it would earn from the fees, and the time needed to resolve those requests would slow down the INS process, possibly making many applicants eligible for work permits because the INS would then exceed its own six-month limit. Martin, 753.

138. 59 Fed. Reg. 62284 (December 5, 1994).

139. See Upswings for Congress, Clinton (graphic) in Richard Morin, "Poll Numbers Up for Clinton Congress," *The Washington Post,* January 3, 1995 (approval rating fell from 60 per-cent in January 1994 to 44 percent in December).

140. The Republicans would hold a majority of six in the Senate, while the new House would have 230 Republicans, 204 Democrats, and one Independent. Kevin Merida, "On Social Agenda, Republicans Remain Far from Consensus," *The Washington Post,* November 22, 1994.

141. Marcus Stern, "U.S. Poised to Reform Immigration," *The San Diego Union-Tribune,* November 10, 1994.

142. Ibid.
143. Ibid.
144. Ibid

Chapter 3: Mr. Smith, Already in Washington

1. *ABC World News Sunday,* ABC, July 2, 1995 (Transcript No. 527).
2. Michael Barone and Grant Ujifusa, *Almanac of American Politics* (1966), 1314.
3. Ibid., 1316.
4. Gwen Ifill, "Panel Endorses Waiting Period to Buy Pistols," *The New York Times,* April 24, 1991.
5. *Almanac of American Politics,* 1314–15.
6. Marcus Stern, "A Former Immigration Quixote Has House Panel Tilting His Way," *The San Diego Union-Tribune,* July 1, 1995.
7. Ibid.
8. Lamar Smith and Edward R. Grant, "Immigration Reform, Seeking the Right Reasons," *St. Mary's Law Journal* 28 (1997): 883, 886.
9. Ibid., 888.
10. Ibid., 891.
11. *1990 Current Biography Yearbook* (1990), 551.
12. Lois Romano, "Simpson, on Second Thought," *The Washington Post,* February 27, 1991.
13. "Senator Simpson and Peter Arnett," *The Washington Post,* February 9, 1991 (editorial).
14. Anthony Lewis, "Slash and Burn," *The New York Times,* October 18, 1991.
15. Claudia Dreifus, "Exit Reasonable Right," *The New York Times Magazine,* June 2, 1996.
16. *Almanac of American Politics,* 1474.
17. Ibid.
18. *1990 Current Biography Yearbook,* 553.
19. Indeed he proclaimed himself "tickled to death" that advocates of Hispanic rights would no longer be able to turn to a Democratic House to reverse the Senate's restrictive immigration bills. Stephen Engelberg, "G.O.P.'s Voice on Aliens Roars Challenge to Party," *The New York Times,* December 8, 1994.
20. Ibid.
21. Simpson regarded Smith as "a very dear, sincere man, coming from the best motives. I admired him very much." Alan Simpson, telephone interview between author and former Senator Alan K. Simpson, July 1, 1998.
22. David L. Wilson and Anne E. Rumsey, "Washington's Movers and Shakers," *National Journal* 19 (1987), 1547.
23. Strom's connection with both subcommittee chairs "helped, naturally so. She knew the players." Simpson interview. She kept the two subcommittees "in communication." "Rep Smith to Unveil Immigration Bill Early Next Month," *Congress Daily,* May 15, 1995.
24. Dan Stein, interview between author and Dan Stein, executive director, FAIR, April 15, 1998.
25. S. 269, January 24, 1995.
26. Dirk Kirschten, "Second Thoughts," *National Journal,* January 21. 1995.
27. "Congress Considers a Major Overhaul of Immigration Laws," *Morning Edition,* National Public Radio, January 26, 1995.
28. Alan Simpson, Statement on Introduction of Immigrant Control and Financial Responsibility Act, *Congressional Record,* S1453 (January 24, 1995, legislative day of January 10, 1995).
29. This number had been suggested by the congressionally created Commission on Immigration Reform, described below. The commission had not yet issued its public report containing a recommended target of fifty thousand refugee admissions, but it had privately discussed this figure with Simpson's staff. Aleinikoff interview, October 29, 1998.
30. Maurice Belanger, interview between author and Maurice Belanger, policy assistant, National Immigration Forum, Aug. 29, 1997.

31. Walter Oleszek, *Congressional Procedures and the Policy Process,* 4th ed. (Washington, D.C.: CQ Press, 1996), 109.
32. Ibid., 110.
33. This hearing was actually held in the full Senate Judiciary Committee, not its immigration subcommittee, but Senator Simpson presided in lieu of Judiciary Chair Orrin Hatch, because Hatch was at a memorial service for his mother. Senate Judiciary Committee, *Proposals to Reduce Illegal Immigration and Control Costs to Taxpayers (S. 269), before the Senate Judiciary Committee,* 104th Cong., First Sess., March 14, 1995 (hereafter referred to as Simpson hearing).
34. Ibid., 13.
35. Ibid., 14.
36. Since about 1990, refugee admissions from the former Soviet Union alone had remained relatively constant at just under 50,000. U.S. Commission on Immigration Reform, *U.S. Refugee Policy: Taking Leadership* (1997), 34.
37. Statement of Phyllis Coven, director, INS Office of International Affairs, at National Conference of the National Immigration Forum, Washington, D.C., May 4, 1995.
38. Simpson hearing, 22–23 (testimony by Janet Reno and Doris Meissner).
39. T. Alexander Aleinikoff, interview between author and T. Alexander Aleinikoff, former executive associate commissioner, INS, October 29, 1998.
40. Ibid., 106–7.
41. Ibid., 164.
42. Ibid., 125–30.
43. Ibid., 133.
44. Ibid., 132–39.
45. Jo Thomas, "Agony Relieved as U.S. Pursues McVeigh Death," *The New York Times,* June 5, 1997.
46. Michael Ross, "Terror in Oklahoma City: Tougher Immigration Laws are Expected in Bomb Aftermath," *The Los Angeles Times,* April 21, 1995.
47. See letter to Alan Simpson from Kent Markus, acting assistant attorney general, June 7, 1995, with views of the administration on the "June 2, 1995 Committee Amendment to S. 269" and noting that "subsequent changes have been made to the Committee Amendment which the Administration is now reviewing." The subcommittee did not meet to consider the bill between the hearing in March and the June 8 mark-up. See LEXIS/NEXIS bill tracking report on S. 269.
48. Simpson interview. Indeed, Simpson thought that "you could have made it shorter." Ibid.
49. National Immigration Forum, Fax Memorandum, May 12, 1995.
50. "Four More Senators Join Senate Subcommittee, Simpson Is New Chairman," *Interpreter Releases* 72 (1995): 94.
51. The council is the coordinating arm of two hundred Jewish Federations, in cities across the nation, which provide health and welfare services to people in need, including refugees resettled from Russia. The council's Washington office lobbies in Congress on behalf of the local federations. Council of Jewish Federations, described on the InterAction website at www.interaction.org/ia/mb/cjf.html.
52. "The Best and Worst of Capitol Hill," *Washingtonian Magazine,* July, 1982, 101.
53. "The Capital Register," *Des Moines Sunday Register,* August 8, 1982.
54. Arnold Leibowitz, interview between author and Arnold Leibowitz, Washington representative, Hebrew Immigrant Aid Society, October 16, 1997.
55. Ally Milder, telephone interview between author and Ally Milder, December 31, 1997.
56. Leibowitz interview; Chris Burbach, "The Angel in Omaha," *The Omaha World-Tribune,* September 6, 1996; Chares E. Grassley, "A Visit with Soviet Jews," *The Saturday Evening Post,* September, 1983.
57. "Freed Soviets Decry Kremlin Emigration Policy," *The Los Angeles Times,* January 24, 1987.
58. Leibowitz interview.

59. John Fredriksson, interview between author and John Fredriksson, former Washington representative of the Lutheran Immigration and Refugee Service, October 10, 1997.

60. Frank Rich, "Mainstream Jews Should Join Specter's Stand against Radical Religious Right," *The Fort Lauderdale Sun-Sentinel,* July 8, 1994.

61. Ibid.

62. Leibowitz interview.

63. White House Briefing, July 27, 1993.

64. U.S. Commission on Immigration Reform, *Legal Immigration: Setting Priorities* (1995), 131.

65. Marcus Stern, "Clinton Endorses Proposal to Slash Legal Immigration," *The San Diego Union-Tribune,* June 8, 1995.

66. Karen Narasaki, executive director of the National Asian Pacific American Legal Consortium, quoted in Robert Pear, "Clinton Embraces a Proposal to Cut Immigration by a Third," *The New York Times,* June 8, 1995.

67. Quoted in Pear.

68. "I am aware of the popular nature of this amendment [to strike the cap]. That was easy to see before we came here." Transcript of Mark-up of Senate Immigration Subcommittee, June 8, 1995 (available in Senate subcommittee records).

69. Simpson hearing, 124.

70. The quotations are drawn from the transcript of the mark-up.

71. "We never would have won had we offered an amendment in subcommittee [and it] would have hurt our chances of success in the full committee." Letter to the author from a Democratic staff member, October 9, 1997.

72. Stein interview. In 1994, FAIR had published the booklet "Ten Steps to Ending Illegal Immigration," which became the basis for the recommendations of Speaker Gingrich's task force in June 1995. Ibid. The composition of the task force changed somewhat over time. In April 1995 it consisted of thirty-three Republicans and eight Democrats. "Insight on the News," *New World Communications,* April 17, 1995. But by the end of June, thirteen additional members had been added. Robert White, "Get Tough, Says Immigration Panel," *Newsday,* June 30, 1995. The task force made more than one hundred recommendations for deterring unlawful entry. Ibid.

73. Strom periodically met with the refugee organizations' representatives but would not show or tell them what she and her colleagues were writing. She parried their questions with questions of her own. "We would say, 'We've been told that you want to change the rules for suspension of deportation [a procedure under which an illegal alien who had lived in the U.S. for many years and proved good moral character could be allowed to remain].' She'd ask, 'Who told you that?'" Fredriksson interview.

74. "Immigration Overhaul Gains Momentum," *The Cleveland Plain Dealer,* July 1, 1995.

75. Stein interview.

76. Memorandum to the author from Dan Stein, executive director, FAIR, April 8, 1999.

77. National Immigration Forum, Fax Memorandum, June 28, 1995.

78. Ibid.

79. Lamar Smith, "Smith to Introduce Immigration Bill" (press release), June 20, 1995 (available on LEXIS/NEXIS).

80. Representative Xavier Beccera, in House Judiciary Committee mark-up, quoted in National Immigration Forum, H.R. 2202 update (fax), October 25, 1995.

81. Grover Joseph Rees, interview between author and Grover Joseph Rees, staff director, House Subcommittee on International Operations and Human Rights, October 17, 1997.

82. H.R. 1915 (104th Cong.).

83. *Hearing on Immigration in the National Interest Act of 1995 (H.R. 1915) before the Subcommittee on Immigration and Claims of the House Committee on the Judiciary,* 104th Cong., 1st Sess., June 29. 1995 (hereafter Smith hearing), 1, 3, 234, 332. The printed hearing record is 490 pages long. It does not include the bill; Smith included in the record only

its table of contents, presumably because of its length. Of the 490 pages, only 27 pages consist of dialogue; the rest are prepared statements or documents submitted for the record.

84. Smith hearing, 14–35, 74. Aleinikoff's statement precisely echoed the remarks of Vice President Al Gore, who a few days earlier had responded to Hispanic criticism of the commission proposals by calling the commission report "not the final word. It is a framework and not a blueprint." Frank Trejo, "Vice President Slams Anti-immigrant Views," *The Dallas Morning News,* June 25, 1995.

85. Smith hearing, 199, 230.

86. Smith hearing, 248–49. Mr. Frelick supported his Refugee Convention argument in a document submitted for the record, 270–74.

87. Smith hearing, 299.

88. Bill McGeveran, interview between author and Bill McGeveran, legislative assistant to Representative Charles Schumer, December 30, 1996.

89. "House Immigration Subcommittee Approves Reform Bill," *Interpreter Releases* 72 (1995): 973, 976.

90. Carmel Fisk, telephone interview between author and Carmel Fisk, former legislative assistant for Representative Bill McCollum, May 19, 1998.

91. Immigration and Naturalization Service, "Asylum Reform Is Making Significant Strides at Helping to Control U.S. Borders After Six Months," news release, July 5, 1995.

92. Immigration and Naturalization Service, "Affirmative Asylum Receipts at INS (Non ABC)," August 2, 1995.

93. Ibid.

94. Carmel Fisk, second telephone interview between author and Carmel Fisk, June 24, 1998.

95. Ibid.

96. Fisk interview, May 19, 1998.

97. Joyce Chiang, telephone interview between author and Joyce Chiang, June 3, 1998.

98. Chiang interview.

99. Stuart Anderson, telephone interview between author and Stuart Anderson, September 28, 1996.

100. "House Immigration Subcommittee Begins Considering Major Reform Bill," *Interpreter Releases* 72 (1995): 943.

101. "House Immigration Subcommittee Approves Reform Bill," *Interpreter Releases* 72 (1995): 973, 974.

102. National Immigration Forum, "National Immigration Forum" (brochure).

103. National Immigration Forum, "Urgent Action Alert, Aug. 1, 1995, and Announcement of Lobby Days in D.C. to Defend Immigration" (undated)

## Chapter 4: Mark-up Hell

1. Greg McCullough, "Report on Mark-up of H.R. 2202 in the House Judiciary Committee," October 11, 1995, *Legislate News Service* (available on LEXIS/NEXIS). A week later, advocating English-only legislation, Bono added, "Enough is enough with this bleeding heart stuff." National Immigration Forum, H.R. 2202 Update (fax), October 18, 1995.

2. National Immigration Forum, "Lobby Days Update," September 1, 1995; Fax Memorandum, September 15, 1995.

3. Ibid.

4. Subcommittee on International Law, Immigration, and Refugees, *Hearing on H.R. 3663 before the House Subcommittee on International Law, Immigration and Refugees,* 103d Cong, 2d Sess., June 15, 1994 (testimony of Rick Swartz); Dick Kirschten and Rick Swartz, "Speaking up for Aliens in Immigration Debates," *National Law Journal* 21 (1989): 2591; *National Law Journal, Immigration Lawyers: Who's Who,* October 3, 1983; John B. Judis, "Huddled Elites," *The New Republic,* December 23, 1996.

5. John Fredriksson, interview between author and John Fredriksson, former Washington representative of the Lutheran Immigration and Refugee Service, October 10, 1997.

6. National Immigration Forum, Fax Memorandum, September 1, 1995.

7. William Branigin, "High-Tech Firms Oppose Major Immigration Cuts," *The Washington Post*, September 13, 1995. The corporations argued that restricting high-tech firms' ability to recruit foreign engineers and scientists "is going to kill us. We would not be able to compete." Ibid.

8. Matthew Purdy, "Unlikely Allies Battle Congress over Anti-Immigration Plans," *The New York Times*, October 11, 1995.

9. See Keith Donoghue, "Immigration Bar Makes Its Mark on Hill," *Legal Times*, April 15, 1996.

10. Fredriksson interview.

11. NIF faxed an Action Alert to its members, advising them that "Controlling the course of [the bill] once it reaches the floor of the House will be very difficult. We need to change the bill now before it gets out of the Judiciary Committee." National Immigration Forum, Action Alert, September 18, 1995.

12. Walter Oleszek, *Congressional Procedures and the Policy Process*, 4th ed. (1996), 138–51.

13. Michael Barone and Grant Ujifusa, *Almanac of American Politics* (1996), 432–33.

14. Andrew Herrmann, "Bernardin Expresses Dismay at Hostility to Immigrants," *The Chicago Sun-Times*, December 10, 1994.

15. See, e.g., "Pope Pays Homage to Immigrants," *The San Diego Union-Tribune*, April 10, 1987 (according to the pope, "a nation open to immigration ... always stays young because, without losing its identity, it is able to renew itself").

16. Mitchell Locin, "Hyde Will Steward Gingrich's Program," *The Chicago Tribune*, November 17, 1994.

17. Angela Kelley, interview between author and Angela Kelley, director of policy, National Immigration Forum, August 29, 1997; Eileen V. Quigley, "Washington's Movers and Shakers," *National Journal*, June 1, 1985 (Hill's previous job).

18. At the time, the tide within the INS was running in the other direction. Memorandum to the author from David Martin, former INS general counsel, November 25, 1998.

19. Letter to Hon. Henry J. Hyde from Deputy Attorney General Jamie S. Gorelick, September 15, 1995. The administration probably had to write a very long letter to put its views on record regarding a very long bill, and it may have been relying on other methods, such as oral briefings of members of Congress willing to meet with INS officials, to make its key points more forcefully. Nevertheless, perhaps the Executive Branch has adopted a style of legislative commentary, including single spacing and long sentences, that is less than an optimal form of communicating with busy members of Congress who receive only its written submissions.

20. Letter to Hon. Henry J. Hyde from Deputy Attorney General Jamie S. Gorelick, September 15, 1995. The proposed "total reduction of employment and family-based immigration to 490,000 annually" appears on page 47. It is not clear from the letter whether that number was indeed the "total" number of business and family immigrants the administration supported at that time, or whether the administration intended to continue to allow, in addition, the approximately 250,000 immediate relatives of U.S. citizens who immigrated outside of the quota.

21. Memorandum to the author from former INS general counsel David Martin, November 25, 1998.

22. The administration's views letter was actually the product of very extensive interagency comment and coordination, a process managed by the Department of Justice and the Office of Management and Budget. Martin memorandum.

23. Elisa Massimino, interview between author and Elisa Massimino, director, Washington Office, Lawyers Committee for Human Rights, June 11, 1997.

24. Fredriksson interview.

25. David S. Broder, "If Starr Goes to Congress," *The Washington Post*, March 23, 1998.

26. "House Judiciary Committee Begins Considering Major Reform Bill," *Interpreter Releases*

72 (1995): 1303. The committee later voted to try out the system with pilot projects in five states before putting it into national use. Ibid.

27. National Immigration Forum, Fax Memorandum, September 21, 1995.

28. H.R. 2202, 104th Cong., 2d Sess, version 2, September 28, 1995.

29. House Judiciary Committee Mark-up, September 20, 1995, *Federal News Service* (available on LEXIS/NEXIS).

30. Amendment III-7 to H.R. 2202 (House Judiciary Committee).

31. Martin memorandum.

32. Transcript, *Federal News Service*, September 20. The INS official may have been the Service's congressional liaison officer, Pamela Berry, its deputy general counsel, Paul Virtue, or another member of the general counsel's staff, Joyce Chiang. The signal may have meant only that the INS did not have the relevant statistics, rather than that it knew that the backlog was overwhelming. Interview with former INS general counsel David A. Martin, November 24, 1998.

33. Ibid.

34. Hyde did not help the opponents of summary exclusion, but he found a different way to demonstrate his concern about Chinese women who sought refuge to avoid compulsory abortion. He successfully proposed an amendment to establish that a person who feared retaliation for resistance to forced abortion was to be considered a victim of persecution. "House Judiciary Committee Marks Up Comprehensive Immigration Bill," *Refugee Reports*, October 30, 1995, 8–9. However, no more than one thousand refugees a year may win asylum or refugee status under this provision, which has become the only numerical limitation on asylum in American law. Immigration and Nationality Act, as amended in 1996, Sec. 207 (a) (5).

35. Massimino interview.

36. Paul A. Gigot, "Uncle Sam Wants Your Papers, Please," *The Wall Street Journal*, September 29, 1995.

37. John Heilemann, "Do You Know the Way to Ban José?" *Wired*, August, 1996.

38. National Immigration Forum, H.R. 2202 Update (fax), October 11, 1995.

39. After being surprised by McCollum's reintroduction and passage in the House Immigration Subcommittee of the old Mazzoli amendment imposing a deadline, Martin and others tried to persuade House members to abandon the concept of a deadline or, at the very least, not to apply it to cases in which a refugee would be eligible for "withholding of deportation"; that is, where the refugee could prove not merely a well-founded fear but that, more probably than not, he would be in danger of losing his life or liberty if deported to his own country. A person who won "withholding" received only a temporary reprieve from deportation, not the opportunity to start on the path to U.S. citizenship. All House members to whom the INS officials spoke told them that because this provision was primarily of interest to McCollum, they should address their case to him. Martin and McCollum had several meetings. Martin was unable to talk McCollum out of imposing a deadline, but he persuaded McCollum that applying it to "withholding" cases would put the U.S. in violation of its international obligations under the Refugee Convention. McCollum told him that the INS had approached him too late to fix the withholding problem in the Judiciary Committee, but that he would see to it that the bill approved on the House floor included a withholding provision with no deadline. David A. Martin, interview between author and David A. Martin, November 19, 1998.

40. Transcript, October 11, 1995.

41. *Almanac of American Politics*, 646–47.

42. Transcript, October 11.

43. Transcript, October 12, 1995.

44. Arnold Leibowitz, interview between author and Arnold Leibowitz, Washington representative, Hebrew Immigrant Aid Society, October 16, 1997.

45. Grover Joseph Rees, interview between author and Grover Joseph Rees, October 17, 1997;

see "Where Refugees Come From" (undated memorandum) ("cutting the Vietnamese and former Soviet categories in half only gets the total down to 64,000. The further reduction would require substantial cuts in the next two largest groups: the 15,000 Bosnian ethnic cleansing victims and the 6000 Cubans.")

46. Jana Mason, interview between author and Jana Mason, September 8, 1997.
47. National Immigration Forum, H.R. 2202 Update (fax), October 12, 1995; "Future of Refugee Resettlement on the Line," *Refugee Reports*, October 30, 1995, 2.
48. Leibowitz interview.
49. Ibid. (*Refugee Reports*), committee records.
50. National Immigration Forum, H.R. 2202 Update (fax), October 25, 1995.
51. "Senate Oks Welfare Bill With Sweeping Immigration Consequences," *Interpreter Releases* 72 (1995): 1365.
52. Letter to Hon. Henry Hyde from Jay Kim et al., October 25, 1995.
53. "House Committee Approves Major Reform Bill, Floor Action Next," *Interpreter Releases* 72 (1995): 1497.
54. National Immigration Forum, Urgent Fax Memorandum, November 9, 1995.
55. "Senate Subcommittee Approves Legal Immigration Reform Measure," *Interpreter Releases* 72 (1995): 1605.
56. Adam Clymer, "Simpson Joins Ranks of Pragmatists Leaving Senate," *The New York Times*, December 4, 1995

## Chapter 5: Someone Else's Problem

1. Pamela Faith Lerman, *Passover Seder*, 3d ed. (1993). I have been informed by my cousin, Rabbi Bob Gluck, that the origin of the concept is found in Pirkei Avot 2:16, reporting that Rabbi Tarfon would say, "It is not up to you to finish the work, yet you are not free to avoid it."
2. Philip G. Schrag and Michael Meltsner, *Reflections on Clinical Legal Education* (Boston: Northeastern University Press, 1998), recounts my development as a clinical teacher and my impressions of the relationship, over the years, between clinical learning and issues of social justice.
3. Gordon Thomas and Max Morgan Witts, *Voyage of the Damned*, 2d ed. (Stillwater, Minn.: Motorbooks International, 1994).
4. Research by the museum through 1998 revealed that a bare majority of the *St. Louis* passengers may have survived, a calculation that may be excessively optimistic because it is based on the assumption that all those not known to have been killed in the camps were in fact survivors. Nicholas Day, "No Turning Back," *The Washington Post*, August 26, 1998.
5. The many decisions that had to be made along the way are described in Philip G. Schrag, "Constructing a Clinic," *Clinical Law Review* 3 (1996): 175, reprinted in Schrag and Meltsner, *supra.*, 239.
6. Letter to Senator Orrin Hatch from Joshua Davis, May 23, 1996.
7. Later, I learned that some of the sponsors of a deadline thought that the great majority of asylum applicants had no colorable claim for asylum, and in their minds, the deadline would discourage these frivolous applications or at least allow the government to dismiss them more rapidly. On the other hand, some of the advocates of a deadline, such as McCollum and Representative John Bryant, believed that even people like Joseph should be able to ask for asylum as soon as they touched U.S. soil.
8. Mary Rawson is the asylum applicant whose story is told in the prologue to this book.
9. Philip G. Schrag, "Don't Gut Political Asylum," *The Washington Post*, November 12, 1995. The internal quotation is from the instructions to the INS's I-589 form (1995 ed.).
10. Letter to the author from Dusa Gyllensvard, November 21, 1995.
11. McCollum later put into the committee report a statement that "INS should take affirmative steps to notify the public of the 30-day filing requirement." *Report 104-469 of the House Judiciary Comm. on H.R. 2202, Immigration in the National Interest Act of 1995*, 104th

Cong., 2d Sess., p. 176. However this vague statement fell short of "requiring" the INS to notify people subject to the time bar.

12. Transcript, "Pork," *America Talking*, November 15, 1995

## Chapter 6: The Committee to Preserve Asylum

1. Michael Perschuk and Wendy Schaetzel, *The People Rising* (New York: Thunder's Mouth Press, 1989), 41, a history of the public interest coalition that fought successfully to defeat President Ronald Reagan's nomination of Robert Bork to be a justice of the Supreme Court.

2. After completing her work on the immigration bill, Pistone applied for and received a fellowship in which she could help to teach asylum advocacy to law students in the author's clinic at Georgetown. The clinic's fellows also write scholarly articles, and the combination of supervised teaching and scholarship prepares them for careers as law professors. Pistone is now a professor and the director of clinical programs, and of the human rights clinic, at the Villanova University School of Law in Pennsylvania.

3. Interview with Michele Pistone, October 15, 1996.

4. The subtitle of this book repeats my omission, and I do not mean to imply that refugees who are threatened with religious or racial persecution are any less entitled to protection than those who face political persecution. I used the word "political" in the subtitle because some people who don't have much contact with immigration or refugee issues might associate the unmodified word "asylum" with a term that was once used to refer to institutions for mental patients. Including all of the categories of persecution was not possible because the subtitle is already rather long.

5. Technically, they are forming an "unincorporated association." If the organization collects money, congressional disclosure rules requiring registration as lobbyists may apply. But our organization never collected money, and we did not have to register.

6. Letter to Members of the Senate Judiciary Committee from the Committee to Preserve Asylum, December 21, 1995.

7. Fax Memorandum to AILA Chapter Chairs from Jeanne Butterfield, December 22, 1995

## Chapter 7: "What's a Senator?"

1. Letter to Senator Russell Feingold, December 28, 1995.

2. Michael Barone and Grant Ujifusa, *Almanac of American Politics* (1996), 856; "Congressmen Focus on Persecuted Believers," *Christianity Today*, July 15, 1996.

3. The leading study of the role of congressional staff members is Michael J. Malbin, *Unelected Representatives: Congressional Staff and the Future of Representative Government* (1979). According to Malbin, the staff members' "ability to run committee investigations, the results of which they can skillfully leak to the media, gives them influence over the items members choose to put on the legislative agenda. Once a bill is on the agenda, the staff works to assemble a coalition behind it, arranging detailed amendments with other staff members and with interest group representatives. . . ." Ibid., 5.

4. Coven seemed to generate the suggestion spontaneously during the meeting, but former executive associate commissioner T. Alexander Aleinikoff thinks that the press conference probably had been planned for some time before the meeting. Aleinikoff interview, October 29, 1998.

5. Michael Pertschuk, *Giant Killers* (New York: W. W. Norton, 1986), 240.

6. Physicians for Human Rights, *Position Paper in Opposition to Proposed Asylum Limit in S. 269 and H.R. 2202*, December 20, 1995.

7. Immigration and Naturalization Service, "INS Successfully Reforms U.S. Asylum System," January 4, 1996 (press release).

8. "INS Holds News Conference on the Asylum Reform Efforts," *Federal Document Clearing House Political Transcripts*, January 4, 1996 (available on LEXIS/NEXIS).

9. William Branigin, "INS Chief Highlights Reform in Political Asylum System," *The*

*Washington Post,* January 5, 1996; "Some Progress at INS," *The Washington Post,* January 15, 1996 (editorial).

10. John Heilemann, "Do You Know the Way to Ban José?" *Wired,* August 1996.

11. Memorandum to the author from David Fry, January 22, 1996.

12. National Immigration Forum, Fax Memo to D.C. members from Angela Kelley, February 1, 1996.

13. See, e.g., letter to members of Senate Judiciary Committee from fifty-four teachers of human rights and immigration law, February 22, 1996. This letter was circulated for signature primarily over the Internet, which has come into its own as a low-cost method of political organizing.

14. Interview with Dan Stein, April 8, 1999.

15. Communication with the author from Lisa Coleman, February, 1996.

16. "Hearing of the Senate Judiciary Committee," February 29, 1996, *Federal News Service* (speech of Sen. Spencer Abraham) (available on LEXIS/NEXIS).

17. Gil Klein, "Should Legal Immigration Be Cut Back?" *The Tampa Tribune,* February 10, 1996.

18. Dan Freedman, "Senators Seek to Save Legal Immigration," *The Fort Lauderdale Sun-Sentinel,* February 28, 1996.

19. Heilemann.

20. "Hearing of the Senate Judiciary Committee," February 29, 1996; Eric Schmitt, "Playing by Senate Rules Wins the Day," *The New York Times,* March 3, 1996; Bureau of National Affairs, "Daily Report for Executives," March 1, 1996.

21. Letter to the author from Senator Paul Simon, "dictated 3-4-96 [but then dated] March 11, 1996."

22. Interview with Michele Pistone, October 15, 1996.

23. "Hearing of the Senate Judiciary Committee," March 14, 1996, *Federal News Service.*

24. "Dear Colleague" letter from Mike DeWine and Edward M. Kennedy, March 18, 1996.

25. The quotations in the debate are drawn from the official transcript in the possession of the Committee. A partial but very garbled and in several places inaccurate transcript is reported at "Senate Judiciary Committee Hearing," March 20, 1996, *Federal News Service* (available on LEXIS/NEXIS). .

26. Report of the Senate Judiciary Committee on the Immigration Control and Financial Responsibility Act of 1996 (S. Rpt. 104-249), 30, records the vote as sixteen to one, with Thompson voting for the DeWine motion (and Biden absent). The official transcript, however, shows that Thompson did not respond to the vote in person or by proxy.

27. Senate Judiciary Committee Report, 21.

28. Senate Judiciary Committee Report, 43

## Chapter 8: The House

1. House Committee on Rules, *Hearing of the House Committee on Rules,* March 14, 1996 (transcript).

2. *1995/2 Congressional Staff Directory* (1995), 1043. The Lutheran Immigration and Refugee Service was, throughout the 104th Congress, one of the leading advocates for refugees. The organization was then about fifty years old. It dated back to 1938, when an organization was needed to resettle German Jews who had converted to Christianity but whom Germany still considered as Jewish. It also did a lot of work with Lutheran displaced persons from Estonia and Latvia. When the displaced person camp work ended in the 1950s, general international resettlement became a part of the Lutheran ministry. John Fredriksson, interview between author and John Fredriksson, former Washington representative for the Lutheran Immigration and Refugee Service, October 10, 1997.

3. Bronwyn Lance, interview between author and Bronwyn Lance, former government relations associate, Lutheran Immigration and Refugee Service, June 17, 1998.

4. Lance interview.

5. The refugee cap and the asylum deadline provisions were in Title V, but summary exclusion was embedded in a different provision of the bill.

6. House Judiciary Committee, *Report 104–469 of the House Judiciary Committee on the Immigration in the National Interest Act of 1995 (H.R. 2202)*, March 4, 1996, 1–106.

7. James Dao, "New York's Democratic Depression Worries the White House," *The New York Times*, September 5, 1995. Schumer later decided that he would instead seek the nomination for senator. Blaine Harden, "N.Y. Gov. Pataki Dumps Running Mate," *The Washington Post*, April 18, 1997. He was elected senator, defeating incumbent Alphonse D'Amato, in November 1998.

8. Celia W. Dugger, "Immigration Bills' Deadlines May Imperil Asylum Seekers," *The New York Times*, February 12, 1996. At the time the article was written, the alien who was featured in it had been denied asylum and had renewed his claim before an immigration judge. The judge granted him asylum. E-mail from Lawyers Committee for Human Rights to Michele Pistone, October 27, 1997.

9. Douglas Shenson, "30 Days or Else," *The New York Times*, February 15, 1996.

10. Letter to Charles E. Schumer from Michael Posner, executive director, Lawyers Committee for Human Rights, February 22, 1996.

11. Letter to Representative Howard Berman from President Bill Clinton, February 13, 1996, responding to letter to President Bill Clinton from Representative Howard Berman, December 18, 1995. Clinton's letter merely restated existing administration policy, but it elevated the expression of that policy from the departmental to the presidential level, perhaps giving it more evident political authority.

12. Clyde Haberman, "Giving Help in the Quest for Refuge," *The New York Times*, March 1, 1996.

13. The donations may not have been as beneficial as McCollum believed. Studies have shown that U.S. drug companies often make third-world donations of drugs that are unusable because they are spoiled and outdated. They take tax deductions based on the nominal value of the drugs and transfer to the receiving countries the two thousand dollars per ton cost of disposing of the useless material. "Unusable Drugs Were Donated in Bosnia," *The Washington Post*, December 18, 1997.

14. The American Immigration Lawyers Association and the U.S. Catholic Conference's Micheal Hill had organized a meeting of staff members of House Republican freshmen (who were on the whole conservative but did not as yet have fixed ideas about immigration) and seasoned Democrats. During this and subsequent meetings, Hill helped to persuade these mutually suspicious groups to work together on splitting the bill. Eventually, the members for whom these staffers worked sent out a bipartisan "Dear Colleague" letter urging others to split the bill. James G. Gimpel and James R. Edwards, Jr., *The Congressional Politics of Immigration Reform* (1999), 255.

15. Within a year, Brownback would move to the Senate to fill the seat vacated by Robert Dole during his presidential campaign. Howard Berman, the immigration subcommittee's ranking Democrat, also sponsored the split-the-bill amendment. But in a Republican-led Congress, the Republican sponsors were more surprising and more essential.

16. John Heilemann, "Do You Know the Way to Ban José?" *Wired*, August 1996.

17. National Immigration Forum, Fax Memorandum, March 6, 1996.

18. Heilemann, August 1996.

19. Joel Najar, interview between author and Joel Najar, former assistant to Representative Howard Berman, June 25, 1998.

20. Lance interview.

21. Najar interview.

22. Najar interview.

23. Keith Donoghue, "Immigration Bar Makes its Mark on Hill," *Legal Times*, week of April 15, 1996.

24. Parole was "the most common way in which we bring Chinese dissidents to the United

States when it has been determined that they would be in danger if they remained in China." Grover Joseph Rees, interview between author and Grover Joseph Rees, October 17, 1997.

25. Stephen H. Legomsky, *Immigration and Refugee Law and Policy,* 2d ed. (1997), 762.
26. House Report 104–469, 140.
27. Immigration and Nationality Act, Sec. 212 (d) (5).
28. House Report Sec. 104–469, 77 (H.R. 2202, Sec. 523).
29. Quoted in Walter J. Oleszek, *Congressional Procedure and the Policy Process,* 4th ed. (1996).
30. Amendment to H.R. 2202 submitted to the Committee on Rules by Reps. Charles E. Schumer, Benjamin A. Gilman, and Christopher Smith (March 13, 1996).
31. Rees interview.
32. Najar interview (timing of the meeting with staff from the Republican leadership).
33. They could have been educated, of course, if Speaker Newt Gingrich or Majority Leader Richard Armey had met with INS Commissioner Doris Meissner, who would have explained to them, as she did to numerous senators, that David Martin's regulation had essentially solved the problem of the ever-increasing asylum backlog and made an application deadline unnecessary. But Commissioner Meissner "never had the opening" to discuss the bill with Gingrich or Armey. Interview with former INS general counsel David Martin, November 24, 1998.
34. Leonard Swinehart, interview between author and Leonard Swinehart, senior floor assistant for Speaker Newt Gingrich, June 23, 1998.
35. Interview between author and a former Republican congressional staff member, June 24, 1998.
36. Swinehart interview.
37. Interview with the former Republican congressional staff member, *supra.*
38. See Remarks of Representative Jerold Nadler, *Congressional Record,* March 19, 1996, H2390 (daily ed.). The amendment, offered by Representatives Christopher Smith and Robert Scott, would have specified that only experienced asylum officers could exercise the power to deny asylum claims and put aliens on return flights. It also would have barred summary removal for aliens fleeing countries that engaged in torture, systematic persecution, or other gross violations of human rights. See Letter to Representative Gerald B.H. Solomon from Representative Chris Smith, March 13, 1996. Joseph Rees had long favored a summary exclusion procedure because he believed that long delays in adjudication aided fraudulent asylum seekers. But he believed safeguards like those in Smith's amendment were essential to any reform, and he had drafted proposals including such safeguards during his last months as INS general counsel, early in the Clinton administration. Rees interview. The Smith-Scott amendment represented a further effort to include those safeguards in a summary exclusion law.
39. National Immigration Forum, Fax Memorandum, March 16, 1996.
40. See "Please Vote YES on Amendment #17" (flyer, undated).
41. Rees interview.
42. Leibowitz interview.
43. Lance interview.
44. Rees interview.
45. *Congressional Record,* March 20, 1996, 2527–2530 (daily ed.).
46. National Immigration Forum, Urgent Action Fax Memo, March 18, 1996.
47. Ibid.
48. National Immigration Forum, Urgent Update/Action Alert, March 20, 1996.
49. A spokesperson for Clinton later said that the president changed his policy quickly because of "opposition [to his support for the Jordan Commission recommendations] across the spectrum [from the] Roman Catholic Church ... to the Microsoft Corportation as well as most of the high-tech industry." He denied that the change resulted as a result of recent large contributions to the Democratic Party from Asian-Americans who wanted to

preserve their ability to sponsor immigration by their siblings. Michael Kranish, "Policy Shift over Fund-Raiser Is Denied," *The Boston Globe*, January 17, 1997.

50. Heilemann, August 1996. James R. Edwards, Jr., who worked on the bill as the staff member for a Republican member of the House Judiciary Commitee, has reported that "the high-tech lobby [had] hired" Norquist to lobby his friend the Speaker, and that the Christian Coalition saw opposing cuts in legal immigration as an opportunity to "improve relationships with some of the other religious interest groups in Washington, including the Catholic Bishops." Gimpel and Edwards, 262.

51. Letter to representatives from Heidi H. Stirrup, director, government relations, the Christian Coalition, March 20, 1996.

52. Angela Kelley, interview between author and Angela Kelley, National Immigration Forum, August 29, 1997.

53. *Congressional Record*, H2589–2600 (March 21, 1966).

54. *Congressional Record*, H2600 (March 21, 1996).

55. *Congressional Record*, H2602–2603 (March 21, 1996).

56. Because the Rules Committee limits the amendments on which floor votes can be taken, it would not have been possible for Chrysler and his allies first to have tried a broader amendment to strike all of Title V and then, if that failed, the actual amendment they sponsored. It is very doubtful that the Rules Committee would have allowed votes on two such similar amendments.

57. *Congressional Record*, H2488 (March 20, 1996).

58. Michael Barone and Grant Ujifusa, *Almanac of American Politics* (1996), 151–53; "Candidates and Issues," *Los Angeles Times*, October 23, 1988.

59. *Plyler v. Doe*, 457 U.S. 202 (1982).

60. *Congressional Record*, H2488–2495 (March 20, 1996).

61. Oleszek, 34.

62. "Teacher Stuns Democrats in a Senate Primary," *The New York Times*, March 14, 1996.

63. In that runoff, Morales beat Bryant. Sam Howe Verhovek, "Running on Dare, Teacher Wins Senate Primary," *The New York Times*, April 11, 1996. Morales later lost to incumbent Gramm in the general election.

64. *Congressional Record*, H2495 (March 20, 1996).

65. Ibid. (remarks of Representative Riggs).

66. *Congressional Record*, H2506–2507 (March 20, 1996).

67. William Branigin, "House Backs State Option to Bar Illegal Immigrant Children from Public School," *The Washington Post*, March 21, 1996.

68. Eric Schmitt, "House Approves Ending Schooling of Illegal Aliens," *The New York Times*, March 21, 1996.

69. National Immigration Forum, Fax Memorandum, March 29, 1996.

70. Ibid.

71. *Congressional Record*, H2639 (March 21, 1996)

**Chapter 9: The Senate**

1. Quoted in Patrick J. McDonnell and William J. Eaton, "Political Asylum System under Fire, Faces Revision," *The Los Angeles Times*, July 19, 1993.

2. See American Bar Association, "The South Texas Pro Bono Asylum Representation Project," on the World Wide Web at http://www.abanet.org/yld/probar.html

3. Cohen was, at the time, minority staff director and chief counsel of the Judiciary's Antitrust Subcommittee, of which Leahy was the ranking Democrat. The immigration bill had nothing to do with antitrust issues, but it is common for senators to ask the senior officials of their subcommittee staffs to work with them on whatever issues are pressing in the full committee. Cohen later became minority chief counsel of the Judiciary Committee.

4. *Current Biography Yearbook* (1990), 391–94.

5. S. 1394 (104th Cong.), Sec. 195.
6. Ibid.
7. Michele Pistone, interview between author and Michele Pistone, December 2, 1997.
8. Readers significantly younger than Senator Simpson or the author may need to brush up on comic books of the 1950s to understand this reference. "Shazam" was the word (actually, an acronym referring to six Greek gods) that Billy Batson uttered to turn into the powerful Captain Marvel. Senator Simpson therefore probably used it to connote a single word or phrase that, when spoken, could transform the speaker's entire life.
9. The debate and roll call are transcribed in "Hearing of the Senate Judiciary Committee," March 14, 1996, *Federal News Service* (available on LEXIS/NEXIS). In a full congressional committee, proposed amendments do not carry when the vote is tied. This rule demonstrates another aspect of the power that subcommittee chairs like Simpson, who have good control over their subcommittees, can assert; it is an uphill battle both psychologically and legally to overturn the subcommittee's work.
10. Joseph Rees was briefed by a House Judiciary Committee staff member about the anti-terrorism bill, but the staff member never mentioned that the legislation included provisions dealing with immigration. He learned about the summary exclusion provisions the day before the bill went to the floor. He asked why new restrictions on all prospective immigrants had been included in a bill about terrorists. A staff member replied that it was obvious that the provision would deter terrorists. By the time Rees learned about the provision, the deadline had passed within which members could propose amendments to the bill. Grover Joseph Rees, interview between author and Grover Joseph Rees, October 17, 1997.
11. H. R. 1710, Secs. 621–623. Depriving such a person of a hearing would also deprive her of the opportunity to apply for "suspension of deportation," a remedy that an immigration judge could grant to someone who had been in the United States for more than seven years, was of good moral character, had not committed a crime, and whose deportation would cause extreme hardship to the alien or a close relative who was a citizen or lawful permanent resident. See Immigration and Nationality Act Sec. 244 as it existed before the 1996 immigration law took effect.
12. John E. Yang, "House Votes to Remove Controversial Provisions From Anti-Terrorism Bill," *The Washington Post*, March 14, 1996; Stephen Labaton, "House Kills Sweeping Provisions in Counterterrorism Legislation," *The New York Times*, March 14, 1996.
13. Letter to Senator Orrin G. Hatch from Deputy Attorney General Jamie S. Gorelick, February 14, 1996.
14. S. 754 (the administration bill, introduced by Sen. Kennedy), 104th Cong., Sec. 106.
15. See, e.g., letter to Hon. Henry Hyde from Rene van Rooyen, Washington representative of the High Commissioner, October 23, 1995 (urging deletion of the deadline and a "manifestly unfounded" standard for credible fear screening); letter to Hon. Orrin G. Hatch from Kate Jastram Balian, acting Washington representative of the High Commissioner, December 13, 1995 (similar recommendations).
16. Letter to Senator Patrick Leahy from Anne Willem Bijleveld, March 19, 1996, citing UNHCR *Executive Committee Conclusions* 15 (1979) and 30 (1983).
17. "UN Agency Objects to US Immigration Bills," *The Boston Globe*, April 2, 1996.
18. Michele Pistone, interview between author and Michele Pistone, October 24, 1996.
19. Rees tried to head off the summary exclusion provisions, but his usual Senate contact, Chief Counsel Mark Disler of the Senate Judiciary Committee, wasn't working on the issue personally and was too busy to focus on it. Rees interview.
20. Walter Oleszek, *Congressional Procedures and the Policy Process*, 4th ed. (1996), 293.
21. *Congressional Record*, S3427–3434 (April 17, 1996).
22. Rene Sanchez, "Clinton Criticizes House for Weakening Terrorism Bill," *The Washington Post*, March 17, 1996.
23. Pistone archives, undated memorandum, apparently sent on or about April 17, 1996.

24.  Statement of the president on signing the Antiterrorism and Effective Death Penalty Act of 1996, April 24, 1996.

25.  Immigration officials misspelled her name, so the now-famous Board of Immigration appeals case that bears her name, and most of the publicity about her, referred to her as Fauziya Kasinga. Celia W. Dugger, "A Refugee's Body Is Intact but Her Family Is Torn," *The New York Times*, Sept. 11, 1996.

26.  Ibid.

27.  Fauziya Kassindja and Layli Miller Bashir, *Do They Hear You When You Cry* (New York: Delacorte Press, 1998), 175–177.

28.  Although entry without a visa is commonly called "illegal" immigration, it is not prosecuted as a crime. In any event, she did not even attempt to enter surreptitiously; she arrived at a border, declared herself to officials, and requested asylum.

29.  Celia W. Dugger, "Woman's Plea for Asylum Puts Tribal Ritual on Trial," *The New York Times*, April 15, 1996.

30.  "Fauziya Kasinga Discusses Why She's Seeking Political Asylum in the United States," *Federal Document Clearing House*, April 29, 1996 (News Conference, statement of Layli Miller Bashir), available on LEXIS/NEXIS.

31.  Keith Donoghue, "A Berkeley Lawyer's Client Could Establish Precedent for Asylum Claims Based on Female Genital Mutilation," *The Recorder*, January 18, 1996.

32.  Judy Mann, "When Judges Fail," *The Washington Post*, January 19, 1996.

33.  Ellen Goodman, "Mutilated by Her Culture," *The Boston Globe*, April 7, 1996; Ellen Goodman, "Refugee Merely Seeks Freedom from Female Genital Mutilation," *The Fresno Bee*, April 9, 1996.

34.  A. M. Rosenthal, "On My Mind; Fighting Female Mutilation," *The New York Times*, April 13, 1996.

35.  Dugger, April 15.

36.  Electronic mail message to the author from Karen Musalo, June 10, 1998.

37.  "Not So Harsh on Refugees," *The New York Times*, April 22, 1996 (editorial).

38.  The table was derived by comparing the Simpson bill, S. 1664 (104th Cong.), Secs. 131, 132, 141, 142, 193; the anti-terrorism law that had recently been enacted, S. 735 (104th Cong.), Secs. 414, 422 and 423; and the Leahy amendment, reprinted at *Congressional Record*, S4457 (May 1, 1996).

39.  The Clinton administration interpreted this provision to permit it to parole the alien out of prison after finding that the alien had credible fear and therefore a plausible asylum claim. Memorandum from former INS general counsel David Martin, November 25, 1998. Its interpretation would not have bound subsequent administrations, however, and in practice, while the Clinton administration believed that a similar provision in the law that was ultimately passed also permitted parole, it delegated parole decisions to individual INS district directors, some of whom almost never paroled anyone. See Michele R. Pistone, "Justice Delayed Is Justice Denied: A Proposal for Ending the Unnecessary Detention of Asylum Seekers," *Harvard Human Rights Journal* 12 (1999): 197.

40.  Such aliens could still seek "withholding," preventing their deportation to the country in which they were endangered, but the standard of proof was much higher than for asylum, and withholding conferred fewer and more temporary benefits.

41.  See "Dole, Angered by Democrats, Takes Immigration Bill off Floor," *The Minneapolis Star Tribune*, April 17, 1996.

42.  Committee to Preserve Asylum, One More Emergency Appeal (fax), April 26, 1996.

43.  Anthony Lewis, "Slamming the Door," *The New York Times*, April 19, 1996.

44.  "Immigrants and Other Ordinary People," *The Washington Times*, April 30, 1996 (editorial).

45.  The continued detention of Ms. Kassindja was a subject of considerable controversy within the INS. Long before her detention made headlines, the general counsel of the INS argued for her release. The INS district director with jurisdiction over her refused to

release her, arguing that an immigration judge had found her not credible, and he did not accept the general counsel's argument that the judge's credibility determination had been colored by his unwillingness to accept the threat of genital mutilation as a type of persecution. The press attention, and particularly Celia Dugger's article in *The New York Times*, began to turn the tide in Kassindja's favor, although the decisive factor favoring her release was the willingness of a cousin of her law student representative to be responsible for her and provide an address at which she could be found for deportation if she lost her appeal. Interview with former INS general counsel David A. Martin, November 24, 1998. For Ms. Kassindja's perspective describing her desperation in the weeks before her release, see Kassindja and Bashir, 431–88.

46. Marilyn Johnson, "Kids Rule," *Life*, January, 1997. The book is Kassindja and Bashir, *supra*.

47. Press conference, April 29, *supra*.

48. Elliot Grossman, "Asylum Is a Painful Victory," *The Allentown Morning Call*, April 22, 1996.

49. William Branigin, "Critics of Immigration Bill Assail Limits on Asylum," *The Washington Post*, May 1, 1996.

50. *Congressional Record*, S4461 (remarks of Senator Leahy, May 1, 1996).

51. *ABC World News Tonight*, ABC, April 29, 1996, Transcript 6085–4. See also *Burden of Proof*, CNN, May 1, 1996, Transcript 151; *All Things Considered*, National Public Radio, May 1, 1996, Transcript 2200–6.

52. "Togolese Teenager Decries Imprisonment," Agence France Presse, April 30, 1996.

53. Pamela Constable, "Togolese Teen Criticizes Detainment," *The Washington Post*, April 30, 1996.

54. "The Terrorism Law Revisited," *The Washington Post*, May 1, 1996 (editorial).

55. *Congressional Record*, S4457–4466 (May 1, 1996).

56. Pistone interview, October 24, 1996.

57. Electronic mail from Musalo, *supra*.

58. Letter to Senator Edward Kennedy from William Danvers, special assistant to the president for legislative affairs, May 1, 1996 (obtained from the administration through the Freedom of Information Act). The letter was sent at 12:08 P.M.

59. *Congressional Record*, S4490–91 (May 1, 1996).

60. Pistone interview, October 24, 1996.

61. *Congressional Record*, S4492 (May 1, 1996).

62. The Lutheran Church has a strong presence in North Dakota, and local members of the Lutheran Immigration and Refugee Service had spoken extensively with the offices of both senators and anticipated favorable votes. Bronwyn Lance, interview between author and Bronwyn Lance, who had been the government relations associate for the Lutheran Immigration Refugee Service, June 17, 1998.

63. Shortly before considering the immigration bill, the Senate had debated the Republican-sponsored "Freedom to Farm" bill, under which federal subsidies for North Dakota wheat farmers, among others, would be slashed. The bill was strongly opposed by Conrad, who said it "takes literally hundreds of thousands of farmers right over the cliff." "Subsidies could be plowed under," *The Houston Chronicle*, February 8, 1996. Democrats at first filibustered the measure and prevented its passage, but then Leahy, the ranking Democrat on the Agriculture Committee, made a deal with the Republicans, delivering enough Democratic votes to defeat the filibuster. Greg Gordon, "GOP's Farm Bill Passes Senate," *The Minneapolis Star Tribune*, February 8, 1996. In exchange, Leahy won the Republicans' agreement to eliminate from the bill certain restrictions on environmental protection and cutbacks in nutrition programs, such as food stamps. In the House-Senate conference, Leahy also obtained a provision permitting the secretary of agriculture to approve the Dairy Compact, under which New England producers could obtain artificially high prices for milk. Guy Gugliotta, "Leahy Ensured His Farm Priorities," *The Washington Post*, March 22, 1996; Gordon; Patrick Jasperse, "State Dairy Farmers May Get Some Relief," *The Milwaukee Journal Sentinel*, March 27, 1996. Conrad, who like Leahy was a member of the

Agriculture Committee and of the House-Senate Conference Committee, "took it very hard" that Leahy had jumped ship; he felt that Leahy had "stabbed him in the back" on an issue of great importance to North Dakota, where agriculture is 35 percent of the economy. Kevin Price, interview between author and Kevin Price, former legislative assistant to Senator Kent Conrad, January 7, 1998. Mr. Price's counterpart in Senator Dorgan's office referred the author's questions to Barry Piatt, the senator's press secretary. Mr. Piatt undertook to find out why Senator Dorgan voted against the Leahy amendment. Barry Piatt, interview between author and Barry Piatt, January 7, 1998. But he did not call the author back with the information. Therefore, it is not clear whether Dorgan's vote represented an accommodation to Senator Conrad, his own distress with Leahy's farm bill decisions, or a desire to curtail more severely the procedural protections for arriving aliens.

64. Oleszek, 248.
65. Senator Simpson later recalled approaching Senator Feinstein during those moments, but he said that his purpose was to discuss an entirely different issue, not the vote she had just cast. Alan Simpson, telephone interview between author and Alan K. Simpson, July 1, 1998. A former Democratic staff member recalls, however, that Simpson's first words to his colleague were, "What the hell do you think you are doing, Dianne?" Democratic staff members then summoned Senators Kennedy, Leahy, and Boxer to talk to Feinstein and support her for her courageous vote.
66. *Congressional Record,* S4493 (May 1, 1996).
67. This effort by Simpson failed by a vote of twenty to eighty. Eric Schmitt, "Senate Bars Plans to Cut Immigration," *The New York Times,* April 26, 1996.
68. *Congressional Record,* S4493 (May 1, 1996).
69. *Congressional Record,* S4596 (May 2, 1996)

## Chapter 10: The Conference

1. Lamar Smith and Edward R. Grant, "Immigration Reform: Seeking the Right Reasons," *St. Mary's Law Journal* 28 (1997): 883, 894.
2. National Immigration Forum, Fax Memorandum, May 2, 1996.
3. National Immigration Forum, "So-Called 'Illegal' Immigration Bill Would Cut Legal Family Immigration by at Least 30 percent," September 26, 1996 (pamphlet).
4. National Immigration Forum, Fax Memorandum, May 16, 1996.
5. American Immigration Lawyers Association, Legislative Alert, May 10, 1996.
6. "A Better Senate Bill on Immigration," *The New York Times,* May 7, 1996 (editorial). See also *All Things Considered,* National Public Radio, Transcript 2211-6 (May 12, 1996) (report on threat to human rights posed by summary exclusion provisions of House bill and anti-terrorism law; no mention of deadlines).
7. Committee to Preserve Asylum, letters to "Dear Supporter," May 13, 1996, and May 20, 1996.
8. *Congressional Record,* S4984 (May 13, 1996).
9. Walter Oleszek, *Congressional Procedures and the Policy Process,* 4th ed. (1996), 282.
10. Democrats had used the same tactic when they had controlled the House. Ibid.
11. Oleszek, 289.
12. Letter to conferees from Spencer Abraham and Mike DeWine, May 20, 1996.
13. Letter to Senator Dianne Feinstein from Representative Lincoln Diaz-Balart and six other representatives, May 15, 1996.
14. Letter to conferees from Christopher Smith et al., June 7, 1996.
15. Interview with former INS general counsel David Martin, November 24, 1998.
16. Special Exclusion in Extraordinary Migration Situations (draft statute dated May 30, 1996, distributed to conference of teachers of immigration law, Boulder, CO, May 31, 1996).
17. Letter to Lamar Smith from Deputy Attorney General Jamie Gorelick, May 31, 1996. The letter said, for example, that the Conference Committee "should adopt provisions for judicial review of special exclusion procedures" without mentioning that the administration contemplated allowing such review only of certain *written* procedures.

18. Martin interview, November 24, 1998.

19. Marcus Stern, "Immigration Bill Turns into Key Election Issue," *The San Diego Union-Tribune,* June 2, 1996.

20. Karen Foerstel and Chuck McCutcheon, "Schooling for Illegal Aliens Could Snag Immigration Talks," *The Congressional Quarterly's Congressional Monitor,* May 23, 1996.

21. Eric Schmitt, "Provision on Legal Immigrants Jeopardize Bill on Illegal Aliens," *The New York Times,* May 28, 1996. The *Times* followed its story with an editorial condemning both Houses' bills as "badly flawed." "Reasonable Immigration Reform," *The New York Times,* May 29, 1996 (editorial).

22. H.R. 3507, S. 1795, S 1823 (104th Cong.).

23. House and Senate versions of H.R. 2202 after passage of each House, but before conference (104th Cong.).

24. My own rate was probably about 33 percent. I was particularly disappointed that I was unable to publish columns in Chicago (to attract Hyde's attention) or Dallas (a double-header, Smith and Bryant).

25. Allen S. Keller, "Congress Should Drop Summary Exclusion from Immigration Bill," *The Salt Lake Tribune,* June 16, 1996.

26. Philip G. Schrag, "Deporting Refugees Who Miss Asylum Deadline Is Dangerous," *Christian Science Monitor,* June 20, 1996.

27. Philip G. Schrag, "Human-Rights Victims Deserve Fair Hearings," *The Miami Herald,* May 31, 1996.

28. Bill McCollum, "Weeding out Asylum Claimants," *The Miami Herald,* June 26, 1996 (letter to the editor). As in our TV debate, his reply failed to meet my critique. An "asylum applicant" would surely see a trained officer, but many refugees would not know enough or be comfortable enough during airport interviews to say that they were "asylum applicants." An airport immigration inspector without special asylum training would have to make the initial determination regarding whether to send them on to an interview by an asylum officer. These inspectors are in fact "low level" officials. The position of immigration inspector is rated GS-5. U.S. Immigration and Naturalization Service, Key INS Jobs (December 1994). As of 1997, GS-5 positions in Miami carried a starting salary of $23,615. "General Schedules by Locality," *Federal Times,* available on the World Wide Web at http://www.federaltimes.com/pay.html.

29. "A lot of people had told us that the administration gets to do its close work [give and take with the legislators about specific wording of provisions] in [the] conference [process]," reported David Martin, who was INS general counsel at the time. "But they didn't show us what they were doing, we didn't get any of that. Commissioner Meissner, [legislative liaison] Pam Berry and I tried to meet with each of the prospective conferees [individually]. We had seven agenda items, our key issues. One was the deadline, which we said was unnecessary and inefficient. We were usually received politely, but few [legislators or staff members] would tip their hands. We wrote various draft [compromises] at the request of staff members, but [those pertaining to the deadline] didn't get incorporated into the final law." Martin interview, November 24, 1998.

30. Letter to Robert J. Dole from Tom Daschle, June 10, 1996.

31. Eric Schmitt, "2 Senior Republican Lawmakers Buck Party to Oppose Effort to Bar Education of Illegal Aliens," *The New York Times,* June 22, 1996. Hyde's stance was consistent with the position of the U.S. Catholic Bishops, whose leader called the bill "inconsistent with the Gospel and ... morally objectionable." "Bishops Denounce Immigration Bill; Church Leaders Fear Impact on Children," *The St. Louis Post Dispatch,* June 23, 1996 (statement by Bishop Anthony Pilla).

32. Ibid.

33. Letter to Orrin G. Hatch from Phil Gramm and Kay Bailey Hutchison, July 2, 1996.

34. Letter to Phil Gramm and Kay Bailey Hutchison from Newt Gingrich, July 3, 1996.

35. Martin interview, November 24, 1998.

36. "Gallegly Plan Draws Opposition from Senate Democrats," *Congress Daily*, September 5, 1996 (Specter role).
37. Eric Schmitt, "Immigration Overhaul Moves toward Vote," *The New York Times*, August 2, 1996.
38. Ibid.
39. Memorandum to Miles Lerman, Lawyers Committee for Human Rights, from Michele Pistone, August 7, 1996. See also National Immigration Forum, Fax Memorandum, August 14, 1996.
40. Memorandum to the author from Michele Pistone, July 28, 1996.
41. Chris Black, "Lott Elected Senate Majority Leader," *The Boston Globe*, June 13,1996.
42. "Immigration Reform Conference Delayed until September," *Congress Daily*, August 2, 1996.
43. Letter to Newt Gingrich from President Bill Clinton, August 2, 1996.
44. See National Immigration Forum, Fax Memorandum, August 14, 1996 (call on membership to oppose Gallegly vigorously).
45. Joshua Bernstein, interview between author and Joshua Bernstein, senior policy advisor, National Immigration Law Center, May 15, 1998.
46. Bernstein interview.
47. See National Immigration Forum, Fax Memorandum, August 21, 1996 (with model letter for advocacy organizations to send to the president, urging him to veto the immigration bill if it "is not changed to correct the harm legal immigrants will undoubtedly suffer," and noting that its provisions will "compound the problems legal immigrants will face as a result of the welfare bill by, for example, subjecting an immigrant student to deportation if he or she were to receive a student loan.")
48. The Republicans allocated themselves eleven conferees, including seven Judiciary Committee members, to eight for the Democrats, including five Judiciary Committee members. As expected, Hyde, Smith, Gallegly, and McCollum led the House delegation. Some of the conferees were appointed because of their membership on committees with interests in specific titles of the legislation, such as the welfare title.
49. Congressional Record, H10189, 10195 (September 11, 1996).
50. National Immigration Forum, Fax Memorandum, September 12, 1996.
51. Eric Schmitt, "Dole's Immigration Stance Splits G.O.P.," *The New York Times*, September 13, 1996.
52. Schmitt, September 13, 1996.
53. *Congressional Record*, S10572 (September 16, 1996).
54. Alan Simpson, quoted in Dan Carney, "Scaled-Back Bill Moves Ahead as GOP Considers Options," *Congressional Quarterly Weekly Report*, September 28, 1996, 2758.
55. Eric Schmitt, "G.O.P. Seems Ready to Drop Political Fight on Children," *The New York Times*, September 18, 1996.
56. The *Washington Post*, read by many members of Congress, did report the Democrats' grievances. William Branigin, "GOP Cancels Conference on Immigration Bill," *The Washington Post*, September 18, 1996.
57. American Immigration Lawyers Assn., Urgent Legislative Update, September 24, 1996.
58. Technically, it split the amendment into a separate bill that could pass the House but had no possibility of passing the Senate.
59. William Branigin, "Conferees Agree on Immigration Bill," *The Washington Post*, September 25, 1996.
60. T. Alexander Aleinikoff, interview between author and T. Alexander Aleinikoff, former INS executive associate commissioner, October 29, 1998.
61. Patrick Leahy, "Asylum Provisions of the Immigration Conference Report," September 25, 1996 (press release), available on LEXIS/NEXIS.
62. See "Final Immigration Vote Scheduled in House Today," *Congress Daily*, September 25, 1996.

63. Eric Schmitt, "Conferees Approve a Tough Immigration Bill," *The New York Times*, September 25, 1996.

64. Leahy press release.

65. Michael D. Towle, "Bill to Retool Immigration Law Passes Committee without Ban on Education," *The Fort Worth Star Telegram*, September 25, 1996.

66. Ibid.

67. *Congressional Record*, H10841, 10891 (September 24, 1996).

68. Chris Black, "Senate Democrats Affirm Distaste for Immigrant Bill," *The Boston Globe*, September 25, 1996.

69. Ibid.

70. The vote was 305–123. The procedural vote on the rule to allow the vote was slightly closer, 254–165. *Congressional Record*, H11079, 11091 (September 25, 1996).

71. National Immigration Forum, Fax Memorandum, September 25, 1996.

## Chapter 11: The President

1. Interview, May 15, 1998.

2. Peter B. Edelman, "The Worst Thing Bill Clinton Has Done," *The Atlantic Monthly*, March 1997, 43, 44.

3. *Congressional Record*, S8076, July 18, 1996.

4. Peter T. Kilborn and Sam Howe Verhovek, "Clinton's Welfare Shift Ends Tortuous Journey," *The New York Times*, August 2, 1996.

5. Edelman, 46.

6. Edelman, 43.

7. Edelman, 48.

8. Lena H. Sun, "Immigrants Will Face Harsher Welfare Deadlines, Advocacy Groups Say," *The Washington Post*, August 1, 1996.

9. Remarks by the president at the signing of the Personal Responsibility and Work Opportunity Reconciliation Act, available on the World Wide Web at http://library.whitehouse.gov.

10. Statement by the president, August 22, 1996, available on the World Wide Web at http://library.whitehouse.gov.

11. William Jefferson Clinton, "A Real Step Forward for Our Country, Our Values and for People," *The Washington Post*, August 1, 1996.

12. "The Welfare Decision," *The Washington Post*, August 1, 1996 (editorial).

13. Barbara Vobejda and Dan Balz, "President Seeks Balm for Anger over Welfare Bill," *The Washington Post*, August 22, 1996.

14. Richard L. Berke, "The Democrats: The Overview," *The New York Times*, August 28, 1996 (Cuomo); David S. Broder, "Parties Trade Policy for Sentiment," *The Washington Post*, August 28, 1996 (Jackson).

15. Barbara Vobejda, "HHS Official Resigns in Protest of Decision to Sign Welfare Bill," *The Washington Post*, August 18, 1996.

16. See, e.g., Craig Crawford, "Clinton to Sign Welfare Overhaul; Senate Approval Is Expected Today," *The Orlando Sentinel*, August 1, 1996 ("'My President will boldly throw 1 million into poverty,' said Rep. Charles Rangel, D-N.Y."); "Clinton Signs Welfare Reform, but Change of Policy Divides Democrats," *The St. Louis Post-Dispatch*, August 23, 1996.

17. National Immigration Forum, Memorandum to Diana Aviv et al., August 26, 1996.

18. Dan Carney, "Scaled-Back Bill Moves Ahead As GOP Considers Options," *Congressional Quarterly Weekly Report*, September 28, 1996, p. 2755.

19. Eric Schmitt, "New Demands by White House Are Made on Immigration Bill," *The New York Times*, September 27, 1996.

20. These provisions and others in the bill as reported by the conference are summarized in Dan Carney, "Conference Agreement Increases Patrols, Makes Deporting Easier," *Congressional Quarterly Weekly Report*, September 28, 1996, 2756–57.

21. "GOP Mulls Dropping Gallegly Plan from Immigration Bill," *Congress Daily,* September 18, 1996.

22. National Immigration Law Center, "Who We Are, What We Do" (undated pamphlet).

23. Joshua Bernstein, interview between author and Joshua Bernstein, May 15, 1998.

24. "Democrats Raise Warnings about Legal Immigration Measures," *Congress Daily,* September 25, 1996.

25. "Fixing Up an Immigration Bill." *The Washington Post,* September 23, 1996 (editorial) (Clinton "claimed to object" to the welfare bill's immigration provisions; "an immigration bill that makes things worse for [those already here legally] should surely invite a veto"); "A Dangerous Immigration Bill," *The New York Times,* September 19, 1996, (editorial) ("the bill also would go further than the recently adopted welfare law in attacking legal immigrants.... It deserves a quick demise."); "Immigration 'Reform' Looks a Lot Like Politics," *The Los Angeles Times,* September 25, 1996 (editorial) ("It comes down harshly on thousands of legal immigrants for no reason other than that immigrant bashing is seen by some in Congress as being good politics these days.... [It] has too many fundamental problems to be acceptable.").

26. *Congressional Record,* H 11091 (September 25, 1996).

27. Mike Dorning, "Senate Democrats Threaten to Stall Immigration Bill," *The Chicago Tribune,* September 27, 1996.

28. Dan Carney, "As White House Calls Shots, Illegal Alien Bill Clears," *Congressional Quarterly Weekly Report,* October 5, 1996, 2865.

29. Ibid.

30. "Bulletin Broadfaxing Network," *The White House Bulletin,* September 27, 1996 (available on LEXIS/NEXIS).

31. "Senate Majority Leader Trent Lott's Regular Briefing," *Federal News Service,* September 27, 1996 (available on LEXIS/NEXIS).

32. Interview between author and a human rights activist close to the negotiations (not Mr. Bernstein) who did not authorize his or her name to be used.

33. *White House Bulletin, supra.*

34. Marcus Stern, "Showdown looms over immigration," *The San Diego Union-Tribune,* September 28, 1996. The agreement would have deleted the provision denying AIDS treatment to legal and unauthorized aliens. Eric Pianin, "Clinton, Hill Near Budget Deal," *The Washington Post,* September 28, 1996.

35. Bernstein interview.

36. Lott briefing, September 27, *supra.*

37. Mike Dorning, "Senate Democrats Threaten to Stall Immigration Bill," *The Chicago Tribune,* September 27, 1996.

38. News Conference, Senators Trent Lott and Mark Hatfield, September 27, 1996, Federal Document Clearing House Political Transcripts (available on LEXIS/NEXIS).

39. Carney, 2865.

40. *White House Bulletin.*

41. The account of Murguia's intervention was provided to the author by a source who claimed to have been present but who did not wish to be identified. It was confirmed by another source.

42. Robert Pear, "Amid Changes Immigration Bill Dies," *The New York Times,* October 12, 1984.

43. *Congressional Record,* S 11503, 11507 (September 27, 1996).

44. Ibid., 11508.

45. Ibid., 11541.

46. Ibid., 11543.

47. Bernstein interview.

48. Eric Pianin, "Clinton Defense of Legal Immigrant Rights Threatens Massive Spending Bill," *The Washington Post,* September 27, 1996.

49. Carney, 2866.
50. Eric Pianin and Helen Dewar, "Immigration, Budget Agreement Reached," *The Washington Post*, September 29, 1996; Carney, 2864 (Simpson and Smith arrival at end of meeting).
51. Dan Carney, "Provisions Deleted," *Congressional Quarterly Weekly Report*, October 5, 1996, 2865; National Immigration Law Center, "Immigrants' Rights Update Reprint," October 10, 1996, 9–10.
52. Bernstein interview.

## Chapter 12: The Regulations

1. Observation in several speeches to the Washington community, repeated in a letter to the author, October 24, 1997.
2. *Congressional Record*, S11839–11840 (September 30, 1996).
3. *Congressional Record*, S11491 (September 27, 1996).
4. INS officials confirmed this statistic in a meeting with non-governmental organizations, August 27, 1997.
5. Immigration and Naturalization Service, Service Center Guide for Form I-589, 10 (February 14, 1995).
6. INA Sec. 212 (a) (9).
7. Michele R. Pistone and Philip G. Schrag, "The 1996 Immigration Act: Asylum and Expedited Removal—What the INS Should Do," *Interpreter Releases* 73 (November 11, 1996), 1565.
8. Meeting of INS officials with non-governmental organizations, December 16, 1996.
9. "Proposed Rule, Inspection and Expedited Removal of Aliens; Detention and Removal of Aliens, Conduct of Removal Proceedings; Asylum Procedures," *Federal Register* 62 (January 3, 1997), 443.
10. *Federal Register*, 62, 447.
11. When the law was passed and when the interim regulation was promulgated, the U.S. had signed no such agreements. It was then negotiating such an agreement with Canada, but the negotiations broke down after the Canadian government studied the immigration reform act that Congress had passed in 1996. See Hon. Lucienne Robillard, Canadian minister of citizenship and immigration, Press Release 98–08, Adjournment of Discussions Between Canada and the United States on Responsibility-Sharing for Asylum Seekers (February 5, 1998).
12. The statute required the INS to have regulations in place when expedited removal took effect on April 1, 1997. INS lawyers worked at breakneck speed, but by the time the INS drafted its proposed regulation, it could not have given the public sixty days to comment and still have reviewed the comments and issued the interim regulation on time.
13. Letter to director, Policy Directives and Instructions Branch, INS, from Philip G. Schrag and Michele Pistone, January 17, 1997.
14. Immigration and Naturalization Service, "Inspection and Expedited Removal of Aliens," *Federal Register* 62 (March 6, 1997), 10312.
15. American Immigration Law Foundation, "List of Comments Filed with the INS on Draft Regulations," March 17, 1997.
16. Letter to director, Policy Directives and Instructions Branch, INS, from Representative Lamar Smith, February 3, 1997.
17. Letter to director, Policy Directives and Instructions Branch, INS, from Senator Spencer Abraham, February 3, 1997.
18. Letter to director, Policy Directives and Instructions Branch, INS, from Senators Edward M. Kennedy and Paul Wellstone, February 3, 1997.
19. "Mary Rawson" was able to enter the United States, where she won asylum, only because an immigration inspector was willing to try to summon her brother, who was waiting for her on the other side of the customs barrier at John F. Kennedy Airport. See the prologue to this book.

20. Immigration and Naturalization Service, "Interim Rule with Request for Comments, Inspection and Expedited Removal of Aliens; Detention and Removal of Aliens; Conduct of Removal Proceedings; Asylum Procedure," *Federal Register* 62 (March 6, 1997), 10312.

21. For the alien to use ineffective assistance of counsel as an excuse for late filing, the alien would have to file an affidavit describing how the counsel had failed to represent her properly, notify the representative and give him an opportunity to respond to the charges, and state whether a complaint had been filed with disciplinary authorities and if not, why not. *Federal Register* 62 (March 6, 1997), 10312, 10339.

22. *Federal Register* 62 (March 6, 1997), 10312, 10316.

23. Ibid.

24. Ibid.

25. 8 C.F.R. Sec. 208.13 (d), *Federal Register* 62 (March 6, 1997), 10312, 10342.

26. *Federal Register* 62 (March 6, 1997), 10312, 10319.

27. Ibid., 10312, 10320.

28. Philip G. Schrag and Michele R. Pistone, "The New Asylum Rule: Not Yet a Model of Fair Procedure," *Georgetown Immigration Law Journal* 11 (1997), 267, 293.

29. "INS Releases Uniform Detention Guidelines," *Interpreter Releases* 75 (February 9, 1998), 199.

30. In our *Interpreter Releases* article and our comments, Pistone and I had recalled that the Supreme Court had implied that a 10 percent chance of being persecuted was sufficient to establish a "well-founded fear" of persecution and qualify for asylum. We therefore urged the INS to interpret the statutory standard for credible-fear determinations—a significant possibility that the alien could establish eligibility for asylum—as requiring only a 10 percent chance of being able to demonstrate a 10 percent chance of persecution. In fact we did not expect that the INS would accept this suggestion, because it would so distress Lamar Smith, who remained chair of its House oversight subcommittee. However, we thought that it would be useful to bring to the agency's attention, in a dramatic way, the idea that the screening standard in credible-fear interviews had to be very low, and that applicants could not be expected at this early stage of proceedings, before they had any opportunity to collect evidence, even to show a 10 percent likelihood of persecution.

31. *Federal Register* 62 (March 6, 1997), 10312, 10317.

32. 8 C.F.R. Sec. 208.30, *Federal Register* 62 (March 6, 1997), 10312, 10345.

33. Ibid.

34. 8 C.F.R. Sec. 3.42, *Federal Register* 62 (March 6, 1997), 10312, 10335. The part of the regulation governing procedure before immigration judges was written by the Justice Department's Executive Office for Immigration Review, in which the judges are located, rather than by the INS.

35. Memorandum to All Assistant Chief Immigration Judges and All Immigration Judges, Interim Operating Policy and Procedure Memorandum 97-3, from Michael D. Creppy, chief immigration judge, March 25, 1997.

36. The regulation also permitted this final appellate review (federal courts being barred by statute from entertaining further appeals) to be held by telephone rather than in person. The combined effect of these two provisions led one human rights organization to complain that "some asylum seekers will be put in a star-chamber proceeding where they have no counsel present, no record to examine, and a judge and interpreter which are faceless voices on the telephone." Letter to Richard A. Sloane, INS, from Martin A. Wenick, Hebrew Immigrant Aid Society, July 7, 1997.

37. Schrag and Pistone, 267.

38. Letter to director, Policy Directives and Instructions Branch, INS, from Philip G. Schrag and Michele R. Pistone, June 12, 1997.

39. The smaller number of comments might be explained by less novelty at the time of the second round of comments, a greater degree of public satisfaction with the regulatory proposal, and the INS's assurance, when it asked for the second round of comments, that sug-

gestions made previously and not yet adopted would be reconsidered in connection with issuance of the final rule. *Federal Register* 62 (March 6, 1997), 10312.

40. Letter to director, Policy Directives and Instructions Branch, INS, from Representative Lamar Smith, July 7, 1997. Representative Smith feared that professional smugglers would be able to coach fraudulent refugees well enough to satisfy the credible-fear standard, though not well enough to fool an immigration judge in a full hearing. Not to be outdone by the tireless Representative Smith, the equally indefatigable Senator Edward M. Kennedy also filed a new set of comments, urging the INS to specify in the regulation itself that the list of exceptional circumstances was not exclusive; to permit outside organizations to monitor some secondary inspections; and to repeal Judge Creppy's instruction barring lawyers from participating in reviews. Letter to director, Policy Directives and Instructions Branch, INS, from Senator Edward M. Kennedy, July 3, 1997.

41. Similarly, for the first six months of the law, thirty-one thousand people were put into the expedited removal process, and 5 percent of them (17 percent of those apprehended at airports) were referred for credible-fear interviews. Immigration and Naturalization Service, Update on Expedited Removals (Fact Sheet, March 24, 1997 [*sic,* should be 1998]). Ninety-one percent of the people removed through the new expedited process were Mexican nationals. Ibid.

42. INS briefing for non-governmental organizations, July 9, 1997.

43. See, e.g., letter to Stephen Rickard, director, Washington Office, Amnesty International, from INS Commissioner Doris Meissner, January 8, 1998, in Karen Musalo and Deborah Anker, "Expedited Removal Study, Report on the First Year of Implementation of Expedited Removal," May, 1998 (Attachment 24) (declining to allow Amnesty International to engage in monitoring, while stating that INS might agree to allow the United Nations High Commissioner on Refugees to do monitoring).

44. *American Immigration Lawyers Association (AILA) v. Reno,* Civ. No. 97-0597 (EGS), U.S.D.C., D.C. (1997). The agency's implication was that observations by advocacy organizations might provide the plaintiffs with evidence that they could use in the case, and that the agency's lawyers would be understandably skittish about opening processes up to observation in the midst of test-case litigation. The suit made two major claims. First, the plaintiffs argued that although the INS explained the credible-fear interview process to aliens who were referred for such interviews, the agency's refusal to explain the possibility of obtaining asylum *before* the interviews in secondary inspection might cause some aliens to refrain from telling the inspectors information that might prevent immediate deportation, and violated the law's requirement that information about the process be given to all those who "may be" eligible for asylum. Second, they claimed that the INS's refusal to allow arriving aliens to consult with attorneys before or during secondary inspection interviews that could lead to their immediate return home, and to assure that competent interpreters were present, denied the due process to which they were entitled under the Fifth Amendment and could cause the United States to violate the Refugee Convention. See amended complaint in *AILA v. Reno,* filed March 31, 1997. In August 1998, the federal district court dismissed the case. Judge Emmet G. Sullivan concluded that Congress did not want aliens to be able to consult with lawyers or family members before secondary inspection, as evidenced by Representative McCollum's statement on the House floor that expedited removal "should deal with these people, especially those who do not make a credible claim of asylum when they first set foot off the plane." The plaintiffs planned to appeal. "District Court Dismisses Expedited Removal Challenges," *Interpreter Releases* 75 (October 9, 1998), 1403.

45. In fact, the inspectors had more power than judges formerly had, because under the new law, a collateral consequence of removal was to bar the alien from re-entering the United States for several years.

46. For a powerful study of the impact of standard operating procedures on preventing changes in government policy, see Graham T. Allison, *Essence of Decision* (1971).

47. The meetings gave us only partial insight into the government's process for drafting and approving the asylum regulations. Officials who attended the meetings came from the Office of the General Counsel, the Asylum Office, and the office that was in charge of preparing all of the agency's regulations. But it was clear that many other offices in other offices of the agency and other parts of the Justice Department were also being consulted by the officials who spoke with us. For example, the inspections and detention divisions of the INS were obviously important participants in the process of developing the new rules on expedited removal.

48. Specifically, the statute required only that the claimed extraordinary circumstances be ones "relating to" the delay, whereas the interim regulation required the alien to show "events or factors beyond the alien's control that caused" the delay. Compare INA Sec. 208 with 8 U.S.C. Sec. 208.4 (a) (5), *Federal Register* 62 (March 6, 1997), 10312, 10339.

49. The federal law governing the process of regulation-writing by agencies, including the right of public comment, is the Administrative Procedure Act, 5 U.S.C. Secs. 551, 553.

50. Letter to Hon. Doris Meissner, commissioner of immigration and naturalization, from Senators Mike DeWine, Edward M. Kennedy, and Russell D. Feingold, February 12, 1998.

51. Letter to Hon. Doris Meissner, commissioner of immigration and naturalization, from Eleanor Acer (the Lawyers Committee's senior coordinator) and Beth Lyon, March 20, 1998. The letter identified two related issues that we also wanted to discuss: the INS's continued detention of most asylum applicants even after they had been found to have credible fear, and the INS's failure to have issued regulations to implement the anti-refoulement provisions of the international Convention Against Torture, to which the United States had become a party.

52. Memorandum to Commissioner Meissner from Eleanor Acer, Beth Lyon, and Philip G. Schrag, April 13, 1998.

53. I knew from my own service as the deputy general counsel of an agency in the Carter administration that congressional relations staffs typically made copies of such letters and sent them to many officials of an agency for comment before trying to draft a suitable reply for the agency director to sign. As a result, congressional letters to senior federal officials often take many weeks to answer, and the replies often reflect only previously stated agency policy or at best the lowest common denominator of what relatively junior agency officials are willing to say. Agency directors are often so deluged with legislative correspondence that they leave their replies to be written through this "clearance" process, forfeiting opportunities to accept legislators' invitations to rethink agency policy.

54. For years, the INS had gone to some lengths to make its application form user-friendly for an unrepresented applicant. Furthermore, 70 percent of affirmative applicants did not have legal help, and INS did not want to intimate in any way that the majority of applicants were disadvantaged. Although the INS did not keep relevant statistics, most advocates firmly believed that the rate at which affirmative applications were granted was much higher for represented aliens. The INS didn't dispute that claim, but its officials believed that the reasons for it were that aliens with stronger cases went to lawyers, and that lawyers refused to accept impossibly weak cases. The advocates believed, however, that a major reason for the much higher grant rate for represented applicants was the weeks of investigative factual research that went into a typical application that professionals put together, which often included dozens of pages of documents to corroborate the applicant's statement and hundreds of pages of research reports to document horrendous human rights abuses by the applicant's government.

## Chapter 13: The Deeper Levels of the Law

1. Commission on Federal Paperwork, *Service Management* (1977), 38.

2. Henry M. Hart, Jr., and Albert M. Sacks, *The Legal Process* (Westbury, N.Y.: Foundation Press, mimeographed tentative edition, 1958, finally published posthumously in book

form in 1994). William N. Eskridge and Philip P. Frickey's awesome introduction to the book traces the enormous influence this course had on an entire generation of lawyers.

3. INS also vetted its new "M-444" form, an explanation of the credible-fear screening process that INS would give to the 5 percent of interviewees who were referred to asylum officers. This form turned out to be much less controversial than the one to be used for secondary-inspection interviews.

4. Immigration and Naturalization Service, Draft Record of Sworn Statement in Proceedings under Section 235 (b) (1) of the Act, February 4, 1997.

5. Ibid.

6. See, e.g., letter to Charlie Fillinger, INS, from American Immigration Law Foundation and American Immigration Lawyers Association, February 12, 1997; letter to Charles Fillinger from Mark Ely Greenwold on behalf of the Washington Lawyers Committee for Civil Rights and Urban Affairs, February 11, 1997; letter to Charles Fillinger from Michele Pistone and Philip G. Schrag, February 10, 1997.

7. Immigration and Naturalization Service, Draft Record of Sworn Statement in Proceedings Under Section 235 (b) (1) of the Act, February 20, 1997. This version of the form was the version later used by INS inspectors, with one additional change: the final form also recorded the identity of the employer of any interpreter used in the interview.

8. 44 U.S. Code Sec. 3501 et seq.

9. 44 U.S. Code Secs. 3506 (c) (2) (A), 3507 (a) (1) (D).

10. Letter to director, Policy Directives and Instructions Branch, INS, from Michele R. Pistone and Philip G. Schrag, January 17, 1997.

11. Immigration and Naturalization Service, "Revision of Existing Collection; Application for Asylum and Withholding of Removal," *Federal Register* 62 (February 11, 1997), 6270.

12. Letter to Bo Cooper, associate general counsel, INS, from Philip G. Schrag, February 21, 1997.

13. Immigration and Naturalization Service, "Request OMB Emergency Approval; Application for Asylum and Withholding of Removal," *Federal Register* 62 (March 3, 1997), 9452.

14. 44 U.S.C. Sec. 3507 (j).

15. Immigration and Naturalization Service, Form I-589, Part D, Question 7 (Rev. 4-01-97) (OMB No. 1115-0086).

16. Immigration and Naturalization Service, "Inspection and Expedited Removal of Aliens; Detention and Removal of Aliens; Conduct of Removal Proceedings; Asylum Procedures," *Federal Register* 62 (March 6, 1997), 10312, 10395 (showing the attorney general's approval on February 26).

17. 8 C.F.R. Sec. 208.4 (a) (2) (B) (2), *Federal Register* 62 (March 6, 1997), 10312, 10338.

18. For example, what was previously called "withholding of deportation" was now "withholding of removal," requiring the INS to change the title of the form because it was a combined application for asylum and withholding.

19. Actually, the period during which the revised form was used might have been shorter, because the INS may not have actually distributed its April 1 revision to its field offices during April.

20. Letter to Charles Fillinger, INS, from Michele R. Pistone and Philip G. Schrag, August 22, 1997.

21. Immigration and Naturalization Service, Clarifying Instruction for I-589 Application for Asylum and for Withholding of Removal (FC-015, September 1997).

22. The INS asked for and obtained from OMB a "90-day emergency extension ... to a currently approved emergency extension for a revision of a currently approved collection." See Immigration and Naturalization Service, "Agency Information Collection Activities; Proposed Collection; Comment Request," *Federal Register* 62 (July 14, 1997), 37604.

23. Ibid., reprinted in *Interpreter Releases* 74 (July 21, 1997), 1116.

24. The only real change was that the extraordinary-circumstances exception was now listed before the changed-circumstances exception.

25. Letter to Richard A. Sloan from Philip G. Schrag, Michele R. Pistone, et al. (on behalf of themselves, Amnesty International, the American Immigration Lawyers Association, the Asylum and Refugee Rights Law Project of the Washington Lawyers Committee for Civil Rights and Urban Affairs, and the American Immigration Law Foundation) to Richard A. Sloan, INS, September 11, 1997; letter to Richard A. Sloan, INS, from Eleanor Acer and Beth Lyon, Lawyers Committee for Human Rights, September 12, 1997.

26. For example, the INS's emergency authority for the old form would expire before April, but the proposed revised form did not exempt those who might use the form before then, and although the form was a combined application for asylum and withholding of removal, it failed to inform applicants that the one-year deadline did not apply to withholding of removal.

27. Immigration and Naturalization Service, "Extension of Existing Collection. Application for Asylum and Withholding of Removal," *Federal Register* 62 (November 18, 1997), 61526, 61530, 61532.

28. Ibid., 61544.

29. Letter to Debra Bond, OMB, from Philip G. Schrag, Michele R. Pistone, Eleanor Acer (Lawyers Committee on Human Rights), Jeanne Butterfield (American Immigration Lawyers Association), Patricia Rengel (Amnesty International), Deborah Ann Sanders (Asylum and Refugee Rights Law Project, Washington Lawyers Committee for Civil Rights and Urban Affairs), Anna Gallagher (American Immigration Law Foundation), and Morton Sklar (World Organization Against Torture USA), December 16, 1997.

30. Memorandum from Debra Bond, OMB, to Rick [*sic*] Sloan, INS, January 7, 1998.

31. Memorandum to Debra Bond, OMB, from Andrea Fleet, INS, January 13, 1998.

32. Memorandum to Rick Sloan, INS, from Debra Bond, OMB, January 15, 1998.

33. Immigration and Naturalization Service, response to OMB suggested revision to I-589, Part D, Question 6 (January 16, 1998).

34. Memorandum to Robert B. Briggs, Department of Justice, from Donald R. Arbuckle, deputy administrator, Office of Information and Regulatory Affairs, OMB, January 16, 1998.

35. E.g., Immigration and Naturalization Service, Detention Standard: Detainee Visitation, January 28, 1998 (providing, *inter alia*, that attorneys shall be permitted to visit the INS's regular detainees seven days a week, and that if a meeting continues through a meal, the detainee shall be provided a substitute meal when the visit ends; that legal assistants and interpreters working for attorneys shall have similar access to clients; that detainees are entitled to retain legal materials for their personal use; and because of the short time periods involved for those facing expedited removal, each detention facility shall develop procedures which "liberally allow the opportunity for" legal consultation before asylum officer interviews).

36. For example, INS officials repeatedly reassured advocates that secondary inspectors would refer for credible-fear interviews any alien who "expresses any fear or concern" about being returned home. See, e.g., letter to Charles Fillinger, INS, from Mark E. Greenwold, on behalf of the Washington Lawyers Committee for Civil Rights and Urban Affairs, February 11, 1997 (summarizing the assurance). But an INS directive instructed secondary inspectors that "if the alien indicates an intention to apply for asylum or a fear of harm or concern about returning home, the inspector should ask enough follow up questions to ascertain the general nature of the fear or concern." Memorandum to Management Team and others (including Port Directors) from Chris Sale, INS deputy commissioner, Implementation of Expedited Removal, March 31, 1997. Although the directive also urged inspectors to "err on the side of caution and apply the criteria generously, referring to the asylum officer any questionable cases," the advocates worried that pursuant to this instruction, even after an alien had expressed a fear, some inspectors would cross-examine the alien until the alien described what might be (at least at first blush) a reason unrelated to persecution, such as a

fear of being beaten by a spouse (which under some circumstances had been held to qualify as fear of persecution under the Refugee Act). Then the inspector might deport the alien without a further interview or hearing. Also, at least one newspaper account reported that an alien from Morocco had been summarily deported after expressing a fear of return to an inspector at the airport in Minneapolis, because he "didn't trust the INS officer" and "would not tell why he left his country and why he was afraid to go back." Greg Gordon, "Tough New Law Evokes Mixed Responses in Minnesota Case," *The Minneapolis Star Tribune,* May 6, 1997. In view of the discrepancy between the INS's oral assurances and at least some of the words of the directive, the advocates sought assurance that inspectors would leave to trained asylum officers any probing of the nature of an alien's fear.

37.  INS also had to write a manual for secondary inspectors and asylum officers to direct them how to deal with aliens subject to expedited removal. Perhaps because litigation was pending, the INS was much less willing to seek or accept comments on drafts of the new training materials pertinent to this issue. Nevertheless, these documents also incorporated some protections for aliens that had not been assured by the statute or the regulations. See., e.g., Immigration and Naturalization Service, Instructor Guide, Asylum Officer Training Course, Asylum Eligibility Part IV: Credible Fear Standard, November 22, 1996 (directing instructors to teach asylum officers that the "standard of proof necessary to establish a credible fear of persecution is a "significant possibility" that the individual could qualify for asylum. "The quantum of proof necessary . . . is less than that required to prove a well-founded fear of persecution. . . ."). Similarly, neither the statute nor the regulation determined whether previous persecution would alone be sufficient to require a determination that an alien had a credible fear of future persecution. But in the training manual, the INS specified that "a finding of past persecution satisfies the credible fear definition, even if there is no threat of future harm. . . . Officers . . . should not evaluate . . . whether country conditions have changed to such an extent that the individual no longer has a reasonable fear of persecution." Ibid., 4. And the training manual instructed asylum officers to "draw all reasonable inferences in favor of the asylum seeker." Ibid., 8. See also Bo Cooper, "Procedures for Expedited Removal and Asylum Screening under the Illegal Immigration Reform and Immigrant Responsibility Act of 1996," *Conn. L. Rev.* 29 (1997), 1501, 1523 (quoting from the INS's "Credible Fear" Training Module, Instructor Guide/ Participant Workbook [1997]).

38.  In particular, it did not recognize any exception based on a demonstration, by the alien, that she had tried in good faith but failed to obtain free or affordable legal representation within the first year after arrival, or that she really did not know about the one-year deadline. Also, while recognition of new exceptions in the training manual was very helpful in orienting asylum officers handing affirmative cases, the manual was not binding on immigration judges in the cases where asylum officers did not grant asylum and referred the aliens to them. In addition, because the judges were not located within the INS, it was difficult for the INS even to inform the judges of the "law" created through this device. Therefore, despite our considerable satisfaction with the manual, we continued to press the INS to revise its regulation, which would bind the immigration judges as well as the asylum officers.

39.  Immigration and Naturalization Service, Asylum Officer Training, One-Year Filing Deadline, Lesson Plan Overview (May 1998), 18.

40.  Ibid., 11.

41.  Ibid., 16. Here, the INS explicitly acknowledged that the source of this guidance in the manual was "comments, both from the public and the INS, on proposed [interim] rule." Ibid.

42.  Ibid., 9.

43.  Compare ibid., 6, with the November 1998 edition, 6. This change made clearer the policy that if a case presented an excuse of a listed type, an asylum officer had to accept it as valid.

44. Such a directive eventually allowed aliens in detention facilities to make local telephone calls, though long distance calls, even to counsel, were not permitted at government expense. "INS Releases Uniform Detention Guidelines," *Interpreter Releases* 75 (February 9, 1998), 199. This limitation on the policy made it difficult for indigent aliens held in detention facilities far from cities to obtain effective legal assistance

## Chapter 14: The Wave

1. Excerpt from the senator's valedictory advice to his colleagues, quoted in Claudia Dreifus, "Exit Reasonable Right," *The New York Times,* June 2, 1996.
2. Similarly, only during the 104th Congress did FAIR have a chance of realizing its goal of cutting legal immigration significantly. The two-year life of that Congress "was a narrow and short-lived window of opporunity." Memorandum to the author from Dan Stein, executive director of FAIR, April 8, 1999.
3. Princeton Survey Research poll for *USA Today* and Public Television, reported in National Immigration Forum, *The Golden Door* (Fall 1997), p. 2.
4. Abraham supported DeWine in opposing the thirty-day deadline, and he voted for the Leahy amendment. He was by no means, however, a senator who put immigration above all other values. He supported Simpson on provisions cracking down on the substantive and procedural rights of aliens who had been convicted of crimes.
5. Even the border-control provisions of the law generated disputes, because tighter border security tends to slow legitimate border traffic. Senator Spencer Abraham, whose state borders Canada, sponsored a bill to repeal the provision of the 1996 law that would have directed the INS to set up an automated system to record all entries and exits at U.S. border crossings. After his bill was approved by the Senate Judiciary Committee, the Senate Appropriations Committee deleted all funding for the system. "Automated Control of Nation's Borders Could Be Derailed by Senate Panel Vote," *The Wall Street Journal,* June 29, 1998. Tightened border controls as a result of the 1996 legislation also generated complaints from owners of large farms, because they had depended on unauthorized aliens to harvest their crops. Before the advent of tighter border controls, 40 percent of all farmworkers in the United States, and 70 percent of such workers in California, were unauthorized. After border enforcement and deportation became more effective in 1997 and 1998, farm owners complained that their crops would rot, and they asked Congress to authorize a new "guest worker" program to permit the importation of Mexican farm hands for the harvest. Lamar Smith responded to their pleas and "switched sides" to pass such a bill through his subcommittee. "Possible Effect of U.S. Crackdown on Illegal Immigrants Rattling Growers," *The San Jose Mercury News,* July 5, 1998. Under pressure from employers, Lamar Smith also eliminated provisions that were originally proposed in the 1996 legislation to require businesses to verify whether workers they wanted to hire had authorization to be employed in the United States. Reportedly, Republican House Majority Leader Richard Armey warned that the immigration bill would die "if even one employer was required to participate" in a pilot project. Marcus Stern, "A Semi-Tough Policy on Illegal Workers," *The Washington Post,* July 5, 1998. In one of its last acts, the 105th Congress delayed implementation of an automated system until March 30, 2001. "Omnibus Measure, Stand-Alone Bills, Provide Substantial Gains to Immigrants," *Interpreter Releases* 75 (Nov. 2, 1998), 1505.
6. As explained below, some of the excesses of the 1996 laws were promptly repealed by the next Congress. Some of the immigrants described below, particularly those from Central America, were "refugees" in the sense in which many people use the word (e.g., refugees from poverty or war), but not refugees from persecution who could qualify for asylum under the Refugee Act. But the civil conflicts in Central America included many brutal human rights violations, so many individuals immigrating from that region were also potential asylum-seekers.
7. Linda Gorov, "Poor Immigrants Face New Hurdles," *The Boston Globe,* November 30, 1997.

In 1997, the required income level was $20,062 for a family of four. Ibid. Refugees and asylees are not required to have sponsors.

8. Patrick J. McDonnell, "U.S. Tightening Rules to Sponsor Immigrants," *The Los Angeles Times,* June 30, 1997.

9. Personal Responsibility and Work Opportunity Reconciliation Act of 1996, Pub. L. No. 104-193 (August 22, 1996), Sec. 402 (a) (1), (3). Refugees and asylees were exempted from this ban. Sec. 406 (b) (2).

10. An excellent description of the restrictions imposed by the welfare law on legal immigrants is Charles Wheeler, "The New Alien Restrictions on Public Benefits: The Full Impact Remains Uncertain," *Interpreter Releases* 73 (September 23, 1996), 1245.

11. Immigration and Nationality Act Secs. 212 (c) and (h) prior to 1996, reprinted in House Committee on the Judiciary, Immigration and Nationality Act (Reflecting Laws Enacted As of May 1, 1995), 10th ed. 1995.

12. See Elise Ackerman, "Tough New Laws Are Booting Out the Bad and the Not-So-Bad," *U.S. News and World Report,* December 7, 1998.

13. Matter of Soriano, Slip op. Attorney General, 1997 WL 159795 (February 21, 1997). For a good description of the new laws, see Juan P. Osuna, "The 1996 Immigration Act: Criminal Aliens and Terrorists," *Interpreter Releases* 73 (December 16, 1996), 1713; Gerald L. Neuman, "Admissions and Denials: A Dialogic Introduction to the Immigration Law Symposium," *Connecticut L. Rev.* 29 (1997), 1395.

14. Cases reported in the press included a fifty-four-year-old woman from Spain who had been living in the United States for thirty-four years, had been convicted in 1987 of stealing perfume at a flea market, and had been paroled after serving eight months of a four-year sentence; a twenty-six-year-old Vietnamese student who had come to the U.S. eleven years earlier and who, applying for citizenship, truthfully revealed that he'd been given a two-year suspended sentence as a result of getting into a fight while in high school; and a forty-year-old Iranian cab driver who had been arrested during a student protest at the White House in the 1970s and given eighteen months' probation. Pamela Constable, "Years Later, Immigrants Pursued by Their Pasts," *The Washington Post,* February 24, 1997; Pamela Constable and William Branigin, "Thousands Confront Deportation Dragnet's Longer Reach," *The Washington Post,* October 26, 1997.

15. Constable and Branigin, *supra.* Representative Lamar Smith said that the Collado case "tugs at your heart" but that "the question is how you could [grant Collado a waiver] without creating a giant loophole through which thousands of others can escape deportation." Anthony Lewis, "A Generous Country," *The New York Times,* December 22, 1997. The Collado case was eventually dismissed and Collado was released from detention, but the law continued to impose hardship on many lawful U.S. immigrants.

16. Mirta Ojito, "Painful Choices for Immigrants in U.S. Illegally," *The New York Times,* September 25, 1997. It could be argued that this group of immigrants deserved less sympathy than others retroactively affected by the new law, because they entered the United States, or overstayed their visas, in plain violation of the immigration law. However, Congress appeared to have accepted this practice in the case of people on line to immigrate, imposing on them only a revenue-raising fine. Federal revenue from the fines exceeded two hundred million dollars annually. "Keep Good Immigration Rule," *The Miami Herald,* September 4, 1997 (editorial). Like other immigration battles, this one continued after its apparent resolution in 1996 and 1997. In 1998, the Senate Appropriation Committee approved a rider reinstating the program. "Panel OK's Fine as Way to Green Card," *The San Diego Union-Tribune,* June 26, 1998.

17. *American Baptist Churches v. Thornburgh,* 760 F. Supp. 796 (N.D. Cal. 1991).

18. Board of Immigration Appeals, In re: N—J—B—, Int. Decision 3309, February 20, 1997.

19. William Branigin, "Court Case Spotlights Possible 'Harsh Effects' of New Immigration Law," *The Washington Post,* August 17, 1997; "The Central American Refugees," *The Washington Post,* July 14, 1997 (editorial).

20. Peter Schuck, interviewed on *All Things Considered,* National Public Radio, August 27, 1997.
21. INA Sec. 242 (e), allowing court review only of whether the alien is an alien and whether the removal was in fact conducted under the expedited removal process.
22. INA Sec. 242 (b). The new statute provides that courts may not review "any judgment regarding the granting" of discretionary relief. Lucas Guttentag, one of the country's most creative immigration advocates, argues that because this provision deals only with judgments "granting" such relief, decisions denying relief may still be appealed. Lucas Guttentag, Federal Court Jurisdiction—Statutory Restrictions and Constitutional Rights, in Juan P. Osuna (ed.), *Understanding the 1996 Immigration Act* (1997). For thorough analyses and critiques of court-stripping provisions of the 1996 legislation, see Lenni B. Benson, "Back to the Future: Congress Attacks the Right to Judicial Review of Immigration Proceedings," *Conn. L. Rev.* 29 (1997), 1411; and M. Isabel Medina, "Judicial Review—A Nice Thing? Article III, Separation of Powers and the Illegal Immigration Reform and Immigrant Responsibility Act of 1996," *Conn. L. Rev.* 29 (1997), 1525. Most asylum decisions were spared from the general "court-stripping" accomplished by the new act, but even in asylum cases, court review was restricted; for example, the courts were forbidden from overturning decisions to the effect that an alien's circumstances didn't qualify for an exception from the one-year deadline. INA Sec. 208 (a) (3).
23. Presidential Determination on Fiscal Year 1997 Refugee Admission Numbers, Presidential Determination No. 96-59, September 30, 1996. See "Clinton Administration to Admit 78,000 Refugees This Year," *Interpreter Releases* 73 (1996), 1619. In fiscal year 1995, the level had been 111,000, approximately the same as in all years after fiscal year 1988. See Stephen H. Legomsky, *Immigration and Refugee Law and Policy,* 2d ed. (1997), 762.
24. "Senators Protest Admissions Decrease," *Refugee Reports,* September 30, 1996, 2.
25. As noted in the chapter on Senate consideration of the immigration bill, these provisions were enacted as part of the anti-terrorism law, but were repealed before they took effect by the somewhat milder provisions of the immigration bill.
26. The federal court upheld the expedited removal scheme in *American Immigration Lawyers Association v. Reno* (Civ. Act. No. 97-0597 EGS, D.D.C. 1998). In addition to challenging the statute and the regulations, the plaintiffs charged that the INS was violating its own regulations, e.g., by denying arriving aliens food, water, and restroom access while they were waiting for extended periods to be interviewed in secondary inspection. But the court dismissed this charge, saying that the statute only authorized the court to review the "written" procedures of the INS, and that therefore, so long as INS officials' misdeeds were not in furtherance of written policies, the court could not prevent those officials from violating the law. The court declared itself "troubled" by the statutory provision tying its hands and therefore "admonishe[d]" the INS to comply with its own regulations.
27. According to INS officials who briefed non-governmental organizations on January 12, 1999, asylum officers interviewed 3,359 applicants who appeared to have filed beyond the deadline during the first eight months that the deadline was in effect. Exceptions were granted in 2,224 of the cases.
28. The statistic is derived from the study attached to the letter to Charles E. Schumer from Michael Posner, executive director, Lawyers Committee for Human Rights, February 22, 1996.
29. Gay rights advocates claim that the new deadline is particularly harmful to those who have fled the persecution of homosexuals, because many "are either facing their sexuality for the first time or they are just afraid of being sent back." One asylum expert in San Francisco said that only about ten percent of his clients who seek asylum because of sexual orientation do so within a year of arrival. Shu Shin Luh, "Activists Say One Year for Applying Is Too Strict; Others Say Limit Needed," *The San Jose Mercury News,* August 24, 1998.
30. As of June 1999, the INS had done no analysis of whether exceptions were granted disproportionately to represented applicants. Even if such analysis is performed, little beyond

anecdotal evidence may ever be known about the validity of the claims that are rejected as late, because these cases are not decided on their merits, and the statute precludes judicial review of the exemption denials. Some data may be gleaned from those cases that are rejected for asylum because of failure to meet the deadline and later adjudicated by immigration judges who disagree with the asylum officers' determinations about the deadline or who grant withholding of removal, which is not subject to the deadline. However, many of these cases will not go to immigration judges. For example, some aliens will leave the United States to seek a different haven. A judge who does hear a "late" case and denies asylum on the merits may never even evaluate the deadline issue. Most important, immigration judge decisions are not made public, making research on this issue very difficult and perhaps impossible.

31. General Accounting Office, "Illegal Aliens: Changes in the Process of Denying Aliens Entry Into the United States" 41 (GAO/GGD-98-81, 1998) (27,774 cases charged under expedited removal in the first six months, plus 1,396 referred for credible-fear interviews). See also Charles Wheeler and Mary McClenahan, Catholic Legal Immigration Network, "Report No. 5 on Credible Fear/Expedited Removal," April 8, 1998 (reporting approximately 1,200 cases per week during the first year). Most aliens arriving at ports of entry without proper documents were intercepted at the Mexican border, but inspectors referred to asylum officers a much higher percentage of such aliens who arrived at airports. The referral rate for such persons was 17 percent rather than 5 percent. INS, Update on Expedited Removals, March 24, 1997 [sic, actually 1998].

32. General Accounting Office, supra, 48.

33. The asylum officers receive extensive training regarding human rights law, human rights conditions, and sensitivity to psychological circumstances that may make it difficult for refugees to tell the officers about rape, torture, or other horrific experiences. See Eric Schmitt, "Asylum Agents Learn to Assess Tales of Torture," The New York Times, December 21, 1997.

34. General Accounting Office, supra, 97.

35. Asylum officers granted less than 1 percent of the 5,376 asylum applications by Mexican nationals in fiscal year 1996. By way of comparison, the approval rate was 53 percent for nationals of Afghanistan, 56 percent for Albania, 17 percent for Colombia, 9 percent for Guatemala, 65 percent for Yugoslavia, and 30 percent for Haiti. Immigration and Naturalization Service, 1996 Statistical Yearbook of the INS (1997).

36. Former INS executive associate commissioner T. Alexander Aleinikoff has argued that "the problem is that we just don't know what's happening in secondary inspection. And I think it's important that there be access for independent monitoring of how the process is working. It may be going just fine, we just don't know." Interview with Peter Kenyon, Morning Edition, National Public Radio, May 16, 1997.

37. In seventy-three days of close observations of secondary inspection at a major airport (apparently the only time INS has allowed a researcher to be present at a substantial number of these proceedings), Janet A. Gilboy found that when aliens arrived on "turnaround" flights, making only brief stopovers at the airport, inspectors sometimes rushed interviews to fit flight schedules, "giving short shrift to foreign nationals' rights," so that the agency would not have to find overnight detention space for them. Janet A. Gilboy, "Implications of 'Third-Party' Involvement in Enforcement: The INS, Illegal Travelers, and International Airlines," Law and Society Review 31 (1997), 505, 515–17. It is possible, of course, that the creation of additional detention space since Gilboy made her observations has reduced the incentive to rush. But other incentives for immediate removal rather than subsequent adjudication remain. Putting aliens on the next flight home "helps to insulate enforcement decisionmaking. From the practical viewpoint of inspectors, it is difficult for outsiders [politicians contacted by the alien's family] successfully to pressure the INS for reversal of a decision when the person is midair on the way home." Ibid., 511.

38. General Accounting Office, supra. GAO officials observed only sixteen secondary

inspections. Ibid., 43. They also reviewed 434 INS case files. Ibid., 42. The study found that except at the Miami airport, "the case files indicated that inspectors did not document asking at least one of the three required questions, or some version thereof, between an estimated 1 and 18 percent of the time." Ibid., 43.

39. Letter to Karen Musalo, Expedited Removal Project Study, from Deputy Attorney General Eric Holder, Jr., March 9, 1988, reprinted in Karen Musalo and Deborah Anker, "Report on the First Year of Implementation of Expedited Removal" (International Human Rights and Migration Project, Markkula Center for Applied Ethics, Santa Clara University, 1998).

40. Written statement of Mohamoud Farah, issued by the Hebrew Immigrant Aid Society, New York, read by Mr. Farah at a conference sponsored by the Lawyers Committee for Human Rights at the U.S. Senate, March 31, 1998. An INS spokesman said that the agency was investigating the charge of mistreatment, but added that Farah had arrived as an "imposter" with a false passport. William Branigin, "INS's Expedited Removal Attacked," *The Washington Post*, April 4, 1998. However, because there is no central government in Somalia, it is apparently impossible to get a Somalian passport. Anthony Lewis, "The Road to Asylum," *The New York Times*, December 8, 1997.

41. Barbara Bradley, "Asylum Law," *Morning Edition*, National Public Radio, October 14, 1997, Transcript No. 97101408–210.

42. Celia W. Dugger, "In New Deportation Process, No Time, or Room, for Error," *The New York Times*, September 20, 1997.

43. Celia W. Dugger, "Albanian Seeking Asylum Is Allowed to Return to U.S.," *The New York Times*, January 14, 1998.

44. "Act Slams Shut America's Open Door," *Texas Lawyer*, January 12, 1998.

45. Anthony Lewis, "Bullies at the Border," *The New York Times*, June 15, 1998. After Mr. Oliver complained to his congressman, who happened to be Jerrold Nadler, an active opponent of the expedited-removal provision when it went through Congress, the INS opened an internal investigation of the case. Ibid.

46. Instances of these practices are described in Lawyers Committee for Human Rights, *Slamming the Golden Door* (1998), 10–13.

47. Ibid., 11.

48. In 1998, Human Rights Watch published a careful, detailed critique of INS detention standards and procedures, including, but not limited to, issues involving the detention of asylum-seekers. Human Rights Watch, *Locked Away: Immigration Detainees in Jails in the United States* (1998).

49. Vanessa Redgrave, "Seek Asylum, Go to Jail," *LA Weekly*, October 10, 1997. The Kern County Lerdo Detention Center Ms. Redgrave apparently visited may have been worse than most INS holding detention areas, but it is not unique. See, e.g., David Gram, "Sudanese Refugee's Joyful Escape Ends behind Bars," *The Los Angeles Times*, March 27, 1994 (describing asylum applicant's detention in a jail in Vermont with "no recreation facilities, library or regular visiting hours" and where the asylum-seeker who was interviewed had been keep indoors for nearly a year. "His cell was as long as the bunk bed that lines one wall, and also included a toilet.")

50. Occasionally, INS detention is even more horrific. In 1998, the chairman of the American Bar Association's Coordinating Committee on Immigration Law reported that the increased detention of aliens required by the 1996 legislation had required the INS to farm detainees out to a local jail in the Florida Panhandle. There, "sadistic jailers apparently constructed an 'electric blanket'" which it "placed over detainees, who are then subjected to intense electric shocks." The detainees were forced to remain there "for hours, worried about repeated shocks, and when refused bathroom privileges, they often soiled themselves.... They [also] endured broken bones, racial slurs, and attacks with Mace and pepper spray." Neal R. Sonnett, "Stop Abusing Imprisoned Immigrants," *The Miami Herald*, October 14, 1998.

51. Memorandum from Michael A. Pearson, INS executive associate commissioner for field

operations, regarding Expedited Removal: Additional Policy Guidance, December 30, 1997.

52. Arthur C. Helton, "A Rational Release Policy for Refugees: Reinvigorating the APSO Program," *Interpreter Releases* 75 (May 18, 1998), 685, 689; Lawyers Committee for Human Rights, *Slamming the Golden Door* (1998), 19; Mirta Ojito, "I.N.S. Handling of Asylum Bids Differs Widely," *The New York Times*, June 22, 1998 ("A recently released study and interviews with more than a dozen lawyers and their clients confirm" advocates' conclusions that "If you come through Miami, you are O.K., but don't come to New York. You'll be stuck in detention"). See also Mae M. Cheng, "Hands-On Manager," *Newsday*, June 14, 1998 (New York INS director Edward McElroy "makes it a point to have them [asylum applicants] detained"). In 1999, Adelaide Abankwah, an African woman who, like Fauziya Kassindja, feared genital mutilation, became the longest-held inmate at the Wackenhut Detention Center in Queens, New York. She'd been found to have a credible fear of persecution, but at her full hearing, the immigration judge did not think that she'd proved that her country's courts would fail to protect her from mutilation. Because the New York district director did not release detainees through the parole process, she remained in jail for two years while her attorneys pursued appeals. Eventually, Charles Schumer, who had been elected a senator in 1998, urged her release. Leonard Glickman, "Without a Home for the Holidays," *The Washington Times*, December 25, 1998; Ginger Thompson, "Asylum Rule Urged for Sex-Based Persecution," *The New York Times*, April 26, 1999. She later won asylum (Kevin McCoy, "African Gains Asylum after 2-Year Struggle," *New York Daily News*, August 20, 1999).

53. "INS Issues Detention Guidelines after Expiration of TPCR," *Interpreter Releases* 75 (1998), 1508, 1509; remarks of former INS executive associate commissioner T. Alexander Aleinikoff at an Immigration Law Teachers Workshop, Berkeley, California, May 30, 1998. See also Ojito, *supra* ("Important decisions—from how long it takes to review an asylum seeker's case to whether he or she is quickly paroled or detained for months—seem to hinge more on the number of beds available at a detention center than on a cohesive national policy.")

54. Helton, *supra*, 690. The "temporary availability" of detention space resulted from increased appropriations for detention of aliens who were not seeking asylum; a new policy allowing the INS to transfer detainees on a space-available basis, rather than having to house those who arrived at Kennedy Airport in the New York area; and the advent of expedited removal itself, which freed jail space by removing immediately many aliens who under the old system would have been imprisoned for months before having hearings. The average jail time until release for aliens detained in expedited removal proceedings ranges from forty-four to ninety-two days, depending on the port of entry. Karen Musalo and Deborah Anker, *supra*, 55.

55. Judith Havemann, "Noncitizen Immigrants Retain Aid in Budget Bills," *The Washington Post*, July 1, 1997; Peter T. Kilborn, "The Budget Deal: the Scorecard," *The New York Times*, August 1, 1997.

56. S. 1150 (105th Cong.); "House Oks Legislation with Food Stamp Restoration for Certain Immigrants," *Interpreter Releases* 75 (June 8, 1998), 806; Memo to the author and others from Charles Wheeler, June 6, 1998 (30 percent estimate). This law passed only because the chairman of the House Agriculture Committee agreed to the restoration in House-Senate negotiations without first obtaining the approval of Speaker Newt Gingrich, who supported Lamar Smith's effort to kill it. Ellen Yan, "Legal Immigrants Aid Restored," *Newsday*, June 6, 1998.

57. William Branigin and Pamela Constable, "Immigration Law Altered Once Again," *The Washington Post*, November 14, 1997. The new law created a presumption that the deportation would cause extreme hardship for the Guatemalans and Salvadorans who had been in the United States for more than seven years, thus easing them past the most restrictive part of the test for suspension. Congressional sources suggested that the presumption

would enable most to become permanent residents of the United States. Ibid. The legislation was the Nicaraguan Adjustment and Central American Relief Act of 1997, enacted as part of the fiscal year 1998 District of Columbia Appropriation Bill.

58. "Omnibus Measure, Stand-Alone Bills, Provide Substantial Gains to Immigrants," *Interpreter Releases* 75 (November 2, 1998), 1505; Merle Augustin, "S. Florida Haitians Rejoice As Refugee Bill Becomes Law," *The Fort Lauderdale Sun-Sentinel*, October 22, 1998.

59. Randal C. Archibold, "Immigrants Pack Agency, Trying to Beat a Deadline," *The New York Times*, January 15, 1998. The privilege of remaining until their visas came through, for a fee, was extended to those on whom the 1996 law imposed a retroactive change, and those for whom family or business visas were sought within two months after Congress passed the law. But it was repealed for future aliens; they would have to wait in their own countries until they were allowed to immigrate within the appropriate quota for the type of immigrant visa they sought.

60. William Branigin, "Court Makes It Harder to Deport Criminals," *The Washington Post*, September 2, 1998 (reporting the decision of the U.S. Court of Appeals for the 9th Circuit in the case of Daniel Magana-Pizano). The decision held that Congress may not suspend all judicial review, including the writ of *habeas corpus*, at least for aliens already in the United States. The Supreme Court later instructed the Court of Appeals to reconsider its decision in the light of a subsequent Supreme Court decision in a case involving a different section of the 1996 immigration law. *INS v. Magana-Pizano*, 119 S. Ct. 1137 (March 8, 1999).

61. *Goncalves v. Reno*, 144 F. 3d 110 (1st Cir. 1998); *Henderson v INS*, 157 F. 3d 106 (2d Cir. 1998). The Supreme Court declined to accept the government's further appeal of these decisions. *Reno v. Goncalves*, 119 S. Ct. 1140 (1999).

62. Mirta Ojito, "U.S. Releases Man Jailed for a 1974 Misdemeanor," *The New York Times*, October 25, 1997.

63. Peter H. Schuck, "The Open Society," *The New Republic*, April 13, 1998.

64. "Omnibus Measure, Stand-Alone Bills, Provide Substantial Gains to Immigrants," *Interpreter Releases* 75 (November 2, 1998), 1505.

65. See Lamar Smith, Release, GAO Report Affirms New Asylum Law Is Working, Smith Fights to Preserve Generous Asylum System, March 30, 1998 (seeing in calls for reform the desire for "billable hour opportunities for immigration lawyers grasping at loopholes for illegal aliens").

66. U.S. Commission on Immigration Reform, *U.S. Refugee Policy: Taking Leadership* (1997), 31. It believed that an exception might be warranted for mass migration emergencies, and that such an exception would be preferable to mass deportations. Ibid.

67. Ibid., 32.

68. U.S. Commission on Immigration Reform, *Becoming an American: Immigration and Immigrant Policy* (1997), 110–111.

69. In their high regard for the ease and speed of turning around aliens arriving without proper documents at U.S. land borders, these officials may not be taking into account the higher recidivism reported by the commission. It is easier to count—and to report to Congress—the larger annual number of total removals from the United States than to track and adjust the statistics for recidivism.

70. Indigent felony defendants jailed as the result of criminal trials are already provided with public defenders at government expense. The adverse consequences of being deported to a country in which one's life is threatened by the government may be greater than those of being imprisoned in the United States. The Commission on Immigration Reform recognized that not only aliens but the INS itself benefit when aliens are represented in the removal process: "cases move more efficiently, economically and expeditiously ... [the] aliens are more likely to appear at their hearings ... [and] hearings take less time.... Representation also decreases anxiety and behavioral problems among detainees." U.S. Commission on Immigration Reform, *Becoming an American: Immigration and Immigrant*

*Policy* (1997), 136. But the commission illogically stopped short of recommending federal funding for representation, suggesting only that the government should "provide funds for services that inform aliens about their rights ... and to otherwise facilitate [privately-funded] legal representation." Ibid., 137.

71. Michele R. Pistone, "Justice Delayed Is Justice Denied: A Proposal for Ending the Unnecessary Detention of Asylum Seekers," *Harvard Human Rights Journal* 12 (1999): 197.

72. INA Sec. 235A, as amended.

73. Of course refugees refused boarding in European airports might seek asylum in Europe, but Europe appears also to be shutting its doors to asylum-seekers, motivated by the same forces that impelled Congress to pass the 1996 Act. See Bill Frelick, "The Year in Review," in *U.S. Committee for Refugees, World Refugee Survey 1997* (1997), 14 (under the Schengen Agreement and Dublin Convention, "each [European] country manages to shift responsibility for examining asylum claims to another. None considers a refugee claim on the merits, averring that another will do that."); U.S. Committee for Refugees, *At Fortress Europe's Moat: The "Safe Third Country" Concept* (1997).

74. I am making the assumption that the United States will continue to apply the Lautenberg amendment so that Jews in the former Soviet Union who have relatives in the United States can qualify rather easily for resettlement. If the United States changes its policy and applies the amendment to Jews from the former Soviet Union who do *not* have U.S. connections, several hundred thousand more people such people will become eligible for favorable treatment within the annual U.S. refugee allotments, and the pressure I describe to increase refugee resettlement from Africa and Asia will not materialize.

75. The Commission on Immigration Reform stated that it was "concerned ... that resettlement could drop to unacceptably low numbers as the need for the two principal resettlement efforts of the 1980s and early 1990s—for refugees from Southeast Asia and the former Soviet Union—declines." U.S. Commission on Immigration Reform, *U.S. Refugee Policy: Taking Leadership* (1997), 46.

76. After the reduction for fiscal year 1997 imposed just as the 1996 immigration bill was being passed, the administrative ceiling climbed back from seventy-eight thousand to eighty-two thousand in fiscal year 1988. Unfortunately, the eighty-two-thousand figure was (as in some previous years) somewhat fictitious, as it included thousands of "unfunded" positions for refugees who would not actually be accepted because funds were not appropriated for their resettlement. For fiscal year 1999, the administration reverted to a ceiling of seventy-eight thousand refugees. See "Clinton Administration Lowers Refugee Admissions to 78,000 for Fiscal Year 1999," *Interpreter Releases* 75 (Oct. 5, 1998), 1378. However, for fiscal year 2000, the Clinton Administration increased the ceiling to 90,000 refugees ("More Refugees Allowed Entry into the U.S." *Washington Post*, August 13, 1999).

77. A State Department official told a human rights advocate that the U.S. resettlement program for Africa has been kept small "because the majority of African refugees have said that they want to eventually go home," even though the refugees' hopes of return may be unrealistic. Bronwyn Lance, "Sorry Policy: Four Ways President Clinton and Congress Can Help African Refugees," Alexis deTocqueville Institution (1998).

78. Some but not all asylum applicants—those on valid student or other visas who apply for asylum (perhaps because a coup occurred while they were in the United States) while those visas are still in force—are also legal aliens.

79. Other developed countries that do not currently have overseas-refugee resettlement programs should initiate them. Prior connections to the United States should not be a requirement for eligibility for U.S. refugee resettlement, but to the extent that applicants for resettlement have connections with a developed country, those connections should play a role in determining the country to which they should be resettled.

80. Departments of State, Justice, and Health and Human Services, "Proposed Refugee Admissions for Fiscal Year 1998," submitted to the House and Senate Committees on the Judiciary, July 1997 (as of Fiscal Year 1997, "a member of any nationality may be referred to

the U.S. Program under Priority One" which includes [among others] "UNHCR-referred or Embassy-identified persons who are facing compelling security concerns in countries of first asylum ... former political prisoners ... women-at-risk [and] victims of torture or violence").

81. The list of countries with the highest percentages of asylum approvals provides a good starting point for such a survey. In 1996 it included two countries whose nationals had approval rates of 70 percent or more (Iraq and Sudan); five of 60 percent or more (Somalia, Yugoslavia, Zaire, Bosnia, and Cuba), and six of 50 percent or more (Iran, Burma, Afghanistan, Albania, Cameroon, and Ethiopia). *1996 Statistical Yearbook of the INS* (1997), 90. By contrast with these "hot spots," sixty thousand of the seventy-four thousand overseas-refugee admissions in the same year were from East Asia, Eastern Europe, and the former Soviet Union. Ibid., 84. These figures do not necessarily show an imbalance; it might be the case, for example, that the United States admitted (among the approximately seven thousand Africans who were helped through the overseas program) every victim of persecution from the Sudan or Cameroon who wanted to resettle in the United States. But the numbers suggest at least that the United States should consider expanding its refugee program in Africa, the Near East, and Burma. It could be argued, of course, that a policy of resettling in the United States a larger number of human rights victims from distant regions would remove from these regions many highly educated people who are devoted to democracy and toleration and therefore work against American efforts to spread liberal values. In this sense, the humanitarian and democratic goals of U.S. human rights policy may conflict. Nevertheless, it does seem very odd that under present practices, the main factor distinguishing refugees from Africa and Asia who can resettle in the United States and those who cannot is the ability to purchase an airline ticket and evade detection at the boarding gate.

82. The administration appears already to be heading in the direction of accepting more overseas refugees from Africa. As recently as fiscal year 1996, only 7.7 percent of the refugee quota was allocated to Africa. See "Administration Proposes 90,000 Refugee Admissions for FY 96," *Refugee Reports*, August 25, 1995, 1. The corresponding figure for fiscal year 1999 was 15 percent. "Clinton Administration to Admit 78,000 Refugees in Fiscal Year 1999, *Interpreter Releases* 75 (July 13, 1998), 959. For fiscal year 2000, the figure was 20 percent ("More Refugees Allowed Entry into the U.S.," *Washington Post*, August 13, 1999).

83. Since 1996, U.S. embassies have had the authority to refer directly to INS those refugees who are urgently in need of resettlement because they are in danger of political reprisal. Telegram 242395 from the Secretary of State to all Diplomatic and Consular Posts, December 31, 1997. But in two years, all embassies combined exercised this authority only four or five times. Lance, supra. Non-governmental organizations may not independently refer refugees to the U.S. refugee program; they may only refer such people to UNHCR or to a U.S. embassy. Therefore, the "vast majority" of top-priority cases (those in which personal security is threatened) "are UNHCR referrals."

84. John Fredriksson, who along with Bill Frelick is one of the most experienced analysts of refugee resettlement, said, "If you opened up a general office for refugee resettlement in Kenya, a million and a half people would apply and the United States office would be overwhelmed." John Fredriksson, interview between author and John Fredriksson, former Washington representative of the Lutheran Immigration and Refugee Service, October 10, 1997.

85. In a recent year, UNHCR devoted only seven million dollars of its fourteen-billion-dollar budget (1/20th of 1 percent) for its resettlement efforts. It allocated only one professional staff position, plus four others in Geneva, for the resettlement program worldwide. John Fredriksson, "Revitalizing Resettlement as a Durable Solution," in *U.S. Committee for Refugees, World Refugee Survey 1997* (1997).

86. Bill Frelick, who has studied UNHCR for many years, concluded that the tripling of the UNHCR budget between 1990 and 1996 took the agency away from its central mission of

helping refugees and turned it into the UN's "leading humanitarian agency," which then tried to use the prospect of humanitarian assistance to prevent refugees from leaving their own countries. Bill Frelick, "Assistance without Protection: Feed the Hungry, Clothe the Naked, and Watch Them Die," in *U.S. Committee for Refugees, World Refugee Survey 1997* (1997).

87. Fredriksson, "Revitalizing Resettlement," *supra*.

88. Testimony of John Fredriksson on U.S. Refugee Admissions for Fiscal Year 1998 before the Senate Subcommittee on Immigration, July 31, 1997.

89. Testimony of Hon. Phyllis E. Oakley, assistant secretary of state, Bureau of Population, Refugees and Migration, before the Senate Immigration Subcommittee, July 31, 1997

## Chapter 15: Public Interest Advocacy in Congress

1. Quoted by Michael Pertschuk, *Giant Killers* (1986), 11. Pertschuk and Cohen are directors of the Advocacy Institute, which trains non-profit legislative advocates in Washington, D.C.

2. Future accounts are necessary, because there appears to be no other book-length study of advocacy by non-profit organizations for the passage or defeat of an Act of Congress. Michael Pertschuk's *Giant Killers*, an excellent series of short accounts of public interest congressional advocacy, does tend to support the conclusions reached here. Ronald D. Elving, *Conflict and Compromise* (1995), 29–34 and 152–59, offers glimpses of another public interest legislative coalition at work (on what became the Family and Medical Leave Act of 1993).

3. A former member of the House Ways and Means (taxation) Committee, who wrote the book *End Legalized Bribery*, explained how money can buy a tax loophole: "The way that the Ways and Means Committee functions, there are certain taxpayers ... who want special legislation in a tax bill which only benefits that taxpayer, 84 million, 165 million, whatever. ... It is a very simple process. You go to the staff of the chairman, you go to the chairman, you go to the political party of the chairman. You discuss access. You discuss whatever kind of support you're going to give to whatever candidates are of interest to the chairman or the party. And lo and behold, when the tax bill's going through the committee, there's a provision for a number of single taxpayers who have been sanctioned by the chairman of the committee so that it goes into the bill." Former representative Cecil Heftel, speaking on *Talk of the Nation*, National Public Radio, June 15, 1998.

4. Representative Scotty Baesler, quoted in David E. Rosenbaum, "Once-Obscure Lawmaker Battles Campaign-Law Status Quo," *The New York Times*, July 2, 1998.

5. Speaking of human rights advocacy on immigration legislation, Senator Russell D. Feingold said, "Without these kinds of groups it's very difficult for members of Congress to work on these issues in a significant way." Remarks at press conference on Capitol Hill, March 31, 1998.

6. John Fredriksson, interview between author and John Fredriksson, former Washington representative of the Lutheran Immigration and Refugee Service, October 10, 1997.

7. Elsewhere, the author has argued that the role of public interest organizations in setting long-term public agendas is very important. Between 1982 and 1993, the United States government did not pay even lip service to the desirability of a treaty to ban all underground nuclear weapon testing, but national and trans-national public interest organizations kept the issue alive in the media and by forcing the United States, Britain, and the Soviet Union to convene an international meeting to discuss the issue. Philip G. Schrag, *Global Action: Nuclear Test Diplomacy at the End of the Cold War* (Boulder, Colo.: Westview Press, 1992). In 1993, the new Clinton administration renewed efforts to negotiate such a treaty, and it was signed in 1996.

8. Of course even in the absence of non-profit advocacy, strong immigration advocates such as Senator Kennedy and Representative Berman would have voted for amendments to kill the Simpson and Smith proposals. But they might not have offered such amendments if

there had been no chance that they would ultimately carry, and if they had not offered the amendments, no other legislators might have offered them either.

9. Memorandum to the author from Dan Stein, Executive Director, FAIR, April 8, 1999.
10. Justice Felix Frankfurter coined the now-famous phrase, "The history of American freedom is, in no small measure, the history of procedure." *Malinski v. New York,* 324 U.S. 401, 414 (1945) (Frankfurter, J., concurring).
11. Senator Simpson later revealed that he never considered reopening the deadline issue on the Senate floor. "I'm not a martyr. That would show a petulant, obsessed legislator." He did try on the floor to recover from his failure to persuade the Judiciary Committee to cut legal immigration quotas, but he lost twenty to eighty. "I stood on the floor for several hours and got that stuck up my ass," he recalled. Alan K. Simpson, interview between author and former Senator Alan K. Simpson, July 1, 1998.
12. On a third occasion, when Representatives Gilman, Smith, and Schumer drafted their floor amendment, the importance of protecting people who needed humanitarian parole may have adversely affected asylum-seekers, because the representatives packaged the two issues into a single amendment, and the House Rules Committee may have been more hostile to allowing a vote to preserve humanitarian parole than one on asylum deadlines.
13. Wendy Young, interview between author and Wendy Young, then a consultant for the U.S. Catholic Conference, more recently Washington liaison for the Women's Commission for Refugee Women and Children, June 17, 1998.
14. The quoted phrase, and the information about the refugee organizations, comes from an interview with Jana Mason, government liaison, Immigrant and Refugee Services of America, September 8, 1997.
15. The nine organizations included the U.S. Catholic Conference, the Hebrew Immigrant Aid Society, Immigrant and Refugee Services of America, the Lutheran Immigration and Refugee Service, World Relief, Church World Service, the International Rescue Committee, the Episcopal Migration Ministries, and the Ethiopian Community Development Council. The first four of these organizations were particularly active in the successful effort to defeat the cap.
16. Simpson interview.

# About the Author

Philip G. Schrag is a professor of law at Georgetown University Law Center, and director of the Center for Applied Legal Studies. The Center's students learn to be advocates while representing asylum applicants under faculty supervision in Immigration Court. To defeat the efforts of the Immigration and Naturalization Service to deport their clients, the students must prove that their clients would have "a well-founded fear" that they would be persecuted if forced to return to their own countries.

Professor Schrag is also the director of Georgetown's Public Interest Law Scholars Program, in which competitively selected students who plan to spend their careers in non-profit organizations or government agencies receive scholarships and take special courses to prepare them for careers in public service. Five of his ten books and several of his articles explore how public interest organizations have helped to make public policy.

Professor Schrag has served twice in government agencies, as the consumer advocate of the City of New York (1970–71) and as the deputy general counsel of the United States Arms Control and Disarmament Agency (1977–81). He now resides in Bethesda, Maryland, with his wife Lisa Lerman (also a law professor), his son Sam and his daughter Sarah, three cats, and two gerbils.

# Index